D0152942

GAY AND LESBIAN ISSUES

A Reference Handbook

Other Titles in ABC-CLIO's
CONTEMPORARY
WORLD ISSUES
Series

Books in the Contemporary World Issues series address vital issues in today's society such as genetic engineering, pollution, and biodiversity. Written by professional writers, scholars, and nonacademic experts, these books are authoritative, clearly written, up-to-date, and objective. They provide a good starting point for research by high school and college students, scholars, and general readers as well as by legislators, businesspeople, activists, and others.

Each book, carefully organized and easy to use, contains an overview of the subject, a detailed chronology, biographical sketches, facts and data and/or documents and other primary-source material, a directory of organizations and agencies, annotated lists of print and nonprint resources, and an index.

Readers of books in the Contemporary World Issues series will find the information they need in order to have a better understanding of the social, political, environmental, and economic issues facing the world today.

GAY AND LESBIAN ISSUES

A Reference Handbook

Chuck Stewart

A B C · C L I O

Santa Barbara, California • Denver, Colorado • Oxford, England

Library of Congress Cataloging-in-Publication Data
Stewart, Chuck, 1951–
     Gay and lesbian issues: a reference handbook / Chuck Stewart.
          p. cm. — (Contemporary world issues)
Includes bibliographical rferences and index.
     ISBN 1-85109-372-9 (hardcover: alk. paper)   ISBN 1-85109-373-7 (e-book)
1. Gays—Social conditions. 2. Gay rights. 3. Homosexuality. 4. Gays—Services for. [1. Gay rights. 2. Homosexuality. 3. Gays—Services for.] I. Title. II. Series.

HQ76.25.S748 2003
305.9'0664—dc21   2003006517

07 06 05 04 03   10 9 8 7 6 5 4 3 2 1

This book is also available on the World Wide Web as an e-book. Visit abc-clio.com for details.

ABC-CLIO, Inc.
130 Cremona Drive, P.O. Box 1911
Santa Barbara, California 93116-1911

This book is printed on acid-free paper ∞.
Manufactured in the United States of America

Contents

Preface and Acknowledgments

The gay civil rights movement parallels the political and social process experienced by African Americans, women, people with disabilities, and other groups in overcoming discrimination against them. Unlike "visible" characteristics such as skin color, sexual orientation can be easily hidden. Many societies do not even have a name for same-sex behaviors or relationships, yet they stigmatize those who are not heterosexual. In these societies, homosexuals have the daunting task of finding each other. The early German homosexual movement created language around sexual orientation that allowed a public dialogue to begin. But the Nazis crushed and exterminated the early gay movement. Not until after World War II did the beginnings of the gay civil rights movement appear in the United States.

A civil rights movement is composed of people. For the movement to progress, its members must pass through stages of overcoming oppression. A homosexual child who grows up in a heterosexist society quickly learns to be silent about his or her sexual orientation and quickly experiences society's animosity. This can cause a sense of self-loathing and self-hatred, otherwise known as internalized homophobia. The first stage of overcoming stigmatization is to overcome internalized homophobia. We see this step in the early stages of the gay rights movement in the 1950s and 1960s. Gay men and lesbians were self-identifying, helping each other, and forming a community. Academic researchers conducted objective investigations and found antigay stereotypes to be untrue. With this new knowledge and increase in self-esteem, some homosexuals became activists willing to stand up to an oppressive society and say, "No more." The 1970s and 1980s were characterized by gay activism, including civil disobedience.

When gay men and lesbians began aspiring to equality with heterosexuals (for example, by seeking the right to marry, adopt

ix

children, and bring their partners to social functions), heterosexuals had to reassess their position. For the first time, heterosexuals had to listen to the concerns of homosexuals. And that is the real power behind a civil rights movement: not a handful of activists willing to demonstrate or argue in courts, but many people educating those in power to overcome their bias and hatred. As lesbians and gay men overcame their internalized homophobia, heterosexuals had to overcome their own homophobia and heterosexism. It was heterosexuals who changed the *Diagnostic and Statistical Manual of Mental Disorders* (DSM) to eliminate homosexuality as a mental illness. It was heterosexuals who changed Vermont law to allow civil unions for same-sex couples. It was heterosexuals who enacted hate crime laws to protect lesbians and gay men. Ultimately, it will be heterosexuals who change the law to ensure equal treatment for homosexuals.

Each year, lesbians and gay men gain more protections. These are not additional rights, but specifications of the law to ensure that it is applied equally to persons of differing sexual orientations—a historically oppressed group. There has been a backlash from the religious right, but its tactics and hysteria reveal how ineffective it is. Full rights for lesbians and gay men may be achieved within two more generations.

Chapter 1 gives a broad analysis of the gay civil rights movement, using specific events in the United States and the world to illustrate the concepts. Chapter 2 discusses a number of controversial issues as they apply to today's political climate. Chapter 3 is a fairly detailed chronology of the events surrounding lesbian and gay civil rights in the United States and elsewhere. Chapter 4 contains more than forty biographic descriptions of both pro- and antigay people. Chapter 5 contains primary research materials, including the positions of a number of major organizations, court decisions, laws and statues, and quotes. Chapter 6 is a list of major organizations, with contact information and a summary of their histories, goals, and accomplishments. Chapter 7 is a detailed list of books, videos, periodicals, television and radio programs, and curricula on lesbian and gay topics, along with a history of homosexuality in the movies. Finally, the book concludes with a Glossary that has a short list of terms for which more details are given.

When I considered this writing assignment, I did not readily see the need for such a reference volume. I believed the Internet made this kind of book superfluous. But during the research phase, I spent more than four months, eight to ten hours a day, surfing the web with my high-speed DSL line, locating organizations, books, films, histories, and more. I now understand that few people have the time or resources to conduct the research this book represents. Reference books with links to the web are still valuable, and I have attempted to bring you timely and accurate information.

Parts of this book were emotionally difficult for me to write. Although I have been a gay activist and academic for more than twenty years, I was not prepared for the hate spewed forth from the religious right. Researching sections of the book necessitated my going to the website of every major antigay organization. There I printed out hundreds of pages and downloaded reports. Although I was aware of the position of these organizations it was very disturbing to see them advocate death to homosexuals—that means me.

I also had a hard time reconciling their outright lies and hypocrisy. For example, the leaders of the reparative therapy movement have *admitted in writing that they cannot change sexual orientation.* Yet they still hold seminars and place ads in newspapers claiming that they can. How many lives have they destroyed through reinforcement of self-hate in homosexuals who seek their help? Documents from the legal counsel for the "no special rights" campaigns reveal that the leaders of the religious right *know the slogan is mistaken.* Their legal counsel has advised them not to use the slogan in legislation. Yet they use it every chance they can to raise money and defeat antidiscrimination statutes. Also, the religious right continues to claim homosexuals are child molesters and are mentally ill. Both claims, and all similar stereotypes, are false and have been known to be false for more than fifty years. Most recently, the Family Research Council (FRC) issued a "report" that sent chills down my back. It claimed in 2002 that gay men account for one third of all child abuse cases. The article is very formal looking, with many footnotes, and it gives the impression of being authoritative. Some of the quoted scientists have written to the FRC and demanded that their names be taken off the report *because the FRC changed their findings.* These scientists reported that homosexuals are no more likely to be child molesters than heterosexuals. The FRC lied and purposefully changed the results of respected researchers. The FRC does not engage in science, it engages in religious propaganda.

Which brings me to hypocrisy. The leaders of the religious right know they are lying. Yet they present themselves as being morally pure and truthful. They are not ignorant. They actually know what they are doing to promote their cause and raise money. I think that is what disturbed me more than anything else.

Acknowledgments

I want to thank ABC-CLIO for having the confidence to let me write a second book for them. I want to thank my dear friend and dance partner Arline Keithe for her generous offer to edit the original manuscript. I also thank Alicia Merritt at ABC-CLIO for her insightful review. These editors form an integral part of my writing process and help make the book as accurate as possible. Thank you all.

Chuck Stewart

1

History of the Gay Rights Movement

There always have been and always will be people who engage in homosexual activities and relationships. But being "gay" is a modern political concept. It reflects the efforts made by homosexuals to fight against a heterosexist society that tells them they are deviant and not deserving of full human rights. Gay rights is the process of claiming the respect due all citizens.

The modern gay rights movement began in Germany during the mid-1800s. The rise of Nazism crushed the fledgling movement. But the idea of equal rights for homosexuals did not die with World War II. Instead, it rose again in the United States, paralleling the civil rights movement that began in the 1950s.

The German Homosexual Emancipation Movement

Karl Heinrich Ulrich published many social and juridical studies in Germany concerning same-sex love between men. His twelve books represented the largest body of work on homosexuality in the 1860s and were collectively known as *Researches on the Riddle of Love between Men.* He used the term *Uranian* in reference to male homosexuality, a term taken from Plato's *Symposium,* which describes love between two men as a beautiful love belonging to the heavenly muse "Urania." Because of his gay-supportive views, Ulrich is recognized as the "grandfather of gay liberation."

The word *homosexual* was coined in 1869 by Hungarian doctor Karoly Maria Benkert (who went by the pseudonym K. M. Kertbeny). The term *heterosexual* was not used publicly until 1880. Initially, heterosexuality meant obsessive sexual behaviors toward the opposite gender and was categorized as sexual deviancy. Some argued that same-sex love was more stable than sexually compulsive heterosexuality. But the medical establishment labeled overt homosexuality dysfunctional, and this opinion influenced political authorities. In 1871, the newly united Germany enacted the New Prussian Penal Code. Paragraph 175 of the code outlawed "unnatural sexual acts between men, and men and beast" and specified imprisonment for up to four years (Plant 1986, 33).

British doctor Havelock Ellis continued the medicalization of homosexuality and coined the phrase *sexual inversion* to characterize homosexual behavior. Sigmund Freud was influenced by the work of Ellis and further characterized homosexuality as an "immature" stage of development. It is important to realize that Freud and other early psychologists did not base their theories on any scientific evidence; they cast social and cultural norms and prejudices into the new field of psychology. Unfortunately, these theories would influence psychology for the next century.

Heterosexuality was medicalized and recast as the norm and homosexuality as "deviant." However, not everyone accepted this assessment. Magnus Hirschfeld founded the Scientific Humanitarian Committee in Germany in 1897 to overcome antigay prejudice and to change the law. He worked tirelessly for three decades for homosexual emancipation. The committee distributed more than 50,000 copies of the pamphlet "What People Should Know about the Third Sex." Although there were forty gay bars in Berlin by World War I, he had little success organizing the many homosexual groups in Germany. But a fledgling homosexual reform movement took root.

Hirschfeld opened the Institute for Sexual Research in 1919. Its library contained more than 20,000 volumes of rare anthropological, medical, legal, and social documents. It employed four physicians and several assistants and included more than 35,000 photographs.

German brownshirts and police often physically beat Hirschfeld. On January 30, 1933, Adolf Hitler was named chancellor of Germany, and all homosexual rights organizations and pornography were banned. Four months later, on May 6, 1933, approximately 100 students surrounded and entered the Institute for Sexual Research. They smashed and then carried everything out. A public ceremony was held four days later in which these materials, along with a bust of Hirschfeld, were burned.

For the next two years, the Nazis staged a campaign against homosexuals. Bars were closed, groups and meetings were banned, and homosexuals were arrested by the thousands. The *SS*, the elite soldiers selected from the brownshirts, acted to consolidate their power under Hitler. On July 3, 1934, the leader of the brownshirts and a known homosexual, Ernst Roehm, was executed, along with hundreds of other members (known as the "Night of the Long Knives"). By 1935, the entire homosexual reform movement had been extinguished, and thousands of homosexuals were thrown into concentration camps, where at least 50,000 of them died. They were identified with a lavender triangle sewn onto their clothes. Tragically, some legal-minded Allied commanders forced homosexuals who survived the camps to return to prison to serve out their sentences as sexual deviants.

The U.S. Homosexual Emancipation Movement

There is very little evidence of efforts toward homosexual emancipation in the United States in the nineteenth and early twentieth centuries. The Chicago Society for Human Rights was the first group in the United States to advocate for gay rights. Henry Gerber, a German American immigrant, along with a number of working-class homosexuals, launched the society in 1924, which was granted nonprofit corporate status by the state of Illinois. They created a newsletter and were able to distribute only two issues before law enforcement arrested (without warrant) all members of the board. The men were jailed, brought to trial, but ultimately set free. Gerber lost his job with the post office, and the society disbanded (Katz 1976).

The early 1920s saw an increase in the number of novels with lesbian and gay themes published in the United States, although not without great controversy. A growing underground developed in Harlem in New York and in other major cities, such as

San Francisco and New Orleans. Homosexuals were fairly free to associate with each other, yet still under the fear of police entrapment and harassment.

World War II and the Migration of Lesbians and Gays to the Cities

Family patterns, social networks, and entire cultural systems were disrupted by World War II. Millions of men and women left their homes to enter the military or to work in factories to help make war supplies. Many of these settings were segregated by race and sex. Soldiers often had to share bunks, and men were often seen sleeping in each other's arms at train depots while waiting to ship out. Men often danced with each other at army canteens. Women lived together in company-provided housing at war factories. Homosexuality was a criminal act in the military in the 1920s and 1930s, but the war provided an excuse for these behaviors. Under these conditions, lesbians and gay men were able to find each other without bringing undue attention to themselves (Blumenfeld and Raymond 1993, 291; D'Emilio and Freedman 1988, 25–26).

An effort was made to reduce the number of personnel in the military after the war. One way to do so was to enforce 1943 regulations banning homosexuals from all branches of the military. Approximately 10,000 men and women were dishonorably discharged from the military for homosexuality during the war and immediately afterward (known as "blue discharges" because the document was printed on blue paper). Many did not return home, but rather flocked to New York, Los Angeles, and San Francisco to form gay enclaves. The gay community found relative safety and, eventually, its identity within these enclaves.

A number of factors led to the development of the modern gay movement after World War II. In 1948 Alfred Kinsey released his study of male sexual habits, *Sexual Behavior in the Human Male*, and in 1953 his corresponding study of female sexual habits, *Sexual Behavior in the Human Female*. The reports sent shock waves through U.S. culture, shattering stereotypes and myths concerning American puritanical codes of sexual conduct. The reports showed, among other things, that many people had sex out of wedlock, had engaged in sex in their teens, and had participated in a variety of sexual behaviors, including bisexuality and homo-sexuality.

Another factor was McCarthyism. Senator Joseph McCarthy (R-WI) led a campaign to purge communists and homosexuals from the federal government. Although many communists lost their jobs, many more homosexuals (thousands) lost theirs. (Interestingly, our history books constantly refer to McCarthyism as the period in which communists were routed out with the question "Are you now or have you ever been a Communist?" Yet the plight of homosexuals is barely mentioned.) However, the hearings gave unprecedented exposure to homosexuals and homosexual oppression. Homosexuality was discussed and writ-ten about in the press in new ways. Much of what was written was negative, but it allowed closeted and isolated homosexuals to know that there were many others like them.

The Homophile Movement

The homophile movement is a period in which people who engaged in homosexual behavior and relationships begin to self-identify and cast off the deficit label put on them by the early sex-ologists. They began to overcome their own homophobia and find love for themselves and other homosexuals. This is the period of *homo* (same) *phile* (love) identity formation.

Harry Hay (previously known as Henry Hay) was one of the key founders of the modern gay movement. He was a communist organizer in Los Angeles and a sought-after teacher of communist theory. In 1950, he assembled friends from the University of Southern California and launched the International Bachelors Fraternal Order for Peace and Social Dignity (sometimes referred to as Bachelors Anonymous). The group was structured as a secret society, with underground guilds separated so that no one would know all other members—a method used by the Old Left to keep members safe.

In 1951 Bachelors Anonymous incorporated in California as the Mattachine Society. The name was inspired by the Société Mattachine, a secret fraternal organization in thirteenth- and fourteenth-century France and Spain of unmarried townsmen who performed music, dances, and rituals while wearing masks, sometimes in protest against oppression. The society wanted to unify homosexuals and educate people about gay issues. At the same time, the Mattachine Foundation was established to provide a legal front for the society.

In the same year the Mattachine Society was formed, Donald Webster Cory published *The Homosexual in America*. He argued that the problems experienced by homosexuals stemmed from societal disapproval rather than from homosexuality itself. This was an important perspective, but U.S. society was not ready for it. The controversy caused the publisher to cease publishing books with homosexual themes.

The United States was a very dangerous place for lesbians and gay men during the 1940s, 1950s, and 1960s. Bars were about the only place gays and lesbians could meet, and often the bars were unmarked and required patrons to enter through a back door so that no one could see them entering from the street. With no provocation or legitimacy, police regularly entrapped men for lewd conduct, raided bars and baths, and suspended business licenses of gay establishments. For example, in some cities and states there were laws that required bar patrons to wear clothing conforming to their gender. Police would enter a lesbian bar and seek out the manliest looking patron. They would take her outside to the sidewalk and make her strip. They were making sure that she was wearing at least three items of clothing that were "feminine." If she wore boxer shorts, she could be arrested.

In 1952, Dale Jennings, one of the members of the Mattachine Society, was arrested and charged with lewd conduct. He claimed that a man he was not overly interested in came home with him. When Jennings went to make him coffee, the man moved to the window and played with the blinds. Police immediately entered the apartment and arrested Jennings. Jennings felt this was entrapment, a very common practice by police at that time (and unfortunately still a problem).

Most people charged with vagrancy and lewd conduct pleaded guilty and paid the fine so as to avoid jail (where they could be raped and beaten) and to prevent employers and families from finding out. Jennings convinced the Mattachine Society to help with the fight. At the trial, Jennings admitted being a homosexual (probably the first time anyone stood in a court of law and made that pronouncement) and insisted that he was neither lewd nor criminal. He helped educate the jury about the process of entrapment and how homosexuals were targets of police abuse. The defense attorney caught the arresting officer lying on the witness stand. The jury was hung (eleven wanted acquittal; one wanted conviction), and the judge dismissed the case. Although this was the first successful defense against police entrapment, none of the mainstream media carried the story.

The Mattachine Society set up another organization to publish a newsletter—*ONE, Incorporated.* It began publication in January 1953 and was the voice of the homophile movement. The U.S. postmaster seized copies of *ONE* on the grounds that it was "obscene, lewd, lascivious, and filthy" and refused to allow the newsletter to be sent by U.S. mail. *ONE* sued, eventually winning a U.S. Supreme Court decision (*One, Inc. v. Olesen*). The Court ruled that homosexual materials were not automatically "obscene" and could be sent via the mail. This was a very important decision: without the right to send materials through the mail, the fledging gay rights movement would have been significantly hampered.

In 1953, Joseph McCarthy called Mattachine Foundation legal adviser Fred M. Snyder to testify before the House Un-American Activities Committee. McCarthy considered Snyder an unfriendly witness and attempted to defame and humiliate him. Snyder was open and professional, not at all conforming to the antigay stereotype. This confused McCarthy and the committee. At the same time, the Mattachine Society held a convention in Los Angeles. With more than 500 representatives, it was the largest such gathering of homosexuals in U.S. history. A power struggle ensued between the founders, who were leftist, and those who wanted a more moderate, liberal organization. The liberal faction won out, and the old Mattachine Foundation board resigned.

Over the next forty years, the Mattachine Society/ONE, Inc. evolved, changed names a number of times, floundered, regrouped, but survived. Currently, it is mostly a library and archive collection located on the campus of the University of Southern California and is named ONE Institute and Archive. It contains the largest collection of homosexual books, magazines, articles, paintings, and memorabilia in the world, with more than 1 million items catalogued.

Soon after the formation of the Mattachine Society in California, homosexuals in New York began meeting informally in a group called The League. Two members of the group, Sam Morford and Tony Segura, became frustrated by the flimsy nature of The League and decided in December 1955 to launch the *Mattachine Review* and Mattachine Society New York (MSNY). Approximately thirty people attended the first meeting of MSNY at the Diplomat Hotel. The organizers had to work with extreme caution because homosexuality was a felony in New York State and punishable by up to twenty years in prison.

Women were always involved with the Mattachine Society, although they constituted a very small percentage of the membership. However, inspired by its success, Del Martin and Phyllis Lyon in 1955 transformed their lesbian social club into a lesbian activist organization named the Daughters of Bilitis (DOB): the first national lesbian organization in the United States. The name came from Pierre Louÿs's narrative "Song of Bilitis," in which Bilitis is a lesbian poet and disciple of Sappho, who lived in ancient Greece on the isle of Lesbos. Chapters of DOB were established in major cities around the country and in Australia. Martin and Lyon produced a newsletter called *The Ladder.* DOB was well connected with the Mattachine Society and other early gay rights organizations.

The early 1960s was a turning point for the homophile movement. The Mattachine Society and Daughters of Bilitis were conservative in their actions and avoided direct politics. For example, when involved in official business, members were required to dress conservatively—suits and ties for men, dresses and heels for women. Both organizations excluded members who were overly effeminate or ultramasculine. They wrote polite letters, planned scholarly publications, and invited experts to lecture on "sexual variation" before serious audiences in respectable halls. Most members were secretive, and even the leaders often used pseudonyms. Because of the fears and inhibitions of these organizations, few people joined. As a result, many homosexuals felt left out and resented professionals who told them they were deviant and immoral. They wanted an organization that would take direct political action to reduce police harassment and to change laws.

Frank Kameny, a Harvard astronomer, was an activist who took direct political action. He was dismissed from his army post in 1957 for being a homosexual. He contested the dismissal all the way to the U.S. Supreme Court. The Court would not review the case and let stand his dismissal. The betrayal he felt toward a legal system that denied his right to employment led him to form the Mattachine Society of Washington (MSW). He wanted the group to take direct political action. He rejected the deviancy label and coined the phrase "Gay Is Good," a paraphrase of African American militants whose motto was "Black Is

Beautiful." He argued "that discrimination was squarely to blame for the homosexual's problems and that boldly challenging discriminatory policies was the most effective way to make progress . . . [and we should take] a militant homophile approach to gay political activity" (Marotta 1981, 25).

The activist approach for MSW threatened Mattachine leadership in New York, San Francisco, and Los Angeles. The leaders responded:

> Mattachine cannot pursue any path but the educational and research. . . . Our charter is placed in jeopardy whenever we try to influence legislation through any other means publicly. . . . We can endorse the action of other agencies working in this field, and "ride on their shirttails," so to speak, with relative safety. But we cannot lobby on our own, and must be careful how we recommend changes of law so that our charter and the right to solicit funds through the mail is not in danger. (Marotta 1981, 15)

Other groups formed outside of Mattachine were more activist oriented. In 1964, ten participants from the Homosexual League of New York and the League for Sexual Freedom picketed in front of the U.S. Army Induction Center on Whitehall Street. In this "first" gay demonstration, they protested the army's dishonorable discharges of gay soldiers.

The next year, 1965, the Mattachine Society held its first public demonstration in front of the White House to protest government discriminatory employment practices. Before they went, they agreed that the men would wear suits and ties and the women would wear conservative dress. That same day, 20,000 antiwar protestors were at the Washington Monument. The coincidence of media being there for the antiwar protesters got national television coverage for this gay demonstration.

In spring 1966, the police began Operation New Broom in New York City in which they "cleaned up" Times Square and Greenwich Village. They raided and closed gay bars, restaurants, bookstores, and taverns. Many men were entrapped and charged with solicitation and lewd conduct. Seven members of the Mattachine Society attended a public meeting at Judson Memorial Church where the chief inspector for the police was holding a community hearing. Randy Wicker and Craig Rodwell from Mattachine spoke and explained how previous efforts by

New York City police to "crack down" on gay bars had left homosexuals with no social outlet and had led to underworld elements opening illegal operations for homosexuals. The illegal bars were sources of police corruption and bribery. The chief inspector responded by saying that gay bars were illegal because of "illicit activities." Wicker pointed out that these illicit activities were mostly undercover policemen soliciting bar patrons for entrapment. The chief inspector denied the allegations. Wicker was shocked by the naïveté of the chief inspector and said, "It's alarming to think that the Chief Inspector doesn't know that a large number of police spend their duty hours dressed in tight pants, sneakers, and polo sweaters . . . to bring about solicitations" (Marotta 1981, 36). The audience at the meeting shouted out, "Bravo!" Soon after, the mayor of New York issued a memorandum ordering the police to cease engaging in entrapment.

It is important to understand the process of overcoming stigmatization and oppression. Initially, those who engaged in homosexual behaviors had no identity concerning their sexual orientation. In much of history and in many cultures today, as long as people meet their familial obligations by marrying and having children, society does not care if they engage in homosexual behaviors. In these cultures, homosexuality is not spoken of. Only if the homosexual relationship interferes with the family or becomes too "obvious" does the culture crack down, often seeking the death of the offender.

As the science of psychology developed, homosexuality was identified as a "sexual inversion" that was deviant. This characterization was based not on science but on social and cultural norms. Nevertheless, this labeling influenced psychologists, legislators, judges, police, schools, universities, churches, and others in power and enabled them to justify the persecution of homosexuals. Those who engaged in homosexual behaviors began to adopt this "identity," even though it was negative and enforced feelings of worthlessness.

But not all homosexuals felt they were mentally ill or deviant. Instead, they recognized that society put this label on them. It was society that expressed homophobia. The Mattachine Society took an educational approach to this matter. It believed that accurate information could dispel stereotypes and influence society. The society issued newsletters and pamphlets, held educational seminars, and challenged the medical establishment.

Society demonstrations were meant to bring attention to problems the media and society refused to face or even name.

The Mattachine Society was the right organization for its time. If gay activists had engaged in direct political action in the 1950s, they would have been jailed and their message would have been obliterated. But by the late 1960s, the Mattachine Society was proving to be too conservative, and few outside the gay community heard its message. Many homosexuals did not accept the negative stereotypes of society and wanted immediate relief from the oppression of police and laws. They wanted to be able to keep their jobs, homes, and families without having to stay in the closet. Thus, they took more political action, such as the public meeting at Judson Memorial Church. They wanted a public hearing with the chief of police to bring the issue of entrapment to his attention. As just described, the chief inspector denied entrapment occurred, yet the gay community knew otherwise and brought it to the attention of the media, the surrounding community, and the mayor.

Bringing the problem to the attention of the community is the first step toward overcoming oppression. Homosexuality was hidden, but no more. Now the arrests, beatings, firings, and more were brought to everyone's attention. Homosexuals were overcoming their internalized homophobia, and so were heterosexuals. The U.S. Constitution and contemporary social mores emphasized fair and equitable treatment. The entrapment of gay men by New York City police was brought to the attention of the mayor and the city council, who saw the unfairness of these actions and stepped in to stop the abuse. It was heterosexuals who understood the oppression of heterosexism and took action. Heterosexuals were overcoming their homophobia.

The next thirty years of gay activism reflect this process. Heterosexuals control the laws and institutions of the United States. Gay activists, especially in the early years, were few in numbers. Yet the truth of their message of equity between homosexuals and heterosexuals was strong enough to convince heterosexuals to intervene and change the power structure. We will see this recurring pattern.

Another major change occurred during the 1950s and 1960s. Psychologists engaged in academic research into homosexuality. Their work changed the social and cultural norms that depicted homosexuality as a mental illness.

The early investigations into homosexuality were performed

on a skewed sample of people who visited gay bars, patients in psychiatric hospital, and prison inmates. Not surprisingly, these studies confirmed the societal beliefs and stereotypes that homosexuals are alcoholic, crazed, and criminal. In the mid-1950s, Evelyn Hooker at the University of California at Los Angeles carried out the first rigorous studies using nonclinical gays and discovered that psychiatrists could not identify lesbians and gay men using psychological testing. Psychiatrists who made money "curing" allegedly insane gays could not even identify them (Hooker 1963). Hooker (who was heterosexual) and other respected academic researchers showed every antigay stereotype to be incorrect. With this evidence, the American Psychiatric Association (APA) dropped homosexuality as a mental illness from the *DSM* in 1973 (Bayer 1981).

The Stonewall Riots and Gay Liberation

There are junctions in history at which many forces come together to create a major shift in the social paradigm. The riot at Stonewall Inn in New York's Greenwich Village was such an event.

On the night of June 27, 1969, officers from the Public Morals Section of the New York City Police Department attempted to shut down the Stonewall Inn—a small local bar. The bar was a favorite place to meet for drag queens, street kids, dopeheads, speed freaks, and other marginal people. As bar patrons were dismissed by the police and allowed to leave, they gathered across the street. Each time someone appeared in the doorway whom the crowd knew, it applauded, which encouraged the brassy individual to pose and make some flippant remark. This infuriated the police even more. When the paddy wagon came to take away the drag queens, bar owner, and bartender, a cry went up from the crowd to overturn the paddy wagon. The wagon drove off, but then the crowd exploded by throwing bottles and stones at the police. The police had to retreat into the bar. A battle cry was heard throughout the Village, and hundreds came out to participate. A small fire began in the window of the Stonewall. Soon after, more police arrived and the crowd scattered.

For the next couple of nights, there were street demonstrations that were more political in nature. Groups of people milled around the streets yelling, "Gay Power," holding hands, and kissing in public. A group of gay cheerleaders was heard singing,

"We are the Stonewall girls/We wear our hair in curls/We have no underwear/We show our pubic hairs" (Marotta 1981, 75). After the first two days of disturbances, the Mattachine Society of New York handed out flyers in the village, capitalizing on the "Christopher Street Riots" and is characterized as the "hairpin drop heard around the world" (Marotta 1981, 77).

Michael Brown was a New Left homosexual who was thrilled to see homosexuals fight against the police. Days after the riots, he met with Dick Leitsch of MSNY to discuss sponsoring more demonstrations. When Leitsch adamantly insisted that MSNY could not engage in such activity, Michael Brown set up an independent action committee that became the Gay Liberation Front (GLF).

Before Stonewall, about a dozen gay organizations existed. Within three months after the riot, more than fifty lesbian and gay organizations formed throughout the United States. These organizations became more radical, with many cities hosting marches and festivals in June to commemorate the anniversary of the Stonewall Riots. It is these events, more than any other, that helped bring unity to the gay community and influenced political and legal progress.

GLF was composed of a series of small groups in the United States and other Western countries. It never became a formal organization. GLF represented an important transitional phase for the homophile movement. It built coalitions with other disenfranchised groups and attempted to dismantle oppressive economic, political, and social structures. Many of its participants had been members of New Left organizations, such as Students for a Democratic Society; others, such as pacifists and "hippies," simply rejected strict social norms. The radical members of GLF believed that a total transformation of society was needed to obtain equality and freedom for all marginalized people. The more moderate reformers attempted to change the system from within. GLF was responsible for the beginnings of many college lesbian and gay student groups.

Primarily, GLF groups engaged in consciousness-raising sessions in people's living rooms, church basements, and storefronts. These groups were nonhierarchical in structure and often did not have a leader. They built on the belief that the "personal is the political" and launched a number of small newsletters and engaged in demonstrations.

The ideological differences among the front's revolutionaries, social radicals, and reformers were too great to maintain, however, and GLF soon broke apart. Many, if not most, of the reformers felt alienated by the radical politics of GLF. Although they had outgrown the conservative homophile groups, they did not want to overthrow the entire political and social system. Instead, they sought a more activist organization that would bring about political change to eliminate discrimination against homosexuals. It was these GLF reformers who created the Gay Activists Alliance (GAA).

GAA engaged in petition drives, political zap actions, and street theater. Zaps are demonstrations in which politicians are directly confronted in public and asked pointed questions or chastised for antigay statements. Street theater included gay-ins or kiss-ins, in which members of the same sex would hold hands or kiss in public, something that heterosexuals are able to do but was (and still is) "shocking" when done by same-sex couples. GAA was successful at obtaining media attention and brought gay issues to the forefront of public discussion. In New York, these actions informed Mayor John Lindsay and city council members, all of whom were heterosexual, about gay issues. Seeing how government was unfair toward gay people, they ended entrapment, police harassment, and public employment discrimination. GAA was able to educate those in power about homophobia, and it was heterosexuals who changed the power structure.

Many groups formed in the early 1970s. They reflected the identity of their members. Separatism was advocated by some as the solution to heterosexual oppression. The National Organization for Women (NOW) was challenged by lesbian feminists over members' fears of being identified as dykes. Bisexuals made their needs known and became a voice within the lesbian and gay liberation movement. The 1969 Eastern Regional Conference of Homophile Organizations proposed a national celebration each June 28 to commemorate the Stonewall Riots. Now, most major cities and many smaller ones hold gay pride festivals and parades that tens of thousands, and sometimes hundreds of thousands of people attend.

Equal Rights and Community-Building

After Stonewall, there was a decline in radical activism. Gay reformers aimed at community-building and political activism.

They worked to educate and overcome oppressive laws, not to overthrow the system. There were more than 1,100 organizations nationwide devoted to lesbian and gay concerns by 1973. This number would more than double by the 1980s and again more than double by the 1990s. There are support organizations for every conceivable group—businesses, students, schools, scientists, lawyers, academics, artists, church members, and racial and ethnic minorities. There was also a flood of publications, media, and more devoted to lesbian and gay concerns.

Government agencies were made aware that homosexuals underutilized government social services. Many cities developed entire centers providing services for lesbians and gay men. Some of the services included mental and physical health clinics, vocational training, counseling, lesbian advocacy, telephone hotlines, roommate referral, rap groups, medical services, and legal help. Often these centers provided professional advice to cities and government agencies about the needs, opinions, and concerns of the gay community.

One of the most influential political groups formed in the United States is the National Gay and Lesbian Task Force (NGLTF). Founded in 1973 as the National Gay Task Force, it blended the old homophile movement with the newer reformist strategies of GAA. Lambda Legal Defense and Education Fund is a national organization that promotes the civil rights of lesbians, gay men, bisexuals, transgender people, and people living with acquired immune deficiency syndrome (AIDS) through litigation, education, and public policy work. When its application for incorporation was rejected by the secretary of state, Lambda took the case to the New York Supreme Court, where the decision was overturned.

Again, we see the process of a handful of gay activists educating heterosexuals to overcome their homophobia. For example, Lambda argued that the U.S. Constitution explicitly allows people to come together to advocate for legal change (otherwise known as the right of assembly guaranteed in the First Amendment) and that this was Lambda's goal concerning gay rights. The New York Supreme Court agreed and rejected the unfairness inherent in denying the application for incorporation. It was heterosexual judges who changed the prohibition against gay groups forming in the state of New York.

Later in 1974, similar arguments were made at the U.S. Supreme Court level in *Gay Students Organization v. Bonner*. Here, gay activists educated the Court about the right of lesbians and gay men to come together and form organizations qualifying for federal tax-exempt status. Again, heterosexual judges found the arguments convincing and ruled that homosexual groups were to receive the same treatment by the IRS as any other qualifying group.

One of the most significant decisions came from the American Psychiatric Association (APA) in 1973–1974. The APA formed a committee in the early 1970s to review the research on homosexuality as related to its classification as a mental illness. The committee reviewed the works of Dr. Evelyn Hooker and many other researchers, along with 1969 recommendations by the National Institute of Mental Health (NIMH) Task Force on Homosexuality, to repeal antisodomy laws and educate the public about homosexuality (Thompson 1994, 69). The committee, along with the APA's Council on Research and Development, Reference Committee, and Assembly, made recommendations to remove homosexuality from its list of mental illness. The APA board unanimously passed a resolution removing homosexuality from the *DSM*. In response, a group of psychoanalysts filed a petition against the resolution. A referendum was held during which more than 58 percent of the 10,000 voting members supported (with 37.8 percent against) the board action. Future challenges to the resolution have been rejected by even larger margins.

Conservatives and members of the religious right often considered that this change in the *DSM* was accomplished by a band of scheming gay activists who pushed through their agenda. This is not true. It was a multiyear review of academic and government research combined with a clear presentation of the findings to the members that convinced the APA to change its position. The membership of the APA reflects society and is mostly heterosexual. It was primarily heterosexuals who reviewed the research and agreed that the change was needed. It was heterosexuals who overcame their bias and homophobia and made a rational decision based on objective research. In the intervening thirty years, no academic research has found any evidence suggesting that homosexuality is a mental illness. If anything, the research has affirmed that there are no differences in psychosocial measures related to sexual orientation.

Gay rights grew nationwide during the 1970s, with individual cities and counties (but no states) adopting antidiscrimination statutes. However, there was a conservative backlash. For example, in 1977 the Miami-Dade County Commission passed an ordinance making it illegal to discriminate on the basis of sexual orientation. This came about because local gay groups had brought their concerns about employment and housing discrimination to the commission. The commission, which was composed of heterosexuals, understood that it was not giving homosexuals additional rights, but rather was providing the city with the legal power to enforce rights already enjoyed by all U.S. citizens but denied homosexuals for historical and social reasons.

Upset by this development, singer and Florida orange juice representative Anita Bryant organized a group called Save Our Children. It used scare tactics, claiming that homosexuals molest children and are mentally ill. It obtained sufficient signatures to place a referendum on the ballot to overturn the ordinance. It was passed overwhelmingly by the county citizens. The Save Our Children campaign is an example of emotional hysteria, caused by religious conservatives and based on false information and stereotypes, overcoming decisions made by heterosexuals educated on the issue. Twenty years later, Dade County passed the same ordinance, and this time religious conservatives were unsuccessful in overturning it.

The very next year, 1978, a similar battle occurred in California. Republican state Senator John Briggs collected signatures and placed Proposition 6 on the ballot. It would have barred homosexuals from teaching in public schools. The Save Our Children slogan and methodology were used to promote the proposition. Nevertheless, teachers, labor unions, Democrats, and many Republicans, including Governor Ronald Reagan, came out against the proposition. It failed to pass. It seems that many people were not ready to give antidiscrimination protection to lesbians and gay men (as happened in Dade County), but also were not ready to discriminate against them outright (as in California's Briggs initiative).

Tragedy hit in 1978. Dan White gunned down Mayor George Moscone and Supervisor Harvey Milk of San Francisco in City Hall. White, a conservative supervisor on the San Francisco City Council, held much animosity toward openly gay supervisor Harvey Milk. In November 1978, White resigned his position on the council. He changed his mind and asked the mayor for his position back. The mayor refused. A week later, White entered City Hall and shot Milk and Moscone to death. The murder of the two men resulted in one of the most impressive memorial services ever seen in San Francisco; more than 40,000 men, women, and children marched by candlelight to City Hall.

At the trial, White's lawyers claimed that White was addicted to junk food and the sugar affected his judgment (what has since become known as the "Twinkie defense"). White was convicted not of first-degree murder but of involuntary manslaughter and was sentenced to seven years in prison. The gay community exploded at the lenient sentence and took to the streets of San Francisco. That night in 1979, known as White Night, police cars were overturned, fires were set, and thousands of people marched to City Hall. More than 150 people were injured, and property damages in excess of $1 million resulted. White was released after serving just five years of his sentence. He committed suicide in 1985.

Anita Bryant's crusade, the Briggs effort, and the murder of Harvey Milk and George Moscone galvanized the gay movement. But it also galvanized conservative religious groups into forming what today is known as the religious right. In 1979, Reverend Jerry Falwell launched the Moral Majority (renamed the Liberty Federation in 1989). In the same year, Beverly LaHaye founded Concerned Women for America (CWA). Pat Robertson, who began the Christian Broadcast Network (CBN) in 1961 and has hosted *The 700 Club* since 1968, opened CBN University in 1977, making his operation one of the best-financed conservative religious organizations in the nation. These three groups would become, and still are, the most powerful antigay organizations in the United States.

Seeing the need to coordinate progay political efforts, the Human Rights Campaign (HRC) was founded in 1980. It focuses on fighting antigay ballot initiatives and supports candidates who promote antidiscrimination policies based on sexual orientation. Its political action committee (PAC) provides financial support for candidates and typically raises and donates more than $1 million a year to candidates at the federal level. For example, in 1998, of the 200 political candidates to whom it contributed money, 91 percent won their respective races.

The 1980s saw a continuation of the trend toward greater recognition and equality for lesbians and gay men. For example, more than 200,000 people participated in the first March on Washington in 1979. In 1981, a court case in Dallas banned police from discriminating against lesbians and gays in employment as police officers (*Childers v. Dallas Police Department*). In 1982, Wisconsin became the first state to pass a wide-reaching law prohibiting discrimination against lesbians and gay men. A high school support program for lesbian and gay children was established in 1984 (Project 10, Los Angeles). In 1987, the second March on Washington took place, with more than 600,000 people attending. The National Education Association (NEA) in 1988 adopted a resolution calling for every school district to provide counseling for students struggling with their sexual orientation.

The U.S. Supreme Court handed down the most significant antigay ruling in 1986 (*Bowers v. Hardwick*). Michael Hardwick was charged with engaging in sodomy in Georgia. Hardwick sued and the case reached the U.S. Supreme Court. The Court ruled against Hardwick in a five to four decision stating that claims for "homosexual sodomy" as a protected right to privacy are "facetious, at best." The Court established that lesbians and gay men have no right to sexual expression under the U.S. Constitution. Soon after retirement, Justice Lewis Powell conceded that he "had made a mistake" and should have voted to strike down Georgia's sex statute (Marcus 1990).

The 1980s also marked the advent of AIDS. The first cases were reported in 1981 in the United States and exclusively involved gay men. Doctors were unsure what caused this "gay plague" and called it gay-related immune deficiency. As more nongays got the disease (Haitians, intravenous drug users, hemophiliacs, and heterosexuals), it became obvious that it was not related to being gay, but rather was an immune deficiency caused by a virus spread through bodily fluids. Bruce Voller, a biological researcher, coined the term *acquired immune deficiency syndrome* (AIDS) to better reflect the nature of the disease.

There was much hysteria about AIDS. People who developed AIDS were often fired from their jobs, forced out of their apartments and housing, lost their health insurance, and more. Children who were asymptomatic but infected with human immunodeficiency virus (HIV) were expelled from schools. Public swimming pools were emptied, scrubbed, disinfected, and refilled after a person with AIDS used the pool. Mortuaries refused to handle the bodies of people who had died from AIDS. Airlines refused to allow people with AIDS to fly. And even heath professionals sometime refused to care for those with AIDS. Massive discrimination resulted, and the government initially ignored the severity of the problem.

The religious right used AIDS to reignite its antigay crusades. Claiming that AIDS was "God's punishment" for the "immoral" gay "lifestyle," religious right organizations called for a general quarantine of people with AIDS, the firing of lesbian and gay teachers, and even more draconian measures. Even the mainstream media refused to cover the AIDS epidemic until the first heterosexuals were reported to be infected (Shilts 1987). It was seven years into the epidemic before President Ronald Reagan publicly mentioned AIDS. Yet Patrick Buchanan, Reagan's chief of communications, was very outspoken, claiming that AIDS was "God's awful retribution" for homosexual behavior and that AIDS patients did not deserve help ("Buchanan Calls AIDS 'Retribution'" 1992). AIDS, unfortunately, is still tied to antigay sentiments in many people's minds, even though it was never a gay disease.

President Reagan appointed a thirteen-member AIDS panel in July 1987. Although there was much in-fighting among the members, it made remarkably progressive recommendations, including a call for massive government funding for research and care. The panel also recommended legislation to prevent discrimination against people with AIDS (PWA) and people infected with the virus. These recommendations impacted the 1990 adoption by Congress of the Americans with Disabilities Act (ADA).

The frustration in the gay community over overt discrimination and government inaction compelled Larry Kramer and other activists to form the AIDS Coalition to Unleash Power (ACT UP) in 1987. ACT UP is a group of individuals united in anger and committed to ending the AIDS crisis through direct action. The slogan "Silence = Death" originated with ACT UP. It engaged in a number of high-profile demonstrations that brought significant media attention to the problem. For example, in 1989 more than 5,000 ACT UP members demonstrated in front and inside of New York's St. Patrick's Cathedral, rallying against the Catholic Church's antigay stance and policies on AIDS.

AIDS made the media, government, and average citizen talk about homosexuality and gay issues in ways they never had before. For example, the *New York Times* used the word *gay* in reference to homosexuality for the first time in 1987. AIDS brought more attention to gay rights than had the previous thirty years of educational efforts and public demonstrations.

To counter the political progress lesbian and gay rights advocates were making and the successes of the HRC, Pat Robertson formed the Christian Coalition in 1989. It is a political organization that works to elect conservative Christians to political office. Formed as a nonprofit religious organization, it violated its tax-exempt status by issuing voters guides and engaging in other direct political action. By 1998, the IRS had revoked its tax exemption.

The gay rights movement in Europe and elsewhere followed a path similar to that of the U.S. movement. Some countries were at the initial stages of simply trying to form support organizations. For example, when twenty gay Finnish citizens attempted to host the first gay pride parade in Helsinki in 1981, all were arrested for "encouraging lewd behavior." In 1989, Nigeria formed the Gentlemen's Alliance and Poland formed its national gay rights group, Lambda.

Other countries were much further along in the process of affirming gay rights. For example, Canada gave postal workers an antidiscrimination contract in 1980, yet conducted a massive raid, arresting 300 gay men in Toronto the next year. The ensuing riot has been called the Canadian Stonewall. Later, in 1988, Canada repealed its antisodomy laws. Ireland was compelled in 1988 by the European Court of Human Rights to eliminate its life imprisonment penalty for homosexual behavior. Britain elected its first openly lesbian mayor in Manchester in 1985. And Israel legalized homosexual acts between consenting adults in 1988.

Norway was further along, having enacted a national antidiscrimination statute that included sexual orientation. In 1984, television evangelist Hans Bratterud was convicted of violating the law. Denmark enacted domestic partnership legislation in 1988 that was just one step away from full marriage for same-sex couples. Full marriage for same-sex couples was granted in 2001 in the Netherlands, placing it ahead of all other countries in recognizing gay rights.

The end of the twentieth century and the beginning of the twenty-first saw a continuation of this process: a forward march toward greater equity for lesbians and gay men, with an occasional step backward. Many more cities and states have enacted hate crime statutes and antidiscrimination statues that include sexual orientation. The U.S. military dropped homosexuality as a trait identifying spies. President William Clinton signed an executive order banning discrimination based on sexual orientation in the federal civilian workforce. And the third March on Washington in 1993 attracted an estimated 1.2 million participants. The development of civil unions in Vermont, the reduction in the number of states having antisodomy laws, and the Supreme Court decision concerning Colorado's Amendment 2 are illustrative of society overcoming its homophobia and heterosexism.

Lesbians and gay men want their relationships to be as valued by society as heterosexual relationships are. A number of lesbians and gay men have sued their states to obtain marriage licenses. In states with constitutions containing a gender equality clause, such as Hawaii and Vermont, lesbians and gay men have successfully argued that denying them the right to marry is a form of gender discrimination. In Vermont, the court handed the problem back to the legislature to solve. The legislature, maintaining its constitutional prohibition on gender discrimination, came to understand that denying same-sex marriage was discriminatory. However, instead of allowing lesbians and gay men to marry, it created a separate category called "civil unions" in 2000. By law, civil unions are completely equal to marriage in Vermont, but other states will not recognize them as such. It is important to remember that the court and legislature are predominately heterosexual and they are the ones that changed the law. It was heterosexuals who took action to overcome societal discrimination against homosexuals.

However, many people were offended by the thought of same-sex marriage. The religious right hooked onto the issue and raised millions of dollars to fend it off. Religious right activists took their antigay message to politicians who then passed legislation defining marriage as the union of one man and one woman. A number of states and the federal government enacted Defense of Marriage Acts (DOMAs) to preempt the possibility of their having to recognize same-sex marriage.

The number of states with antisodomy laws has dropped significantly. Gay activists and attorneys have brought the unfairness of these laws to the attention of state courts. Antisodomy laws are a violation of privacy and result in the unequal application of the law (a violation of the equal protection clause of the U.S. Constitution). Many courts have revoked their states' antisodomy laws. By 2002, less than one third of the states still had them on the books. Again, it is important to remember that it is predominantly heterosexual judges who came to understand that antisodomy laws are discriminatory and invasive and ruled them invalid.

Colorado's Amendment 2 was one of the watershed decisions made by the U.S. Supreme Court concerning gay rights. Early in the 1990s, a number of cities and counties in the state of Colorado enacted antidiscrimination statutes that included sexual orientation. This angered a number of conservative residents.

Colorado for Family Values (CFV) was formed and successfully placed an amendment to the Colorado Constitution on the ballot. Amendment 2 sought to repeal any existing law or policy that protected people with "homosexual, lesbian, or bisexual orientation" from discrimination in the state and to prohibit future adoption or enforcement of any such law or policy. CFV claimed the amendment provided "special rights" to lesbians, gay men, and bisexuals that they neither "deserved" nor "needed."

The special rights argument has a long history. Originally used by opponents of laws prohibiting discrimination based on race, the slogan implies that a particular class of people will be given rights or privileges beyond what the majority have. "In truth, the laws simply ensured that minorities would have the same rights the majority already had, to participate in society without fear of discrimination" (Keen and Goldberg 1999, 10). Brian McCormick, staff counsel for Pat Robertson's National Legal Foundation, coached CFV to keep the term *special rights* out of the initiative, but to use it in all campaign promotions. As McCormick explained: "If language denying special privileges to homosexuals is in the amendment it could possibly allow homosexuals to argue that they are not asking for special privileges, just those granted to everyone else. [However] I believe that 'No Special Privileges' is a good motto for the amendment's public campaign" (Keen and Goldberg 1999, 11). It is important to realize the religious right knows that the special rights argument is not valid, but uses it anyway to influence voters and raise money.

On November 3, 1992, Colorado voters passed the amendment, with 53 percent in favor and 46 percent against. A temporary injunction was granted, and six months later Judge Jeffrey Bayless of the Colorado District Court for Denver heard the case. He rejected all state claims. The state appealed to the state supreme court, which upheld Judge Bayless's decision.

In 1995, the U.S. Supreme Court agreed to review the Colorado Supreme Court's decision (*Romer v. Evans*). The Court characterized Amendment 2 as "unprecedented in our jurisprudence" in that it identified "persons by a single trait and then denies them protection across the board .... A law declaring in general that it shall be more difficult for one group of citizens than for all others to seek aid from government is itself a denial of equal protection of the laws in the most literal sense." Also, Amendment 2 "inflicts on [gay people] immediate, continuing, and real injuries that outrun and belie any legitimate justifications that may be claimed for it."

The Court ruled 6–1 that Amendment 2 appeared to violate the fundamental right of lesbians, gay men, and bisexuals to participate in the political process on a basis equal to other Coloradans. Justice Anthony Kennedy stated: "We conclude that Amendment 2 classifies homosexuals not to further a proper legislative end but to make them unequal to everyone else. This Colorado cannot do. A state cannot so deem a class of persons a stranger to its laws."

The Court made a number of findings important to the rights of lesbians and gay men. First, the Court agreed that homosexuals have a long history of being persecuted. Second, the Court accepted the medical, psychological, social, and scientific evidence that homosexuality is not a medical disorder and is equivalent to heterosexuality. These two findings have significantly impacted other courts and administrative decisions nationwide. For example, at the trial of the two men who brutally murdered Matthew Shepard in 1998, the judge refused to allow the "homosexual panic" defense (see the Glossary for a further description), a completely discredited stereotype. Likewise, fewer judges are willing to allow antigay stereotypes to be used as the basis for taking children away from gay and lesbian parents during child custody and adoption proceedings.

Another major development occurred in the public schools. Many schools faced having to accept a gay-straight alliance student group on campus. A number of schools refused to accept these groups, but the courts consistently upheld the Equal Access Act, which requires schools to accept all noncurricular student groups on an equal footing. This trend should continue with many more, if not most, schools having gay-supportive programs on campus.

Schools have traditionally been a dangerous place for gay and lesbian students. One celebrated case has changed this situation. Jamie Nabozny experienced terrible abuse from other students while attending an Ashland, Wisconsin, high school. He was attacked by other students, mock-raped, urinated upon, and kicked so badly he required surgery to stop internal bleeding. His parents complained to school officials who told them he "had to expect that kind of stuff" because he was a homosexual. He eventually sued the school administration, and a jury found that school officials had violated Jamie's rights under the Fourteenth Amendment's Equal Protection Clause. The district was forced to pay $962,000 in damages (*Nabozny v. Podlesny*).

The 1990s also brought to the forefront the potential conflict between antidiscrimination statutes and the desires of private organizations. Two U.S. Supreme Court decisions illustrate this problem. Each year the Boston St. Patrick's Day Parade is sponsored by the South Boston Allied War Veterans Council. They refused to allow a gay marching group to participate. The gay group sued, and the court initially sided with the gay group. The parade organizers canceled the event and appealed to the U.S. Supreme Court. In *Hurley v. Irish-American Gay, Lesbian, and Bisexual Group of Boston* (1995), the Court upheld the First Amendment right of the organizers to exclude gays from their event because the "private" organizers of the event had the right to control the message of the event.

Likewise, the U.S. Supreme Court upheld the right of the Boy Scouts to exclude openly gay men from serving as troop leaders or participating as members (*Boy Scouts of America v. Dale,* 2000). The Court held that requiring the Boy Scouts to include James Dale in its ranks would violate the organization's First Amendment right of "expressive association" (see Chapter 5).

Although many lesbians and gay men saw the Boston St. Patrick's Day Parade and Boy Scout cases as losses, some civil libertarians believe they were the right decisions. Private organizations need to retain the right to select their members and promote their cause. However, the dividing line between public and private is not clear. The aftermath of the Boy Scouts case has been a withdrawal of support for the Boy Scouts by many cities, school districts, and local governments. They often have nondiscrimination conditions for use of facilities, and the Boy Scouts is open about its discrimination. Many of these agencies have withdrawn their support of the Boy Scouts in favor of organizations that do not discriminate (such as the Camp Fire Girls, Girl Scouts, Indian Guides, and Police Cadets).

The Culture Wars

Some political analysts believe lesbians and gay men have already won the culture wars and that the complete elimination of antisodomy laws, the right to marriage, and so forth are simply mopping-up activities, albeit ones that may take another generation or two to achieve. They point to the fact that more and more cities, counties, and states are enacting antidiscrimination statutes and hate crime reporting procedures and enforcement, businesses are extending domestic partnership benefits to their employees with same-sex partners, and more. Television has gay characters on many programs, from MTV's *The Real World*, to NBC's *Will & Grace*, to Showtime's *Queer as Folk*. Most bookstores have a gay and lesbian section. And schools nationwide are having to accept gay-straight student groups on campus and are incorporating lesbian and gay educational materials into their curriculum from kindergarten to high school.

The knowledge that homosexuals are virtually indistinguishable from heterosexuals and that both orientations are equally valid has gradually filtered into society. It was scientists in the 1950s to 1970s, most of whom were heterosexual, whose studies influenced the APA to recognize that homosexuality is as valid as heterosexuality. The predominately heterosexual membership of APA supported removing homosexuality as a mental illness. This knowledge spread to city councils, state legislatures, courts, places of religious service, schools, and more. Public attitude has shifted significantly, with most people in the United States accepting the idea of gay adoption, gays in the military, and support for nondiscrimination laws. Changes in laws and policies have come about because heterosexuals understood that discrimination against homosexuals was unfounded and unfair.

The religious right has always recognized homosexuality as an issue that generates significant funds. For example, Robert Billings, the first executive director of the Moral Majority, stated: "I know what you feel about these queers, these fairies. We wish we could get in our cars and run them down when they march. . . . We need an emotionally charged issue to stir up people. . . . I believe that the homosexual issue is the issue we should use" (Young 1982, 78). Throughout the 1990s, the religious right increased the use of homophobic rhetoric to raise money and recruit followers (Berlet 1998; Mookas 1998).

By the late 1990s, there was a shift in tactics by the religious right. Claiming that homosexuals are child molesters and mentally ill just does not have the impact that it used to have. Likewise, "no special rights" is still used but, it, too, is losing impact. Too many people, courts, and politicians know that these stereotypes and slogans are inaccurate.

In July 1998, full-page paid advertisements were placed in major national newspapers promoting the "ex-gay" movement. The ads were purchased through a coalition of fifteen Christian right organizations. They condemned homosexuality as a sin but emphasized curing homosexuality as a prolife act. They hoped to plant the idea that homosexuality is a chosen "lifestyle" and is therefore alterable. Logically, this assumption implies that homosexuals "choose" to endure discrimination and pain. The movement claims that all homosexuals need to do is choose heterosexuality to receive full rights. Acceptance of the ex-gay movement's position would undermine lesbians' and gay men's claim to civil rights. "The ex-gay movement poses a significant new threat to efforts to secure civil rights legal protections for gay/lesbian/bisexual/transgender people. Potentially, it is the most damaging manifestation of an ongoing backlash against this community. . . . The long-term goal of the Christian Right in using the ex-gay movement to convince people that lesbian, gay, and bisexual people can become heterosexual is to create a restrictive legal environment in which equal rights are only accorded to heterosexual men and women" (Khan 1998, 17–18).

It is important to remember the religious right's goal is to create a theocratic state, a "nation whose laws are based on fundamentalist's interpretation of the Bible" ("We've Come a Long Way . . . Maybe" 2000). Founder and director of the Christian Coalition Pat Robertson stated: "The country was founded by Christians. It was founded as a Christian nation. They're trying to sell us this nonsense about separation of church and state. And that's what it is, it's a fanatical interpretation of the First Amendment. . . . We're going to win this battle but we've got to stand together, all the Christians in America need to join hands together and say we've had enough of this utter nonsense" (White 1997). Similarly, Dean Wycoff, director of the Moral Majority of Santa Clara County, California, stated: "I agree with capital punishment and I believe that homosexuality . . . could be coupled with murder. . . . It would be the government that sits upon this land who will be executing the homosexuals" (Young 1982, 77). Thus, the agenda of the religious right is to take control of the United States and use state power to discriminate, incarcerate, and kill those who do not agree with it—particularly homosexuals.

Separate but Equal

The process of overcoming systemic discrimination is the same whether the bias is race, gender, or sexual orientation. The gay rights movement, like the civil rights movement, is a human rights approach that deconstructs social bias. Comparing the gay rights movement with the civil rights movement gives some insight as to how the gay rights movement is progressing toward the future.

Initially, Africans were brought to the United States as slaves. They were legally and socially treated as property. Many questioned this arrangement and argued that blacks were humans due rights afforded all U.S. citizens. It took a civil war with a terrible death toll to get the Fourteenth Amendment to the U.S. Constitution enacted, which recognized full citizenship for African Americans. But there was a backlash by Christian conservatives who influenced state and local authorities to enact Jim Crow laws. These laws kept the races segregated. African Americans could attend school, but they were separated from whites—this was also true at restaurants, hotels, public transportation systems, swimming pools, and more. For almost 100 years, separate-but-equal was the law of the land and terror perpetrated by white supremacists was used to keep blacks "in their place." Slowly, state by state, city by city, Jim Crow laws were overturned and replaced with laws recognizing full equality regardless of race. This process culminated in 1954 when the U.S. Supreme Court ruled in *Brown v. Board of Education of Topeka, Kansas* that separate was inherently unequal. Only then was the United States faced with fully integrating African Americans into all levels of society. Even still, the Civil Rights Act of 1964 and other legislative acts were required to ensure the equal participation of people of different races. This process deconstructed the allocation of rights and privileges associated with race.

Lesbians and gay men are entering the separate-but-equal stage of their legal status. Until recently, homosexual behavior was illegal. Lesbians and gay men were often arrested, prosecuted, imprisoned, and killed. They were constantly at risk of losing their jobs, homes, and children. Slowly, businesses and schools included sexual orientation in their antidiscrimination codes. Similarly, cities and states removed antigay laws and replaced them with antidiscrimination statutes aimed at providing some protection in the areas of employment and housing. Even with this progress, as of 2003, approximately one-third of the states still had sodomy laws on the books that render homosexuality illegal.

The possibility of same-sex marriages being recognized has created a backlash by Christian conservatives. They have influenced federal and state governments to define marriage as an exclusively heterosexual institution. By 2003, more than two-thirds of the states and the federal government had enacted their own Defense of Marriage Acts (DOMAs). However, some states are attempting to ameliorate the situation by providing "super" domestic partnership for same-sex couples. Vermont implemented a program called civil unions, which confers all the same legal rights and responsibilities associated with marriage to same-sex couples. Civil unions are supposedly equal to "marriage" without using the word *marriage*—a separate-but-equal status for homosexuals.

But civil unions are not the full equivalent of marriage; other states do not recognize them nor does the federal government. As with segregated schools in the 1950s, civil unions are never equal. The U.S. Supreme Court recognized that separate schools for blacks do not confer all the same benefits that whites enjoy in segregated schools. It is expected that the courts will eventually come to a similar understanding about sexual orientation and rule that any scheme attempting to give lesbians and gays "equal" rights to those enjoyed by heterosexuals without giving them exactly the same rights is inherently unequal. Ultimately, gay liberation will deconstruct sexual orientation just as African American liberation deconstructed race and the women's movement deconstructed gender.

The major impediment to African Americans gaining equal rights has been white supremacists and Christian fundamentalists. The major impediment to women's rights has been male supremacists and Christian fundamentalists. The major impediment to gay rights has been heterosexist people and Christian fundamentalists. The arguments used by bigots and Christian fundamentalists are always the same—that blacks are inferior to whites, that women are inferior to men, and that homosexuals are inferior to heterosexuals. However, the stereotypes used to stigmatize these classes of people as being inferior are false. Discrimination against a class of people is never justified; the real issue is not science or scripture, but a *culture war* involving those in power and those who are stigmatized.

The way a culture is changed is through education and positive personal experiences. As more and more gay people come out, more and more heterosexuals have the direct experience of knowing someone gay. Many heterosexuals have learned that gay people are just like them. They have learned that antigay stereotypes are false. Although we sometimes forget, people in power—judges, politicians, and religious leaders—are people too, and they too are experiencing more contact with gay people. When heterosexuals overcome their homophobia and heterosexism, society becomes safer for people of differing sexual orientations to coexist with them. Heterosexuals are an important and necessary ally for lesbians, gay men, bisexuals, transgenders, transsexuals, and intersex people.

References

Bayer, R. 1981. *Homosexuality and American Psychiatry.* New York: Basic Books.

Berlet, C. 1998. "Who Is Mediating the Storm? Right-Wing Alternative Information Networks." In L. Kintz and J. Lesage, eds., *Media, Culture, and the Religious Right.* Minneapolis: University of Minnesota Press, pp. 249–274.

Blumenfeld, W. J., and D. Raymond, eds. 1993. *Looking at Gay and Lesbian Life.* Rev. ed. Boston: Beacon Press.

Bowers v. Hardwick, 106 S.Ct. 2841, 2843 (1986).

Boy Scouts of America v. Dale, No. 99–699 U.S. (2000).

"Buchanan Calls AIDS 'Retribution.'" 1992. *Boston Globe,* February 28.

Childers v. Dallas Police Department, 513 F. Supp. 134 (N.D. Tex. 1981).

D'Emilio, J., and E. B. Freedman. 1988. *Intimate Matters: A History of Sexuality in America.* New York: Harper & Row.

Gay Students Organization v. Bonner, 367 F. Supp. 1088 (D.N.H.), *aff'd,* 509 F.2d 652 (1st Cir. 1974).

Hooker, E. 1963. "The Adjustment of the Male Overt Homosexual." In H. M. Ruitenbeed, ed., *The Problem of Homosexuality.* New York: Dutton, pp. 141–161. (Reprinted from *Journal of Projective Techniques* 21 [1959]: 18–31.)

Hurley v. Irish-American Gay, Lesbian, and Bisexual Group of Boston, No. 94–749 (1995).

Katz, J. 1976. *Gay American History: Lesbians and Gay Men in the U.S.A.* New York: Thomas Y. Crowell.

Keen, L., and S. B. Goldberg. 1999. *Strangers to the Law: Gay People on Trial.* Ann Arbor: University of Michigan Press.

Khan, S. October 1998. *Calculated Compassion: How the Ex-Gay Movement Serves the Right's Attack on Democracy.* New York: Political Research Associates, the Policy Institute of the National Gay and Lesbian Task Force, and Equal Partners in Faith.

Kinsey, A. C., W. B. Pomeroy, and C. E. Martin. 1948. *Sexual Behavior in the Human Male.* Philadelphia: W. B. Saunders Co.

Kinsey, A. C., W. B. Pomeroy, C. E. Martin, and R. H. Gebhard. 1953. *Sexual Behavior in the Human Female.* Philadelphia: W. B. Saunders Co.

Marcus, R. 1990. "Powell Regrets Backing Sodomy Law." *Washington Post,* October 26, A3.

Marotta, T. 1981. *The Politics of Homosexuality.* Boston: Houghton Mifflin.

Mookas, I. 1998. "Faultlines: Homophobic Innovation in Gay Rights/Special Rights." In L. Kintz and J. Lesage, eds., *Media, Culture, and the Religious Right.* Minneapolis: University of Minnesota Press, pp. 319–328.

Nabozny v. Podlesny, 92 F.3d 446, 7th Cir. (1996).

One, Inc. v. Olesen, 355 U.S. 371 (1958).

Plant, R. 1986. *The Pink Triangle: The Nazi War against Homosexuals.* New York: New Republic Books/Henry Holt.

Romer v. Evans, 517 U.S. S.Ct. 620 (1996).

Shilts, R. 1987. *And the Band Played On: Politics, People, and the AIDS Epidemic.* New York: St. Martin's Press.

Stewart, C. K. 2001. *Homosexuality and the Law: A Dictionary.* Santa Barbara, CA: ABC-CLIO.

Thompson, M., ed. 1994. *Long Road to Freedom:* The Advocate *History of the Gay and Lesbian Movement.* New York: St. Martin's Press.

"We've Come a Long Way . . . Maybe." 2000. *Frontiers* 18, no. 22 (March 3): 12.

White, M. 1997. "Selected Quotes from the *700 Club.*" In *The Justice Report.* Special edition. Laguna Beach, CA: Soulforce.

Young, P. D. 1982. *God's Bullies: Native Reflections on Preachers and Politics.* New York: Holt, Rinehart & Winston.

2

Problems, Controversies, and Solutions

"**B**ut I'm her partner," screams Rose at the admitting nurse of a large South Carolina hospital who has denied Rose the right to visit her badly injured partner and their son. "I want to see her and Justin now." Rose shoves a copy of her Vermont civil union certificate at the nurse. "We are married and Ruth is my spouse and Justin is our son."

"Is Justin your biological son?" asks the nurse.

"No, Ruth gave birth to him. But I'm legally his parent in Vermont."

"Do you have any legal documents showing that you have the power of attorney over Ruth? Or adoption papers for Justin?" the nurse continues. "If not, you cannot enter the hospital room, and Justin will stay with Child Protective Services."

"But we're married," cries Rose.

"Not in South Carolina," retorts the nurse.

Although the names have been changed, this story is based on an actual incident that occurred soon after Vermont adopted its civil union for same-sex couples. A civil union confers most of the rights and responsibilities for same-sex couples as does marriage for opposite-sex couples, but only in Vermont. The specter of same-sex marriage released a maelstrom of opposition in many states, and the federal government enacted preemptive legislation otherwise known as Defense of Marriage Acts (DOMAs).

Gay marriages hit a nerve with many Americans, as do other family issues, such as child adoption and child custody and gay kids in school. However, for many lesbians, gay men, bisexuals, and transgender people who face daily legal discrimination in securing employment and a safe place to live, same-sex marriages seem a far-off dream. In this chapter, we review some of these controversies.

Actual Causes of Homosexuality and Numbers of Homosexuals

Two questions are repeatedly asked when the topic of homosexuality is discussed: (1) What causes homosexuality, and (2) how many people are gay or lesbian? These important questions are often a source of conflict between gay activists and the religious right, and are used to sway public opinion.

• What causes homosexuality?

Antigay: The National Association for Research and Therapy of Homosexuality (NARTH), an organization committed to changing sexual orientation, claims that homosexuality is caused in males by poor relationships with their father, difficulty individuating from their mother, a sense of masculine deficit, and a persistent belief of having been different from, and misunderstood by, same-sex childhood peers. NARTH does not give explanations for lesbianism. The ex-gay movement of the religious right claims that homosexuality is chosen as a sin against God.

Progay: The distant father, strong mother claim as the cause of homosexuality has been discredited by psychoanalytic theory. The American Psychiatric Association states:

> No one knows what causes heterosexuality, homosexuality, or bisexuality. Homosexuality was once thought to be the result of troubled family dynamics or faulty psychological development. Those assumptions are now understood to have been based on misinformation and prejudice ... to date there are no replicated scientific studies supporting any specific biological etiology for homosexuality. Similarly, no specific psychosocial or family dynamic cause for homosexuality has been identified, including histories of childhood sexual abuse. Sexual abuse does not appear to be more prevalent in children who grow up to identify as

gay, lesbian, or bisexual, than in children who identify
as heterosexual. ("APA Fact Sheet" 1994)

• How many people are homosexual?

Antigay: The number of gay people is very small, perhaps
less than 2 percent.

Progay: Estimating the number of lesbians, gay men, and
bisexuals is impossible. Many gay activists claim that approximately 6–10 percent of the population is homosexual. The primary estimation problems include underreporting, definition of
gay or homosexual, setting of studies, and ability of research to
construct an objective and representative sample.

Underreporting: "[Homosexuality] is one of the most difficult
things to measure," says Tom Smith, director of General Social
Survey at the National Opinion Research Center (NORC). "It's
personal and intimate, some people won't admit to it, and its
practice is [legally] questionable in some states. Many people
won't give a true response which leads to under-reporting"
(Giger 1991). Research by Clark and Tifft (1966) discovered
underreporting of homosexual behaviors by more than 200 percent between what students stated on a written survey and what
they revealed during polygraph testing.

Definition: What is gay? What is homosexuality? Just exactly
what is being measured—the number of people who have a gay
identity or the number of people who engage in homosexual sex?
How many times does someone have to engage in homosexual
sex before she or he is considered homosexual? Do childhood
experiences count, or do only adult experiences result in a person
being categorized as gay? Is a gay identity the same as homosexual behavior? What about feelings—are people who have homosexual fantasies and feelings, yet never act on them, gay? Are
people who masturbate to same-sex images gay, even if they
engage only in opposite-sex sexual behaviors? As you can see,
how gay and homosexual are defined drastically changes
research results. Likewise, what is sex? The Bill Clinton/Monica
Lewinsky scandal demonstrated that there are varying views
about what constitutes sex and what does not. Thus, how one
defines sex also affects research results.

Kinsey, Pomeroy, and Martin's (1948) famous study of sexuality used a behavioral model for their definition—that is, they
defined sex as achieving orgasm and sexual orientation as the
ratio of heterosexual to homosexual behaviors. Although the
research was flawed, it represented an important milestone in sex

research and is where the infamous 10 percent figure representing the number of people who were mostly homosexual came from.

The term *gay* is a modern word and reflects the politics of people who identify with other homosexuals in their fight to obtain equality with heterosexuals within a heterosexist society. Being gay is not synonymous with engaging in homosexual behaviors, however. For example, the AIDS health community quickly faced the situation of working with men who have sex with other men but do not categorize themselves as gay. In fact, the health community has created a special acronym, MSM (men who have sex with men) for these men. Gay reflects the oppression of homosexuals. Most people who engage in homosexual behaviors do not eventually take on a gay identity. Thus, research that attempts to measure the number of gay people is not reflective of the number of homosexuals or those who engage in homosexual behavior.

Setting: Our Western culture is heterosexist and homophobic. Until recently, people accused of engaging in homosexual sexual behavior faced prison terms or even death. Gay and fag bashings are on the upswing. One third of the states still have sex statutes that make homosexual behavior illegal. Very few cities or states have laws that provide protection in employment, housing, child custody, and other areas based on sexual orientation. Considering these extremely negative environments, we can reasonably assume that many, if not most, people who engage in homosexual behavior will not be truthful to researchers.

Thus, measuring the incidence of homosexuality is dependent on the definition of terms, the negativity of the environment in which the research is conducted, and the truthfulness of the respondents. Estimates as to the incidence of homosexuality (usually 10 percent or lower) should be suspected to be underestimates (Friedman and Downey 1994; Michael, Gagnon, Laumann, and Kolata 1995; Tremblay 1995).

The incidence of homosexuality is more than an item of curiosity. Corporations, cities, counties, and states are considering offering domestic partnership benefits to same-sex couples. During planning for these extended benefits, the question of additional cost comes up. So far, the experience of businesses and governmental agencies that have granted these benefits has shown the costs to be minimal. Very few same-sex couples take advantage of the programs. In fact, often more opposite-sex couples avail themselves of the programs than same-sex couples. Similarly, conservatives sometimes block research into lesbian and gay concerns because they believe it may lead to affirmative action and quotas in hiring. No national or major lesbian and gay organization has called for affirmative action. Thus, the conservative concerns are unfounded, and this reason should not be used to block legitimate research.

AIDS

AIDS is expected to surpass the Black Death as the world's worst pandemic. Since the early 1980s, at least 25 million people have died from AIDS and 40 million people are HIV-positive. It is estimated that 14,000 people become infected each day. In the United States, approximately 900,000 residents are currently infected with HIV, with an additional 40,000 people becoming infected each year ("AIDS" 2002).

AIDS can be contracted only through the exchange of blood, which includes blood transfusions; use of infected needles (primarily sharing of needles between drug addicts); and sex. Discussing AIDS transmission and drug use is controversial in erotophobic (fear of sensuous feelings and behaviors) societies. Fundamentalist Christians, Muslims, Jews, and many other conservative religions and cultures are erotophobic. Developing educational programs in these settings has been difficult.

The United States led the way in developing safe-sex programs. At first, educational pamphlets could not show the proper use of condoms. Eventually, the pamphlets became more and more sexually explicit. Still, there has been a conservative backlash. In 2002, federal inspectors embarked on a comprehensive review of AIDS prevention grants. This occurred because a number of Republican politicians and religious right leaders felt some of the prevention programs went too far. For example, a San Francisco prevention agency sponsored two events called the "Great Sex Workshop" and the "Booty Call." Irate phone calls were received in Washington claiming the programs promoted promiscuity. Likewise, the mayor of St. Louis ordered the removal of billboards that featured two bare-chested African American men in an embrace, with the message "Before the love begins, get tested. Know your HIV status" (Ornstein 2002, 1).

The AIDS groups claim that it is more effective to combine prevention messages with positive images of sex. But critics are uncomfortable with the explicit sex and would prefer messages that encouraged abstinence from anal intercourse. Dana Williams, one of the people who developed the St. Louis campaign, remarks, "People need to take their heads out of the sand and get real about this issue" (Ornstein 2002, 1).

Iran, China, and other highly restrictive countries are in the initial stages of developing their educational programs—and the problems are daunting. In Iran, the word *condom* cannot be used. The pamphlet designed by the Iranian Center for Disease Control for adolescents says: "The best way to avoid AIDS is to be faithful to moral and family obligations and to avoid loose sexual relations. Trust in God in order to resist satanic temptations" (MacFarquhar 2002, 1).

China had a blood donation program that bought unscreened blood, mixed together in vats, and resold it without testing. This spread HIV quickly such that the city of Donghu has an infection rate of 80 percent—the highest in the world. By late 2001, China admitted having a "very serious" AIDS epidemic, with HIV cases up by two thirds in one year. Experts expect that China will soon be devastated by AIDS because of its large size, isolated communities, and culture that does not discuss sex or drug use.

Similar problems have stymied AIDS prevention programs in Africa, Eastern Europe, the former Soviet Union (Maugh 2001), and much of the Middle East, Mexico, and Latin America. Ninety-five percent of new infections occur in the world's poorest countries ("AIDS" 2002).

Antidiscrimination Statutes

Many cities and a few states have enacted antidiscrimination statutes based on sexual orientation. The protections are often limited to public employment, but some are more comprehensive and extend to private employment and public accommodations. As lesbians and gay men gained more protections, conservatives and members of the religious right attempted to squash these protections. A chilling example was the passage of Amendment 2 in the state of Colorado in 1992. This amendment rescinded all existing antidiscrimination laws based on sexual orientation in the state and precluded the adoption of future laws that would provide protections against discrimination based on sexual orientation. The U.S. Supreme Court reviewed the case in 1995 and ruled that Amendment 2 violated the fundamental right of lesbians, gay men, and bisexuals to participate in the political process on an equal basis with other Coloradans.

This was an important ruling because similar attacks were being mounted in other states. What was most revealing from the entire process was the deeper understanding gained about the motivation and strategies used by the religious right in mounting its antigay campaigns. Correspondence between the lawyers and leaders of the religious right showed that they understood that antidiscrimination laws are meant to help stigmatized groups attain status equal to the dominant group. These lawyers advised against using the term special rights in the wording of the law because it was obviously incorrect and would invalidate the law. The term was therefore not used. However, the amendment sponsors purposely chose the motto "no special rights" in their advertising campaign because of its impact on the minds of voters and its ability to raise money (Keen and Goldberg 1998). The religious right's mantra "no special rights" is a deception of which its members are fully aware. Because of the slogan's effectiveness, it will probably be used in future attempts to keep lesbians and gay men from gaining equality with heterosexuals.

Most often, antidiscrimination statutes are enacted by legislative bodies. These are sometimes overturned by public referendum and then sometimes reinstated by courts. In the year 2001, there were approximately 300 gay-related bills pending in state legislatures. About one half of them were antigay. Gay and antigay forces are acutely aware that the battle over gay rights has moved from Washington to the states.

There is a common belief that once an antidiscrimination statute is enacted, the problem of discrimination is solved and the government aggressively protects the people. But just how effective are government agencies at protecting the rights of citizens? Stewart (1996) obtained data from the California Department of Labor Standards Enforcement (DLSE) concerning the outcome of complaints filed with the agency claiming discrimination based on sexual orientation in employment. Of the 372 cases disposed within the first three years after enactment of an antidiscrimination law (AB 2601), 143 (40 percent) were dismissed, 98 (27 percent) were abandoned, 97 (24 percent) were withdrawn, and 34 (9 percent) were settled in favor of the complainant.

DLSE was not able to explain why 91 percent of the complaints were not successful, and the department had no plan to review the cases or to conduct a follow-up to determine if there was a pattern to the unsuccessful complaints. With only *one* full-time investigator on staff for *all* of California reviewing *all* complaints of labor law (not just sexual orientation discrimination), DLSE had no idea how effective it was at enforcing the law. Yet DLSE expresses pride in the quality of its investigations.

Lesbians, gay men, bisexuals, transgender, transsexual, and intersex people need to be aware that antidiscrimination statutes are mostly symbolic and reflect societal attitudes, not actual effectiveness of enforcement.

Child Custody and Adoption

An equally volatile issue is the right of lesbians and gay men to retain legal rights to their children or to gain custody of children through second-parent adoptions or foster care. It has been estimated that as many as one quarter of all gay men and one half of all lesbians have been married at some time in their lives and many of them have children (Gottman 1990; Patterson 1992). Child custody is a real issue, and many same-sex couples want to adopt children of their own. The desire to be a parent is not confined to heterosexuals.

The hysteria over these issues originates with antigay stereotyping that homosexuals are unfit parents, that they molest children, and that they will influence the child to be homosexual. Let us look at these stereotypes.

• Lesbians and gay men are unfit parents.

Counterpoint: The research on children raised by lesbian mothers or gay fathers reveals that there are no significant differences between these children and children raised in heterosexual households. The intellectual development (Flaks, Ficher, Masterpasqua, and Joseph 1995; Green, Mandel, Hotvedt, Gray, and Smith 1986; Kirkpatrick, Smith, and Roy 1981), gender identity (Golombok, Spence, and Rutter 1983), sexual orientation (Bailey, Bobrow, Wolfe, and Mikach 1995; Golombok et al. 1983; Miller 1979), peer group relations (Green et al. 1986), and self-esteem (Huggins 1989) are the same regardless of whether the child is raised in a homosexual or a heterosexual family. Children of homosexual parents do not suffer disproportionate amounts of turmoil (Flaks et al. 1995; Weeks, Derdeyn, and Langman 1975) or depression (Tasker and Golombok 1995; Pennington 1987).

• Homosexuals molest children.

Counterpoint: One of the major stereotypes used to denigrate lesbians and gay men is that homosexuals molest children. This is not true. Many studies have concluded that "gay men are no more likely than heterosexual men to molest children" (Newton 1978, 42). For example, in response to the state of Colorado's attempt to deny rights to homosexuals with Amendment 2, Jenny, Roesler, and Poyer (1994) reviewed the charts of all sexually abused children seen in one year in a Colorado children's hospital. The study revealed that children were abused by homosexuals only 0–3.1 percent—a rate significantly lower than expected. From these studies, Groth and Birnbaum (1978) concluded that children are unlikely to be molested by homosexuals. In contrast, children are primarily (82 percent) molested by heterosexual partners of a close relative of the child.

Many of the antigay stereotypes have been bolstered by the "research" of Paul Cameron. Since 1985, Cameron has self-published a number of pamphlets purporting that most serial killers, child molesters, and others who commit heinous crimes are homosexual. His publications misrepresented the findings of Groth and Birnbaum and contained his own methodologically unsound research. Cameron came under investigation by the American Psychological Association for breach of ethics and poor research methodology. His membership was terminated. Still, he continues to be a one-man propaganda machine of "scientific research" that the religious right has appropriated for its antigay agenda. Unfortunately, his exclusion from the APA made him a martyr for the religious right. (For a comprehensive up-to-date review of this topic, see the website maintained by Gregory Herek at the University of California at Davis Department of Psychology: psychology.ucdavis.edu/rainbow/html/facts_molestation.html# cameron.)

In June 2002, the Family Research Council (FRC) issued a "report" claiming that gay men account for one third of all child abuse cases (available at www.frc.org, *Homosexuality and Child Sexual Abuse*, by Timothy J. Dailey, Ph.D.). The article, very formal looking with many footnotes, gives the impression of being authoritative. However, this is a case of the religious right purposefully misrepresenting the findings of other researchers. The conclusions of every respected academic researcher cited in the study are opposite to the statements made by the FRC. For example, Kurt Freund has stated that "homosexuals are no more likely than heterosexuals to be attracted to children" ("Pathetic Propaganda" 2002). Further, A. Nicholas Groth, one of the most respected academic researchers on the topic, issued an angry letter to the FRC in which he writes that he "objects to my name and research being associated in any way, shape, or form to lend legitimacy to the views proposed in your paper" (Groth 2002). The FRC misrepresents the work of respected scientist to further its hateful goals.

• Homosexual parents will make their children homosexuals.
Counterpoint: The sexual orientation of the parent has no influence on the gender identity of the child (Green 1978) or on his or her independence (Steckel 1987). Children prefer sex-typed toys consistent with their biological gender regardless of their parent's sexual orientation (Hoeffer 1981). There is ample evidence that the sexual orientation of the parent has no influence on the sexual orientation of the child (Bailey et al. 1995; Flaks et al. 1995; Miller 1979; Tasker and Golombok 1995).

Antigay stereotypes are false and have been used to oppress lesbians and gay men. These stereotypes are slowly fading away. For example, the American Academy of Pediatrics ("Co-parent" 2002) recently came out in support of same-sex couples adopting children. These important findings are making their way into court decisions and legislative debate.

Child Custody

Child custody and visitation issues arise when there are competing interests between adults in regard to their legal relationship to children. The most common dispute regarding child custody comes about during divorce. All states use the "best interest of the child" as the rule guiding their decisions. Such a rule is obviously vague and open to a wide range of interpretations. Courts have developed a list of factors to determine what is best for the child and have shown bias toward keeping children in conventional, heterosexual, middle- or upper-class homes.

When one or both parents are lesbian, gay, bisexual, transgender, transsexual, or intersex, the court considers this information. Historically, courts have held many of the antigay stereotypes discussed previously and have taken a narrow view of sexual orientation—usually awarding custody to the heterosexual parent regardless of how abusive he or she may be. Courts are slowly taking a more moderate view and are allowing placement of children with homosexual parents, but only if the parents are "parents first," that is, the parent does not "flaunt" his or her homosexuality. Parents who are politically active in the gay community or have a live-in lover have often been denied custody or visitation rights with their children.

For example, Colorado district judge Thomas Curry barred a bisexual father from taking his nine-year-old daughter to Metropolitan Community Church (a predominantly gay church) or from having overnight guests. The mother, who belonged to a conservative Christian church, was not ordered to adhere to similar restrictions. The father fought back, and in 2001 the Colorado court of appeals reversed the lower court ruling, stating that parenting time in custody cases may not be restricted based on sexual orientation. This is the first time a higher court has ruled on the legitimacy of child custody in relation to lesbian or gay parents.

At the same time this decision was made, in another part of the country, Alabama Supreme Court chief justice Roy Moore concurred with a unanimous decision to deny custody of three children to their lesbian mother and stated that homosexuality is "an inherent evil, and if a person openly engages in such a practice, that fact alone would render him or her an unfit parent" (Bohling 2002). Thus, local law and opinion have a significant impact on the success of lesbians and gay men in retaining custody of their children.

Adoption

The laws concerning adoption of children by lesbians and gay men and same-sex couples are rapidly changing. Often referred to as "second-parent adoptions" or "coparent adoptions," these are a new development in the law. Here, one partner of a same-sex couple adopts the child of the other partner, who is the legal parent—similar to stepparent adoptions. Courts have had difficulty with these arrangements because the act of adopting a child has historically terminated the rights of the legal parent (Clark 1988). Some courts still do not recognize these types of adoptions.

A few states allow joint adoptions. These are adoptions in which two people simultaneously adopt a child who is not legally related to either person. Courts have recognized that having two parents provides a safety for children that is absent when there is only one parent. However, there is still much controversy about allowing children to be adopted into a lesbian or gay male family. For example, the Utah state legislature in March 2000 and the state of Mississippi in May 2000 both approved a ban on all adoptions by unmarried couples. This was the first time since 1988 that a state approved a bill to restrict the rights of lesbians and gay men to adopt or foster children (Freiberg 2000). In that same year, eight similar bans in other states were eliminated. This left only Florida, Arkansas, Utah, and Mississippi with legislation prohibiting adoptions and foster care by lesbians and gay men. Interestingly, Mississippi's ban went further, not only banning same-sex couples from adopting but also refusing to recognize gay adoptions performed in other states.

Domestic Partnership

Domestic partnership programs provide some of the legal and financial benefits of marriage to couples who are not married. Domestic partnership programs vary tremendously in what they provide and in who qualifies. Sometimes they apply only to same-sex couples; other times they apply to both opposite-sex and same-sex couples. In 2002, California enacted the most comprehensive domestic partnership program (AB 25) in the United States, a program that confers virtually all the same rights as marriage.

Many large businesses have instituted domestic partnership benefit programs for partners of same-sex employee couples. Benefit programs are a tool to attract and retain employees. By providing employment benefits only to married couples, companies ignore the desires and needs of same-sex couples. It is simply an issue of fairness. Employment benefits have monetary value (up to 40 percent of an employee's salary can come from benefits), and granting them only to traditional married employees gives these employees financial benefits that are unavailable to employees in same-sex relationships. It is expected that more companies will provide benefits to their gay and lesbian employees.

But not all steps with domestic partnership are forward. For example, when the city of San Francisco instituted a new law in 1997 requiring all companies doing business with the city to extend domestic benefits to same-sex partners of employees, the Salvation Army refused to do so and lost a $3.5 million contract.

In 2001, the Salvation Army's Western Corporation, which covers thirteen states, decided to extend domestic partner benefits to same-sex partners of employees. Religious conservatives, headed by the American Family Association, claimed that "homosexual relationships are not legitimate in God's eyes," and asked members to contact the Salvation Army to persuade it to change the policy (www.afa.net/activism/aa110701.asp). The pressure worked and the Salvation Army rescinded its domestic partnership program two weeks later.

Sometimes it is argued that implementing domestic partnership benefits for same-sex couples will cost too much. But cities and businesses have not found this to be true. For example, Home Box Office found that its health care program for gay partners cost 17 percent less than for heterosexual partners. Likewise, the cities of Seattle, West Hollywood, Berkeley, and Santa Cruz found domestic partner costs to be equivalent to adding an equal number of married spouses (Becker 1995). Although insurance companies initially added surcharges to their premiums to companies providing domestic partnership programs, most reduced or eliminated these charges once they learned that costs were no higher than for spouses of married employees (*Report of the CUNY Study* 1993).

Employment and Housing

Gay marriage, adoption by same-sex couples, and other topics make headlines, are fodder for late-night talk shows, and are used for urgent requests from religious groups asking for donations to stop the impending doom. For most lesbians and gay men, however, these are minor issues compared with the right to work and have a place to live. Without the antidiscrimination statutes discussed in the previous section, lesbians, gay men, bisexuals, and transgender people can be and are fired from their jobs and are often denied housing or evicted from their homes solely for not being heterosexual. These are survival issues that make all other rights secondary.

Employment

The 1884 case of *Payne v. Western Alt. R.R.* established the doctrine of "employment at will." This doctrine allowed both private and public employers to hire and fire without cause. Slowly, this absolute doctrine has been modified by the Civil Rights Act of 1964 and by recent state and city enactment of antidiscrimination statutes that included sexual orientation as a protected class. In general, however, lesbians and gay men are not protected from willful termination by private employers.

Historically, being lesbian or gay automatically disqualified people from obtaining state licensing and other employment credentials. Many lesbians and gay men, once found out, have been terminated from their jobs and have had their credentials revoked. The McCarthy witch-hunts in the 1950s resulted in thousands of homosexuals being fired from government employment.

Not until 1969 in *Morrison v. State Board of Education* did a court rule that homosexuality itself could not be used as a cause for termination. Instead, the court shifted the emphasis to the employer (in this case a school district), who had to demonstrate that the actions of open lesbian or gay employees affected their ability to work efficiency. However, working in schools and with children entails other risks that have resulted in some courts ruling that homosexuality, in itself, is cause for dismissal. Even today, lesbian and gay teachers run great risk of losing their jobs if they are open.

The U.S. government is the single largest employer in the United States. The U.S. Civil Service Commission in 1973 issued a bulletin (December 21) informing federal agencies that they could not deny employment to gay men or lesbians solely on the basis of sexual orientation. Later this concept was expanded by the enactment of the Civil Service Reform Act of 1978. Supervisors were directed not to discriminate against employees on the basis of conduct that does not adversely affect their performance or the performance of others. Finally, in 1998, President Clinton signed an executive order specifically banning discrimination based on sexual orientation in the federal civilian workforce.

President George W. Bush proposed a "faith-based initiative" that would funnel government money to religious organizations providing social services. Many civil libertarians expressed concern over the initiative, fearing these organizations would use government money to promote their religions—a condition expressly forbidden by the U. S. Constitution.

A glimpse of how this could affect homosexual people was demonstrated in a Kentucky federal court. The Kentucky Baptist Homes for Children (KBHC) fired its top therapist upon discovering she was a lesbian. KBHC claimed that because she was a lesbian, she would be incapable of inculcating Baptist views in children. KBHC, which receives more than one half of its annual $17 million budget from the state, argued that it had the right to enforce its religious views, which meant excluding lesbian employees. The woman sued, but the court upheld the firing. According to Christopher E. Anders, legislative counsel for the American Civil Liberties Union (ACLU), "There can now be no question that if the Bush initiative is passed, the result will be government-funded discrimination" ("Court Allows Baptist Homes Firing" 2001).

Currently, the military and any government job that deals with security or intelligence may legally exclude homosexuals because they are considered security risks. The premise is that homosexuals are susceptible to blackmail, an accusation disproved by many military studies. Although the FBI, CIA, and other agencies officially no longer discriminate against homosexuals, openly lesbian and gay applicants are invariably turned down.

Unless expressly forbidden by state or local law, private employers may discriminate against lesbian and gay employees and applicants. There are no federal laws preventing discrimination in private business against employees based on sexual orientation. A few states and many cities have enacted antidiscrimination statutes and ordinances that provide employment protection for lesbians and gay men, and sometimes for gender.

Much of the controversy that surrounds housing and employment issues for lesbians and gay men is the enactment of antidiscrimination ordinances specifying sexual orientation. Conservatives and members of the religious right see antidiscrimination statutes as special rights, whereas lesbians and gay men see them as necessary enforcement of basic constitutional rights. Some conservative lesbians and gay men believe that antidiscrimination laws are unnecessary, that the Constitution already contains language providing protection for every citizen's right to housing and employment. But as any marginalized group can attest, characteristics such as race, religion, nationality, and now gender and sexual orientation have long histories of being targeted for oppression by the dominant power structure, which has failed to enforce constitutional protections. Thus, the need to reaffirm these rights through antidiscrimination statutes is necessary. Antidiscrimination statutes are not special or additional rights, but rather affirmations of existing rights.

Housing

Even with housing antidiscrimination statutes, courts have allowed religious exemptions. For example, Alaska forbids discrimination in housing based on marital status. Two Christian landlords in Anchorage, Alaska, claimed that compliance with city and state fair housing laws by renting to unmarried couples would force them to "facilitate sin." The Ninth U.S. Circuit Court of Appeals ruled in 2000 (*Thomas v. Anchorage*) that the landlords had the right to discriminate against tenants based on their religious beliefs. Further, "the court said the state and city discrimination laws unconstitutionally forced landlords to choose between their businesses and their religious beliefs. The court also said prohibiting landlords from asking about a prospective tenant's marital status violates freedom of speech" (Egelko 1999). The decision was dismissed the next year because the case was "purely hypothetical" since the landlords had never encountered the actual situation. However, this case could be a harbinger of things to come and has implications for lesbian and gay couples, who are precluded from marriage.

Rent control or rent stabilization statutes can be used to protect same-sex couples. For example, a New York City gay man faced eviction from his apartment when his lover of eleven years died from AIDS. The survivor's name did not appear on the lease. Rent control provisions precluded landlords from evicting "either the surviving spouse of the deceased tenant or some other member of the deceased tenant's family who has been living with the tenant." The man argued that he was "family," and the court of appeals agreed with that position (*Braschi v. Stahl Associates Co.*). This was precedent setting and helped to establish the idea that lesbians and gay men could form legitimate families.

Hate Crimes

Hate crimes are bias-motivated violence. When aimed at lesbians, gay men, transgender people, or those perceived to be non-heterosexual, these crimes are commonly referred to as fag bashing or gay bashing.

The reported incidents of antigay violence increased nationally almost 400 percent between 1988 and 1996 and continues to rise ("Anti-Lesbian, Gay, Bisexual, and Transgendered Violence"

2001). Of those hate crimes that were reported, 50 percent of all victims were injured, 25 percent received serious injuries, and 2 percent were killed. The majority of bias crimes are directed at individuals (95 percent)—not property (5 percent) as popularly believed ("Anti-Lesbian, Gay, Bisexual, and Transgendered Violence" 1996). Furthermore, hate crimes are underreported. The National Gay and Lesbian Task Force (NGLTF) reports "[Hate crime] figures released today by the Federal Bureau of Investigation demonstrate that local law enforcement entities across the United States are massively underreporting hate crimes based on sexual orientation, and show the necessity for more effective legislation mandating that hate crimes be reported to the federal government" ("FBI Hate Crimes Data" 2001).

In 1990 the federal government passed the Hate Crime Statistics Act. The act provides for the collection of statistics on hate crimes, including crimes based on sexual orientation. Because of conservative forces in Congress, the act specifically excludes taking action on sexual orientation hate crimes. Senator Jesse Helms (R-NC) effectively blocked passage of the act in its first form in 1986, claiming that "studying hate crimes against homosexuals is a crucial first step toward achieving homosexual rights and legitimacy in American society" (Yeoman 1996). At this time, there is still no national hate crime prevention act that increases punishment for bias-based crimes.

Perpetrators of antigay and lesbian violence tend to be teenage or young adult males who are unknown to their victims. Gay men and lesbians of color experience significantly more victimization by white perpetrators. In antigay hate crimes, it is usually small groups of perpetrators who attack small groups of gays and lesbians. During the attack, the perpetrators often verbally condemn the victims based on religious grounds. Studies have found that the potential to be a gay basher results from (1) learned beliefs and religious biases against gays and lesbians, sometimes (2) combined with a latent fear of being homosexual (Adams, Wright, and Lohr 1996; Goleman 1990).

There is controversy concerning hate crime legislation. Some people believe that some crimes are worse than others and therefore require special consideration. This *special model* is the approach taken by the Hate Crime Statistics Act and most hate crime statutes. Laws created using the special model impose greater penalties for crimes in which bias hate is a major motivation. Here, judges can impose stiffer fines and longer sentences for hate crimes that, for example, involve robbery than for robbery itself.

However, some lesbian and gay legal advisers argue against such a special model. They propose a *neutral model* that requires rigorous enforcement of already existing criminal laws and penalties, regardless of who the victim is. They argue that the primary problem facing lesbians and gays is a long history of police and courts showing leniency toward people who commit crimes against nonheterosexuals or of prosecutors who refuse to prosecute those who commit these crimes. These advocates point out that enacting hate crime laws possibly encroaches on the First Amendment right to free speech. Lesbian and gay activists and legal thinkers understand the importance of free speech and are hesitant to impose limitations in this area for fear the limitations could be used against gay liberation.

Marriage

The hysteria that surrounded gay marriage in the 1990s and 2000s stemmed from the possibility that Hawaii, Vermont, or both were going to allow same-sex marriage. The constitutions of both states provide antidiscrimination protections based on sex or gender. The courts interpreted this to mean that disallowing same-sex marriage was a form of sex discrimination. Before the Hawaii Supreme Court could render a decision, however, the voters of Hawaii enacted a DOMA amendment to their state constitution that mooted the suit. Vermont took a different approach. Again, the Vermont Supreme Court determined that barring same-sex marriage was a form of sex discrimination. Instead of the court mandating same-sex marriage, it referred the issue back to state legislators to find a solution that would place same-sex relationships on the same legal footing as opposite-sex relationships. The legislators created a civil union designation for same-sex couples that conferred all rights associated with marriage.

Civil unions are marriage in all aspects except in name. However, civil unions extend only as far as the Vermont border. Other states and the federal government do not recognize civil unions. In the first case testing the validity of civil unions, the Georgia appeals court ruled in January 2002 that civil unions are not valid marriages in Georgia ("Ga. Appeals" 2002).

In April 2001, the Netherlands became the first country in the world to legalize same-sex marriage. It is unknown if these marriages will be recognized in the United States. A number of U.S. citizens have been married in the Netherlands (which has a four-month residency requirement), but none have come back to the United States to challenge the law.

Religious conservatives have expressed a number of concerns over allowing same-sex marriage. Some of these include the following:

• Marriage should be reserved for monogamous male-female attachments to further the goal of raising psychologically, emotionally, and educationally balanced offspring.

Counterpoint: This statement is based on two false concepts. The first is that the primary purpose of marriage is reproduction. If this were true, then opposite-sex couples who cannot have children, such as older couples or those who are infertile, would also be barred from marrying. But our society does not stop these classes of people from marrying. Thus, reproduction is not a necessary condition for marriage. Second, the belief that only heterosexual married couples can provide emotionally stable environments for children is false. Same-sex couples provide equally healthy family environments for children, as demonstrated by the recent decision by the American Association of Pediatrics ("Co-parent" 2002) advocating same-sex-couple adoption of children.

• Government policy should encourage marriage and intact families because they are the basic units of social order, stability, and growth.

Counterpoint: Most lesbians and gay men would agree with this statement. However, there is an underlying assumption that only a traditional heterosexual family structure can fulfill this role. This is not true. Many different family structures can provide order, stability, and growth. Same-sex marriages would help provide legal stability for children in those families.

• Even domestic partnerships are reason for alarm. The apparent evenhandedness of the law is deceptive. Heterosexuals, who have the option of marriage, will not use domestic partnership registration. Instead, this is a homosexual rights ordinance, and it promotes behavior that increases the likelihood of transmission of AIDS.

Counterpoint: Cities that have enacted domestic partnership programs have found that a majority of enrollees are opposite-sex couples, not lesbian or gay male couples. The belief that a homosexual "lifestyle" spreads disease is false, and suggesting that it is true is one of the strategies used by the religious right to smear the gay community.

• This is part of the gay agenda. Asking that persecution end and demanding recognition and full marriage rights will lead to demands for preferential treatment to counter historic discrimination.

Counterpoint: The gay agenda, if there is such a thing, is to obtain equal rights, not special rights. Marriage is an institution through which heterosexuals have obtained at least 1,049 federal laws and regulations that are not available to same-sex couples. It is heterosexuals, not lesbians and gay men, who have obtained special rights. No gay activist organization, lesbian and gay student group, or gay academic has ever requested special rights, affirmative action, or preferential treatment. Linking the drive for equal rights with affirmative action is misleading.

• Approving of gay marriage will lead to the sanctioning of polygamy or worse.

Counterpoint: This has been a scare tactic used by religious conservatives who claim that approving same-sex marriages will create a domino effect allowing all kinds of marriages. This is faulty logic and was used during the debate over interracial marriages. Although white supremacists preached that society would be ruined if interracial marriages were allowed, that did not happen. Similarly, allowing same-sex marriage will not destroy society and is not related to the issue of polygamy. Whether polygamy or other marriage forms are allowed will be determined by debate on the merits of the issue.

Every argument given to promote marriage applies equally to opposite-sex or same-sex couples.

The Military

Gays in the military became a controversial issue when presidential candidate Bill Clinton announced that he would lift the ban on homosexuals serving in the military if elected. Clinton won the presidency and immediately launched an investigation into the feasibility of lifting the ban. There was much resistance by the military, Congress, and the public. Georgia's Democratic senator Sam Nunn blocked the president's efforts and was able to insert into the Department of Defense budget a policy that has become known as "Don't Ask, Don't Tell, Don't Pursue," which allows gays to serve in the military only if they remain closeted.

The military has given a number of arguments for why gay men and lesbians should not serve.

• Homosexuals are easily blackmailed and cannot be trusted with classified information.

Counterpoint: In 1957 the secretary of the navy put together a board chaired by Captain S. H. Crittenden, Jr., USN. The findings, known as the Crittenden Report, examined the stereotype that homosexuals are easy targets of blackmail by enemy agents who might threaten to expose their sexuality. He found that "the number of cases of blackmail as a result of past investigations of homosexuals is negligible. No factual data exist to support the contention that homosexuals are a greater risk than heterosexuals" (Dyer 1990, xvi). There is no sound basis to the belief that homosexuals pose a security risk

• Homosexuality is incompatible with military service.

Counterpoint: Besides the Crittenden Report, two more research projects were commissioned by the military to analyze the participation of lesbians and gay men in military service. Again, both the 1988 and 1989 Personnel Security and Education Center (PERSEC) reports found no reason to deny lesbians and gay men the right to serve in the military (Sarbin and Karois 1988; McDaniel 1989). The reports were buried, but leaks to Congress and the press brought them, and the Crittenden Report, to the surface.

• Homosexuals disrupt military morale, and they cannot be effectively integrated into the service.

Counterpoint: Britain lifted its ban on homosexuals in the military in 2000. With the exception of the United States, all member countries of the North Atlantic Treaty Organization now accept homosexual personnel into their military. These countries report integrating lesbians and gays into their militaries successfully.

• Don't Ask, Don't Tell has been stabilizing for the military.

Counterpoint: The persecution of lesbian and gay military personnel soared, instead of declining, after Don't Ask, Don't Tell was implemented, and the rate of discharge from the military for homosexuality increased by 73 percent ("New Gay Discharge Figures Up" 2000). Likewise, antigay harassment increased. The Servicemembers Legal Defense Network reported that antigay harassment increased by 142 percent in 1999 over 1998 ("Antigay Harassment" 2000). In March 2000, the Pentagon inspector general released a report based on the responses of 72,000 troops stationed around the world. The survey found "disturbing" levels of gay harassment in the U.S. military. Secretary of Defense William S. Cohen said the survey showed that additional efforts were needed to end the terrible harassment (Richter 2000).

A number of lawsuits were filed against the military in the 1980s and 1990s by lesbian and gay personnel discharged for homosexuality. With few exceptions, the suits were not successful, and the Supreme Court refused to review any of the cases that directly challenged Don't Ask, Don't Tell. Courts often made illogical and irrational decisions in this area. For example, the Ninth Circuit U.S. Court of Appeals ruled in *Holmes/Watson v. California Army* that the Don't Ask, Don't Tell policy was not discriminatory since it treated "homosexuals and heterosexuals equally because neither are allowed to say they are gay." This utterly confusing ruling shows to what extent courts are willing to avoid resolving conflicts over military policy. Until some president is willing to take the lead, as did President Harry Truman with the integration of African Americans into the armed forces, the military will remain a dangerous place for lesbians and gay men.

Public Attitudes about Gays and Lesbians

There was a striking change in public attitude about key gay and lesbian rights issues in the last decade of the twentieth century. A very large study in 2000 was conducted by the University of Michigan to measure public attitude on a number of key issues (Burns, Kinder, Rosenstone, Shapiro, National Election Studies 2001). The research is part of a longitudinal study spanning more than a decade. The study found:

- Public support for *gay adoption* had increased 15 percent since 1992. In 2000, the American people were divided on this issue, with 41.4 percent supporting gay adoptions and 50.5 percent opposed (8.1 percent had no opinion).
- Public support for allowing gay men and lesbians to *serve in the military* had increased 16 percent since 1992. In 2000, approximately 71.2 percent of Americans believed gays should be allowed to serve in the military, whereas 22.9 percent opposed this (5.9 percent had no opinion).
- Public support for enactment of *nondiscrimination laws*

based on sexual orientation had increased 17 percent since 1988. In 2000, Americans supported this idea by a two to one margin, with 63.9 percent in favor and 30.9 percent opposed (5.2 percent had no opinion). For the first time since this question was asked, a majority of Republicans (55.6 percent) supported enacting such laws.

- The National Election Studies ask respondents to rate their *feelings* concerning various groups of people. In 1988, lesbians and gay men rated the lowest among all groups (feminists, blacks, Hispanics, environmentalists, Christian fundamentalists, people on welfare, and "illegal aliens"), at 28.5. This improved in 2000 to 47.5, yet it is still lower than any other group. Thus, there seems to be a general thaw in feelings toward minority groups, including lesbians and gay men.

The general improvement in the public's attitude toward lesbians and gay men shows up in the passage of antidiscrimination statutes, acceptance of same-sex couples, and a multitude of areas. However, as lesbians and gay men reach greater levels of acceptance, members of the religious right feel greater rage and marginalization and lash back with lawsuits, antigay legislation, and violence.

Reparative Therapy

There are some who claim that sexual orientation can be changed. An entire industry has sprung up to "help" homosexuals become heterosexual. This effort is often referred to as reparative therapy, through which the gay persons "brokenness of homosexuality" is "repaired." Usually conducted by ex-gay ministries, these programs are always religious based (Christian fundamentalist), target homosexuals who hate their sexuality and who want to be heterosexual, and use a number of behavior modification techniques including shock and aversion therapy, psychoanalysis, "deprogramming," and twelve-step model. Since the programs are conducted under the guise of "religious counseling," they do not need to conform to professional or state psychotherapy guidelines. Although these ministries publicly promise "change," they "acknowledge that celibacy is the realistic goal to which homosexuals must aspire" (Haldeman 1991, 156).

The ex-gay movement makes a number of claims:
• Reparative therapy is successful from 38 percent to 71.6 percent of the time.

Counterpoint: A number of reports issued by conversion programs make claims of high success rates. For example, in the 1994 PBS documentary *One Nation under God*, Exodus International, the largest ex-gay organization in the world, claimed to have treated hundreds of thousands of homosexuals and boasted a success rate of 71.6 percent. Yet Exodus keeps no follow-up records, does not make its records available to outside researchers, and refuses to publish its findings in peer-reviewed academic journals.

The founders of Exodus, Michael Bussee and Gary Cooper, became infamous when they fell in love, divorced their wives, held their own commitment ceremony, and became outspoken opponents of the ex-gay movement—otherwise known as "ex-ex-gay." "Some people who went through the Exodus program had breakdowns or committed suicide. . . . After dealing with hundreds of people, [he hadn't] met one who went from gay to straight. . . . If you got them away from the Christian limelight . . . not one person said, 'Yes, I am actually now heterosexual'" (Mills 1999, 17). If Exodus wanted respectability, it would conduct longitudinal studies using respected academic researchers who know how to structure objective studies.

Leaders of ex-gay ministries have a history of engaging in sex with their clients. This has led to the demise of many groups and attempted cover-ups by the sponsoring religious organizations. Perhaps the most notorious of these scandals involved Colin Clark of the Seventh Day Adventist Church; he had sex with his patients and the church tried to cover up the abuse (Lawson 1987). Indeed, "the tradition of conflicted homosexual pastors using their ministries to gain sexual access to vulnerable gay people is as long-standing as the conversion movement itself" (Haldeman 1991, 157). And as reported by Exodus International, "[The program was] ineffective. . . . Not one person was healed" (Newswatch Briefs 1990). These religious-based programs often exacerbated already prominent feelings of guilt and personal failure among the counselees; many were driven to suicidal thoughts as a result of the failed "reparative therapy" (Haldeman 1991, 159).

In June 2001, two conflicting studies on the success rate of reparative therapy were released. Robert Spitzer, a psychiatrist from Columbia University and author of the 1973 resolution to remove homosexuality from the APA list of disorders, reported that "good heterosexual functioning" was achieved in 66 percent of the men and 44 percent of the women in his study who underwent reparative therapy. However, there are many problems with this study. Many of the participants were suicidal and acknowledged that they still had attractions to the same sex. More than 65 percent of the participants came from ex-gay ministries or NARTH. The study was based on a single forty-five-minute phone call, there was no control group, and Spitzer himself is a member of NARTH and thus not an impartial researcher. In addition, Spitzer self-released the report and did not submit it for professional review (Dezotos 2001).

At the same time, Shidlo and Schroeder presented their research at the American Psychiatric Association's annual conference. They found that 88 percent of interviewees were unable to "convert" their sexual orientation, another 9 percent reported that they were struggling or celibate, and just 3 percent reported being successful and living contently as heterosexuals. Of the 3 percent who reported successful change in their sexual orientation, all but one made their living as "conversion" counselors, thus reflecting possible bias. This was one of the few studies that attempted to be objective, in which subjects were interviewed repeatedly over a five-year period ("Spitzer's Study" 2002).

In an older study conducted in the 1970s, behavioral psychotherapist Birk claimed that 38 percent of his patients achieved a solid heterosexual shift. Yet he stated: "Most, if not all, people who have been homosexual continue to have some homosexual feelings, fantasies, and interests. More often than not, they also have occasional, or more than occasional, homosexual outlets, even while being 'happily married'" (Birk 1980). By what criteria are these people heterosexual?

Claims of conversion are made by religious groups or "researchers" from antigay organizations that do not use objective measures or methodology. Academic researchers consistently find few, if any, people who change their sexual orientation. "[There is] no scientific evidence . . . to support the effectiveness of any of the conversion therapies that try to change sexual orientation. These interventions do not shift sexual orientation at all. Rather, they instruct or coerce heterosexual activity in a minority of subjects which is not the same as reversing sexual orientation" ("APA Fact Sheet" 1994).

- People can be changed from homosexual to heterosexual.

Counterpoint: According to the American Psychiatric Association: "There is no published scientific evidence supporting the efficacy of reparative therapy as a treatment to change one's sexual orientation. . . . Gay men and lesbians who have accepted their sexual orientation positively are better adjusted than those who have not done so" ("APA Fact Sheet" 1994). In 1990 the APA stated "that scientific evidence does not show that conversion therapy works and that it can do more harm than good" ("Health Care Needs" 1994).

- The APA was taken over by gay activists who were responsible for removing homosexuality from its list of mental disorders in 1973.

Counterpoint: NARTH has claimed that the APA was hijacked by gay activists and forced into removing homosexuality from its list of mental disorders. But in fact, the decision to remove homosexuality as a disorder was voted on by the entire membership of the APA and other professional organizations after careful review.

- Homosexuality is a mental disorder. Only when a person becomes heterosexual can he or she achieve true emotional stability.

Counterpoint: The APA has stated "For nearly three decades, it has been known that homosexuality is not a mental illness. Medical and mental health professionals also now know that sexual orientation is not a choice and cannot be altered. Groups who try to change the sexual orientation of people through so-called conversion therapy are misguided and run the risk of causing a great deal of psychological harm to those they say they are trying to help" ("Health Care Needs" 1994). All sexual orientations are equally healthy.

Schools

Homosexuality and schools are a volatile mix. There always have been and always will be homosexual students and teachers. Schools have been dangerous places for lesbian and gay students (and teachers). Academic researcher K. Carter estimated in 1997 that a child hears twenty-five antigay remarks each day in public schools. When these are said in front of a teacher, 97 percent of those teachers will make no effort to stop the comments.

Sexual Harassment

The experience of Jamie Nabozny illustrates the dangers in school. Nabozny was harassed in school. He was mock-raped by two boys in front of twenty other students, urinated on in the bathroom, and beaten so badly that he required surgery to stop the internal bleeding. When Jamie and his parents complained to school officials, they said he should "get used to it" because he was homosexual. Nabozny sued and, for the first time, a court found a school liable for the mistreatment (*Nabozny v. Podlesny*). The school was fined almost $1 million. The court upheld the notion that harassment of lesbian and gay students that is sexual in nature constitutes sexual harassment. In 1997, the U.S. Department of Education clarified that Title IX made schools responsible for providing a safe environment for all students, that is, an environment free from sexual harassment—including harassment toward lesbian and gay students. Only now is this ruling and its implications filtering down to local schools.

Equal Access Act

Religious groups wanting the right to conduct Bible study on pub-lic school property during lunch and after school lobbied Congress in the early 1980s. The debate in Congress demonstrated that such a law could lead to lesbian and gay student groups wanting the same right to assemble as other extracurricular groups on campus. Although the bill in its original form addressed only the problem of schools barring religious groups, it was amended to include all extracurricular groups without preference.

In 1984, the Equal Access Act was passed, requiring schools to give access to *all* groups equally. With the formation of lesbian and gay clubs, some schools rebelled against the law. For exam-ple, the Salt Lake City School District board cancelled all extracur-ricular clubs and activities rather than allow lesbian and gay stu-dents the same access. Unfortunately, many parents and students blamed the lesbian and gay students for cancellation of the clubs instead of blaming the school board.

Particularly since the *Nabozny v. Podlesny* case and the expan-sion of Title IX, courts have been issuing injunctions against school districts that try to block lesbian and gay students from organizing. We should expect these conflicts to continue in the future, particularly in conservative communities.

Prom

The prom is an example of an extracurricular activity that traditionally has excluded same-sex couples. In a celebrated case, Aaron Fricke wanted to bring his friend Paul Guilbert to the Cumberland High School 1980 senior prom. The principal denied the request, saying that there was a "real and present threat of physical harm" to the two boys. Fricke sued. At the trial of *Fricke v. Lynch,* the judge acknowledged that the principal's fears were real, but that the school should have looked into ways of increasing security and instituting other safety measures rather than denying the couple the right to attend. The court recognized that attendance at a prom is "symbolic speech," much like marching in a parade, and thus merits First Amendment protection. Aaron and Paul were allowed to attend the prom.

Even though this groundbreaking case occurred more than twenty years ago, lesbians and gay student are still sometimes prevented from going to their prom. As recently as May 2002, Cy Scott and his date, Paul Alexander, were turned away at the door of the prom. It was claimed that there was an "unwritten rule" barring the selling of tickets to same-sex couples at Robert E. Lee High School in Baton Rouge, Louisiana. When Scott sued, the principal, Jack Stokeld, apologized, claiming that the action was not deliberate. Still, the young man was denied a once-in-a-lifetime experience.

Sodomy

Antisodomy statutes are used by about one third of the states to criminalize adult consensual sexual behavior. The statutes are inconsistent in defining sodomy, however. In some states, sodomy is defined as sex between people of the same sex, whereas in other states sodomy is defined as sex between any two people who are not married to each other. Even which sexual acts constitute sodomy varies greatly from state to state. Some limit sodomy to anal penetration, others include mouth-to-genital contact, and still others only vaguely refer to "detestable and abominable crimes against nature." Antisodomy provisions are often found in other laws covering indecent exposure, lewd conduct, loitering, and disorderly conduct.

The term *sodomy* comes from the biblical city of Sodom. The

Bible tells of its destruction by God because of the evils practiced by its citizens. Some people believe homosexual sex was the evil practiced in Sodom and Gomorrah. Although most current biblical scholars acknowledge that Sodom's sin was the sin of inhospitality, certain Jewish and Christian sects have interpreted the destruction of Sodom as God's wrath against homosexuals (Blumenfeld and Raymond 1993, 173).

In 1961, Illinois became the first state to eliminate sex statutes against consensual homosexual sex. It took another ten years before another state followed suit (Connecticut). By the mid-1980s, about one half of the states still had antisodomy statutes.

Antisodomy statutes were directly challenged at the federal level in 1986. The U.S. Supreme Court in *Bowers v. Hardwick* refused to strike down a Georgia law criminalizing sodomy. In a five to four vote, the majority opinion in *Bowers v. Hardwick* stated that there was no constitutional right to engage in "homosexual sodomy." This affirmed the right of states to enact and enforce antisodomy statutes.

The battle over antisodomy statutes is being fought state by state. In 1992, the Kentucky Supreme Court struck down its sex statutes in *Commonwealth v. Wasson*. This was an important decision because the court rejected many of the points made by the majority of judges in *Bowers v. Hardwick* and recognized that privacy extended to adult consensual sex regardless of whether it was homosexual. Other courts have concluded that antisodomy statutes violate the right to privacy and/or violate the equal protection laws.

A recent tragic case (*Kansas v. Matthew Limon* 2002) demonstrates the conflict between antisodomy statutes and equal protection provisions. Matthew Limon, an eighteen-year-old boy who suffers from intellectual disability and lived as a resident of the Lakemary Center (a school for developmentally disabled youths in Paola, Kansas), engaged in oral sex with another developmentally disabled resident of the school, who was fourteen. When the younger boy asked Limon to stop, he did so. The case came to the attention of police, and Limon was charged with sodomy. The court found him guilty and sentenced him to seventeen years in prison.

Limon's defense agreed that Limon had engaged in illegal behavior, but that the sentence violated equal protection provisions. In the state of Kansas, if a teen between fourteen and sixteen engages in sex with a teen of the opposite sex who is no more than four years older, the older teen can be prosecuted under the "Romeo and Juliet Law" and imprisoned for not more than one year. The law is routinely ignored. The defense argued that because Limon engaged in same-sex behavior, he was given a much harsher sentence that violated the state's equal protection provisions. The court responded by saying the U.S. Supreme Court in *Bowers v. Hardwick* allowed states to treat homosexual acts differently from heterosexual ones, and as such, there was no violation of the equal protection provisions.

As of 2002, consensual sodomy was still criminalized in about one third of the states. Some states are confused, having enacted legal protections based on sexual orientation and at the same time retaining their antisodomy laws.

Although antisodomy statutes are rarely enforced, they have an impact on lesbians and gay men. Their existence makes homosexuals de facto criminals. This often affects child custody decisions, state professional licensing, employment, government housing, and other areas that exclude "criminals." Further, those opposed to gay rights point to antisodomy statutes as justification for their belief that homosexuals are criminals not deserving equal treatment under the law.

Speech and Association

The First Amendment to the U.S. Constitution provides protected status for the right of free speech and association. Many court cases have upheld the right to discuss homosexuality; publish books, magazines, pamphlets, movies, videos, and other forms of media about homosexuality; form organizations both publicly and privately to promote and educate on homosexual causes; and more.

Probably the most important U.S. Supreme Court decision to impact the gay community was made in 1958. At that time, homosexual materials were automatically classified as "obscene, lewd, lascivious and filthy" and were not allowed to be distributed by the U.S. Postal Service. In a lawsuit brought by the ONE, Inc., the Court ruled against the government and allowed gay materials to be mailed through the U.S. postal system (*One, Inc. v. Olesen*). This led to a boom in the publishing and distribution of lesbian and gay information. The dissemination of knowledge concerning lesbian and gay issues within the lesbian and gay community helped reduce internalized homophobia and spur political organizing. Similarly, the dissemination of knowledge about lesbians and gay men helped heterosexuals overcome their own homophobia and recognize that homosexuals should be treated fairly and equally.

Currently, there are three areas of controversy surrounding free speech and homosexuality. First, many people fear the spread of an uncontrolled Internet. Some parents and religious conservatives want to block information they believe is harmful to minors. Attempts by Congress to regulate the Internet have been struck down by the Supreme Court in *ACLU v. Reno I* and *ACLU v. Reno II*. Most recently, the Court struck down the Children's Internet Protection Act (2002) as being an unconstitutional infringement of the First Amendment. Legislators seem unable to construct laws that clearly define "harmful," "offensive," and "community standards," or that include regulatory schemes that can be upheld by courts. Further, there is no scientific evidence that any information, including pornography, is "harmful" to minors. ACLU Legal Director Stefan Presser states, "The technology cannot block simply obscene speech, or speech that is harmful to minors, without blocking an enormous amount of speech that is constitutionally protected" (Caruso 2002).

Second, just what does it mean for lesbian, gay, bisexual, transgender, transsexual, and intersex people to come out and be open about their sexuality? For example, the California Supreme Court ruled in 1979 in *Gay Law Students* that a person's affirmation of homosexuality was analogous to expressing a political view and as such was protected under the state labor code. But what constitutes "affirming" one's homosexuality? Does this mean a person has the right to declare that he or she is gay? What about answering questions about beliefs or personal life? Is that protected?

With homosexuals, these First Amendment rights are undeveloped. For example, teachers who share that they are lesbian or gay with students may be accused of acting unprofessionally and promoting homosexuality. Often they will be fired from their job. Interestingly, no city, state, or union contract has ever specified what constitutes "professional" conduct by teachers. Thus, charging teachers with "unprofessional" conduct for sharing their sexual orientation with students is a smoke screen for homophobia. Courts have not been helpful in this area.

In some cases, teachers can declare they are gay but are not allowed to answer any questions. If they do answer questions about their personal life, they are accused of talking about sex. Because sex education is highly regulated by state boards of education, the teachers' employment will often be terminated.

Third, a current legal strategy being used by a number of religious individuals and groups is to claim "religious freedom" as a way to circumvent antidiscrimination statutes. For example, J. Barrett Hyman launched two civil cases in Kentucky in which he claimed local human rights ordinances made him vulnerable to prosecution because his antigay religious beliefs required him to not hire gay employees. The U.S. District Court for Western Kentucky rejected Hyman's plea. Chief Judge Charles Simpson wrote that the human rights ordinances "do not regulate the beliefs of Dr. Hyman. . . . [They] merely seek to regulate the conduct of all individuals who are engaged in the employment of others" (*Hyman v. Louisville City and Jefferson County*).

Similarly, some employees with conservative or fundamentalist religious beliefs have sued their employers for creating a "religiously hostile work environment" when they hire openly gay employees. Here, employees who hold antigay beliefs feel they are antagonized by the presence of openly gay employees. Taking their direction from sexual harassment laws and cases, they claim that their First Amendment right to choose with whom to associate is compromised by the company, which creates a hostile work environment. So far, courts have rejected these claims.

The Terrorist Attacks of September 11, 2001

In the early morning of September 11, 2001, four commercial jumbo jets were hijacked from airports in the eastern United States. Two of the jets crashed into the twin towers of the World Trade Center in New York City. Both towers collapsed a short time later, killing thousands of people. A third jet crashed into the Pentagon, causing much damage and loss of life. A fourth jet crashed in the countryside of Pennsylvania, killing all on board. It is thought that jet was headed for either the White House or the Capitol and that a rebellion by passengers and crew caused the plane to crash before hitting its target.

These attacks made by terrorists constituted the single greatest attack ever made against the United States on American soil.

It was a day no one will forget and a day that profoundly changed America.

Two days later, Jerry Falwell was interviewed on Pat Robertson's *The 700 Club* television show. There he stated:

> ACLU's got to take a lot of blame for this. And, I know that I'll hear from them for this. But, throwing God out successfully with the help of the federal court system, throwing God out of the public square, out of the schools. The abortionists have to bear some burden for this because God will not be mocked. And when we destroy 40 million little innocent babies, we make God mad. I really believe that the pagans, and the abortionists, and the feminists, and the gays and the lesbians who are actively trying to make that an alternative lifestyle, the ACLU, People for the American Way, all of them who have tried to secularize America. I point the finger in their face and say, 'You helped this happen.'

Pat Robertson nodded his head in agreement.

Immediately, other religious leaders distanced themselves from these comments. There was an outcry from both conservatives and liberals condemning these actions. Both Jerry Falwell and Pat Robertson made public corrections and apologized for their comments, but this only intensified the controversy. (For a day-by-day accounting, see GLAAD New Pop, September 21, 2001 at www.glaad.org/org/publications/documents/index.html?record=2846.)

Rush Limbaugh, a leading conservative voice in the United States, responded by saying: "Suggestions of this kind are one of the reasons why all conservatives get tarred and feathered with this extremist, bigoted, racist, sexist, homophobic label or image that isn't true. . . . All I can say is I was profoundly embarrassed and disappointed by their comments" (www://rushlimbaugh.com/home/daily/site_091701/content/stack_a.guest.html; see also Aravosis 2001).

After the terrorist attack, the U.S. government set up the September 11 Victims Compensation Fund. It was designed to give up to $1 million to each surviving family of someone who had died in the attacks. But what constituted families? Many debates occurred on the question of whether to provide compensation to the surviving same-sex partner of a lesbian or gay man who had died in the attack. Reverend Louis P. Sheldon came out and said, "[Red Cross aid] should be first giving priority to those widows who were at home with their babies and those widowers who lost their wives . . . and assistance should be given on the basis and priority of one man and one woman in a marital relationship" (Edsall 2001). Eventually, some gay and lesbian survivors got compensation, while others did not.

References

ACLU v. Reno, 117 S.Ct. 2329 (1997).

ACLU v. Reno II, 31 F.Supp.2d 473 (E.D. Pa. 1999).

Adams, H. E., L. W. Wright, and B. A. Lohr. 1996. "Is Homophobia Associated with Homosexual Arousal?" *Journal of Abnormal Psychology* 105, no. 3: 440–445.

"AIDS Set to Surpass Black Death as Worst Pandemic." 2002. Reuters, January 25.

"Antigay Harassment in Military Surges Even after Pentagon Announces Zero Tolerance for Harassment." 2000. Press release by the Servicemembers Legal Defense Network, March 10. Available at http://www.sldn-list@digitopia.net.

"Anti-Lesbian, Gay, Bisexual, and Transgendered Violence in 1996." 1996. New York: New York City Gay and Lesbian Anti-Violence Project.

"Anti-Lesbian, Gay, Bisexual, and Transgendered Violence in 2001." 2001. New York: New York City Gay and Lesbian Anti-Violence Project.

"APA Fact Sheet: Gay, Lesbian, and Bisexual Issues." 1994. www.psych.org/public_info/gaylesbianandbisexualissues22701.pdf.

Aravosis, John. "The List." Available at www.gayadvocacy.com. Cited September 18, 2001.

Bailey, J. M., D. Bobrow, M. Wolfe, and S. Mikach. 1995. "Sexual Orientation of Adult Sons of Gay Fathers." *Developmental Psychology* 31: 124–129.

Becker, L. 1995. "Recognition of Domestic Partnerships by Governmental Entities and Private Employers." *National Journal of Sexual Orientation Law* 1, no. 1: 91–104.

Birk, L. 1980. "The Myth of Classical Homosexuality: Views of a Behavioral Psychotherapist." In J. Marmor, ed., *Homosexual Behavior: A*

Modern Reappraisal. New York: Basic Books, pp. 376–390.

Blumenfeld, W. J., and D. Raymond, eds. 1993. *Looking at Gay and Lesbian Life*. Rev. ed. Boston: Beacon Press.

Bohling, J. 2002. "Harsh Judgment." *Frontiers* (March 15): 28.

Bowers v. Hardwick, 106 S.Ct. 2841, 2843 (1986).

Braschi v. Stahl Associates Co., 74 N.Y.2d 201, 544 N.Y.S.2d 784, 543 N.E.2d 49 (1989).

Burns, J., D. R. Kinder, S. J. Rosenstone, V. Sapiro, and the National Election Studies. 2001. "National Election Studies, 2000: Pre-/Post-Election Study." Data set of the Center for Political Studies. Ann Arbor: University of Michigan Press.

Carter, K. 1997. "Group Monitors Pervasiveness of Comments: Gay Slurs Abound, Students Say." *Des Moines Register*, March 7, B3.

Caruso, D. B. 2002. "Judges Toss Out Online Porn Law." *Los Angeles Times*, May 31.

Clark, H. 1988. *The Law of Domestic Relations in the United States*. 2nd ed. St. Paul, MN: West Publishing.

Clark, J. P., and L. L. Tifft. 1966. "Polygraph and Interview Validation of Self-Reported Deviant Behavior." *American Sociological Review* 31, no. 4 (August): 516–523.

Commonwealth v. Wasson, 842 S.W.2d 487 (Ky. 1992) (Wintersheimer, J., dissenting).

"Co-Parent or Second-Parent Adoption by Same-Sex Parents." 2002. Pp. 339–340 of the policy statement of the American Association of Pediatrics. Available at www.aap.org/policy/020008.html.

"Court Allows Baptist Homes Firing of Alicia Pedreira." 2001. Press release by the American Civil Liberties Union of Kentucky, July 24.

Dezotos, B. 2001. "The 'Ex' Files." *Frontiers* (June 8): 22.

Dyer, K. 1990. *Gays in Uniform: The Pentagon's Secret Reports*. Los Angeles: Alyson Publications.

Edsall, T. B. 2001. "Minister Says Gays Should Not Get Aid." *Washington Post*, October 5, A22.

Egelko, B. 1999. "Court to Reconsider Ruling on Renting to Unmarried Couples." Associated Press, October 19.

"FBI Hate Crimes Data Woefully Underreports Crimes against GLBT People." 2001. Press release by the National Gay and Lesbian Task Force, February 13.

Flaks, D. K., I. Ficher, F. Masterpasqua, and G. Joseph. 1995. "Lesbians Choosing Motherhood: A Comparative Study of Lesbian and Heterosexual Parents and Their Children." *Developmental Psychology* 31: 105–114.

Freiberg, P. 2000. "Utah Approves Gay Adoption Ban." *Washington Blade* 31, no. 9 (March 3): 12.

Freund, K., et al. 1984. "Pedophilia and Heterosexuality vs. Homosexuality." *Journal of Sex and Marital Therapy* 10 (Fall).

Fricke v. Lynch, 491 F.Supp 381 (R.R.I. 1980).

Friedman, R. C., and J. I. Downey. 1994. "Homosexuality." *New England Journal of Medicine* 331, no. 14: 923–930.

"Ga. Appeals Court Rules Civil Unions Not Equal to Marriage." 2002. *Gay and Lesbian Times,* January 31, 24.

Gay Law Students Ass'n v. Pacific Tele. and Tel. Co., 24 Cal. 3d 458, 156 Cal. Rptr. 14, 595 P.2d 592 (1979).

Giger, B. 1991. "Is 10% Too High?" *Frontiers* 10, no. 4 (June 21): 43.

Goleman, D. 1990. "Studies Discover Clues to the Roots of Homophobia." *New York Times,* July 10. Also available at http://www. youth. org/loco/PERSONProject/Resources/ResearchStudies/homophobia. html.

Golombok, S., A. Spence, and M. Rutter. 1983. "Children in Lesbian and Single Parent Households: Psychosexual and Psychiatric Appraisal." *Journal of Child Psychology and Psychiatry* 24: 551–572.

Gottman, J. S. 1990. "Children of Gay and Lesbian Parents." In F. W. Bozett and M. B. Sussman, eds., *Homosexuality and Family Relations.* Binghamton, NY: Harrington Park Press.

Green, R. 1978. "Sexual Identity of 37 Children Raised by Homosexual or Transsexual Parents." *American Journal of Psychiatry* 135, no. 6 (June): 692–697.

Green, R., J. B. Mandel, M. E. Hotvedt, J. Gray, and L. Smith. 1986. "Lesbian Mothers and Their Children: A Comparison with Solo Parent Heterosexual Mothers and Their Children." *Archives of Sexual Behavior* 15, no. 2: 167–184.

Groth, A. N. June 10, 2002. Personal correspondence to Family Research Council. Copy of letter available from A. Nicholas Groth by e-mail at a.n.groth@att.net or by mail at P.O. Box 690817, Orlando, FL 32869–0817; (407) 351–2308.

Groth, A. N., and H. J. Birnbaum. 1978. "Adult Sexual Orientation and Attraction to Underage Persons." *Archives of Sexual Behavior* 7, no. 3: 175–181.

Haldeman, D. C. 1991. "Sexual Orientation Conversion Therapy for Gay Men and Lesbians: A Scientific Examination." In J. C. Gonsiorek and J. D. Weinrich, eds., *Homosexuality: Research Implications for Public Policy.* Newbury Park, CA: Sage, pp. 149–160.

"Health Care Needs of Gay Men and Lesbians in the U.S." December 1994. A report presented by the Council on Scientific Affairs to the AMA House of Delegates interim meeting.

Hoeffer, B. 1981. "Children's Acquisition of Sex-Role Behavior in Lesbian-Mother Families. *American Journal of Orthopsychiatry* 51: 536–544.

Holmes/Watson v. California Army, no. 9615855 (9th Cir., April 7, 1997).

Huggins, S. L. 1989. "A Comparative Study of Self-Esteem of Adolescent Children of Divorced Mothers and Divorced Heterosexual Mothers." In F. W. Bozett, ed., *Homosexuality and the Family.* New York: Hawthorn, pp. 123–135.

Hyman v. Louisville City and Jefferson County, U.S. Dist. Ct., Western Dist. of Kentucky, Louisville Division, civil action 3:99CV-597-S (August 14, 2000).

Jenny, C., T. Roesler, and K. Poyer. 1994. "Are Children at Risk for Sexual Abuse by Homosexuals?" *Pediatrics* 94, no. 1 (July): 41–44.

Kansas v. Matthew Limon, Kansas Court of Appeals No. 85, 898 (2002).

Keen, L., and S. B. Goldberg. 1998. *Strangers to the Law: Gay People on Trial.* Ann Arbor: University of Michigan Press.

Kinsey, A. C., W. B. Pomeroy, and C. E. Martin. 1948. *Sexual Behavior in the Human Male.* Philadelphia: W. B. Saunders Co.

Kinsey, A. C., W. B. Pomeroy, C. E. Martin, and R. H. Gebhard. 1953. *Sexual Behavior in the Human Female.* Philadelphia: W. B. Saunders Co.

Kirkpatrick, M., A. Smith, and R. Roy. 1981. "Lesbian Mothers and Their Children: A Comparative Study." *American Journal of Orthopsychiatry* 51: 545–551.

Lawson, R. 1987. "Scandal in the Adventist-Funded Program to 'Heal' Homosexuals: Failure, Sexual Exploitation, Official Silence, and Attempts to Rehabilitate the Exploiter and His Methods." Paper given at a meeting of the American Sociological Association, Chicago.

MacFarquhar, N. 2002. "Condom as a Problem Word: Iran Grapples with a Surge in AIDS." *New York Times*, April 4.

Maugh, T. H. 2001. "Former Soviet Bloc Hit by Skyrocketing Rate of HIV." *Los Angeles Times*, November 29.

McDaniel, M. A. January 1989. *Preservice Adjustment of Homosexual and Heterosexual Military Accessions: Implications for Security Clearance Suitability*. Monterey, CA: Defense Personnel Security Research and Education Center.

Michael, R. T., J. H. Gagnon, E. O. Laumann, and G. Kolata. 1995. *Sex in America: A Definitive Survey*. New York: Little, Brown.

Miller, B. 1979. "Gay Fathers and Their Children." *The Family Coordinator* (October): 545–552.

Mills, K. I. 1999. *Mission Impossible: Why Reparative Therapy and Ex-Gay Ministries Fail*. Washington, DC: Human Rights Campaign.

Morrison v. State Board of Education, 82 Cal. Rptr. 175, 461 P. 2d 375 (Cal. 1969).

Nabozny v. Podlesny, 92 F.3d 446 (7th Cir. 1996).

"New Gay Discharge Figures Up 73% since 'Don't Ask, Don't Tell, Don't Pursue' First Implemented." 2000. Press release by the Servicemembers Legal Defense Network, February 1. Available at sldn-list@digitopia.net.

Newswatch Briefs. 1990. *Gay Chicago Magazine* 8 (February 22): 43.

Newton, D. E. 1978. "Homosexual Behavior and Child Molestation: A Review of the Evidence." *Adolescence* 13: 29–43.

One, Inc. v. Olesen, 355 U.S. 371 (1958).

Ornstein, C. 2002. "Explicit Ads Prompt Review of U.S. AIDS Prevention Grants." *Los Angeles Times*, January 4.

"Pathetic Propaganda: NGLTF Leader Blasts Anti-gay Group's 'Report' on Gays." 2002. *Frontiers* (June 21): 42.

Patterson, C. J. 1992. "Children of Lesbian and Gay Parents." *Child Development* 63 (October): 1025–1042.

Payne v. Western Atl. R.R., 81 Tenn. 507, 519–20 (1884), *rev'd on other grounds sub nom. Hutton v. Watters*, 132 Tenn. 527, 179 S. W. 134 (1915).

Pennington, S. B. 1987. "Children of Lesbian Mothers." In F. W. Bozett, ed., *Gay and Lesbian Parents.* New York: Praeger, pp. 58–74.

Report of the CUNY Study Group on Domestic Partnerships. 1993. New York: City University of New York.

Richter, P. 2000. "Armed Forces Find 'Disturbing' Level of Gay Harassment." *Los Angeles Times,* March 25, A1.

Sarbin, T. R., and K. E. Karois. December 1988. *Nonconforming Sexual Orientation and Military Suitability.* Monterey, CA: Defense Personnel Security Research and Education Center.

"Spitzer's Study Is Biased and Unscientific." 2002. *Frontiers* (June 8): 51.

Steckel, A. 1987. "Psychosocial Development of Children of Lesbian Mothers." In F. W. Bozett, ed., *Gay and Lesbian Parents.* New York: Praeger, pp. 75–85.

Stewart, Chuck. 1996. "How Effective Is the Department of Labor Standards Enforcement at Protecting Our Rights under AB 2601?" *Edge* 341 (August 7): 30.

Tasker, F., and S. Golombok. 1995. "Adults Raised as Children in Lesbian Families." *American Journal of Orthopsychiatry* 65: 203–215.

Thomas v. Anchorage Equal Rights Commission, No. 97–35220 (August 4, 2000).

Tremblay, P. J. 1995. "The Homosexuality Factor in the Youth Suicide Problem." Paper presented at the Sixth Annual Conference of the Canadian Association for Suicide Prevention, Banff, Alberta, Canada, October 11–14.

Weeks, R. B., A. P. Derdeyn, and M. Langman. 1975. "Two Cases of Children of Homosexuals." *Child Psychiatry and Human Development* 6: 26–32.

Yeoman, B. 1996. "Out." Available at http://www.out.com/out-cgi-bin/article?a=9605/hesse.

3

Chronology

U ntil recently, history courses amounted to little more than reading about the activities of wealthy white men who engaged in war against one another. Rarely did the histories and lives of people of color or women appear, and if they did, it was as a sidebar in textbooks and presented in relation to men. Homosexuality was completely ignored unless it pertained to particular "scandals."

The civil rights movement and women's rights movement in the 1960s and 1970s brought significant changes to historical textbooks. The process of consciousness-raising initiated by the women's movement included reclaiming women's history—a process adopted by other marginalized groups, including lesbians and gay men.

Even though people such as U.S. archivist Jim Kepner privately collected material on the early American gay movement, many of the current lesbian and gay historical collections did not begin until the aftermath of the Stonewall Riots. The Lesbian Herstory and Archives, founded in 1973, and the San Francisco Lesbian and Gay History Project, begun in 1977, are examples of two new collections. Now lesbian and gay archives can be found at most universities, all around the country, and around the world.

Nevertheless, deciding on which events to include in this chapter is problematic. Before the twentieth century, there were virtually no writings, either personal letters or books, that included explicit sexual descriptions. We have very little information about the actual lives of people in earlier times. Identifying someone as gay or lesbian is exceedingly difficult. We mostly have court documents of people who were arrested and convicted of sexual crimes or the passage of legislation criminalizing sodomy. Gay identity as an idea and a term is a decidedly modern invention and cannot be properly applied to people of earlier cultures and times.

Since Stonewall, and particularly since the mid-1980s, gay rights have come to the forefront of world politics. Every day there is some act of gay protest, opposition to gay rights, laws being passed or rescinded that specifically identify sexual orientation. Thus, any chronology, including this one, will be incomplete. Readers are encouraged to use this list as a starting point in their own research.

Homosexuality Prior to the Nineteenth Century

Until the Industrial Revolution, the lives of most people were unchanging. The development of steam power, the use of fossil fuels, and the invention of electricity were technical developments that increased the ability of humans to communicate and be productive. These events occurred during the 1800s. Before that, most people worked on farms. A farmer in seventeenth-century England would be virtually indistinguishable from a farmer in c.e. 180 Rome or a farmer in Egypt or China or Africa in 2000 b.c.e. Cultures slowly evolved and most accepted homosexuality. In general, as long as a person fulfilled his or her familial obligations of producing children, the gender of sexual partners was relatively immaterial.

Native Americans, Polynesians, Indians, Asiatic Eskimos

Before the influence of Christianity, many of these societies saw sex as a gift from the spirit world. In general, the gender of sexual partners was unimportant and homosexuality was accepted. Also accepted were transgender people who adopted the behaviors and clothing of both men and women. Known as *berdaches* (also as *yirka-la ul, mahu, hijras*), they were thought to have two spirits and often held the position of teacher and shaman in these societies.

Amazons

When explorer Pedro de Magalhaes de Gandavo explored north-eastern Brazil in 1576, he discovered women who imitated men, wore their hair like men, and had another woman as a wife. He was impressed by these women and, in tribute, named the river that flowed through the area "River of the Amazons" in reference to the ancient Greek legend of women warriors. At least thirty-three North American cultural groups included Amazons in their societies. Other Amazon societies could be found around the world and in other times.

Institutionalized Homosexuality

Throughout history and into the modern age, many societies institutionalized homosexual behaviors and relationships. Such cultures included seventeenth-century Mayan society, Buddhist monks, the samurai class of early Japan, and Melanesia in southern New Guinea. In these societies, all members engaged in homosexual relationships for the majority of their lives.

Ancient Greece

Sex for the Greeks was mostly value neutral. Exclusive homosexuality was discouraged. Sexual relationships between older men and young boys were considered a crucial part of the younger man's maturation process. Not much is known of lesbianism except for a limited number of poems written by Sappho extolling the virtues of love between women.

Ancient Rome

There is widespread evidence of homosexual behavior being accepted in the republic and early empire. Neither the Romans nor Greeks identified homosexuality as a problem. Around the third century C.E., due to the influence of Christianity, Rome began to enact a series of laws regulating various aspects of homosexual relationships.

China

For 300 years beginning in the third century B.C.E., many historical documents show that homosexuality was accepted, particularly among the ruling class. It is from these stories that common euphemisms for male homosexual love, *fen tao zhi ai* (literally, "the love of shared peach") and *duanxiu* (literally, "the cut sleeve"), came.

The Roman Catholic Church and the Twelfth-Century European Transformation

For most of the first thousand years of the Roman Catholic Church, homosexual marriages were sanctioned by church ritual. Unlike heterosexual ceremonies, which were mostly about property rights and were held outdoors, gay marriages were identified with love and held inside the church. But by the twelfth century, the church solidified its hold over Europe and Thomas Aquinas constructed a framework in which homosexual acts were classified as less worthy than heterosexual ones. In fifty short years, from 1250 to 1300, homosexuality went from being completely legal in most of Europe to meriting the death penalty.

Ming Dynasty, 1368–1644

Homosexuality was tolerated in China as long as it was not an exclusive sexual expression and as long as men fulfilled their familial procreative duties. When the Manchu entered the city in the summer of 1644, overthrowing the Ming dynasty, the first male homosexual rape law was enacted and male homosexuality was severely punished.

Russia

There is much evidence that male homosexuality was widespread and tolerated in all strata of Russian society prior to the westernization reforms of Peter the Great (early eighteenth century). The first law penalizing consensual male homosexuality was enacted in 1706 and required burning at the stake. Peter the Great (who was bisexual) mitigated the penalty, and there are no known instances of its application. The criminalization of male homosexuality came later, under the brutal rule of Nicolas I, when Article 995 was enacted in the legal code of 1832.

United States

1610   The Virginia Colony passes the first antisodomy law in America. It requires the death penalty for offenders and does not include women in its definition of "sodomites."

1624   Richard Cornish, master of the ship *Ambrose*, is executed in Virginia Colony by hanging for alleged "buggery" of his indentured servant, William Cowse, ship steward.

1629   Thomas/Thomasina Hall is proclaimed by the governor to be both "a man and a woman" and ordered to wear articles of clothing appropriate for each sex.

Reverend Francis Higginson discovers "5 beastly Sodomiticall boyes [*sic*], which confessed their wickedness not to be named" on a ship bound for New England. The incident is reported to the governor of the Massachusetts Bay Colony, who sends the boys back to England for punishment. At that time, males over fourteen years of age could be hanged for sodomy. It is not known what happened to the boys.

1641   The Massachusetts Bay Colony includes sodomy as a capital crime in its newly adopted code of laws. It defines sodomy as "man lying with mankind as he lies with a woman"—wording taken directly from Leviticus 20:13.

1646   "Jan Creoli, a negro" in New Netherland is executed by choking for engaging in sodomy. Ten-year-old Manuel Congo, whom Creoli allegedly sodomized, is flogged in public.

1649   Sarah Norman and Mary Hammond, two married women, are charged with lewd behavior. Hammond, who is younger, has her charges dropped. Norman receives a warning that her punishment will be greater if there are any subsequent charges.

1673–   On his voyage down the Mississippi River, Father
1677   Jacques Marquette recounts that some Indians assume the garb of women, which they wear throughout their lives. Many other travelers to the American frontier make similar observations.

1720   By this time, every colony has adopted a law making sodomy a capital offense.

1778   Baron Frederich von Steuben is the first soldier known to
       be dismissed from the U.S. military for engaging in
       homosexuality. Steuben was recognized as one of Eu-
       rope's greatest military minds and was engaged by the
       U.S. military to train the disparate armies of the thirteen
       colonies. He was discovered in bed with Lieutenant Gott-
       hold Frederick Enslin.

1848   The first women's rights convention is held at Seneca
       Falls, New York. Susan B. Anthony and other women are
       ejected from the convention, propelling them into the na-
       tional limelight.

1860   Walt Whitman publishes his homoerotic *Leaves of Grass*.

The Homophile Movement

The homophile movement is marked by the medicalization of
homosexuality and an increase in public discourse on the topic.

1869   Karoly Maria Benkert (who uses the pseudonym K. M.
       Kertbeny), a Hungarian physician, coins the term *homo-
       sexual*. The word *heterosexual* does not appear for another
       ten years. Heterosexuality initially is used to denote a
       sexual perversion.

1865– At least 100,000 women form a community and political
1935   movement that resists marriage in the districts of Pearl
       River Delta, Hong Kong. The *sou hei* vows to remain sin-
       gle and forms emotional and physical bonds only with
       her "sworn sisters."

1885   Homosexual acts are recriminalized by the British Parlia-
       ment.

1896   The first periodical addressing the issue of homo-
       sexuality, *Der Eigene* ("The Community of the Special"), is
       published in Germany.

       Two women hug and kiss for the first time on an American stage in the play *A Florida Enchantment*. The scene is so controversial (although the play is not lesbian in content) that ushers offer ice water during intermission to audience members who feel faint.

1897   The Scientific-Humanitarian Committee is founded by Magnus Hirschfeld, Max Sphor, and Eric Oberg in Germany.

Havelock Ellis, English sexologist, publishes *Sexual Inversion*. This book is considered the first book in English to treat homosexuality as a natural condition, not as an illness or crime.

1901   New York politician Maury Hall dies and is discovered to have been a woman passing as a man.

1908   English writer Edward Carpenter publishes his book *The Intermediate Sex*. It is his most influential book on gay issues.

Edward Stevenson releases *The Intersexes*, the first review of gay issues within the United States.

1912   A group of "unorthodox women" begins to meet at Polly Halliday's restaurant in York City. The group, Heterodoxy, meets bimonthly and has among its membership many prominent lesbians, including Helen Hall, Katharine Anthony, Dr. Sara Josephine Baker, and Elisabeth Irwin. Heterodoxy continues to meet until the 1940s.

1914   A dictionary of criminal slang published in Portland, Oregon, describes the word faggot for the first time as referring to male homosexuals.

1916   For the first time in the United States, the Articles of War make homosexuality and the intent to commit sodomy in the U.S. military capital crimes.

1919   The Institute for Sexual Research is established by Magnus Hirschfeld in Berlin. It is one of the world's first organizations to explore sexual topics from a scientific

1919,   standpoint. Hirschfeld becomes aware of the need to for-
cont.   mally organize to help reform attitudes and laws concerning homosexuality. In 1921 he establishes the World
League for Sexual Reform, whose membership grows to
130,000 people worldwide. It is through the league that
Hirschfeld campaigns in German courts and legislature
for the overturn of Paragraph 175—the legal code that
criminalizes homosexual behaviors.

The U.S. Navy, under orders from Assistant Secretary of
the Navy Franklin Roosevelt, uses a squad of young enlisted men to search for "sexual perverts" at the Newport
Rhode Island Naval Training Station. Sixteen civilians and
twenty sailors are arrested on morals charges and prosecuted by naval and municipal authorities.

1920–   The Harlem Renaissance heralds an unprecedented
1935   flourishing of African American culture. Many lesbian
and gay writers, artists, and musicians are central to this
cultural explosion. These include Claude McKay, Bessie
Smith, Langston Hughes, Countee Cullen, Ma Rainey,
Bruce Nugent, Alain Locke, and Ethel Waters.

1923   Sholom Asch's *God of Vengeance* opens on Broadway. It is
the first play with a lesbian content to reach Broadway. It
was originally written in Yiddish and first produced in
Berlin in 1907.

1924   *Inversions,* the first gay French journal, is founded.

Henry Gerber and others found the Society for Human
Rights in Chicago. It is the first gay rights group in the
United States. It survives only a short time. It publishes
two issues of *Friendship and Freedom,* its gay liberation
magazine (the first in the country), before police confis-
cate them. The members of the society are arrested and
imprisoned.

1926   Bruce Nugent's narrative poem "Smoke, Lilies, and Jade"
is published in the periodical *Fire!* This poem is considered to be the first published piece about homosexuality
to be written by an African American.

1927 Mae West writes and produces *The Drag,* the first play produced in the United States with a gay male content. It closes before reaching Broadway.

1929 The German constitution is modified by the removal of Paragraph 175. This will prove to be a hollow victory for Magnus Hirschfeld and the World League for Sexual Reform as the Nazis will soon assume power and recriminalize homosexuality (in 1934).

   Radclyffe Hall's lesbian novel *The Well of Loneliness* is published by Covici-Friede in New York. The publisher is convicted of obscenity; the conviction is later overturned.

1930 The Motion Picture Production Code is enacted by Hollywood studios. It prohibits all references to homosexuality or "sexual perversion" in movies. The code is strengthened in 1934 under pressure from the Catholic-led Legion for Decency, which is influential until the code's revision in the 1960s.

1933 Hirschfeld's Institute for Sexual Research is ransacked by Nazi students and destroyed. Vast collections of library and artistic works are burned.

1934 Lillian Hellman's play *The Children's Hour* opens on Broadway. It escapes the censors because of its moralistic ending: the lesbian character kills herself.

1941– Almost 10,000 enlisted personnel in the U.S. military
1945 receive dishonorable discharges for homosexuality. These are called "blue discharges" because the orders are typed on blue paper.

1942 The U.S. military issues official prohibitions against homosexuality and homosexuals in the armed forces.

   Jim Kepner begins his private collection of gay-related clippings, artifacts, books, and photographs in Los Angeles.

The Modern Gay Movement

World War II dislocated millions of people and brought large numbers of lesbians and gay men to the city. There, they began to organize, reject the medical deviancy label, and create the modern gay movement.

1948   The first U.S. lesbian magazine, *Vice Versa*, begins publishing in Los Angeles. From her desk at RKO Studios, Lisa Ben (anagram for "lesbian") types each issue twice, using four carbons, then circulates it among her friends, who then circulate it among their friends.

Alfred Kinsey and the Kinsey Institute publish their groundbreaking study of sexual behavior in U.S. men. *Sexual Behavior in the Human Male*, finds that more than 50 percent of those surveyed admitted erotic responses to other men and that approximately 10 percent were exclusively homosexual. The Kinsey findings shake the heterosexual world and help get the fledgling gay community off the ground.

1948–   McCarthyism purges homosexuals and communists from
1953   the federal government, and thousands lose their jobs. More homosexuals lose their jobs than do those accused of being communist. Ironically, Roy Cohn, Joseph McCarthy's right-hand man, is found to be gay.

1951–   The International Conference for Sexual Equality is spon-
1958   sored by the Amsterdam-based Cultaur-en-Ontspannings Centrum. The issue of gay rights is prominent on the agenda.

1951   The Mattachine Society is founded by Harry Hay, Bob Hull, and Chuck Rowland in Los Angeles. It evolves into the ONE Institute and Archives located on the campus of the University of Southern California and becomes the most celebrated and long-lived gay rights organization in the United States.

Edward Sagarin, under the pseudonym Donald Webster

Cory, publishes *The Homosexual in America*. It is one of the first books written by a gay author to describe gay life and ask for tolerance.

1952   "Sexual deviants" are barred from immigrating into the United States by the McCarran-Walters Act. The U.S. Supreme Court extends this definition to lesbians and gay men in 1967.

1953   The Kinsey Institute publishes *Sexual Behavior in the Human Female*. This second historic study finds that 28 percent of women surveyed responded erotically to other women and that between 2 and 6 percent identified their sex orientation as lesbian.

ONE begins publishing in Los Angeles as an adjunct to the Mattachine Society. This is the first national gay male publication.

Executive Order 10450, signed by President Dwight Eisenhower, makes "sexual perversion" grounds for being barred from federal employment.

Evelyn Hooker begins studying male homosexual personalities. It is this research that leads to the findings that there are no discernible psychosocial differences between homosexual and heterosexual men. Her research eventually enables the overturning of medical theories of homosexuality as a sickness.

Gay concentration camp survivors are rearrested by the German government for being "repeat offenders."

1954   Copies of *ONE* magazine are seized by the Los Angeles postmaster, who refuses to mail them on the grounds that they are "obscene, lewd, lascivious, and filthy." *ONE* editors sue, are ruled against by two lower courts, but eventually prevail in 1958 in the U.S. Supreme Court (*One, Inc. v. Olesen*). Without this favorable decision, the gay rights movement would have been severely hampered.

1955   The Daughters of Bilitis is founded by Del Martin and

1955,   Phyllis Lyon in San Francisco. This is the first national
cont.   lesbian organization in the United States and soon begins
        publication of *The Ladder*.

1957   The Crittenden Report, a 639-page navy document, con-
        cludes there is "no sound basis" for the belief that homo-
        sexuals pose a military security risk. The Pentagon
        denies the existence of this report for more than twenty
        years.

1960   The first national convention of the Daughters of Bilitis
        (the first national lesbian conference) is held in San Fran-
        cisco.

1961   Illinois becomes the first state to decriminalize consen-
        sual homosexual sex conducted in private.

1962   After five years of study, the United Kingdom's Com-
        mittee on Homosexual Offenses and Prostitution (com-
        monly known as the Wolfenden Committee) recom-
        mends the decriminalization of homosexual behavior.

1964   The "first" street protests for homosexual rights are con-
        ducted by the Homosexual League of New York and the
        League for Sexual Freedom in front of the U.S. Army In-
        duction Center located at Whitehall Street, New York.
        The ten members carry signs protesting the army's dis-
        honorable discharges of lesbian and gay soldiers.

        The Conference of East Coast Homophile Organizations
        in Washington, D.C., produces the first homosexual
        rights button.

        The first homophile organization in Canada appears, the
        Association of Social Knowledge (ASK), along with the
        first gay magazine, *TWO*.

1965   The Mattachine Society New York leads the first protest
        demonstration in front of the White House. The seven
        gay men and three lesbians receive national television
        coverage.

1966   The Society for Individual Rights (SIR) Center opens in San Francisco and is the first gay community center in the United States. Later in the same year, ASK opens a community center in Vancouver, becoming the first such center in Canada.

The North American Conference of Homophile Organizations is created to coordinate protest efforts against the federal government's antigay discrimination policies.

1967   *The Advocate*, currently the oldest national gay publication, begins publishing in Los Angeles.

The American Civil Liberties Union declares its opposition to state antisodomy laws.

The first protest demonstration by gay activists against any police department is held in front of the Black Cat and New Faces bars in Silver Lake, California. The demonstration is held to protest Los Angeles police officers' treatment of bar patrons during a New Year's Eve party.

The British government acts on the recommendations made by the Wolfenden Committee ten years earlier and decriminalizes homosexual behavior between consenting adults.

The Oscar Wilde Memorial Bookshop, now the oldest gay bookstore in the United States, opens in New York. In 1973, the bookstore relocates to the junction of Christopher and Gay Streets.

1968   The Reverend Troy Perry in Los Angeles begins the first gay church, the Metropolitan Community Church.

John Money at Johns Hopkins University performs the first complete male-to-female sex-change operation in the United States.

The university of Sorbonne, Paris, is taken over by rioting gay French students led by David Cohn-Bendit.

The Birth of Gay Liberation

1969   New York City police raid the Stonewall Inn on June 27. The bar's patrons, including transvestites, butch lesbians, and gay teenagers, violently resist. This event is considered the birth of the modern gay liberation movement and is commemorated each year by parades and festivals around the United States.

Building on the participants of the Stonewall Riots, the Gay Liberation Front is founded New York.

Time magazine contains articles on national gay rights and has on its cover "The Homosexual in America."

Canada amends its criminal code to legalize sexual acts, including homosexuality, between consenting adults.

West Germany repeals its antihomosexual sodomy laws.

1970   New York City's Gay Pride Parade, the first in the nation to commemorate the Stonewall Riots, draws about 10,000 marchers.

Three New York State Assembly members convene the first legislative hearing on gay rights in United States.

The New York–based lesbian-feminist group Radicalesbians publishes its manifesto, "The Woman Identified Woman," which defines lesbians as "the rage of all women condensed to the point of explosion."

Amazon bookstore in Minneapolis opens for business. It is the first lesbian/feminist bookstore in the United States. Later that year, A Woman's Place bookstore opens in Oakland, California.

Rita Hauser, U.S. permanent representative to the United Nations, advocates same-sex marriages as a tool for controlling world population growth.

Carl Wittman releases his "Gay Manifesto," which summarizes many of the goals of the gay rights movement.

1971 The Lesbian and Gay Community Services Center is founded in Los Angeles and becomes the world's largest such center.

   The National Organization for Women (NOW) passes a resolution supporting lesbian rights. Just a few years earlier, Betty Friedan, the first president of NOW, had attacked similar resolutions and labeled lesbians "the Lavender Menace."

   The American Library Association launches its annual Gay Book Award and gives the first award to Isabel Miller for her novel *Patience and Sarah*.

   Connecticut becomes the second state to repeal its antisodomy law. Idaho attempts to do the same. It repeals the law, but then, under pressure from religious and conservative leaders, reinstates the law, which criminalizes homosexual behavior with felony punishment of up to five years in prison.

   After years of meeting, the President's National Commission on Reform of Federal Criminal Laws recommends the repeal of all state antisodomy laws.

   Canadian gay groups call for legal reform and issue a "We Demand" brief to the federal government. The first gay public demonstration in Canada takes place shortly after in support of the brief.

1972 Beth Chayim Chadashim, the first gay synagogue in the United States, is founded in Los Angeles.

   A U.S. district judge rules that the Civil Service Commission cannot discriminate against employees based on sexual orientation unless the commission can prove that being gay impacts the workplace.

   East Lansing, Michigan, becomes the first city in the United States to ban discrimination based on sexual orientation in city hiring.

1972, cont.   The United Church of Christ, California, ordains William Johnson as the first openly gay minister of any major religious denomination.

Ann Arbor, Michigan, becomes the first city in the United States to officially proclaim Gay Pride Week.

1973   The American Psychiatric Association removes homosexuality from its list of mental disorders.

The American Bar Association adopts a resolution supporting the repeal of all state laws regulating sexual acts between consenting adults.

Howard Brown declares at a medical convention that he is gay. As the former New York City commissioner of health, he is, at this time, the highest-ranked person to publicly declare his homosexuality. He is later instrumental in the formation of the National Gay Task Force.

The National Gay Task Force, later renamed the National Gay and Lesbian Task Force (NGLTF), is founded in New York by activists Martin Duberman, Ron Gold, Barbara Gittings, Frank Kameny, Howard Brown, Bruce Voeller, and Nathalie Rockhill.

A lesbian-feminist collective begins Olivia Records.

Naiad Press, currently the oldest surviving lesbian book publisher, is launched in Florida.

Lambda Legal Defense and Education Fund is founded to help gay civil rights court action.

1974   Massachusetts's Elaine Nobel becomes the first openly gay person ever elected to a state legislature.

New York City Democratic congressmember Bella Abzug introduces a federal gay and lesbian civil rights bill (HR-14752) in the U.S. House of Representatives. The bill fails and is reintroduced, without success, in subsequent sessions of Congress.

Halton Renaissance Committee is formed by fundamentalist minister Ken Campbell in Canada to oppose gay rights.

Lesbian Connection begins publishing in East Lansing, Michigan, and become the largest circulation lesbian periodical in the United States.

1975   Santa Cruz County, California, becomes the first county in the United States to ban antigay discrimination.

Sergeant Leonard Matlovich is discharged from the U.S. Air Force because of his homosexuality. Matlovich wins a five-year court battle with the Air Force but chooses to accept a financial settlement of $160,000 instead of reenlisting.

The American Association for the Advancement of Science (AAAS) passes a resolution opposing discrimination based on sexual orientation.

A county clerk in Boulder, Colorado, issues a marriage license to a same-sex couple. The state attorney general later revokes this license.

The Arkansas state legislature repeals the state's antisodomy laws, but two years later reinstates them.

The U.S. Supreme Court rules in *Rose v. Locke* that cunnilingus is covered by Tennessee's "crimes against nature" statute.

1976   Montreal police launch many raids against gay bars to "clean up" the city before the opening of the Summer Olympics. The gay community fights back with many large demonstrations. Emerging from those demonstrations is the Association pour les droits des gai(e)s du Quebec (ADGQ).

Willard Eugene Allen is released after spending twenty-six years in a Florida state mental institution for having been convicted of "lewdness" (having sex with another man). His doctors had recommended his release for nearly twenty years.

1976, *Tales of the City*, by Amistead Maupin, begins its serialized
cont. run in the *San Francisco Chronicle*.

1977 Fundamentalist singer Anita Bryant and the Save Our
Children campaign are successful at convincing voters in
Dade County, Florida, to repeal a gay rights law.

Harvey Milk is elected as San Francisco's first openly gay
supervisor.

Toronto police raid the offices of Canada's leading gay
publication, *The Body Politic*, claiming "indecent" materials are being distributed. After a long and costly court
battle and another police raid in 1982, the paper is acquitted, but the financial strain pushes it under in 1987.

The National Gay Task Force meets with presidential assistant Midge Constanza at the White House to discuss
gay rights issues. This is the first such meeting between a
gay organization and the Office of the President.

Both the International Association of Chiefs of Police and
the Fraternal Order of Police adopt resolutions opposing
the hiring of lesbian and gay police officers.

The African American lesbian-feminist group the Com-
bahee River Collective, publishes "A Black Feminist
Statement." The manifesto recognizes the interconnec-
tedness of oppression based on race and sexual identity.

Ellen Marie Barrett is ordained as the first openly lesbian
priest of the Episcopal Church.

The province of Quebec passes a charter of human rights
that bans antigay discrimination in employment, housing,
and public accommodations. This makes Quebec the first
major province in North America to offer such protection.

1978 Supervisor Harvey Milk and Mayor George Moscone of
San Francisco are shot to death at City Hall by ex-
supervisor Dan White. White is later convicted of involuntary manslaughter, sentenced to seven years in prison

(of which he serves only five), and commits suicide in 1985.

The Briggs initiative (Proposition 6), which would have barred lesbians and gay men from teaching in state public schools, is defeated by California voters.

San Francisco's Gilbert Baker designs the rainbow flag, which becomes the international symbol for gay liberation.

Ed Koch, the mayor of New York City, issues an executive order forbidding discrimination based on sexual orientation in government employment. The order is eventually overturned through efforts of the Roman Catholic Archdiocese.

In *Federal Communications Commission v. Pacifica Foundation*, the U.S. Supreme Court approves restrictions on broadcast material that is "indecent" but not "obscene." Such a distinction affects future broadcasts of gay-themed programs.

1979   When Dan White is found guilty of involuntary manslaughter in the deaths of Mayor George Moscone and Supervisor Harvey Milk, lesbians and gay men take to the streets and riot on the night of May 21 in response to the light sentence. The White Night riots cause more than $1 million in property damage, and more than 150 people are injured.

The Moral Majority is founded by Jerry Falwell and his associates. It later becomes one of the major opponents to gay rights in the United States.

The First National March on Washington for Lesbian and Gay Rights draws more than 100,000 marchers.

Stephen Lachs becomes the first openly gay judge to be appointed to the Superior Court of Los Angeles.

The Japan Gay Center opens in Tokyo. The first center of its kind in Japan, it is designed to educate the general public about homosexuality.

1979,   The first gay pride march in Mexico City is hosted by
cont.   Frente Homosexual de Acción Revolucionaria (Homo-
          sexual Revolutionary Action Front).

The San Francisco Police Department swears in its first
openly lesbian and gay police officers.

AIDS and Coalition-Building

1980   Aaron Fricke sues his high school in Providence, Rhode
         Island, to allow him to bring his male date to the senior
         prom. He wins the suit and goes to the dance with Paul
         Guilbert. Fricke chronicles these events in the popular
         book *Reflections of a Rock Lobster.*

The Democratic National Convention accepts a plank supporting federal gay rights legislation. At the same convention, Mel Boozer, a gay black man, is nominated for vice
president and is allowed to speak to the assembly.

Sasha Alyson launches Alyson Publications, which becomes the largest gay press in the United States.

Congressman Robert Bauman (R-MD), a leading opponent of gay rights legislation and a prominent member of
the Moral Majority, is arrested for soliciting sex from a
sixteen-year-old boy in Washington, D.C. Initially he dis-
avows his homosexuality, but in 1983 he appears before
the American Bar Association recommending adoption
of a gay rights resolution.

The Canadian Union of Postal Workers adopts a contract
that includes nondiscrimination based on sexual orientation. This is the first such contract covering federal employees anywhere in the world.

The gay student group at Georgetown University is expelled and forbidden from using university facilities. It
takes eight years for the student group to win its case and
return to campus.

1981   The U.S. Department of Defense (DOD) revises its policy concerning lesbians and gays in the military. For the first time the DOD explicitly states that homosexuality is "incompatible with military service." Its new policy requires all recruits to be questioned about their sexual orientation.

More than 300 gay men are arrested by Toronto police in a massive raid on gay bathhouses. This is the largest mass arrest of gay men in Canadian history and in all of North America. A riot ensues that is called the Canadian Stonewall.

The New York Supreme Court overturns the state's anti-sodomy laws as being unconstitutional.

All twenty participants in Finland's first gay pride parade are arrested in Helsinki for "encouraging lewd behavior."

The first cases of HIV-related illnesses are reported by the Centers for Disease Control and the *New York Times.*

A group of mothers and fathers organize the Parents and Friends of Lesbians and Gays (PFLAG) in Los Angeles. It becomes the most influential parent group supporting gay rights in the United States.

The first publishing house in the United States dedicated to work by and about women of color, Kitchen Table: Women of Color Press, is founded in New York.

The Kinsey Institute releases a report showing that neither parental nor societal influences have much effect on a person's sexual orientation.

Mary Morgan is appointed to the California Supreme Court by Governor Jerry Brown, making her the first openly lesbian judge.

Wisconsin becomes the first state to pass antidiscrimination laws based on sexual orientation in the areas of employment, housing, and public accommodation.

1981,   The New York City Gay Men's Chorus performs at
cont.   Carnegie Hall. It is the first openly gay group allowed to
        perform there and is followed a year later by openly les-
        bian singers Meg Christian and Cris Williamson.

        The Family Protection Act is defeated in Congress. Its
        provisions include withholding social security, welfare,
        and pension benefits to anyone who is homosexual or
        who supports a homosexual "lifestyle." Its sponsor, Rep-
        resentative Roger Jepsen (R-IA), is later defeated for re-
        election when it is discovered that the "health spa" to
        which he belonged was actually a house of prostitution.

        Florida governor Bob Graham signs the Task Amend-
        ment to the state constitution. It withholds money to any
        state institution that recognizes gay student groups. The
        state supreme court later overturns this legislation.

1982   Wisconsin becomes the first state in the United States to
        pass statewide gay rights legislation.

        The first Gay Games are held in San Francisco, with
        1,300 people from twelve countries participating. Ini-
        tially the Gay Games are called the Gay Olympics, but
        the U.S. Olympic Committee sues and blocks use of the
        word Olympics even though it allows that usage in the
        Rat Olympics and Dog Olympics.

        The voters in Austin, Texas, reject a ballot initiative de-
        signed to allow discrimination against lesbians and gay
        men.

        Bruce Voeller suggests that gay-related immune disorder
        be renamed acquired immune deficiency syndrome
        (AIDS) as a better reflection of the characteristics of the
        disease. The terminology is adopted by the medical com-
        munity.

        Quebec passes legislation that gives homosexual rela-
        tionships status equal to heterosexual ones.

        A social service and education agency, Gay Men's Health

Crisis (GMHC), is formed in New York and serves as the model for other AIDS organizations throughout the nation.

The Texas antisodomy law is ruled unconstitutional by a federal judge.

A federal judge declares unconstitutional the U.S. Immigration and Naturalization Service policy of excluding homosexuals from entering the country.

The 1,700 delegates to the National Convention of the American Federation of State, County, and Municipal Employees adopt, by unanimous vote, a resolution calling for laws to be passed prohibiting discrimination against lesbians and gay men at the federal, state, and local levels.

The Philadelphia Board of Education establishes the first high school for gay and lesbian students at Byton High. A similar school, Harvey Milk School, is established three years later by the New York City Board of Education.

1983   Representative Gerry Studds (D-MA) states that he is gay on the floor of the U.S. House of Representatives.

The Lesbian and Gay Community Services Center of New York is founded in a former public high school building.

A man whose partner of twenty-seven years has died is awarded $25,000 in survivor benefits by the California Compensation Appeals Board. This appears to be the first such award by a government agency in the United States.

A West Virginia kindergarten teacher, Linda Conway, is fired because school administrators believe she looks like a lesbian.

1984   Mervyn Silverman, head of San Francisco's Health Department, closes fourteen gay bathhouses because of high-risk behavior by patrons.

1984,   Television evangelist Hans Bratterud is convicted of vio-
cont.   lating Norway's antidiscrimination law when he calls for
        the dismissal of gay men and lesbians from their jobs.
        The Norwegian Supreme Court upholds the conviction
        because his statements were of "an aggravated insulting
        nature . . . [against] homosexual tendencies, way of life or
        orientation" (Newton 1994, 44).

        Berkeley, California, is the first city in the United States to
        extend domestic partnership benefits to employees in
        same-sex relationships.

        The city of West Hollywood becomes incorporated as a
        separate municipality and elects a mostly gay city coun-
        cil, with a lesbian mayor.

        A gay rights bill passes both houses in the California leg-
        islature, but Governor George Deukmejian vetoes the
        bill.

        Louie Welch loses a race for mayor of Houston when,
        days before the election, he is heard on an open micro-
        phone stating that the best way to contain the HIV epi-
        demic is to "shoot the queers."

1985   The Gay and Lesbian Alliance Against Defamation
        (GLAAD) is founded in New York City as a watchdog or-
        ganization over the media's poor coverage of AIDS and
        gay and lesbian issues.

        Margaret Roff is elected mayor of Manchester, England;
        she is the first open lesbian in British history to be elected
        to public office.

        A native Australian man who was involved in a ten-year
        monogamous relationship with another man who was a
        U.S. citizen faces being deported to his native country. He
        contests the deportation and receives an official notice
        from the U.S. Immigration and Naturalization Service
        stating, "A bona fide marital relationship cannot exist be-
        tween two faggots" (Newton 1994, 45). A court upholds
        the deportation ruling.

The U.S. Food and Drug Administration (FDA) licenses a test for HIV antibodies.

Movie and television actor Rock Hudson, after repeated denials of being gay or having AIDS, issues a public statement that he has AIDS. He dies three months later.

Hundreds of well-known women sign a *Ms.* magazine petition condemning government interference in the sexual lives of consenting adults.

The Texas legislature adopts legislation that bans homosexual sodomy only, which is approved by the judiciary. This overcomes the Texas Supreme Court's 1982 decision invalidating the state's antisodomy laws, which applied to both opposite-sex and same-sex behaviors.

Lesbian and gay men are prohibited from acting as foster parents by orders implemented by the Massachusetts House of Representatives.

1986   The U.S. Supreme Court, in the Georgia *Bowers v. Hardwick* case, upholds the right of states to enforce antisodomy laws.

Pope John Paul II issues a pastoral letter stating that homosexuality is intrinsically a disorder and forbids all Catholics from supporting civil rights legislation for lesbians and gay men.

A gay rights ordinance is passed by the province of Ontario, Canada.

The experimental drug azidothymidine zidovudine (AZT) is released by the U.S. Public Health Service for people with pneumocystis carninii pneumonia.

The Nevada Supreme Court upholds the state's antisodomy laws. Ironically, Nevada is the only state with legalized prostitution.

Outspoken opponent of homosexuality and prominent

1986,   conservative Republican Terry Dolan dies from HIV-
cont.   related illnesses. He is believed to have been gay.

Voters reject an initiative on the California ballot that requires the quarantine of people with AIDS.

1987   Approximately 500,000 people attend the second National March on Washington for Lesbian and Gay Rights.
At the event, 2,000 lesbian and gay couples participate in
a mass wedding held on the steps of the IRS building.
Also, sections equivalent to two football fields in size of
the NAMES Project quilt are displayed on the mall in
front of the U.S. Capitol.

Congressman Barney Frank (D-MA) becomes the second
member of the House to announce that he is gay.

The *New York Times*, for the first time in its history, uses
the word *gay* in reference to homosexuality.

Vermont becomes the first state to distribute condoms to
prison inmates.

Larry Kramer, along with other activists, begin the AIDS
Coalition to Unleash Power (ACT UP). Its goal is to bring
public and government attention to the need for AIDS
funding and research.

1988   The World Health Organization hosts its first World
AIDS Day.

NGLTF designates October 11 as National Coming Out
Day in honor of the historic 1987 lesbian and gay march
on Washington.

Ireland is ordered by the European Court of Human
Rights to eliminate its life imprisonment penalty for
homosexual behavior.

Measure 8, an amendment to the Oregon Constitution
that repeals an executive order issued by the governor
prohibiting discrimination in employment of gay men

and lesbians, is passed by the voters. This paves the way for other antigay legislation to be passed in Oregon.

Clause 28, issued by the British government, prohibits all local governments from "promoting" homosexuality. This means all gay and lesbian groups are prohibited from obtaining local government funding for community centers, educational activities, health organizations, or other programs.

The National AIDS Commission releases a report with more than 500 recommendations. An adviser to President Ronald Reagan reduces this list to ten items.

Canada eliminates its antisodomy laws.

The national lesbian and gay quarterly magazine *Out/Look* begins publication.

After the District of Columbia enacts a gay rights ordinance, the U.S. Congress orders that it revoke the ordinance or face losing all funding.

Leonard Matlovich, who was discharged by the U.S. Army in 1973 after he announced that he was gay, then sued and won, dies from HIV-related illnesses.

In response to an escalating national epidemic of violence against gay men and lesbians, the Campaign to End Homophobia holds its first conference in Washington, D.C.

Homosexual acts between consenting adults are legalized in the state of Israel.

1989   A federal court orders the reinstatement of Perry Watkins into the U.S. Army (*Watkins v. United States Army*). Changes in the military code render the precedent set in this case ineffective against future antigay discharges.

San Francisco passes domestic partnership legislation that includes lesbian and gay relationships.

1989,   Denmark enacts domestic partnership legislation that is
cont.   just one step away from actual marriage for same-sex
        couples. Full marriage for same-sex couples is granted in
        2001.

The U.S. Supreme Court rules in *Price Waterhouse v. Hopkins* that an accounting firm violated sex discrimination laws when it dismissed a woman for "masculine behavior."

A retrospective of Robert Mapplethorpe's photographs is cancelled at the Corcoran Art Gallery in Washington, D.C. The exhibit is attacked by Senator Jesse Helms for its homoerotic content. The gallery director resigns, and the ensuing media attention makes Mapplethorpe's name synonymous with protests against artistic censorship.

Massachusetts becomes the second state to enact a gay rights law.

Over 5,000 ACT UP members demonstrate in front and inside of New York's St. Patrick's Cathedral. They rally against the Catholic Church's antigay stance and policies on AIDS.

Artwork from gay artist Keith Haring is used by the U.S. Post Office to issue a commemorative stamp in honor of the twentieth anniversary of the Stonewall Riots.

A New York judge rules that a gay male couple constitutes a "family" for purposes of housing rules.

The Gentlemen's Alliance is formed as Nigeria's first gay male organization.

Poland forms its first national gay rights group (Lambda), launches an information center, and begins publishing a journal (*Filo*).

When Larry Kramer's play *The Natural Heart* is scheduled to play at a local college in Springfield, Missouri, residents react with animosity. Many believe the topic of the play, the early years of the AIDS epidemic, is not appropriate for public discussion. Efforts made to close the show include bomb threats sent to the college and a student home being burned down. However, the play gives eight sold-out performances.

Two internal Pentagon reports conclude that homosexuals pose no military security risks. The reports are released by members of Congress after having been hidden for years.

1990   The Americans with Disability Act (ADA) is signed into law. It explicitly prohibits AIDS-based discrimination.

Queer Nation is founded in New York City as a direct action, in-your-face group with the rallying cry, "We're here, we're queer, get used to it!"

Hong Kong repeals its sodomy laws.

Congress votes to end the national immigration policy that bans homosexual immigrants.

The National Endowment for the Arts (NEA) revokes grants already awarded to four solo theater artists. This is unprecedented in the history of the NEA. The four—Karen Finley, John Fleck, Holly Hughes, and Tim Miller—soon become known as "The NEA Four." Their defunding was initiated by Senator Jesse Helms. Three of the four artists are homosexual, and their performance art is sexually explicit. They become a cause célèbre for the lesbian and gay community. The four artists sue the NEA in 1993 and settle out of court for $252,000.

After ordaining two lesbians and a gay man as ministers, two Lutheran churches in San Francisco are suspended from their national organization.

The Michigan Supreme Court declares the state's antisodomy laws unconstitutional.

Dennis Barrie, director of the Cincinnati Museum of Art,

1990, cont.
is charged with obscenity, and then acquitted, when he books the homoerotic photographs of Robert Mapplethorpe for an exhibition.

The Hate Crime Statistics Act is approved by Congress and signed by President George Bush. It requires the Department of Justice to collect, maintain, and report statistics on hate crimes motivated by race, religion, national origin, or sexual orientation. It is the first federal legislation to include sexual orientation as a specific class. Senator Jesse Helms is instrumental in holding up the act. He believes it is a conspiracy initiated by "the radical elements of the homosexual movement" (Newton 1994, 49).

Polk County, Florida, jail officials discontinue the practice of requiring gay prisoners to wear pink bracelets. The practice was used to distinguish gay from nongay prisoners in the mistaken hope of reducing the spread of HIV.

Twenty-seven percent of Russians interviewed for a survey conducted by the *Moscow News* support the death penalty for homosexuality.

General Motors develops a promotional videotape in which it refers to Japanese-made trucks as "little faggot trucks." Later, the company apologizes for the statement.

Two men are sentenced to five years in prison by a judge in Adrian, Michigan, for having sex in a public park.

The lesbian and gay community boycotts Miller beer and Marlboro cigarettes, products of the Philip Morris Company, when it is discovered that Philip Morris provided campaign financing to antigay senator Jesse Helms.

When the local chapter of PFLAG is asked to participate in the St. Louis adopt-a-roadway program, the St. Louis County Board of Highways and Traffic initially decides to cancel the entire program. Eventually, it changes its mind and allows PFLAG to participate.

Conservative Backlash

1991   Karen Thompson is awarded guardianship of her lover, Sharon Kowalski, who is in a coma due to a car accident, over the objections of Kowalski's parents.

The International Lesbian and Gay Association cancels its Thirteenth Annual Conference in Guadalajara, Mexico, because the mayor threatens to use force to stop the function.

NOW's president, Patricia Ireland, discloses that she has a female lover in addition to being married to a man.

In situations of domestic violence, an Ohio appellate court rules that lesbian and gay couples have a "spousal relationship."

Simon LeVay releases his findings suggesting a biological influence on brain structure and sexual orientation, otherwise known as "the gay brain."

For the first time, gay men and lesbians are included in Amnesty International's campaign to free individuals imprisoned because of sexual orientation and political crimes.

Department of Defense spokesperson Pete Williams is outed by *The Advocate*.

A request by the Irish Lesbian and Gay Organization (ILGO) to march in the annual New York City's St. Patrick's Day Parade is denied. The parade is protested by 1,000 members of ILGO.

Marlon Riggs's documentary about African American gay men, *Tongues Untied*, is aired on PBS. The Federal Communications Commission receives many complaints from homophobic viewers.

Because of the U.S. immigration policy banning the admission of HIV-positive visitors to the United States, the

1991,   Eighth Annual International AIDS Conference is can-
cont.   celled in Boston and moved to Amsterdam.

Baltimore's first Black Gay and Lesbian Pride March is held in Washington, D.C.

Audrey Lorde, a lesbian poet, teacher, and activist, is named poet laureate of New York State.

Connecticut becomes the fourth state to enact a gay rights bill.

The Milwaukee School Board approves a gay sensitivity training program for teachers and staff. It enrages conservative citizens and community groups, which demand a recall of the board members.

1992   The General Accounting Office reports that between 1981 and 1990, approximately 17,000 service men and women were discharged from the military for homosexuality, at a cost of almost $500 million.

Voters in Colorado approve Amendment 2 to the state constitution, which prohibits equal rights ordinances for gays. A similar ballot initiative in Oregon, Proposition 9, is defeated.

Canadian country and pop singer k. d. lang becomes the first major female recording artist to come out as a lesbian.

The (San Francisco) Bay Area United Way publicly states that it will no longer support the Boy Scouts of America because of its antigay policies.

At the Democratic National Convention, Bill Clinton becomes the first presidential nominee to mention gay people in his acceptance speech.

After three years of effort, the government of Argentina grants legal recognition to the gay and lesbian group Comunidad Homosexual Argentina.

U.S. Navy cadet Terry Helvey beats to death sailor Allen Schindler, who had just come out. The case receives national media attention due to its brutality and the fact that Schindler reported these problems to his superiors months in advance. Schindler was so badly beaten that his mother is unable to identify his body. Helvey states during questioning, "I'd do it again." Helvey is sentenced to life in prison.

New Jersey becomes the fifth state to pass a gay rights law.

For the first time at the Democratic National Convention, in New York, an open lesbian, a gay man with AIDS, and a HIV-positive heterosexual woman address the members.

Levi Strauss, with 23,000 employees, becomes the largest company in the United States to grant health benefits to employee domestic partners.

Lesbian Avengers, International, is launched by a group of activists in New York City. Within two years, the organization grows to more than thirty-five chapters in North America and Europe.

Massachusetts becomes the first state to grant lesbian and gay state workers the same bereavement and family leave rights as heterosexual workers.

Antisodomy laws are abolished in the country of Estonia.

Canada removes its ban on lesbians and gays in the military.

For the first time in North America, the Canadian immigration service grants immigration status to an Irish lesbian whose partner is a Canadian citizen.

Statewide bans on antigay discrimination are enacted by Vermont, California, and New Jersey.

1993   Soon after taking office as president of the United States, Bill Clinton directs the secretary of defense to look into overturning the 1981 ban on gays in the military. Fierce opposition from conservative members of Congress and fundamentalist religious groups throughout the nation force Clinton to settle for the Don't Ask, Don't Tell compromise, which does not significantly change the current status of gays in the military.

The Hawaii Supreme Court rules that lower courts in the state improperly dismissed a challenge to the state's policy restricting marriage to opposite-sex couples only. The court decides that denying same-sex marriage constitutes sex discrimination, which is prohibited by Hawaii's state constitution.

Once again, the Irish Lesbian and Gay Organization is excluded from New York's annual St. Patrick's Day Parade. Both Governor Mario Cuomo and Mayor David Dinkins, along with thousands of others, stay away from the parade. More than 200 people are arrested when they try to stage an alternative parade on the same day.

The Nevada legislature votes to repeal its state's antisodomy laws.

The March on Washington for Gay, Lesbian, and Bi Equal Rights draws a crowd between 300,000 (estimated by the National Park Service) and 1 million (estimated by the *New York Times*). President Clinton, along with most legislators, leave town. The three largest newsmagazines in the nation, *Time, Newsweek,* and *U.S. News and World Report,* fail to mention the march even though its size places it in the top ten of such demonstrations in Washington, D.C.

The First International Dyke March, organized by the Lesbian Avengers, takes place the evening before the March on Washington.

Antigay ballot measures are approved by the voters of Cincinnati, Ohio; Portsmouth, New Hampshire; and Lewiston, Maine.

California becomes the sixth state to enact employment antidiscrimination provisions protecting the rights of lesbian and gay public employees.

The Tenth Circuit Court of Appeals rules that Kansas's school officials may legally refuse to hire teachers suspected of being gay, even if a teacher/applicant is not gay.

The Christian right embraces findings of the Battelle Human Affairs Research Center that concludes that only 2.3 percent of U.S. men have had sex with other men and that only 1.1 percent consider themselves exclusively homosexual.

Three high school teachers are suspended after several lesbian mothers are allowed to speak to a parenting class in Meridian, Idaho. The teachers are reinstated two weeks later after vigorous protests by students.

The adoption of a multicultural, gay-tolerant "Rainbow Curriculum" causes much controversy in the New York City schools. Five of thirty-two local school boards refuse to adopt the curriculum. City schools Chancellor Joseph Fernandez does not have his employment contract renewed, primarily because of the Rainbow Curriculum.

Roberta Achtenberg is approved by the U.S. Senate as assistant housing secretary over the objections of many conservatives, including Senator Jesse Helms, who calls her "a damned lesbian." She becomes the highest-ranked acknowledged lesbian in the U.S. government.

President Clinton appoints the first "AIDS czar," Kristine Gebbie. She is widely criticized by AIDS activists and is forced to resign within a year.

The Wisconsin Supreme Court decides that landlords may refuse to rent to unrelated couples because it would undermine the stability of marriage and family.

President Clinton restores the ban on HIV-positive visitors to the United States.

1993,   The U.S. Post Office issues a red ribbon stamp depicting
cont.   AIDS awareness.

The Oregon Citizens Alliance (OCA) is successful at getting the town of Cornelius to adopt a law similar to
Proposition 9, which banned civil rights protection for
lesbian and gay men. This success leads the alliance to affiliate with other groups and target eleven states for similar initiatives.

Ireland eliminates its 132-year-old law banning homosexual acts.

Minnesota becomes the seventh state to pass gay rights
legislation.

Sharon Bottoms, a twenty-three-year-old lesbian mother,
loses custody of her son Tyler to her mother. Henrico
County (Virginia) circuit judge Buford Parsons, Jr. rules
that Virginia's antisodomy law makes Sharon Bottoms a
criminal and therefore by definition unfit to be a mother.
Judge Parsons states that he fears the boy will grow up
unable to distinguish between women and men. In 1997,
the Virginia Court of Appeals overturns this decision, re-
turning Tyler to his mother.

Russia repeals its antisodomy laws.

The U.S. Supreme Court rules that the antigay Colorado
Amendment 2 is unconstitutional.

1994   Organizers cancel the Boston St. Patrick's Day Parade
rather than comply with a court order allowing the Irish-
American Gay, Lesbian, and Bisexual Group to participate.

For the first time, the U.S. Immigration and Naturalization Service grants political asylum based on sexual orientation to a gay Mexican who claims his life will be
threatened if he returns to Mexico.

Amnesty International mounts a six-month campaign in

the United States to combat civil rights abuses against lesbians and gay men.

The Academy Award for best actor is given to straight actor Tom Hanks for his portrayal of a gay man with AIDS in the movie *Philadelphia*.

The United Nations Human Rights Committee decides that laws criminalizing consensual sex between adult men is a breach of privacy and that no nation should have such laws.

Approximately 15,000 people from two dozen nations participate in Gay Games IV, in New York City. This becomes the largest single athletic event in the world, with more than 500,000 spectators.

Randy Shilts, author of *And the Band Played On* and *Conduct Unbecoming*, dies from AIDS-related causes in San Francisco. His funeral is picketed by Westboro Baptist Church (WBC) members carrying signs that read, "Filthy Face of Fag Evil."

The age of consent for homosexual acts is lowered by the British Parliament from twenty-one to eighteen. However, the age of consent for heterosexual acts is sixteen.

Surgeon General Joycelyn Elders, in an interview with *The Advocate* magazine, says: "We have to be more open about sex, and we need to speak out to tell people that sex is good, sex is wonderful. It's a normal part and healthy part of our being, whether it is homosexual or heterosexual" (Newton 1994, 58). Conservatives press President Clinton to "publicly disavow" Elders's views.

The consultative status granted to the International Lesbian and Gay Association (ILGA) in 1993 is revoked by the United Nations based on an unsubstantiated claim that some of its members are affiliated with pedophile groups.

The American Medical Association (AMA) adopts policy

1994,
cont.

to remove all references in the *Diagnostic and Statistical Manual (DSM)* to "sexual orientation related disorders." By doing so, medical doctors are no longer justified in conducting "therapies" for "treating" homosexuality.

Massachusetts becomes the first state to provide protection from antigay harassment to public school children.

The Brazilian newspaper *Folha de São Paulo* estimates that one antigay killing occurs every four days in the nation.

In national midterm elections, Republicans obtain a majority in both houses of Congress and win many gubernatorial elections. Because these wins were made with major backing from the homophobic Christian right, there is much fear within the lesbian and gay community about its future civil rights.

In a vote of 159 in favor and 96 against, the European Parliament recommends that lesbian and gay couples be allowed to marry and adopt children.

With the end of apartheid in South Africa, its new constitution includes sexual orientation as a protected class—the only country in the world to do so.

An attempt is made by residents of Ovett, Mississippi, to close down Camp Sister Spirit because of their fear that the lesbian-run camp will be a haven for violent crime and transform unborn children in the community into lesbians. The camp provides food, lodging, and support for women who are victims of abuse or are homeless. Field marshals are sent by Attorney General Janet Reno to protect the lesbians when it becomes evident there is a potential for physical danger.

1995

Rhode Island becomes the ninth state to pass a statewide gay rights bill. In another ruling at year's end, the Rhode Island Supreme Court upholds the state's antisodomy laws.

Greg Louganis, four-time Olympic gold medalist in diving, reveals in a television interview with Barbara Walters on *20/20* that he has AIDS.

Congress passes the draconian Illegal Immigration Control and Immigrant Responsibility Act. The law deprives many binational couples and HIV-positive immigrants of the opportunity to stay in United States on humanitarian "hardship" grounds.

Zimbabwe president Robert Mugabe says homosexuals are "lower than dogs and pigs" (Predrag 2001).

Protease inhibitors, a new generation of AIDS drugs, show considerable success and receive approval from the Food and Drug Administration.

The state of South Dakota bans same-sex marriages as a preemptive strike against the potential of gay marriages being approved in Hawaii. Other states soon follow.

Jonathan Tyler Schmitz kills Scott Amedure by shooting him twice in the chest. Three days earlier, both men appeared on a *Jenny Jones Show* episode in which Amedure revealed his romantic feelings to an unsuspecting Schmitz. Schmitz is convicted of second-degree murder in 1996. His defense attorney argues that humiliation on the talk show and past mental problems reduce Schmitz's responsibility for the killings. The *Jenny Jones Show* is sued by the Amedure family and is ordered to pay the family $25 million. These events lead shock television to reexamine its programming.

Federal judge Eugene Nickerson declares the Don't Ask, Don't Tell policy unconstitutional. By year's end, there are a number of conflicted rulings on this policy—some for, some against.

When a group of gay and lesbian leaders comes to meet with President Clinton, White House security personnel put on latex gloves to meet the group. At the same time, Marsha Scott, a straight woman, is appointed by Clinton as his liaison to the gay and lesbian community. Both incidents cause uproar in the gay community.

1995,   The Hawaii Supreme Court postpones until 1996 a deci-
cont.   sion on same-sex marriage in the state. The court allows
        a special state commission to review the issue. The com-
        mission later recommends legalizing same-sex mar-
        riages.

        The Ryan White Comprehensive AIDS Resources Emer-
        gency Act is approved by the House over delaying tactics
        by Senator Jesse Helms.

        The Zimbabwe government forces Africa's biggest book
        fair to remove a gay exhibit and sparks more antigay re-
        marks from President Robert Mugabe.

        President Clinton signs an executive order ending the
        policy of denying security clearances to gay men and les-
        bians.

        Penny Culliton, a schoolteacher in Mascenic, New
        Hampshire, is fired when she uses the gay-themed books
        Maurice, by E. M. Forster, and *The Education of Harriet Hat-
        field,* by May Sarton, in her high school English class.

        More than 100 transvestite, transgender, and transsexual
        activists gather for the First National Gender Lobbying
        Day on Capitol Hill.

        Dean Hammer releases a new study suggesting that
        genes inherited from the mother influence whether a
        man becomes gay.

        The New York Supreme Court grants the right of unmar-
        ried couples, whether gay or not, to adopt their partner's
        children. This is a landmark ruling.

        PFLAG use quotes from televangelist Pat Robertson's
        own television show to create television ads showing the
        impact that hate speech has on gay and lesbian youths.
        Threats of lawsuits from Robertson keep most television
        stations from showing the spots.

1996   Murder and assisting suicide charges against Keith W.

Green are dropped after the gay community protests. Green helped reattach an auto exhaust hose being used by his AIDS-stricken lover to commit suicide.

Magic Johnson returns to the National Basketball Association after a five-year absence since his announcement of being HIV-positive.

District judge Jeffrey Sherlock rules Montana's antisodomy laws unconstitutional. The state appeals the ruling.

Utah passes two bills designed to eliminate gay-straight student alliances at state-financed high schools. One bill prohibits teachers from promoting "illegal activities" (sodomy is illegal in Utah), and the second bill requires students to obtain parental approval before joining any club.

The Virginia Federal Appeals Court upholds a ban on gays in the military.

The U.S. Olympic Committee decides to bypass Cobb County, Georgia, during the torch run for the Atlanta Summer Games because of an antigay resolution passed by the county.

The U.S. Supreme Court declares Colorado's Amendment 2, which denies legal protection based on sexual orientation, unconstitutional.

President Clinton signs the federal Defense of Marriage Act in which marriage is defined as the union of one man and one woman. Interestingly, no local, state, or federal law defines "man" or "woman."

President Clinton boosts funding for the Ryan White AIDS CARE fund.

Robert James Acemant admits killing Roxanne Ellis and Michele Abdill of Medford, Oregon, because they were lesbians. The bodies of the women were found bound and gagged in the back of a pickup truck; they had been

1996,   shot execution style. Acemant is convicted of the murders
cont.   but not of a hate crime.

Two research teams report finding that about 1 percent of
the male population is resistant to HIV due to a defective
gene.

The last viewing of the complete AIDS Quilt (38,000 pan-
els) is held at the National Mall in Washington, D.C.

The Harvard AIDS Institute International Advisory
Council predicts that blacks will account for one half of
all U.S. AIDS cases by the year 2000.

Jamie Nabozny wins a $962,000 judgment against his
Wisconsin high school for failure to protect him from
antigay harassment while he was a student there. This
ruling has significant impact for all gay and lesbian students and the nation's schools.

1997   An Atlanta lesbian nightclub is attacked with a bomb
laced with nails. Five people are injured. This is the third
such attack in seven months and may be related to the
bomber responsible for the 1996 Summer Olympics bomb
and a blast at a local family planning clinic.

The Centers for Disease Control and Prevention reports
the first decline in the number of AIDS-related deaths.

More than 500 AIDS activists converge on Wall Street and
stop traffic in lower Manhattan. ACT UP protests alleged
price-gouging by pharmaceutical companies.

Hawaii becomes the first state to enact a domestic registry and at the same time passes a constitutional amendment limiting marriage to opposite-sex couples only.

Lesbian actor Ellen DeGeneres's character comes out as a
lesbian on her television show *Ellen*. This is the first time
the primary character on a commercial television program is openly gay.

New Hampshire becomes the tenth state to ban discrimination against lesbians and gays in employment, housing, and public accommodations. Two days later, Maine becomes the eleventh state to enact similar legislation.

President Clinton makes a promise to find an AIDS vaccine within ten years. Activists are unimpressed by the promise since the initiative includes no new research funds.

The city of San Francisco passes an ordinance requiring all companies doing business with the city to provide domestic partnership benefits to employees. The ordinance is challenged in court, but ultimately upheld in most situations.

Delegates at the Southern Baptist Convention call on its 15.7 million members to boycott the Walt Disney Company for ownership of *Ellen* and Disney's employee domestic partnership policy.

Andrew Cunanan murders gay fashion designer Gianni Versace on July 15. While hiding out on a houseboat in Miami, Florida, Cunanan fatally shoots himself. He is wanted for a series of murders and is on the FBI's most-wanted list.

Many lesbians and gay men grieve the death of Britain's Princess Diana. The community remembers her for her charitable activities, including help in the fight against AIDS.

Hundreds of AIDS activists protest in front of the Department of Health and Human Services against a federal ban on funding for needle-exchange programs.

The National Conference of Catholic Bishops distributes the groundbreaking document titled "Always Our Children," which encourages parents to give first priority to love and support of their lesbian daughters and gay sons over church doctrine condemning homosexuality.

1997, cont.
The lesbian and gay community expresses concern over a rally of the Promise Keepers in Washington, D.C., that attracts more than 700,000 men. Although they claim to be apolitical, they have deep ties to the religious right and espouse antigay rhetoric.

Openly gay businessman James Hormel is nominated to be the U.S. ambassador to Luxembourg. Acrimonious debate in the U.S. Senate delays his confirmation until 1998.

President Clinton becomes the first sitting president to speak to a gay rights group. At a speech given at a dinner for the Human Rights Campaign, he calls for all Americans to overcome prejudice.

Researchers confirm that drug therapies using protease inhibitors are unable to completely eradicate HIV from all cells in the body.

1998
In the Afghan city of Heat, eighteen-year-old Abdul Sami and twenty-two-year-old Bismillah are placed beside a mud wall that is then bulldozed on top of them. The men were found guilty of engaging in sodomy and are killed as part of a public execution.

A Dutch man dying of pneumonia is granted the right to "marry" his partner of forty years to become the first same-sex couple to marry in the Netherlands. Full marriage rights do not become effective in the Netherlands until 2001.

The Cayman Islands gives in to religious activists and prohibits a gay cruise ship from docking at its harbor.

U.S. district judge Stanley Sporkin rules that the U.S. Navy went too far by illegally obtaining confidential information about dismissed Senior Chief Petty Officer Timothy McVeigh.

The voters of Maine throw out a gay rights ordinance enacted the previous year.

The U.S. Supreme Court decides in *Oncale v. Sundowner* that sexual harassment laws apply to same-sex cases.

Two court decisions in March concerning the Boy Scouts' ban on gays are conflicted. In the case of James Dale, the court finds that the Scouts must abide by New Jersey's antidiscrimination laws. In the Timothy Curran case, the California Supreme Court rules the Scouts is not a business and therefore the state's antidiscrimination laws do not apply.

Nebraska minister Reverend Jimmy Creech is acquitted of misdeed by the United Methodist Church for performing a union ceremony between two lesbians. Although he wins, he is eventually forced out of the church.

While addressing the Wisconsin State Assembly, Green Bay Packer Reggie White makes a speech full of homophobic comments and ethnic slurs that stuns the audience.

Pop star George Michael is arrested for lewd conduct in a Beverly Hill's public restroom. This leads to his coming out as bisexual and releasing a music video that spoofs his arrest.

A Pentagon report confirms that discharges from the military for being gay skyrocketed 67 percent since Don't Ask, Don't Tell took effect in 1994.

In response to the anti–affirmative action measure California Proposition 209 passed by voters, the Los Angeles City Board of Education eliminates its Gay and Lesbian Education Commission, along with six other minority education commissions.

Although the Clinton administration issues a report showing that needle-exchange programs are effective at reducing the spread of AIDS, it still refuses to lift the ban on federal funding for these programs.

Lawmakers in Rhode Island vote to eliminate the state's 102-year-old antisodomy laws.

1998,   The United Methodist Church warns pastors that they
cont.   will be tried, reprimanded, or defrocked if they perform
same-sex union ceremonies.

The Second U.S. Court of Appeals rules that Congress has
complete authority to exclude gays from the military as
part of personnel policies.

University of Wyoming gay student Matthew Shepard is
found hanging spread-eagle on a fencepost in subzero
weather beside a remote road in Laramie, Wyoming. His
death a few days later becomes the springboard for many
organizations to push for hate crime laws in their states.

A Cincinnati city charter banning any policies favorable
to gays and lesbians is ruled constitutional by the U.S.
Supreme Court. The ruling infuriates the gay community
since the U.S. Supreme Court had already decided in a
similar case, Colorado's Amendment 2, that such prohibitions are not constitutional.

Circuit court judge Richard Rombow rules that Maryland's
1916 antisodomy laws violate the state's constitution.

The Georgia Supreme Court rules that the state's 165-
year-old antisodomy law violates its constitutional guarantee of privacy. This ruling comes twelve years after the
U.S. Supreme Court ruled in *Bowers v. Hardwick* that
Georgia had the right to enforce this law.

The Miami-Dade County Board of Commissioners votes
to approve a new antigay discrimination ordinance. This
occurs twenty-one years after Anita Bryant successfully
helped overturn a previous gay rights ordinance.

1999   Both the states of New Hampshire and Connecticut remove barriers to child adoption by gay couples, whereas
the states of Arkansas and Utah institute antigay policies
against gay adoptions.

The Ninth U.S. Circuit Court of Appeals rules that landlords in Anchorage, Alaska, can refuse to rent to unmar-

ried couples if it is against their religious beliefs. This could have significant impact for gay and lesbian couples.

Almost 13,000 people witness the holy union between long-time lesbian couple Jeanne Barnett and Ellie Charlton in Sacramento, California. Eighty United Methodist ministers attending the ecclesiastically disobedient event may face formal charges from the church.

Jerry Falwell outs Tinky Winky, the purple Teletubby, in his *National Liberty Journal*. The national media and gay press have a field day with the absurdity of the accusation.

Billy Jack Gaither, a thirty-nine-year-old man, is found burned to death on the banks of Pockerwood Creek in Alabama. He was bludgeoned with an ax handle and his body thrown on two burning tires. Two men are convicted of his murder and sentenced to life in prison without parole.

Tracey Thompson, a thirty-three-year-old transgender woman, is found beaten to death with a baseball bat on a rural south Georgia road. No perpetrator is charged.

New York City police officer Justin Volpe is convicted of sodomizing Haitian immigrant Abner Louima with a broken broomstick handle while Louima was in custody.

A coalition of eighteen religious right organizations launches phase two of its "Truth in Love" ad campaign, which urges gay men and lesbians to enter therapy to convert to heterosexuality.

The Canadian Supreme Court rules that same-sex couples must have the same rights as opposite-sex couples.

Pat Robertson's Christian Coalition loses its tax-exempt status from the IRS.

Bill Clinton becomes the first president ever to proclaim June as Gay and Lesbian Pride Month.

1999,
cont.

Gary Matson and Winfield Scott Mowder of Happy Valley, California, are killed by two white supremacist brothers connected to the antigay, racist World Church of the Creator. The two brothers, Benjamin Matthew Williams and James Tyler Williams, are also charged with setting fire to three synagogues and a medical clinic in Sacramento, California.

Army PFC Barry Winchell is attacked by Private Calvin N. Glover with a baseball bat while asleep in his barracks. Prosecutors acknowledge the killing is an antigay hate crime, and Glover is convicted of premeditated murder. In 2000, Spc. Justin R. Fisher is sentenced to thirteen years in prison for obstructing justice in the murder investigation and for providing Glover with the murder weapon.

Reverend Robert Nugent and Sister Jeannie Gramick are ordered by the Vatican to end their twenty-two-year-old ministry to gay men and lesbians.

During the San Diego Gay Pride Parade, a tear-gas canister is thrown into the middle of a group of seventy children, parents, and grandparents. The parade is temporarily disrupted, and approximately fifteen people are treated for injuries.

The European Court in Strasbourg finds Britain to be in violation of the European Convention of Human Rights with its ban on gays and lesbians serving in the military. As a result, the British Defense Ministry draws up a new military code of conduct that allows gays to serve in the military.

Reverend Mel White leads a delegate of some 200 gay activists to meet with Reverend Jerry Falwell in an effort to get him to tone down his antigay rhetoric.

Dana Rivers, a transgender woman ousted from her teaching position with Antelope School District, California, settles out of court for $150,000 not to seek her job back.

The Orange County School District Board of Trustees, in a unanimous vote, denies a gay-straight alliance from meeting at El Modina High School. The board members openly acknowledge that they are in violation of federal law and that other gay-straight alliance student groups are already meeting in other district high schools.

2000   California enacts the first statewide domestic partnership registry in the nation.

President Clinton calls on Congress to pass the Hate Crimes Prevention Act and the Employment Nondiscrimination Act.

Laura Schlessinger gets a $3 million contract from Paramount Studios to place her daily "Dr. Laura" antigay radio talk show on TV. In response, the StopDrLaura.com effort is launched. Cincinnati-based Proctor and Gamble announces that it will not sponsor her upcoming television show and also pulls out of her radio show. Soon, most advertisers cease funding her show, and as a result it lasts only a short time on television.

Proposition 22, the Knight Initiative outlawing same-sex marriages, is passed overwhelmingly in California.

Hilary Swank wins the Oscar for best actress for her portrayal of transgender murder victim Brandon Teena in *Boys Don't Cry.*

The New Jersey Supreme Court makes a landmark decision when it declares the nonbiological parent of a same-sex couple who broke up is the "psychological parent" of the twin girls she helped raise.

The Vermont House approves the state's civil union law as a way of providing marriage to same-sex couples without calling it marriage.

The U.S. Supreme Court rules that the Boy Scouts of America has the right to ban gays from its ranks.

2000,
cont.

"J. R" Carl Warren, Jr., of Grant Town in Marion County, West Virginia, is found dead on a lonely road. Two seventeen-year-old males confess that they were afraid he was going to reveal a sexual liaison he had with one or both of them. They beat and kicked him to death, then placed his body into the trunk of a car, drove to an isolated spot, placed his body on the ground, and ran over it several times to make the murder look like a hit-and-run accident.

The California State Board of Equalization votes to grant a nonbiological lesbian parent the tax status of "head of household."

Two lesbians are ejected from Dodger Stadium, Los Angeles, California, for kissing to celebrate two home runs by their team. When the situation hits the media, Dodger president and CEO Bob Graziano publicly apologizes to the women and the gay community—which are all the damages the women requested.

Ronald Gay, fifty-three, kills one and injures six patrons at a gay bar in Roanoke, Virginia. He defends his actions by saying that he was made fun of his entire life because of his surname and that he wanted to get rid of "faggots."

Exodus International ex-gay chair John Paulk is removed from his position when he is discovered by three employees of the Human Rights Campaign sitting in a gay bar in Washington, D.C. At first he claims that he entered the bar to use the bathroom not knowing what kind of bar it was, but later admits that he knew it was a gay bar. Paulk and his "ex-lesbian" wife, Anne, advocate reparative therapy for homosexuals wanting to be heterosexual.

The Virginia Court of Appeals rejects a challenge to the state's antisodomy laws.

2001

In April, the Netherlands becomes the first country in the world to legally sanctify same-sex marriage.

The Permanent Partners Immigration Act is reintroduced

to Congress by Representative Jerold Nadler (D-NY). The act offers same-sex couples the same privileges currently afforded to legal spouses under federal immigration law.

The Chinese Psychiatric Association decides to drop all references to homosexuality as a pathological condition. This brings China's mental health establishment in closer line with that of Western nations.

Seven gay and lesbian couples in Massachusetts apply for marriage licenses and are denied. They begin the process of suing the state.

The *Washington Post* reports that a Washington, D.C., Health Department's AIDS pamphlet (paid for by the government) makes statements such as, "Jesus is our hope!" and contains a fifteen-page tract, "A Christian Response to AIDS," in which the Bible is cited thirty times.

The James Byrd Jr. Hate Crimes Act is passed in Texas after a long, hard-fought battle. Passage is achieved when Lieutenant Governor Bill Ratliff and five other Republicans break rank and vote with all fifteen senate Democrats.

Police and the Egyptian State Security Intelligence raid the *Queen Boat* while it is moored on the Nile in Cairo's Zamalek district. They arrest fifty-five men, many teenagers, while they are partying. The arrests are made because the men are suspected of engaging in a gay sex party. As the months unfold and the matter is brought to trial, there is an international outcry over the proceedings and harsh sentences. U.S. Representative Barney Frank obtains signatures from thirty-five members of the House and sends a letter expressing "strong disapproval" to Egyptian president Hosni Mubarak over the arrest of the men.

The U.S. Supreme Court rules 8–0 that marijuana cannot be used for any debilitating diseases, including AIDS.

The U.S. Census releases figures showing that the number of American households reporting same-sex couples has skyrocketed.

2001,
cont.

Namibia president Sam Nujoma declares, "The Republic of Namibia does not allow homosexuality [or] lesbianism here" (Amnesty 2001).

Senator Jesse Helms is successful at getting the Senate to pass an amendment that denies federal funding to school districts that apply their antidiscrimination policies to the Boy Scouts.

The U.N. General Assembly issues a worldwide plan to fight the spread of AIDS and to provide better care for the approximately 36 million people currently infected.

The *Washington Post* reveals that White House senior adviser Karl Rove brokered a deal with the antigay Salvation Army, which would receive between $88,000 to $100,000 a month in exchange for its support of President George W. Bush's faith-based initiative, HR 7. Initially, the White House vehemently denies that the meetings took place, but only days later admits that they had.

Fred Martinez, Jr., a two-spirit sixteen-year-old Native American, is beaten to death by Shaun Murphy, eighteen, near Cortez, Colorado. Still, the Colorado legislature fails to pass a hate crimes bill.

The firing of a lesbian because of her sexual orientation from the Kentucky Baptist Homes for Children is upheld by a federal judge in Louisville, Kentucky.

On September 11, terrorists in the northeastern United States hijack four airliners. Two airliners crash into the World Trade Center towers, destroying both. One crashes into the Pentagon, and another, believed to be headed for the White House, crashes into the countryside of Pennsylvania. A few days after the attacks, while on *The 700 Club* television program, Reverend Jerry Falwell blames gays and lesbians, among others, for the attacks. While Falwell makes these statements, Pat Robertson nods his head in agreement. There is a swift and furious outcry by liberals, conservatives, other religious leaders, and gay activists over their comments. Falwell and Robertson attempt damage control, but without success. Also, there is continuing debate over whether to provide survivor funds to partners of lesbians and gay men who died in the attack.

HIV/AIDS and prevention workers are arrested in India under antisodomy and antiobscenity statutes.

Openly gay Michael Guest is confirmed by the Senate to act as the United States ambassador to Romania. The antigay Family Research Council protests his appointment. Secretary of State Colin Powell presides over the swearing in and publicly acknowledges Guest's lover of six years.

Switzerland's two largest banks agree to pay $1.25 billion in settlement to five groups of people, including lesbians and gay men. This represents more than 50,000 bank accounts placed with them in an effort to keep assets out of the hands of the Nazis during World War II. After the war, the banks failed to return the money. Although other European governments have created funds to provide for victims redressed for Nazi crimes, this is the first time gays have been specifically mentioned and documented.

AB 25, California's Domestic Partnership bill, is signed into law by Governor Gray Davis, making California second only to Vermont in the support of gay and lesbian relationships and families.

Three antigay measures are defeated in Michigan, while two progay measures in Dade County, Florida, effectively erase the legacy of Anita Bryant.

Germany comes close to legalizing same-sex marriages but is blocked at the last moment by conservative regional states.

Los Angeles County sheriff Lee Boca announces that condoms will be distributed in county jails as part of a HIV prevention program.

2002   On the first day of the new year, Saudi Arabia, in a public execution, beheads three men found guilty of "engaging in the extreme obscenity and ugly acts of homosexuality."

Alaska governor Tony Knowles signs an administrative order prohibiting discrimination based on sexual orientation in state employment.

The Australian High Court reaffirms the right of single and lesbian women to have *in vitro* fertilization treatment.

Bill Flanigan sues the University of Maryland medical system in Baltimore City Circuit Court for refusing him the right to visit his dying life partner because only "family" members are qualified to visit. Flanigan and his partner had a five-year legal California domestic partnership, and Flanigan possessed a specified health care power of attorney, which the hospital refused to acknowledge.

Two widowed domestic partners file claims with the New York State Workers' Compensation Board after being denied spousal benefits by their partners' life insurance companies as an aftermath of the September 11, 2001, terrorist attack.

A leading Jerusalem rabbi, David Batzri, states that gays should be "put to death."

An Ohio lesbian couple goes to court to secure name changes so that the couple's children will have the same surname. The Ohio Supreme Court has not ruled but has affirmed Ohio's law not recognizing de facto parenting.

More homosexual men are arrested in Egypt in an apparent crackdown.

In the first National Day of Silence, on April 10, students at more than 1,900 high schools and colleges across the nation choose not to speak in order to bring attention to antigay bias in schools.

The Jamaican government rejects a recommendation by parliament to decriminalize homosexuality.

The state of Washington enacts an antibullying bill in its public schools that prohibits bias-motivated harassment.

U.N. AIDS chief Peter Piot reports that Russia has the fastest-growing HIV infection rate in the world.

Pi Kappa Phi's national council removes all members of its Michigan State University fraternity for using antigay epithets and slogans during pledging rituals.

Britain repeals sex statutes that banned "gross indecency" between men, "soliciting for the immoral purpose," and "buggery." These were the same statutes used to prosecute Oscar Wilde.

The city of Dallas, Texas, enacts an antidiscrimination ordinance that includes sexual orientation and gender identity.

Romania bans discrimination based on sexual orientation and eliminates its antisodomy laws.

J'Noel Gardiner, a transgender woman, is denied the right to inherit her late husband's estate because the Kansas Supreme Court rules that she is not a woman under Kansas law and thus her marriage to Marshall Gardiner is not valid.

A thirty-seven-year-old gay man, Clint Scott Risetter, is killed when gasoline is poured over him while he sleeps and he is set on fire. The killer, Martin Thomas Hartman, tells the police that he "has a lot of hatred" toward gays.

References

Amnesty International. 2001. *Namibia: Gays and Lesbians under Attack.* Available at http://web.amnesty.org/802568F7005C4453/8F1CEB4390F 1142AF80256A23003CB68A!Open&Highlight=2,gay

Blumenfeld, W. J., and D. Raymond, eds. 1993. *Looking at Gay and Lesbian Life*. Rev. ed. Boston: Beacon Press.

Bowers v. Hardwick, 106 S.Ct. 2841, 2843 (1986).

Duberman, M., M. Vicinus, and G. Chauncey, eds. 1989. *Hidden from History: Reclaiming the Gay and Lesbian Past*. New York: Meridian.

Federal Communications Commission v. Pacifica Foundation, 438 U.S. 726, 98 S.Ct. 3026, 57 L.Ed. 2d 1073 (1978).

Frontiers Magazine. Year-end reviews for 1995–2001.

Katz, J. 1976. *Gay American History: Lesbians and Gay Men in the U.S.A.* New York: Thomas Y. Crowell.

Marcus, R. 1990. "Powell Regrets Backing Sodomy Law." *Washington Post*, October 26, A3.

National Museum and Archive of Lesbian and Gay History, comp. 1996. *The Gay Almanac*. New York: Berkley Books.

Newton, D. E. 1994. *Gay and Lesbian Rights: A Reference Handbook*. Santa Barbara, CA: ABC-CLIO.

Oncale v. Sundowner Offshore Services, Inc, 523 U.S. 75 (1998).

One, Inc. v. Olesen, 355 U.S. 371 (1958).

Predrag, S. 2001. "Slow Progress: Despite Changes in South Africa, Gays in Neighboring Counties Sorely Lack Rights." *Frontiers* (September 14): 56.

Price Waterhouse v. Hopkins, 490 US 228 1989.

Radicalesbians. (1970). "The Woman Identified Woman." *Notes from the Third Year*. This celebrated article is available at www.cwluherstory. com/CWLUArchive/womidwom.html and may be obtained for reprint from the Herstory Project from the Women's Studies Resources, Duke Special Collections Library, a project of The Digital Scriptorium, Special Collections Library at Duke University at http://scriptorium.lib.duke.edu/wim.

Rose v. Locke, 423 U.S. 48 (1975).

Stewart, C. K. 2001. *Homosexuality and the Law: A Dictionary*. Santa Barbara, CA: ABC-CLIO.

Thompson, M., ed. 1994. *Long Road to Freedom:* The Advocate *History of the Gay and Lesbian Movement*. New York: St. Martin's Press.

Watkins v. United States Army, 875 F.2d 699 (9th Cir. 1989) (en banc).

4

Biographical Sketches

Deciding which people and events to include in this chapter is a daunting challenge. There are many books and lists of famous gays and lesbians. Surf the web to the Queer Resources Directory, or to the Gay, Lesbian, and Straight Education Network (GLSEN), or elsewhere and you will find hundreds, if not thousands, of names and biographies. The list here contains only a few of these names.

People such as Harry Hay, Magnus Hirschfeld, Phyllis Lyon, and Del Martin have had significant impact on the development of gay and lesbian consciousness. Others, such as Leonard Matlovich and Yukio Mishima, were not gay activists per se, but by living openly nonconformist lives, they became role models for others, as did Evelyn Hooker, a heterosexual psychologist who in the 1950s was instrumental in overturning the illness model of homosexuality. Antigay activists such as Anita Bryant, Paul Drummond Cameron, Jerry Falwell, and Lon Mabon still have a major influence in contemporary U.S. politics.

Susan B. Anthony (1820–1906)

Susan B. Anthony was one of the major activists behind the early suffragette movement. She was born to the family of a Quaker abolitionist on February 15, 1820, in Adams, Massachusetts. She was able to read at an early age and was sent to boarding school in Philadelphia to finish her education. She became a teacher at Eunice Kenyon's Quaker Academy in New Rochelle, New York.

By 1846, she moved to Rochester, New York, where she became headmistress of the female department at the Canajoharie Academy. She joined the temperance movement and began to identify the inequalities between the sexes. Soon, in 1851, she met Elizabeth Cady Stanton. They formed a fifty-year-long personal and political partnership that significantly impacted nineteenth-century America.

Anthony discovered that male temperance leaders were not interested in the participation of women. Thus, in 1852, she founded the Women's State Temperance Society of New York. The Civil War pushed the struggle for women's rights to the back burner. Once the war was over, Anthony spoke across the country on the issues of women's right to control property, to their guardianship of their children, and to divorce. When the debate on the Fourteenth Amendment was held in Congress in 1868, which granted all males the right to vote, she led an unsuccessful attempt to have women included.

One by one, the women Anthony associated with married. Her loneliness was swept away in 1868 when she met Anna Dickinson—a woman twenty years her junior and popular lecturer on women's rights.

In 1872 Anthony tested the legality of the right of women to vote in Rochester, New York. She attempted to vote and was arrested, tried, and fined. She refused to pay the fine on moral grounds garnering much publicity for the cause. Susan B. Anthony died on March 13, 1906, in Rochester, New York, fourteen years before passage of the Nineteenth Amendment to the U.S. Constitution—the so-called Anthony amendment that granted women the right to vote.

James Baldwin (1924–1987)

James Baldwin was an African American gay writer who addressed racism in his books and essays. Born on August 2, 1924, in Harlem, New York, Baldwin was raised by a Bible-thumping, white-hating preacher stepfather. Baldwin read his way through two Harlem libraries by age thirteen. He initially followed in his stepfather's footsteps, and at age fourteen became a Holy Roller minister at the Fireside Pentecostal Church in Harlem. For those two years, Baldwin was out of school preaching in the streets.

After high school, Baldwin moved to Greenwich Village, working at low-paying jobs to help support his siblings. He began to publish reviews and essays in respected magazines such as *The Nation, New Leader,* and *Commentary.* But he felt trapped as a black man in racist America and as a gay man in the homophobic African American community. Thus, in 1948, with a passport and a little pocket money, he went to Paris.

His fiction writing flourished in France. He was encouraged by his lover, Lucien Happersberger, and published the novel *Go Tell It on the Mountain* in 1953. His next two books, *Giovanni's Room* (1956) and *Another Country* (1962), brought critical acclaim to Baldwin. But the homosexuality depicted in *Another Country* brought savage criticism from the black community. It was virtually impossible to depict such a taboo subject at that time. Even today, the contributions made by Baldwin in his discussion of race and homosexuality are undervalued. For the next forty years, he continued to write novels, plays, and essays that were controversial and often dealt with the civil rights movement as it related to the black experience. He died of cancer on December 1, 1987, in the south of France.

Tammy Baldwin (1962–)

The first open lesbian to be directly elected to Congress, Tammy Baldwin was born in Madison, Wisconsin, in 1962. Raised by her mother and maternal grandparents, she graduated first in her class at Madison West High School. She received an A.B. degree from Smith College in Northampton, Massachusetts, in 1984 with majors in government and mathematics. She earned her J.D. from the University of Wisconsin Law School while an active member of the Dane County Board of Supervisors. She was a member of the Wisconsin State Legislature for six years. Not only is she the first woman from the state of Wisconsin elected to Congress in 1998, but also she did this while being an open lesbian. In Congress she serves on the House Budget and Judiciary Committees and was reelected in 2000.

She is dedicated to enacting laws that benefit her constituents in Wisconsin. She is a leading advocate for health care reform, preserving and protecting Social Security and Medicare, and assisting people with disabilities in their efforts to lead productive lives. As a first-term congressmember, Baldwin led the successful effort to reauthorize the Violence Against Women Act.

Elizabeth M. Birch (1959–)

Elizabeth Birch is currently the director of the Human Rights Campaign and has been responsible for tripling the size of the organization in fewer than ten years.

Birch was born in Dayton, Ohio, in September 1959 to Canadian parents. He father was in the Canadian Air Force and the family spent much of their time in Winnipeg. Birch left home in her teens to join the cast of Up With People (an organization dedicated to developing leaders with a global perspective). She then earned a bachelor's degree at the University of Hawaii and earned her law degree from Santa Clara (with honors). While in law school, she clerked with California Supreme Court justice Mosk.

After law school, she worked as a commercial litigator at the firm of McCutchen, Doyle, Brown & Enersen in San Francisco. She moved onto Apple Computer, Inc. where she was Worldwide Director of Litigation and Human Resources counsel. She has authored a number of AIDS antidiscrimination policies that became law in California. She is the founder of AIDS Legal Services in northern California.

In 1995, she began serving as executive director of the Human Rights Campaign. She has represented HRC and the community throughout the country and in the media, including such programs as *Good Morning America, 20/20, This Week, Face the Nation, Nightline, Crossfire, Larry King Live,* and *Newshour with Jim Lehrer.* HRC has developed a reputation for innovative communications strategies and products. During Birch's eight-year tenure, HRC has been successful in defeating every antigay and anti-AIDS initiatives, except for one, in the United States. This is a major achievement considering that during this time the congressional cycles were very conservative. In the 2000 election cycle, HRC was able to invest over $1 million supporting 210 races with a 90 percent success rate. HRC has expanded its foundation efforts through launching the National Coming Out Day Program, HRC WorkNet, and the Lesbian Health Project.

Birch has received numerous legal awards in California, including Pro Bono Lawyer of the Year. Birch lives in Chevy Chase, Maryland, with her partner Hilary Rosen and their two children.

Rita Mae Brown (1944–)

Rita Mae Brown is the author of *Rubyfruit Jungle,* the first lesbian novel with a happy ending. Brown was born November 28, 1944, in Hanover, Pennsylvania, and was adopted in infancy. The family moved to Fort Lauderdale, Florida, in 1955, where Brown attended high school and had sex with both boys and girls. When she was sixteen, love letters she had written to a female schoolmate were discovered by a friend. They were shown to the girl's father, and Brown was dismissed from the student council and lost friends.

She attended the University of Florida. Her scholarship was revoked in 1964 because of her involvement in the civil rights movement and her public statement that she had the right to love the person of her choice—black, white, male, or female. The dean of the university ordered her to therapy on a daily basis with the campus psychiatrist. She dropped out of school and hitchhiked to New York City. There she lived for a while with a gay black man and an orphaned cat in an abandoned car. The cat, named Baby Jesus, would remain her companion for the next seventeen years.

Brown returned to college in 1967 and founded the Student Homophile League at New York University. She graduated with a bachelor's degree in English in 1968 and joined the New York chapter of the National Organization for Women (NOW). She brought the issue of lesbian rights to the attention of NOW and authored the Radicalesbians manifesto "The Woman Identified Woman." The members of NOW responded poorly, and Brown quit the organization to form a more radical feminist group, Redstockings, in 1970. Later, in 1971, she was an organizing member of the Furies Collective in Washington, D.C.

Brown's semiautobiographical novel *Rubyfruit Jungle* was released in 1973 by a small feminist press. It sold astonishingly well; more than 70,000 copies were sold through word of mouth. Bantam Books bought the rights to *Rubyfruit Jungle* for $250,000 and printed 300,000 copies. This infusion of cash allowed Brown to devote herself full-time to writing.

She has written many novels and essays, published two books of poetry, translated six plays by the medieval nun Hrotsvitha, and written award-winning screenplays for television. In 1978, Brown moved to Charlottesville, Virginia, where she shared a house with Fannie Flagg (author of *Fried Green Tomatoes at the Whistle-Stop Café*). Brown met Czechoslovakian tennis star Martina Navratilova in 1979. The two fell in love and bought a mansion outside Charlottesville. The relationship lasted only two years. Brown then moved to Los Angeles to work on a number of screenplays for television. Her 1982 ABC series *I Love Liberty* won an Emmy nomination.

Brown moved back to Charlottesville and began her own company, American Artists, Inc., to help produce *Rubyfruit Jungle* and other novels for television. After ten years of solitude, she began a relationship with Judy Nelson, a former lover of Navratilova. Rita Mae Brown continues to be a prolific writer.

Anita Bryant (1940–)

Anita Bryant launched the Save Our Children organization to stop gay and lesbian rights in Dade County, Florida. This became the galvanizing force behind what would become the religious right.

Born into a devoutly Southern Baptist family in Barnsdall, Oklahoma, Anita Bryant accepted Jesus Christ as her savior when she was eight. In 1958 she was chosen Miss Oklahoma and later runner-up Miss America. She was a talented singer and was chosen by Bob Hope in 1961 to participate in his Christmas junket entertaining GIs in the Caribbean. For seven years, Anita traveled with Bob Hope to the Arctic, the Pacific, and the Far East, including Vietnam, to sing in his Holiday Troupe.

Her trademark song was a rousing rendition of the "Battle Hymn of the Republic," which she sang at the 1976 Super Bowl halftime, Bob Hope's Christmas specials, and presidential performances. From 1960 to 1980, Bryant was a spokesperson for the Florida Citrus Growers. She became known as the Sunshine-Tree Girl. During those eleven years she made seventy-six television commercials and orange juice sales climbed from 382 million gallons to more than 800 million gallons a year.

In 1977, the Miami-Dade County Commission passed an ordinance making it illegal to discriminate on the basis of sexual orientation. Upset by this development, Bryant organized a group called Save Our Children. She obtained sufficient signatures to place a referendum on the ballot to overturn the ordinance. It was passed overwhelmingly by the county citizens. Her crusade galvanized the gay pride movement to organize and coordinate a national protest and spurred conservative religious groups into what is today known as the religious right. A successful boycott by the gay community of orange juice resulted in the termination of her contract with the Florida Citrus Growers. At the same time, her marriage dissolved.

Twenty-one years later, in 1998, a new law outlawing discrimination based on sexual orientation was approved by the Miami-Dade County Commission. Bryant has made no comments about this new law, as she is preoccupied with the bankruptcy of the Anita Bryant Theater.

Ron Buckmire (1968–)

Ron Buckmire is an African American professor of mathematics who is the creator of the Queer Resources Directory—the largest and oldest source of gay/lesbian/bisexual/transgender and AIDS/HIV information on the Internet. Born May 21, 1968, in Grenville, Grenada, Buckmire was recognized early as having strong mathematical skills. He was three-time Barbados Junior Chess Champion (1983–1986) and three-time Barbados Senior Chess Champion (1983–1986). He was accepted to Rensselaer Polytechnic Institute in Troy, New York, where he completed his bachelor of science degree, magna cum laude, in mathematics in 1989. He continued on to receive his master's degree (1992) and then his Ph.D. in applied mathematics (1994). While at Rensselaer, Buckmire designed and launched the Queer Resources Directory (www.qrd.org).

In 1991, Buckmire met his life partner, Dean Elzinga. They both moved to Los Angeles when Buckmire accepted a teaching position at Occidental College in 1996. Besides teaching, Buckmire continues his chess playing and is currently ranked in the top 250 of the United States. He is also a board member of PlanetOut Corp., on the steering committee of the Los Angeles Freedom to Marry Coalition, cofounder of Digital Queers Los Angeles (1995), and manager of numerous Internet mailing lists, such as Queerlaw, Marriage, GLBPOC, Queer Politics, and NA-teach.

Charlotte Bunch (1944–)

Charlotte Bunch is considered one of the most important theorists on gay and lesbian politics and is an expert on feminism. Bunch was born October 13, 1944, in West Jefferson, North Carolina, but grew up in a small town in northern New Mexico. Graduating high school in 1962 with highest honors, she went to Duke University because "the men there would be more willing to accept such an independent woman" (Newton 1994, 61). At Duke, she became deeply involved in social and political actions and later organized demonstrations against racism and the Vietnam War.

Bunch married Jim Weeks in the spring of 1967. However, they grew apart as Bunch became aware of her lesbianism. She became deeply involved in the emerging lesbian feminist movement and helped found the Furies Collective.

Over the years she became very involved with one or another civil rights or antiwar organizations, including the National Organization for Women, the University Christian Movement, the National Gay and Lesbian Task Force, the National Women's Program of the American Friends Service Committee, the New York City Commission on the Status of Women, and the National Council for Research on Women.

As a professor of urban studies at Case Western Reserve University and Rutgers University, she has lectured and written extensively on feminist theory. She has developed a core course on feminist theory used by many universities. She has edited eight books on feminist thought besides having her essays published by St. Martin's Press in 1986 (*Passion and Politics*).

Paul Drummond Cameron (1939–)

Paul Cameron is the primary source of antigay "research." Cameron was born November 9, 1939, in Pittsburgh, Pennsylvania. He received his bachelor's degree from Los Angeles Pacific University in 1961, obtained a master's degree from California State University Los Angeles in 1962, and earned his Ph.D. from the University Colorado in 1966. He was affiliated with various colleges and universities until 1980, including Wayne State University (1967–1968), University of Louisville (1970–1973), Fuller Graduate School of Psychology (part of the Fuller Theological Seminary, 1976–1979), and the University of Nebraska (1979– 1980).

In 1980, his teaching contract with the Department of Psychology of the University of Nebraska was not renewed. At that time, he began publishing hysterical pamphlets alleging that gays were disproportionately responsible for serial killings, child molestation, and other heinous crimes. In these pamphlets, Cameron misrepresented the findings of academic researchers. Cameron was asked to retract his statements, but he refused. Complaints were filed, and the American Psychological Association investigated Cameron and found that he not only misrepresented the works of others but also used unsound methods in his own studies. For this ethical breach, he was expelled from the association in 1983. Cameron has also been expelled from the Nebraska Psychological Association and the American Sociological Association. In *Baker v. Wade* (the case in which a Texas court found the state's prohibition against consensual sodomy between homosexuals to be unconstitutional), Judge Buchmeyer of the U.S. district court in Dallas states, "Dr. Paul Cameron . . . has himself made misrepresentations to this court" and "there have been no fraud or misrepresentation except by Dr. Cameron" (536).

Cameron conducted a large research study in the early 1980s from which he has made outrageous claims—such as the short life expectancy of gay men. The professional censure of Cameron has not stopped his antigay agenda. In 1987, Cameron founded the Family Research Institute and has been a virtual one-man propaganda press, periodically revising his brochures and distributing them to policymakers. Yet with all these problems of poor science, the religious right latched onto and helped fund Cameron's work to substantiate its religious agenda. When challenges are made concerning Cameron's ethical breach, unsound research methodology, and misinformation, the religious right dismisses the problems, holds him up as a martyr, and continues to promote his work.

Edward Carpenter (1844–1929)

Carpenter was one of the first authors to write about homosexuality in a positive light. He took great chances with his writing at a time when people such as Oscar Wilde were being imprisoned for homosexual acts.

Born in Brighton, England, on August 29, 1844, Edward Carpenter grew up in a home dominated by his retired naval officer father. Carpenter was educated in Brighton College and then studied for the priesthood at Trinity Hall at Cambridge in 1864. He was ordained in 1869 and appointed to the parish of St. Edward's in Cambridge in 1870.

Soon, he had developed serious doubts about the church. He resigned from the priesthood in 1874. He supported himself teaching classes on astronomy in northern England. At the same time, he became active in the socialist movement and wrote a half-dozen books exploring change in society.

Carpenter became aware of his own sexual awakening and was influenced by Walt Whitman's homoerotic poetry. In April

1877, Carpenter traveled to the United States to speak with Whitman and found the poet reluctant to discuss social and political issues as they related to his work. Carpenter was disappointed by these meetings with Whitman but began to integrate a positive homosexual view into his socialist writings. Carpenter saw the Uranian (homosexual) spirit to be more enlightened than that of the common man and believed that Uranians were the new prophets of the coming social revolution.

Carpenter inherited a large sum of money on the death of his father in 1882, which allowed him to build a home isolated on seven acres in Millthorpe, Chesterfield. He lived there for the next forty years. In 1891, Carpenter met and fell in love with George Merrill, with whom he lived until the latter's death in 1928. Heartbroken, Carpenter moved to a small cottage in nearby Guilford and died a year later.

Martin Bauml Duberman (1930–)

For more than two decades, Martin Duberman has been one of the leading academic spokespersons on lesbian and gay rights. He was one of the founding members of the Gay Academic Union in the 1970s and is the founder/director of the Center for Lesbian and Gay Studies at the graduate school of the City University of New York.

Born in New York City on August 6, 1930, he earned his bachelor of arts degree from Yale in 1952 and a Ph.D. in history from Harvard in 1957. In his book *Cures: A Gay Man's Odyssey*, he reports being sexually attracted to men as far back as he could remember. He did not act on his homosexual feelings until his freshman year at Yale. For many years, he was in and out of therapy to help him understand and deal with those feelings.

His life has seen a series of increasingly prestigious academic appointments, from his early days as an instructor of history at Yale to his professorship of history at Lehman Graduate Center of the City University of New York. He has also been a prolific writer of more than a dozen books, many of which have won major awards. In 1992, he became the editor of a fifty-volume series on the lives of *Notable Gay Men and Lesbians*.

Duberman has written four major books chronicling the gay rights movement: *About Time: Exploring the Gay Past* (1986, 1991); *Hidden from History: Reclaiming the Gay and Lesbian Past* (1989); *Cures: A Gay Man's Odyssey* (1991); and *Stonewall* (1993).

Jerry L. Falwell (1933–)

Jerry Falwell founded the Moral Majority and is one of the major forces representing fundamentalist Christian principles in U.S. politics. Falwell was born on August 11, 1933, in Lynchburg, Virginia. He received a bachelor's degree from the Baptist Bible College of Springfield, Missouri, in 1956 and was married two years later to Macel Pate (with whom he has three children).

Falwell founded the Thomas Road Baptist Church in Lynchburg in 1956, where he continues to this day as pastor. He saw the need for a Christian-based school of higher education and founded Liberty University in Lynchburg in 1971. Recognizing the power of radio and television, he hosted the *Old-Time Gospel Hour* television program for many years.

In 1979, as a reaction to the political battle over homosexuality in Florida and elsewhere, he branched out into political action and founded the Moral Majority. Unlike the church or university or television programs, the Moral Majority allowed Falwell to directly participate in local and national elections. The Moral Majority has been one of the major opponents of gay rights legislation in the United States. In 1989, the Moral Majority changed its name to the Liberty Federation.

Falwell has written many books, with the most influential being *Listen, America!* (1980); *The Fundamentalist Phenomenon* (1981); *Champions for God* (1985); and his autobiography, *Strength for the Journey* (1987).

A national outcry occurred when Jerry Falwell blamed feminists, lesbians, and gays as well as others on national television for the bombing of the World Trade Center on September 11, 2001.

Michel Foucault (1926–1984)

Michel Foucault brought academic research and language concerning sexual deconstruction to queer theory and AIDS activism. Foucault was born in Poitiers, France, on October 15, 1926. He was the son of an eminent surgeon and excelled in school. In 1946 he attended Ecole Normale Supérièure and was the fourth-highest-ranked student. There he received his *license* in philosophy in 1948 and in psychology in 1950; he was awarded diplomas in psychopathology in 1952. He taught in France, Sweden, Poland, and Germany and returned to France in 1960 as head of the Philosophy Department at the University Claremont-Ferrard.

There he published his landmark work *Madness and Civilization* (1965). For this book he won the *doctorate d'état*. He argued that "madness" is an invention of the age of reason.

In that same year, Foucault met Daniel Defret, a philosophy student ten years his junior. They formed a relationship that lasted more than eighteen years. It would be Defret's political activism that influenced Foucault's future theoretical work.

In 1966, Foucault's second major work, *The Order of Things*, became a best-seller in France and made Foucault a household name. The combination of economics, the natural sciences, and linguistics in the eighteenth and nineteenth century was, in his opinion, coming to an end. He predicted that "man" (the construct) would be "erased, like a face drawn in sand at the edge of the sea" (Russell 1995, 132).

Foucault's influential work that has impacted gay and lesbian thought was his monumental unfinished project *The History of Sexuality. Volume 1: An Introduction*, which caused much controversy when it was released in 1976. The second and third volumes—*The Uses of Pleasure* and *The Care of the Self*—came out just before his death in 1984.

It was Foucault's experiences in San Francisco during 1975 when he was teaching at the University California, Berkeley that influenced the development of *The History of Sexuality*. He was impressed by liberated gay sexuality, particularly in the bathhouses. He wrote: "I think that is politically important that sexuality be able to function as it functions in the bath houses. You meet men there who are to you as you are to them: nothing but a body with which combinations in production of pleasure are possible. You cease to be imprisoned in your own face, in your own past, in your own identity" (Russell 1995, 133).

The History of Sexuality articulated what is known as the theory of social constructionism. It states that sexuality is far from being "natural" and unmediated. Rather, it is a cultural construction that varies considerably from culture to culture and over time. Our modern notions of gay and lesbian, of homosexual and heterosexual, are comparatively recent inventions. Michel Foucault died on June 25, 1984, in Paris from complications resulting from AIDS.

Barney Frank (1940–)

Barney Frank is an openly gay Democratic congressmember from the state of Massachusetts who wields significant power in the

House of Representatives. Born in Bayonne, New Jersey, on March 31, 1940, Frank earned his bachelor's degree from Harvard College in 1962 and then entered a doctoral program in political science. He left graduate school in 1967 to become involved in Kevin White's campaign for mayor of Boston. White was elected and appointed Frank as his executive assistant. That allowed Frank an inside look at the workings of politics in Boston and in Massachusetts.

Frank won election to the Massachusetts House of Representatives in 1972 and earned a reputation as being very outspoken, extremely liberal, and sometimes one of the most abrasive personalities in the state. He easily won reelection in 1974, 1976, and since. Frank has weathered a number of very close elections, each time improving his winning margin.

In 1989, the conservative *Washington Times* discovered and reported on a male prostitute, Steve Gobie, who was living in Frank's home at the time. The *Times'* investigation discovered that Gobie had used Frank's apartment to operate a bisexual prostitution business. Frank claimed not to know anything about the illegal behavior, but he nevertheless came under investigation by the House Ethics Committee. The House officially reprimanded Frank by a vote of 408 to 18.

After the incident, Frank spoke out more often on gay and lesbian issues. Frank has said very little about his own personal life other than "he lives with Herb Moses." Disclosure of his homosexuality has had little effect on his career.

Although Frank is openly gay and promotes gay rights legislation, he has sometimes been chastised by lesbian and gay civil rights leaders. For instance, the debate over President Bill Clinton's promise to revoke the ban on gays and lesbians in the armed forces resulted in Frank supporting Clinton's compromise. Frank explained this as being an expedient decision.

Barbara Gittings (1932–)

Gittings began the New York chapter of the Daughters of Bilitis, and was editor of the lesbian magazine *The Ladder* during its formative years. Born in Vienna, Austria, in 1932, Gittings grew up in a diplomat's household. At the beginning of World War II, the family returned to the United States, where Gittings completed high school and entered Northwestern University to study drama. At Northwestern she had her first homosexual experiences. She was accused of being a lesbian by other students because of her close friendships with other women. She went into counseling with a psychiatrist, who confirmed that she was a lesbian. Gittings spent the remainder of her first year trying to find out exactly what that meant. She spent much of her time at the library reading fiction works, such as Radclyffe Hall's *The Well of Loneliness*.

Discovering her lesbianism was very important to Gittings, and she dropped out of Northwestern. She visited San Francisco in 1956 and met Del Martin and Phyllis Lyon, founders of the Daughters of Bilitis. This was an uplifting experience, and she returned to New York to begin her own DOB chapter in 1958. In 1962 she became editor of *The Ladder* and held that position until 1966.

For much of the 1960s, Gittings was active in many of the early homophile organizations, including New York City's Gay Activists Alliance. However, by the 1970s, her interest had shifted, and she decided to work more within the system. She joined the gay caucus of the American Library Association (ALA), which allowed her to address her early frustrations at not finding gay- and lesbian-related books in public libraries. She has been instrumental in developing lists of these books and has written material designed to help librarians locate lesbian and gay materials.

Radclyffe Hall (1880–1943)

Radclyffe's Hall's book *The Well of Loneliness* (1928) was banned in Britain and caused far-ranging discussions of the topic of lesbianism in the United States. Hall was born Margaret Radclyffe-Hall Bournemouth in Hampshire, England, on August 12, 1880. She came from a wealthy family and was educated at King's College, London. She wore very short hair and men's clothing and was known to her friends as John. By age twenty-seven, she is reported to have "probably loved more women than she had read books" (Russell 1995, 114). At that time, she met Mabel Batten (a woman twenty years her senior), fell in love, and moved in with her.

At a London tea party in 1915, they met Una, Lady Troubridge, an admiral's wife. Batten unexpectedly died a few months later from a heart attack. This facilitated the development of a close relationship between Hall and Troubridge that lasted for the next thirty years.

Hall wrote and published a considerable volume of poetry and a set of short stories with lesbian themes in 1924. Soon after she won a number of coveted prizes for her writing. In 1928 she published *The Well of Loneliness*. For its time, it was a sexually explosive story of a masculine girl who loves and loses women. Although the book seems very tame by today's standards, it was declared obscene by London magistrate Chartres Biron.

The book was initially withheld in the United States but eventually was published and distributed. For many women, *The Well of Loneliness* was a beacon of light in an otherwise dark time for lesbians. For years it was known as "the lesbian Bible." Today, the book is difficult to read, couched as it is in old terminology and early-twentieth-century vernacular.

Henry (Harry) Hay (1912–2002)

Harry Hay is considered by many to be the founder of the modern gay rights movement. Hay was born April 7, 1912, in Worthing Sussex, England. His family was American and returned to Los Angeles in 1917. He graduated from Los Angeles High School with honors in 1929 and worked as an apprentice for a local attorney's office. At the age of seventeen, he enticed older gentlemen for sex at the notorious Pershing Square in downtown Los Angeles.

From one of these older men, Hay learned of the Society for Human Rights formed in Chicago many years earlier. The society was the earliest gay rights group in the United States. Hay found the idea of men getting together for anything other than sex "an eye opener of an idea" (Newton 1994, 69).

He enrolled in the Drama Department at Stanford University in 1930. Hay was tired of hiding his sexual orientation and told his friends. Many avoided contact with him, but his closest friends were not perturbed by the information. Hay quickly realized that acting was unlikely to provide a living for him, so he became active in guerrilla theater productions focused on workers' rights and demonstrations. From there he joined the Communist Party, working as union organizer and a developer of cultural projects for the next fifteen years. The party was decidedly anti-homosexual, however, and under its pressure, Hay married another party member, Anita Platky. Their marriage lasted for fifteen years, producing two daughters.

In 1948 during a "beer bust" at the University of Southern California, Hay and a group of gay friends developed the idea of an organization named Bachelors for Wallace in support of presidential candidate Henry Wallace of the Progressive Party. Hay realized that gay men needed to organize themselves to combat the rising tide of Senator Joseph McCarthy's anticommunist and antihomosexual campaign. Two years later, Bob Hull, Chuck Rowland, and Dale Jennings, along with Hay, founded the International Bachelors Fraternal Order for Peace and Social Dignity. Later the organization was renamed the Mattachine Society. The Mattachine Society grew and became the longest-lived homophile organization in the United States. It has been at the forefront of activism on behalf of freedom of the press and archiving gay history.

Hay was instrumental in organizing the first gay pride parade in Los Angeles (and perhaps the nation) and other political actions that put Los Angeles at the forefront of gay liberation in the 1960s. He and his lover John Burnside, with whom he formed The Circle of Loving Companions, opened a kaleidoscope factory. The Stonewall Riots in New York in 1969 did not impress Hay. As far as he was concerned, the East Coast was finally catching up with Los Angeles. But Hay got caught up in the excitement of the times and was elected chair of the Southern California Gay Liberation Front in 1969 and hosted "Gay-In" and "funky dances" despite police warnings against such activities since same-sex couple dancing was illegal under California law at the time.

In 1970, Hay and Burnside moved their mail-order kaleidoscope factory to New Mexico. The area had always enchanted Hay ever since traveling there in the 1950s on his research into berdache. He became increasingly interested in spiritual issues and formed the Radical Faeries—a movement devoted to spiritual truth, ecology, and gay life. The first gathering of the Radical Faeries was in the Arizona desert in 1978 with more than 200 men in attendance. The Radical Faeries movement grew, but, like the Mattachine experience, Hay's politics came in conflict with many of the Faeries and he was ousted from its leadership.

In their later years, Hay and Burnside were provided housing and care as a tribute for his pioneering work by the gay community. Hay died in San Francisco, October 24, 2002.

Jesse Helms (1921–)

For more than thirty years, Jesse Helms had been the most outspoken opponent of gay and lesbian rights in the U.S. Senate.

Born on October 18, 1921, in Monroe, North Carolina, Helms received his bachelor's degree from Wake Forest University. He served in the U.S. Navy during World War II and after the war took a job with the *Raleigh North Carolina Times*. He later became city editor. From 1948 to 1970 he was the administrative assistant to a number of U.S. senators, executive director of the North Carolina Bankers Association, and an executive vice president and vice chairman of the Capitol Broadcasting Company.

He became disenchanted with the Democratic Party and switched to the Republican Party in 1970. He was elected U.S. senator in 1972 and has since become one of the most powerful conservative voices in the U.S. Senate.

Helms consistently blocked gay and lesbian rights legislation in the Senate. For example, in 1990 he was one of only four senators to vote against the Hate Crime Statistics Act. He believed the U.S. Congress was being "hoodwinked" into adopting legislation that would promote homosexuality. Helms was also a major opponent of AIDS research and education. In 1990, he attempted to persuade the U.S. Senate to amend the Americans with Disabilities Act (ADA) to permit restaurant owners to discharge HIV-infected individuals, but he was unsuccessful. Helms retired from politics in 2002, announcing that he had had a change of heart with regard to AIDS funding but not homosexuals.

Magnus Hirschfeld (1868–1935)

Hirschfeld founded the Scientific Humanitarian Committee in Germany, which was the leading homosexual rights organization in the world until its destruction by the Nazi government in 1933. Hirschfeld was born in Kolberg, Germany, on May 14, 1868. He earned a medical degree in 1887 and traveled to numerous foreign countries in the early 1890s, including visiting the 1893 Chicago World's Fair, Asia, Africa, and Europe. Finally, in 1895 he settled down and opened a medical practice in Charlottenburg, which he transferred to Berlin in 1909. He specialized in the human nervous system and sexuality.

Hirschfeld was a homosexual and a Jew and wrote more than 200 books in his lifetime. He viewed sexual orientation as a deep and internal state over which one did not have a choice. He became an advocate of homosexual rights, claiming that homosexuality was neither a sin nor an illness. He believed the goal of the medical profession should be to help homosexuals adjust to society's treatment of them and not try to change their sexual orientation.

Hirschfeld, along with two friends, Max Sphor and Erich Oberg, founded the Scientific Humanitarian Committee on May 15, 1897. Hirschfeld devoted nearly every waking moment of his life to organizing, writing, and speaking for homosexual rights. Hirschfeld helped found the Medical Society for Sexual Science and Eugenics. Five years later he establish his own foundation—the Magnus Hirschfeld Foundation for Sex Research—and later the Institute for Sexual Research.

The constitution of Germany at this time contained Paragraph 175, which outlawed homosexual acts. Hirschfeld worked diligently to have the paragraph revoked. Eventually, the Reichstag removed homosexuality from the national penal code in 1929, but the up-and-coming Nazi Party reinstated persecution of homosexuals. Hirschfeld was constantly harassed by the Nazi Party and was often badly beaten. He fled to Switzerland in 1932 and then later to France. His last few years of life were spent in France, where he died in Nice on May 15, 1935. His partner of many years, Kurt Giese, committed suicide in Prague in 1936.

About 100 students attacked Hirschfeld's Institute for Sexual Research on May 6, 1933. They removed its contents of more than 20,000 books and 35,000 photographs, made a bonfire of the items, and burned the building. The infamous pictures of Nazi book burning shown in history books are pictures of the destruction of Hirschfeld's library, and the books being burned are mostly on the topic of homosexuality.

Evelyn Hooker (1907–1996)

Evelyn Hooker's research in psychology in the early 1950s opened the door to scientific demonstration that homosexuals are not mentally ill. Born on September 2, 1907, Hooker was the sixth of nine children. She lived next door to Buffalo Bill's home in North Platte, Nebraska. Her parents were extremely poor. They had lived in a sod house in Sand Hills just months before her birth. Her family lived on a succession of small farms, and she attended one-room schoolhouses.

She entered the University of Colorado on a tuition scholarship in 1924. She chose the Psychology Department because, in part, it allowed her to work in the department and pay her own way through college. In her senior year, Hooker accepted an instructor position that enabled her to work on a master's degree. In 1930 Hooker was determined to go to an eastern university for her doctoral degree. She wanted to attend Yale University, but the chair of the department refused to recommend a woman. She went to Johns Hopkins University instead. She completed her Ph.D. in 1932 at the height of the Depression. There was no academic position for her other than a teaching position at a small women's college near Baltimore.

In the fall of 1934, she came down with tuberculosis and went west to a sanitarium in California. She recovered, and after two years of convalescence she obtain a part-time teaching position at Whittier College. There she received an anonymous fellowship that allowed her to travel to Germany and Russia in 1937 and 1938. Experiencing these totalitarian states intensified her feelings that she wanted to do something important with her life to help correct social injustices.

Soon, she was offered a research associate position in the Psychology Department of the University California, Los Angeles (UCLA), where she remained until 1970. She enjoyed teaching, and it was at the suggestion of some of her students that she decided to conduct research with homosexuals. She conducted exploratory research, but her divorce in 1947 and subsequent remarriage in 1951 postponed the project.

In 1953, Hooker applied to the National Institute of Mental Health for a six-month grant to study the adjustments of nonclinical homosexual men and to compare them to a similar group of heterosexual men. This had never been done. All previous research had included only homosexuals who either were in prison or were mental patients. John Eberhart, chief of the grants division of the institute, explained that her application was quite extraordinary considering this was the height of the McCarthy witch-hunt era. Even so, she received the grant, which was continually renewed until 1961. In her 1957 research, Hooker found that expert clinical judges could not distinguish the projective test protocols of nonclinical homosexual men from those of a comparable group of heterosexual men, nor were there differences in adjustment ratings. Her findings were soon validated by other academic investigators. Research by Hooker and others directly led to the American Psychiatric Association deleting homosexuality from the *DSM* in 1973. Hooker gained great satisfaction from contributing to the freedom of and lifting of the stigma from this marginalized group.

Hooker entered private practice in the 1970s and was appointed chair of the National Institute of Mental Health Task Force on Homosexuals. She won many awards and acclaims. She died at her home in Santa Monica, California, on November 19, 1996, at the age of eighty-nine.

Larry Kramer (1935–)

Larry Kramer was a founder of ACT UP and was one of the earliest AIDS activists. Kramer was born in Bridgeport, Connecticut, on June 25, 1935. He grew up in a middle-class household, received his bachelor of arts degree from Yale, and served a brief stint in the army. He found work as an agent with the William Morris Agency in New York City. Within a year, he began working for Columbia Pictures as an assistant story editor and then production executive. United Artists hired him to be the assistant to the president in 1965.

By 1969, he was a respected screenwriter and wrote the screenplay for and produced Ken Russell's film *Women in Love*. For his effort, Kramer was nominated for an Academy Award. The movie was famous for its homoerotic elements, something unseen at the time.

In 1978 Kramer published his first novel, called *Faggots*. It was a satire of a gay man's search for love in bathhouses and bars. Many in the gay community denounced the work but Kramer argued that it was meant to be a serious critique of the excesses of certain people within the gay community.

Kramer was one of the first to write essays on what we now know as AIDS. In his famous "1,112 and Counting" article, he wrote: "If this article doesn't scare the shit out of you, we're in real trouble. If this article doesn't rouse you to anger, fury, rage, and action, gay men may have no future on this earth. Our continued existence depends on just how angry you can get" (Russell 1995, 187).

Seeing the potential devastation from AIDS, Kramer, along with five other men, founded the Gay Men's Health Crisis (GMHC) in 1982. Kramer's combative personality forced him to resign one year later. He used that experience to frame his 1985 drama, *The Normal Heart*. Although many agents and directors initially turned the drama down, eventually it was produced and won the 1986 Dramatists Guide Marton Award, the City Lights Award, and the Sarah Siddons Award for best play of the year. It was later made into a movie. The purpose of the play was to make people see gay men as men who love men and are supportive during the dying process.

In 1987 Kramer was the primary force behind the creation of the AIDS Coalition to Unleash Power (ACT UP). Its purpose was to encourage public disobedience to draw attention to the AIDS crisis. Its first demonstration was on March 24, 1987, on Wall Street in New York City. Almost 300 men and women tied up traffic for several hours chanting for AIDS reform. Many were arrested, and the story garnered widespread media attention. ACT UP spread across the country, with chapters found in every major city.

Kramer learned he was HIV-positive in 1988. He responded by writing the critically acclaimed 1992 play, *The Destiny of Me*. His in-your-face activism has made him one the most influential gay men in America today.

Audre Lorde (1934–1992)

Audre Lorde was an African American poet whose book of essays *Sister Outsider* has become a feminist classic and is used as a staple in women's studies courses. Lorde was born in Harlem, New York, on February 18, 1934. Her parents were from Granada and believed they were going to return to their Caribbean home. As such, Lorde had a profound nostalgia for her lost "home."

She picked up languages easily and memorized poems voraciously. She attended Hunter College High School and in 1954 attended the National University of Mexico for a year. "For the first time in my life," she wrote, "I walked down the streets of the city where most of the people were brown-skinned, everywhere I went. It was like coming into sunlight" (Russell 1995, 201).

She returned to the United States and entered the "gay-girl" scene in Greenwich Village. However, she was distressed to find only three or four black women in the lesbian community. At Hunter College she worked as a librarian and continued to write poetry. She attempted to become part of the Harlem Writers Guild, but was driven away by the groups' homophobia. In 1959 she received a bachelor of arts degree in literature and philosophy and went on to Columbia University School of Library Services where she earned a master's of library science in 1960.

She published her first book of poems, *The First Cities*, in 1968. Because of its success, she spent six weeks as a writer-in-residence at Tougaloo College in Mississippi. It was there that she met Frances Clayton, the woman who would become her life partner.

Lorde returned to New York City and taught courses for the SEEK program at City College. There she met writers Alice Walker and Adrienne Rich, an enriching experience for Lorde. Through their encouragement, Lorde publicly read a lesbian love poem for the first time in 1971. Although it was later published in *Ms.* magazine, her book editor rejected it for inclusion in her third volume of poetry, *From a Land Where Other People Live.* That book was nominated for a National Book Award in 1974.

Lorde contracted breast cancer in the late 1970s, which later recurred She wrote about her mastectomy and decision to forgo additional surgery in her autobiographical *Cancer Journals* (1980). In 1984 she wrote *Sister Outsider,* a collection of essays on feminism and race that has become a staple of women's studies courses. She died on November 17, 1992.

Phyllis Lyon (1924–)

Phyllis Lyon cofounded the Daughters of Bilitis and the nation's first lesbian periodical, *The Ladder.* Lyon was born on November 10, 1924, in Tulsa, Oklahoma. Her family moved many times during her childhood and she lived in Seattle, Southern California, and the San Francisco Bay area. She eventually graduated from Sacramento High School in 1943 and received a bachelor of arts degree in journalism in 1946 from the University of California, Berkeley.

Lyon, like many women of her day, believed that she would eventually have to marry and center her life on a man. However, while working as a writer for a trade magazine in Seattle, she met Del Martin and fell in love. They have been together ever since.

Phyllis Lyon and Del Martin together founded the Daughters of Bilitis in 1955. A year later, they founded the nation's first lesbian periodical, *The Ladder.* In 1972, Lyons and Martin wrote *Lesbian/Woman,* a book that *Publishers Weekly* considers one of the twenty most important books of our time.

Lyon focused on the study of human sexuality and in 1970 cofounded the Institute for the Advanced Study of Human Sexuality in San Francisco. It is there that she earned her doctorate in education in 1976. She has also served for many years on the San Francisco Human Rights Commission.

Lon T. Mabon (1947–)

Lon Mabon founded Oregon Citizens Alliance (OCA), which was instrumental in the passage of Measure 8 (which revoked the governor's executive order giving equal legal protection based on sexual orientation). Mabon was born May 12, 1947, in Minnesota. As an adult, he lived in southern Oregon with his wife, Bonnie, and their three children. He and his wife owned an adult retirement home. Lon Mabon is a Bible teacher involved in his local church.

In 1986, Mabon was the southern Oregon regional director for fundamentalist Baptist preacher Joe Lutz in his challenge for Robert Packwood's Senate seat. From that experience and his religious teachings, Mabon launched OCA and the No Special Rights Committee. Their goal was to overturn Governor Neil Goldschmidt's executive order giving equal legal protection based on sexual orientation. OCA collected the necessary signatures to place Measure 8 on the ballot, and the measure won by an overwhelming majority. Thus, the executive order was revoked. OCA has been instrumental in developing other initiatives and political movements in Oregon with the goal of preventing antidiscrimination laws based on sexual orientation, stopping abortions, and prohibiting public schools from "promoting the homosexual lifestyle." Most of these other efforts have been unsuccessful.

During a 1991 antigay event, gay rights activist Catherine Stauffer was roughed up by OCA spokesman Scott Lively. She sued and won a $30,000 judgment against OCA. The Mabons refused to pay, and the case went back to court a number of times. The Mabons claimed that OCA did not have the $30,000 to make restitution, even though it is estimated that more than $1 million went through the organization in a few years. The court required the Mabons to produce OCA's financial records. Lon Mabon refused to comply with the court order and was jailed for contempt of court. Bonnie Mabon avoided going to jail when she agreed to bring the records in. Stauffer continued suing Lon Mabon, claiming he fraudulently transferred money out of OCA to avoid paying the 1992 judgment to her.

Del Martin (1921–)

Del Martin cofounded the Daughters of Bilitis and the nation's first lesbian periodical, *The Ladder*. Born in San Francisco on May

5, 1921, Martin graduated from George Washington High School in 1937. As a young woman living in the United States before World War II, Martin was uncomfortable with the expected life path of marriage and family. In a 1971 interview, Martin related that when she double-dated, she had little interest in her male date and was more interested in the other girls. Still, she married and gave birth to a daughter.

Her feelings for other women were strong, and eventually she divorced her husband. She read Radclyffe Hall's *The Well of Loneliness* and other books that helped her recognize her sexual orientation. She came out to friends when she was twenty-six, and several years later met Phyllis Lyon, who became her life partner.

Martin, Lyon, and six other women were dissatisfied with the limited social outlets available to lesbians. They wanted an alternative to the bars and formed an organization named the Daughters of Bilitis. Although it began as a social club, DOB quickly expanded into educational programs for lesbians and the general community and engaged in political activism. Within a year, Martin and Lyon founded *The Ladder*, the nation's first lesbian periodical.

Martin and Lyon have been together for more than four decades and have been deeply involved in political activism. Martin was a founding member of the Council of Religion and the Homosexual in 1964 and San Francisco's Alice B. Toklas Memorial Democratic Club in 1972. The National Organization for Women accepted Martin on the board of directors in 1973 as NOW's first open lesbian representative. In 1972 Martin, along with Lyon, wrote one of the most important books on gay love in the lesbian movement—*Lesbian/Woman*. Martin also wrote *Battered Wives*, a book that has had significant impact on the national movement against domestic violence.

Leonard Matlovich (1943–1988)

Leonard Matlovich was involved in one of the earliest legal test cases against the U.S. military's discharge of gay personnel. Matlovich was born July 6, 1943, in Savannah, Georgia. Since his father was a sergeant in the U.S. Air Force, Matlovich grew up at various bases in the United States and England. After graduating from high school, he enlisted in the Air Force and was trained in its electrical school. Upon completing his training, he eagerly accepted an assignment to Vietnam. Matlovich revealed in an interview many years later that he had been aware of his homosexual feelings since age twelve and it was important for him to "prove that he was a man" (Newton 1994, 76). Thus, he often volunteered for the most dangerous missions in Vietnam. By the time he returned to the United States, he had been awarded the Bronze Star and Purple Heart, along with other medals.

After the war, Matlovich was assigned to teach classes on racism at U.S. military bases. Matlovich found this to be a somewhat ironic assignment because of his self-acknowledged racist views. As he taught, he found that he began to include discussions about homosexuality. However, at age thirty, Matlovich was still a virgin. He decided that he needed to find other gay people and discover what it meant to be gay; so he went to a gay bar. Matlovich expected the worst. He later told interviewers that "seeing the real thing was totally different. In an instant, a billion pounds of pressure fell from my shoulders" (Newton 1994, 76).

Matlovich decided he could not continue living a double life. In discussions with the ACLU and other legal representatives, Matlovich volunteered to become a test case to challenge the U.S. military's discrimination against lesbians and gays. He announced his homosexuality to a commanding officer and was immediately expelled. Although he had twelve years of perfect performance reviews in the military, homosexuality caused his discharge. For many years, his case was bounced back and forth between courts. Eventually, the U.S. military offered Matlovich $160,000 not to return to duty, an offer he accepted. Matlovich explained he was no longer the person he used to be and did not want to return to the Air Force.

Matlovich moved to San Francisco in 1978 and was unsuccessful at gaining a seat on the city's Board of Supervisors. In 1986 he was diagnosed with AIDS and spent the remaining two years of life working as an HIV activist. He died in San Francisco on June 23, 1988, and two years later President George H. W. Bush issued a special citation to Matlovich's parents, stating: "The United States of America honors the memory of Leonard P. Matlovich. This certificate is awarded by a grateful nation in recognition of devoted and selfless consecration to the service of our country in the armed forces of the United States" (Newton 1994, 77). Matlovich is buried at the Congressional Cemetery in Washington, D.C., where his tombstone states, "When I was in the military, they gave me a medal for killing two men, and a discharge for loving one."

Harvey Milk (1930–1978)

Harvey Milk was one of the first openly gay officials elected to office in a major U.S. city; he was murdered by Dan White on November 27, 1978. Born in New York City on May 22, 1930, Milk grew up in a middle-class family where he constantly battled to keep his rigorous school activities and his homosexual interests separate from each other. He received a bachelor's degree in mathematics in 1950 from New York State College for Teachers and enlisted in the U.S. Navy. He rose to the rank of petty officer and was discharged in August 1955. He worked as an actuarial statistician and researcher for a Wall Street investment firm. In 1963, he was transferred to Dallas for a short time, after which he resigned his job to follow his partner to San Francisco.

San Francisco changed Milk. He abandoned his Republican conservatism and became a brash Democratic liberal. He opened a camera shop on Castro Street that became a center for social and political life for the growing gay community. Milk soon earned the nickname "the mayor of Castro Street."

Milk ran for the city's Board of Supervisors in 1973 but was not elected. He ran again in 1975 and in a stunning upset won with more than 30 percent of the votes. In November 1978, conservative supervisor Dan White resigned his position on the board citing personal pressures. White changed his mind and asked for his position back. The mayor refused. A week later Dan White entered City Hall and shot Harvey Milk and Mayor George Moscone to death. White had had a long-standing feud with Milk and believed that he was partially responsible for Moscone's decision.

The murder of the two men resulted in one of the most impressive memorial services ever seen in San Francisco, with more than 40,000 men, women, and children marching by candlelight to City Hall. Days before his assassination, Milk recorded his political will. One statement stood out from all the rest. He said: "if a bullet should enter my brain, let that bullet destroy every closet door" (Russell 1995, 951). Later that year, when White was given a short seven-year sentence for the two murders, the largest riot in San Francisco's history occurred, with police cars overturned, fires set, and hundreds of thousand of people marching to City Hall in what is known as White Night.

Yukio Mishima (1925–1970)

Yukio Mishima was a charismatic Japanese writer who was nominated for the Nobel Prize three times. Born on January 14, 1925, in Tokyo, Hiraoka Kimitake was the son of a high-level civil servant. He was slight and sickly by nature and allowed to be raised as a girl by his grandmother. He wrote and published his first short story when he was sixteen under the pseudonym Yukio Mishima.

He worked in a factory during World War II and after the defeat studied law at the University of Tokyo. His second novel, *Confessions of a Mask*, was published in 1949 and brought immediate fame. Although the story revolves around a young boy recognizing his homosexuality and the need to conceal it behind a mask, Japanese audiences seemed to miss the homosexual theme and saw the story as a coming-of-age tale. After the success of the novel, Mishima wrote numerous books and plays, including the famous *Madame de Sade*.

He became obsessed with the military samurai past of Japan and saw it as a solution to the materialism and isolation of the modern world. Through exercise, karate, and kendo (a traditional Japanese form of swordsmanship), he transformed himself physically into the samurai he wanted to be. Although dutiful as a husband and father, his main sexual attraction was to male "rough trade." He celebrated and engaged in the tradition of homosexual love between samurai warriors.

His writings and beliefs attracted many followers. He built his own private army, the Shield Society, to defend the emperor in the event of a leftist uprising. On November 25, 1970, Mishima and his followers took an army general hostage in Tokyo's Ichigaya military headquarters and encouraged an assembly of 1,500 soldiers to reject Japan's democratic constitution and restore worship of the emperor. The soldiers were unimpressed with the demand. Two hours later, Mishima had himself beheaded and his devoted young collaborators committed hara-kiri.

Martina Navratilova (1956–)

Martina Navratilova was the number-one ranked tennis player in the world for a number of years and has been one of the few sports personalities who has been open about her homosexuality. Born in Prague, Czechoslovakia, on October 18, 1956, Navratilova was brought up in a sports enthusiast's family. She took up tennis and won tournaments around Czechoslovakia. She visited West Germany in 1969 as part of a tennis club exchange program. It was a revealing experience for her. By age fifteen, she was touring Czechoslovakia and the Eastern bloc countries; she was better known abroad than at home.

In the early 1970s, she was granted permission to play in the United States in a number of tours, where she was managed by Beverly Hills businessman Fred Barman. In 1975, while participating in the U.S. Open in New York, she contacted the New York office of the Immigration and Naturalization Service through Fred Barman and was granted asylum.

It was during these tours of the United States that she discovered that she was attracted to women. She had a number of relationships over the years, including a three-year affair with her new manager, Sandra Haynie.

In 1978, Navratilova beat Chris Everett at Wimbledon to become the number-one ranked tennis player in the world. That same year she met novelist Rita Mae Brown and began a short-lived, intense affair. Brown's divergent opinions concerning sports split the relationship apart. Navratilova learned that celebrity status has a price in a free-press society, as her name often showed up in the tabloids.

Navratilova worried that her homosexuality would affect her career and pending application for U.S. citizenship. However, citizenship was granted without incident in 1981, and tennis sponsors did not withdraw their funding.

Martina Navratilova had a spectacular tennis career, including nine singles wins at Wimbledon, and four U.S. Opens. Her very public affairs with other well-known lesbians made her the most highly visible lesbian sports celebrity in the world.

Holly Near (1949–)

Holly Near was one of the first and probably the most influential lesbian singer to emerge from the women's music movement. Born on June 6, 1949, in Ukiah, California, Near grew up in a musical family. She made her public singing debut when she was seven years old. By her teens, she had appeared in a number of films and television programs. After high school, she traveled to New York, where she landed the lead in the Broadway production of the musical *Hair*.

She was very politically active and campaigned against the Vietnam War. She toured with the controversial Jane Fonda's "Free the Army" show. Throughout the 1970s, Near traveled constantly on the vocal music circuit. Although she was approached by major record companies, she did not take up their offers. She did not want to give up control over material that included lesbian-themed songs. Instead, she established her own record company, Redwood Records.

Redwood released its first album, *Hang in There*, in 1973. By 1979, Redwood had sold more than 155,000 copies of this album, which is considered highly successful for a small independent label. One of her songs, "Singing for Our Lives," with the refrain "We are gay and lesbian people/And we are singing, singing for our lives," was considered by many to be the anthem for the gay civil rights movement.

Another feminist music company to rise in the 1970s was Olivia Records. It was dedicated to women making music for women and operated nonhierarchically as a collective. Its first record was *Meg Christian: I Know You Know*, which included the well-known song "Ode to a Gym Teacher." Its second album was by Cris Williamson, *The Changer and the Changed*. Holly Near also sang for Olivia Records, and the three singers created what is known as the Olivia sound.

Olivia Records flourished throughout the 1970s and early 1980s, but by the mid-1980s was floundering because of financial undercapitalization. Olivia abandoned some of its initial lesbian feminist principles and became more mainstream in its business operations. With the changes at Olivia, Holly Near went on with her solo career and continued playing at college concerts and on the coffeehouse circuit. She is well loved and admired by her lesbian followers.

Will Perkins (1928–)

Perkins founded Colorado for Family Values (CFV) and was responsible for placing Amendment 2 (outlawing antidiscrimination statutes based on sexual orientation) on the Colorado ballot in 1992. Born in Montrose, Colorado, on August 22, 1928, Perkins received his bachelor's degree in business from Colorado College in 1950. While in college, he was a respected athlete and was head baseball coach at Colorado College during the 1951–1952 season. Later he played professional baseball for the Chicago White Sox for one year. He married his wife, Bess, with whom he has three daughters and one son.

He worked for many years as a car salesman and eventually became chairman of the board of the Perkins Chrysler Plymouth Company in Colorado Springs. Frustrated with what he perceived as the antifamily gay agenda that was gaining support in many cities throughout the state of Colorado, he founded CFV in 1991. He was able to convince a number of city councils to refuse to adopt or to rescind antigay discrimination ordinances. Perkins was successful at obtaining wide support for his efforts and getting Amendment 2 placed on the 1992 statewide ballot. The initiative passed in November 1992 and was immediately challenged in courts. It was eventually ruled unconstitutional in *Romer v. Evans* (1996). Perkins continues as chair of the board of CFV and provides expert advice to other conservative organizations battling gay right ordinances.

Troy Perry (1940–)

Troy Perry founded Metropolitan Community Church (MCC), the world's largest gay and lesbian religious organization. Born in Tallahassee, Florida, on July 27, 1940, Perry did not come from a particularly religious family. However, at an early age Perry decided he wanted to become a minister and was influenced by local Baptist and Pentecostal churches. He adopted their strict moral code and did not attend movies or dances or play cards or games involving dice. Before he would go out on a date, he made his date kneel with him and pray to have the strength to avoid temptation.

Perry had his first homosexual experiences by the age of nine but did not believe that he was homosexual. When he married a pastor's daughter in 1958 at the age of eighteen, he was convinced that his homosexual fantasies were of minor importance. Five years later, after having two sons, he divorced his wife.

Perry attended Midwest Bible College and Moody Bible Institute in Chicago and became an ordained minister in the Church of God in 1962. He became pastor of a church in Santa Ana, California, but found it increasingly difficult to reconcile his religious beliefs with his homosexual feelings. He therefore left the church in 1964 and worked at Sears Roebuck.

Perry joined the army for a brief time and felt worthless after a failed relationship with another man. He attempted suicide.

These experiences made him confront the pain of being a stigmatized outsider. The only solution he saw was to start his own church, providing supportive religious messages for the gay and lesbian community. A small group of twelve people attended the first service of MCC in Perry's living room on October 16, 1968. Of the twelve people, nine were friends who "came to console me and to laugh at me" while the other three came as a result of an ad placed in *The Advocate* (Newton 1994, 81).

The church grew so spectacularly that by March 7, 1971, MCC had purchased its own building in Los Angeles, with 1,012 people attending the dedication service. Today MCC has more than 400 churches throughout the world, with a membership of more than 50,000 people, of which 84 percent are lesbian and gay.

Perry has written an autobiography, *The Lord Is My Shepherd and He Knows I'm Gay*, and coauthored two additional books—*Don't be Afraid Anymore* and *Profiles in Gay and Lesbian Courage*.

Adrienne Rich (1929–)

Adrienne Rich is a major poet and essayist who has been a tremendously influential writer on women's issues and lesbian identity. Rich was born on May 16, 1929, in Baltimore, Maryland. Her father was a professor of medicine and her mother a composer and pianist. In 1951 she graduated from Radcliffe College and her first collection of poems, *A Change of World*, was chosen for the Yale Younger Poets Award. In 1953 she married Harvard economist Alfred Conrad and lived as a model faculty wife in Cambridge, Massachusetts.

She wrote a number of other books between 1959 and 1966 while trying to balance her traditional female role with her life as a poet. In 1966 she began teaching at City College in New York City. This position brought her into contact with African American poets Alice Walker and Audre Lorde. Rich's 1973 collection of poems, *Diving into the Wreck*, was given a National Book Award. Rich rejected the award as an individual and instead accepted it "in the name of all women whose voices have gone and still go unheard in a patriarchal world" (Russell 1995, 184).

Rich became an outspoken radical feminist and lesbian separatist after the suicide of her husband in 1970. Besides publishing her poems in mainstream magazines, she reached out to feminist and lesbian journals. Probably her most influential essay is "Compulsory Heterosexuality and Lesbian Existence." In this essay, Rich argues that "heterosexuality, like motherhood, needs to be recognized and studied as a political institution" (Rich 1980). She believes that women are forced into compulsory heterosexuality by the power wielded by men against women. However, she observes that women have resisted through a number of ways, which she defines as "lesbian continuum." The lesbian continuum is "a range, through each woman's life and through history—of women-identified experience: not simply the fact that a woman has had or consciously desired genital sexual experience with another woman . . . [but includes] the sharing of rich inner life, the bonding against male tyranny, the giving and receiving of practical and political support. . . . [that far exceeds the] clinical definitions of 'lesbianism'" (Rich 1980). Rich continues writing and teaching at Stanford University as a professor of English.

Marion Gordon (Pat) Robertson (1930–)

Pat Robertson founded the Christian Broadcast Network (CBN) and *The 700 Club* television program and is one of the primary spokespeople against lesbian and gay rights. Born on March 22, 1930, in Lexington, Virginia, Robertson grew up in a religious household. He received his bachelor's degree from Washington and Lee University in 1950, a law degree from Yale University in 1955, and a master's degree from the New York Theological Seminary in 1959. He was ordained a minister in the Southern Baptist Church in 1961, at the same time founding CBN. The TV program gave him national exposure such that he was able to begin CBN University in 1977. He has hosted *The 700 Club* since its beginnings in 1968 and continues to be active in CBN. He is author or coauthor of a number of books, including *My Prayer for You* (1977), *The Secret Kingdom* (1982), *Beyond Reason* (1984), and *America's Date with Destiny* (1986).

Robertson campaigned for the Republican nomination for president of the United States in 1988. Although not successful, his campaign significantly impacted conservative politics in the United States. From his efforts sprang the Christian Coalition, which sought to transform the United States into a Christian theocratic state.

A national outcry occurred when on *The 700 Club* Pat Robertson agreed with Jerry Falwell that feminists, lesbians and gays, and others were to blame for the destruction of the World Trade Center on September 11, 2001.

Sappho (sixth century B.C.E.)

Sappho has been a significant influence on lesbian identity for 2,500 years. Sappho was born on the Aegean island of Lesbos off the coast of Asia Minor, probably in the early sixth century B.C.E. We know virtually nothing about this woman whose very name has come to signify women who love women. It is believed that she was married to a wealthy merchant, had a daughter named Cleis, and plotted against the tyrant Pittacus. It is also believed that she spent most of her life on Lesbos.

The island of Lesbos in the sixth century was a gathering place for aristocratic women who formed informal societies to compose and recite poetry. Sappho headed one of these societies and wrote mostly about her relationships with other women. Her lyrics are passionate and simple rather than literary. Although no complete poem of hers still exists, with the largest fragment being only twenty-eight lines long, we know that her works were collected into ten books in the third or second century B.C.E. These books survived until the Middle Ages, when they were either lost or destroyed. Many writers and religious leaders have attempted to disparage Lesbos and Sappho. Yet the idea of a band of women living with women who were poetic and passionate manages to survive. When American lesbians in the 1950s decided to organize a national organization, they called themselves the Daughters of Bilitis in homage to Sappho's fictitious disciple.

Phyllis Stewart Schlafly (1924–)

Phyllis Schlafly is one of the major conservative voices in the United States and led the successful fight to stop passage of the Equal Rights Amendment (ERA).

Schlafly was born in 1924 in St. Louis, Missouri. Her family quickly realized how intelligent she was and entered her into college as a young teenager. She graduated at age twenty with a B.A. from Washington University in St. Louis with honors (Phi Beta Kappa, Pi Sigma Alpha, Final Honors). She received her master's in Government from Harvard University the next year (1945). She worked her way through college on the night shift at the St. Louis Ordnance Plant where, as a laboratory technician investigating misfires, tested ammunition by firing rifles and machine guns.

Her appetite for politics was wetted when she worked as the campaign manager for a Republican candidate for Congress in St.

Louis in 1946. The campaign was successful which encouraged her to run for an Illinois congressional seat in 1952 and later in 1970. Although she was not successful at these efforts, she later was elected delegate to six different Republican National Conventions beginning in 1956.

In support of Barry Goldwater's 1964 presidential campaign, she wrote *A Choice, Not An Echo*. It became a best-seller and put Schlafly on the conservative map as author and speaker. She began in 1967 to publish a regularly syndicated column—*The Phyllis Schlafly Report*—which continues today in 100 newspapers and with radio commentaries heard daily on 460 stations. Mainstream press seeks her conservative, profamily, prolife, and antigay comments and she has testified before more than fifty congressional and state legislative committees. She also wrote a monthly article for the ultraconservative *Daughters of the American Revolution Magazine* from 1977 to 1995.

In the 1970s, she started the Eagle Forum, a conservative think tank and political action organization. At the same time, she launched the Stop ERA campaign. Schlafly was the major force behind defeat of the Equal Rights Amendment. She believes a constitutional amendment should be passed to put prayer back into the schools, "but to the real God, the Christian God, the one referred to on our currency. Don't let the atheists and the communists run this country. Put it back in the hands of good, Christian, white males. That's my opinion" (Schlafly 1998).

She has authored more than twenty books and was selected the 1992 Illinois Mother of the Year. She and her late husband are the parents of six children. Her oldest son, John, is gay. He was outed by Queer World in 1992. At age forty-one, he still lived with his mother. Schlafly conceded that she knew from John's earliest years that he was homosexual. During interviews where questions are asked about her gay son, Schlafly becomes irritated and often refuses to answer. While speaking on *Meet the Press* in 1993, she was asked about her son's homosexuality. She became angry and said, "The only reason people bring it up is to embarrass me "(Voboril 1993). The National Gay and Lesbian Task Force assail her as one of the "top five most powerful anti-gay forces in the country" (Voboril 1993).

Michelangelo Signorile (1960–)

Michelangelo Signorile launched the newsmagazine *Outweek*,

which outed public figures. Signorile was born in Brooklyn, New York, in 1960 to a tight-knit Roman Catholic family. He did not enjoy baseball but instead played with dolls and his female cousin. He was called a sissy and faggot and queer in school and fought back. He later wrote, "I became a queer-basher to prove I wasn't queer" (Russell 1995, 371).

He had his first sexual experience when he was twelve years old with a thirty-five-year-old male neighbor. He felt insurmountable guilt and was physically ill for days. In an attempt to "cure himself," he took up football and became very athletic. However, he discovered other Italian boys his own age along the Franklin D. Roosevelt boardwalk at South Beach with whom he could have sex.

He attended a prestigious high school where he played football and continued to queer-bash. He was called in by his principal to explain his violent behavior. He replied that he got into fights because the other boys called him faggot or queer.

He tried Brooklyn College for a short time but was dissatisfied. He transferred to Syracuse University to study journalism. There, he was able to come out of the closet. He reported, "I was the happiest I had ever been" (Russell 1995, 372).

He graduated from Syracuse, moved to New York City, and began working for a public relations firm that placed celebrity gossip in the news. Signorile noticed that everything was fair game in the gossip trade except homosexuality. He saw this as a vast conspiracy of silence.

He began to attend ACT UP meetings as one friend after another became HIV-positive or died of AIDS. His friend Gabriel Rotello asked him in 1989 to start a controversial gay and lesbian publication named *Outweek.* Its purpose was to publicly identify and disclose closeted gay and lesbian public figures. *Outweek* garnered a large readership of not only those who approved of his methods but also of those who were offended. Signorile was accused of engaging in McCarthyism and invasion of privacy.

It was *Outweek* that revealed that Malcolm Forbes, one of the wealthiest men in the United States and owner of the business magazine *Forbes,* was homosexual. The firestorm over the Forbes revelation was nothing compared to what occurred in 1991 when Signorile revealed in *The Advocate* that Pete Williams, senior civilian Department of Defense spokesman and protégé of Secretary of Defense Dick Cheney, was gay. Signorile saw this as the greatest hypocrisy: the U.S. military, which regularly discharged homosexual personnel, had as its spokesperson a gay man. Signorile came under much abuse for the revelation. In 1993, Signorile presented his case for outing in his book *Queer in America: Sex, the Media, and the Closets of Power.*

Socrates (469–399 B.C.E.)

Socrates was one of the earliest Western philosophers to promote same-sex love. Socrates was born in 469 B.C.E. in the Greek city-state of Athens. Very little known about his childhood, but he did serve as a foot soldier in the Athenian army during the Peloponnesian War. In his adult life, Socrates spent much of his time sitting under the shade of olive trees discussing philosophical questions of justice, virtue, and the soul with well-born youths. He was a teacher and lover of young men and embodied the Athenian institution of *paiderasteia,* or "boy love."

The Great Oracle at Delphi declared Socrates to be the wisest among men. He held no firm philosophical doctrines of his own but asked students a series of questions and then directed them to examine the implications of their answers. This became known as the Socratic method. Socrates criticized Athenian politics and religious institutions. He was arrested, tried, convicted of corrupting the morals of Athenian youths and speaking religious heresy, and sentenced to death. He fulfilled the sentence by drinking hemlock, a poison prescribed by law.

None of Socrates's writings has survived. Instead, we have the writings of his famous student Plato with which to better understand this man and his influence. Plato's *Symposium* and *Phaedrus* have had the greatest impact on gay thought. Socrates discussed how the love between an older man and a beautiful boy begins as erotic passion, then evolves as the older man becomes a teacher, as well as lover, of the beautiful boy. This is the essence of what is known as platonic love.

John Addington Symonds (1840–1893)

John Symonds is credited with writing the first essay to review all existing research on homosexuality and to show that same-sex love was admirable and normal. Born in Bristol, England, on October 5, 1840, Symonds came from the family of a physician. He attended Balliol College and earned high honors in classics. He suffered from many health problems and began to travel extensively in hopes of finding a climate where he could live.

He married a woman while on a visit to Italy in 1864 and had three daughters. He was still in poor health and devoted himself to a literary life. Over the next three decades, he produced many volumes of literary works, travel articles, biographies, and translations. Modern scholars are mostly interested in his essay entitled "A Problem in Greek Ethics," an essay not listed in his official biography. He had fifty copies of it printed at his own expense and distributed it in 1891. In the essay, he systematically reviewed all that was known about homosexuality and took the position that same-sex love was both normal and admirable.

Although Symonds was married, he had homosexual feelings throughout his life. While in high school he fell in love with a boy three years younger than himself, and he referred to this as his "birth," an experience similar to what could be construed in modern life as coming out.

Symonds wrote extensively to Walt Whitman. This concerned Whitman so much that he abruptly discontinued corresponding with Symonds. Symonds formed relatively long-lasting homosexual relationships with other men.

Alan Turing (1912–1954)

Alan Turing developed the basic theories used for creating the computer. Turing was born in London on June 23, 1912. His parents were British civil servants stationed in India. He and his brother were placed with an English family to attend school at Sheborne, one of England's oldest public schools. There, the headmaster characterized Turing as being "antisocial." Turing developed a deep, affectionate relationship with one of the boys in the school and was devastated when the lad died at the age of eighteen.

Turing was only twenty-three and studying mathematical logic at King's College, Cambridge, when in 1938 he wrote the article "On Computable Numbers, with an Application to the *Entscheidungsproblem*." The theories presented in the article about unsolvable problems became the basis for the development of computer theory. Turing conceived of a universal machine—a Turing machine—that eventually became what we now know as a digital computer.

Turing came to the United States in 1938, where he received his doctoral degree in mathematics from Princeton University. He returned to England at the beginning of World War II and worked with the British Code and Cipher School. He is credited with inventing the machines the broke the German code, otherwise known as Enigma, and contributed directly to the defeat of Germany by the Allies.

Turing helped design and construct the Automatic Computing Engine and became director of Manchester Automatic Digital Machine (MADAM). His far-ranging theories about mathematics, machines, and intelligence led to the development of the computer and were the beginnings of research into the field of artificial intelligence.

Immediately after the war, Turing's top-secret clearance was revoked because of his known homosexuality. In 1952, a burglary of his apartment by a former lover resulted in the police charging him with "gross indecency" for being a homosexual. He was subjected to "chemical castration" by means of hormone injections that left him physically and emotionally scarred. On June 7, 1954, he committed suicide by eating an apple dipped in cyanide.

Karl Heinrich Ulrichs (1825–1895)

Karl Ulrichs was one of the earliest writers on the subject of homosexuality and suggested that homosexuals constituted a third sex situated between male and female (he referred to it as Uranian).

Born in Hanover, Germany, in 1825, Ulrichs spent a significant portion of his life writing about the issues of human sexuality. He first published a twelve-volume work under the pseudonym Numa Numantius in 1864. Over the next six years he published another dozen books, but this time under his own name. Ulrichs believed homosexuals constituted a third sex that was inborn, natural, and thus not sinful, depraved, or perverted. Although his belief that Uranians are a third sex is considered primitive by our modern science, other ideas, such as the immutability of sexual orientation, have sustained.

He attempted to bring the issue of rights for gays and lesbians to the Congress of German Jurists in 1867, but was shouted down and prevented from speaking. In 1870 Ulrich left Germany for Italy and lived a quiet life. Even though he was an early pioneer, very little of his work influenced the burgeoning gay rights movement in Germany.

Urvashi Vaid (1958–)

Urvashi Vaid was responsible for transforming the National Gay and Lesbian Task Force (NGLTF) into the principal source of information in the United States on lesbian and gay rights issues.

Vaid was born in India in 1958 to Indian parents and moved to the United States when she was eight years old. She was an awkward young girl with very thick glasses and long, thick, straight Indian hair that extended to her waist. She was socially shy and an intellectual who spent her time voraciously reading.

Vaid describes herself as feeling as an outsider because of her ethnicity, accent, and intellectual interests. She became politically aware and involved at very early age. She participated in her first antiwar march when she was twelve years old.

She graduated high school early and attended New York's Vassar College on an academic scholarship. She was impressed by Vassar and attracted to the feminist movement, though she was concerned about oppression in all its forms. She graduated college in 1979 with a bachelor's degree in English and political science. She worked as a legal secretary while serving on the steering committee of the Allston-Brighton Greenlight Safehouse Network, an antiviolence neighborhood project that she cofounded.

In 1980, she enrolled in law school at Northeastern University in Boston. At that time, she also cofounded the Boston Lesbian/Gay Political Alliance. Immediately after graduating law school in 1983, she worked as a staff attorney with the ACLU's National Prisons Project in Washington, D.C. In 1984 she initiated the National Prisons Project's work with prisoners who had contracted the HIV virus.

Vaid was appointed to the board of directors of NGLTF in 1985. She became the group's director of public information and brought with her a degree of professionalism and media savvy it had not known before. In doing so, she increased coverage of NGLTF's activities and agenda and established the organization as a principal source of information on issues concerning gay and lesbian rights.

In 1989 Vaid became executive director of NGLTF's Policy Institute in Washington, D.C. There, she tripled the group's operating budget and increased staff while beginning major fundraising and public outreach programs. As always, Vaid was working to increase visibility, believing that the more gays and lesbians are seen by the media as ordinary citizens participating in society just like anyone else, the fewer barriers there will be to acceptance. She also cofounded the NGLTF's Creating Change conference, which remains the only national gay and lesbian political conference.

In 1992 she resigned her position to work on *Virtual Equality*, which was published in 1995. She returned to the Policy Institute in 1997.

Bruce Voeller (1934–1994)

Bruce Voeller coined the term *acquired immune deficiency syndrome* (AIDS). Voeller was born in Minneapolis, Minnesota, on May 12, 1934. He experienced homosexual feelings as early as junior high school, but a school counselor and minister assured him he was not gay because, unlike sick perverts, he "was emotionally healthy, a good athlete and not effeminate" (Newton 1994, 90).

He graduated Reed College with a bachelor's degree in 1956 and received his Ph.D. in biology in 1961 from the Rockefeller Institute in New York City. He became a research assistant, assistant professor, and then associate professor at Rockefeller.

He met and married a woman from graduate school and fathered three children. His life seemed to be following a traditional academic and personal path, but he could no longer ignore his homosexual feelings. He left his academic life and marriage in 1971 to concentrate full-time on the growing gay liberation movement.

He became president of the New York Gay Activists Alliance (GAA) and soon found that it was too limited in scope. Sitting at his kitchen table in October 1973 with four other friends, they drew up plans for a new national organization called the National Gay Task Force (later known as the National Gay and Lesbian Task Force).

Voeller worked for the task force until 1978, by which time it had achieved most of its early goals including establishing contacts with more than 2,000 local gay groups throughout the country and building a national membership of more than 10,000.

Voeller move to California and became president of the Mariposa Foundation, an organization devoted to sex research and education. As a biological researcher and gay activist, he felt the term *gay related immune defense disorder* continued to stigmatize homosexuals. He coined the term *acquired immune deficiency syn-*

drome (AIDS) and wrote more than sixty scholarly papers on the topic. Voeller died from AIDS in California on February 13, 1994.

Tom Waddell (1937–1987)

Tom Waddell founded the Gay Games. He was born Tom Flubacher on November 1, 1937, in Paterson, New Jersey. At an early age he befriended Gene Waddell, who was a vaudevillian acrobat, and his wife, Hazel Waddell, who was a dancer. They fueled Tom's interest in sports. Tom's closeness with the Waddells eventually led to his decision to change his name to Waddell. As a child he studied ballet. In secondary school he took up athletics, but he dropped athletics while in college to pursue a medical degree.

Passionately opposed to the Vietnam War, Waddell avoided fighting by excelling in military athletics. As a thirty-three-year-old, he trained for the 1968 Olympic Games in Mexico City and placed sixth in the decathlon. It was at this Olympics that two African American athletes gave the Black Power salute during the U.S. national anthem. Waddell supported their actions and was threatened with court-martial by his commanding officers.

In 1980, Waddell proposed the idea for a gay Olympics that would be inclusive rather than exclusive. He intended that anyone, regardless of sex, age, sexual orientation, race, national origin, or athletic ability, be allowed to participate. As a committed socialist, he believed the Gay Olympics should promote equality and universal participation.

When the U.S. Olympic Committee (USOC) heard about the Gay Olympics, its members were outraged. Shortly before the first Gay Olympics were to take place in 1982, the committee filed a court action claiming that it had exclusive use of the word *Olympic*. The Gay Olympics therefore changed its name to the Gay Games.

The first Gay Games (1982) were held in San Francisco, with 1,300 female and male athletes competing. Two years later, a lien was placed against Waddell's house by the USOC in an attempt to recover $96,000 in legal fees it had spent in the court case against the Gay Olympics.

At the next Gay Games (1986), more than 3,000 athletes competed. Sadly, Waddell was diagnosed with AIDS-related pneumocystis carninii pneumonia. He still competed and won, but the disease was taking its toll. He was forced to resign his position as chief physician at San Francisco's Central Emergency Facility. His last few years were spent fighting the USOC's lawsuit. A month before his death, the U.S. Supreme Court upheld USOC's legal authority "to bar homosexual rights group from using the generic word *Olympic* in the names of its games" (Russell 1995, 328).

Thomas Waddell died on July 11, 1987, at his home. Just three years after his death, in 1990, the Gay Games in Vancouver attracted more than 7,000 athletes from around the world. The Gay Games have become the largest amateur sporting event in the world.

We'wha (1849–1896)

We'wha was a Zuni two-spirit (berdache) who became the toast of Washington, D.C., society and whose legacy has had an impact on our modern understanding of transgenderism. We'wha was born at Anthill at the Middle of the World, of the Pueblo of Zuni (near the present-day border of New Mexico and Arizona), in 1849. His parents died from smallpox brought by white American settlers passing through. His father's sister adopted him and his brother. In matrilineal Zuni society, this would mean that he retained membership in his mother's clan, the Badger People, while also maintaining lifelong ties to his father's clan, the Dogwood People. We'wha's adoptive family was very powerful within the pueblo.

As a child, perhaps as early as three or four, We'wha showed signs of being a woman. The Zuni saw gender as an acquired trait, not something inborn. Biological sex was not the determining factor as to whether someone was male or female. Thus, We'wha was identified as a *lhamana* (what anthropologists refer to as berdache or two-spirited) and trained in the customs and skills of a woman.

During We'wha's childhood, there was great intertribal conflict between the Zunis and the neighboring Navajos and Apaches. The U.S. Army defeated the Navajos in 1864 and forced their removal to distant reservations. Peace brought increasing contacts between the Zunis and white people. Mormon missionaries converted hundreds of Zunis in 1876 and set up a mission. Presbyterians moved in two years later, hoping to run the Mormons out. It was then that anthropologist Matilda Stevenson discovered We'wha and assumed him to be a Zuni "girl."

A friendship developed between Stevenson and We'wha. In

1885, We'wha, along with Stevenson and several others Zunis, went to Washington, D.C. We'wha quickly learned English and soon became the toast of the town. People did not know that he was not a woman. He was introduced as an Indian princess, and receptions were held in his honor. On June 23, 1886, We'wha shook hands with President Grover Cleveland.

We'wha returned to his pueblo. There were conflicts between the Zuni leaders and the U.S. military. We'wha was arrested along with five of the Zuni leaders. We'wha was charged with engaging in witchcraft and served a month in prison.

While participating in the annual Sha'lako festival in December 1896, We'wha died from heart failure at the age of forty-seven. His death was viewed as a great "calamity" and disrupted the calm of the clan. Some Zuni took to their horses and raided nearby lands. This provided the U.S. government with an excuse to exert complete authority over the Zunis. Understanding We'wha's place in Zuni culture sheds light on how gender is constructed in Western societies.

Walt Whitman (1819–1892)

Walt Whitman was an influential poet of early America whose homosexual themes encouraged closeted gay men and women. Born in Huntington, New York, on May 31, 1819, Whitman began working in a printing shop at eleven years of age and continued in the publishing business for the next twenty-four years. He met his heart's companion, Peter Doyal, an eighteen-year-old streetcar conductor, in 1865 and depicted their relationship in the collection of poems *Leaves of Grass*. The section called "Calamus " contained overtly homosexual poems. During the Civil War, Whitman volunteered to visit soldiers in hospitals and was appreciated for his ability to bring cheer and boost the men's spirits in the camps.

In 1873, Whitman had a stroke that partially paralyzed him. He moved to Camden, New Jersey, leaving Doyal behind. While there he met an eighteen-year-old boy named Harry Stafford. Their relationship lasted a number of years, but Whitman finally disengaged himself from the boy.

By 1884, the Philadelphia edition of *Leaves of Grass* brought financial rewards that enabled him to purchase a house in Camden, New Jersey. However, another stroke in 1888 left him very incapacitated. He died at home on March 26, 1892.

Oscar Wilde (1854–1900)

Oscar Wilde was a famous British writer who was arrested and convicted in a very public trial for his "love that dare not speak its name." Born on October 16, 1854, in Dublin, Ireland, Wilde came from a professional family. His father was a famous eye and ear surgeon, and his mother was a folklorist and poet. He graduated with honors in 1878 from Oxford University. He had a reputation as a serious classic scholar, but he was also an aesthete who favored gorgeously decorated rooms and gaudy clothing.

Acting as the advance agent for London's Gilbert and Sullivan touring companies, he was able to lecture in more than seventy U.S. cities on arts and literature. He became a celebrity hound and was well known for being well known. Although he married and had two sons, he led a double life with a widening circle of available young men.

In 1891, Wilde completed his novel *The Picture of Dorian Gray*. It caused a storm of indignation for its "purple patches" and thinly veiled allusions to homosexual life. At the same time, Wilde was introduced to Lord Alfred Douglas. The beauty of this twenty-one-year-old stunned Wilde. Within the year they were reckless lovers and Wilde was completely in love. Personal letters between them found their way to Douglas's father, the Marquis of Queensberry. The father left a card with a scrawled insult at Wilde's hotel. Douglas egged on Wilde, who sued Queensberry for criminal libel. When the case came to court, the tables were turned, and Wilde was placed on trial for sodomy. Wilde was convicted and sentenced to two years of hard labor. After his release from prison, Wilde moved to France and was reunited with Douglas. Wilde died November 30, 1900, at the age of forty-six in Paris.

References

Baker v. Wade, 553 F. Supp. 1121 (N.D. Tex. 1982), *aff'd on other grounds*, 743 F.2d 236 (5th Cir. 1984), *rev'd*, 769 F.2d 289 (5th Cir. 1985).

Newton, D. E. 1994. *Gay and Lesbian Rights: A Reference Handbook*. Santa Barbara, CA: ABC-CLIO.

Rich, Adrienne. 1980. "Compulsory Heterosexuality and Lesbian Existence." *Signs: Journal of Women in Culture and Society* 5 (Summer): 631–660.

Russell, P. 1995. *The Gay 100*. New York: Kensington Books.

Schlafly, Phyllis. 1998. "None Dare Call It Reason." *Phyllis Schlafly Report* 31(8) (March): 1. Available at www.mattneuman.com/schlafly.htm.

Voboril, M. 1993. "Conservative Leader Schlafly Says 'Outing' of Son Was 'Strike at Me.'" *Knight-Ridder Newspapers*, April 28. Available at www. qrd.org/qrd/misc/text/schlafly.outing.reaction-KNIGHT.RIDDER.

5

Documents, Cases, Laws, and Quotations

Documents

Antidiscrimination Policies and Statutes: Wisconsin's Antidiscrimination Law

Antidiscrimination statutes are laws passed to provide protection against discrimination. The Civil Rights Act of 1964 was the most significant step taken by the federal government to enact antidiscrimination provisions. It provided protections for a few categories of people based on race, color, religion, sex, and national origin.

Interestingly, sex was not initially included in the draft of the Civil Rights Act. It was put there by conservatives hoping that its inclusion would ensure that the act did not pass. But it did pass, and it opened the door for local and state antidiscrimination policy and laws specifying gender and eventually sexual orientation.

Every state has some types of laws providing protection from discrimination. Only a few explicitly include sexual orientation. In the other states, courts have made wide interpretations that sometimes exclude and other times include sexual orientation as a protected class. More than 100 towns, cities, and counties have passed antidiscrimination laws based on sexual orientation.

Wisconsin became the first state in the nation to adopt a statewide nondiscrimination law for gay men and lesbians. Following is an excerpt from Chapter 12, Laws of 1981.

175

SECTION 12: It is the intent of this section to render unlawful discrimination in housing. It is the declared policy of this state that all persons shall have an equal opportunity for housing regardless of sex, race, color, sexual orientation as defined in [Section 15], handicap, religion, national origin, sex or marital status of the person maintaining the household, lawful source of income, age or ancestry and it is the duty of the local units of government to assist in the orderly prevention or removal of all discrimination in housing through the power granted to municipalities. The legislature hereby extends the state law governing equal housing opportunities to cover single-family residences which are owner-occupied. The legislature finds that the sale and rental of single-family residences constitutes a significant portion of the housing business in this state and should be regulated. This section shall be deemed an exercise of the police powers of the state for the protection of the welfare, health, peace, dignity, and human rights of the people of this state.

SECTION 13: The Equal Rights Council shall disseminate information and attempt by means of discussion as well as other proper means to educate the people of the state to a greater understanding, appreciation and practice of human rights for all people, of whatever race, creed, color, sexual orientation, national origin, to the end that this state will be a better place in which to live. . . .

SECTION 17: It is discrimination because of sexual orientation:

1. For any employer, labor organization, licensing agency or employment agency or other person to refuse to hire, employ, admit or license, or to bar or terminate from employment, membership or licensure any individual, or to discriminate against an individual in promotion, compensation or in terms, conditions or privileges of employment because of the individual's sexual orientation. . . .

SECTION 25: [A person is guilty of a Class A misdemeanor who] denies to another or charges another a higher price than the regular rate for the full and equal enjoyment of any public place of accommodation or amusement because of sex, race, color, creed, physical condition, developmental disability . . . sexual orientation . . . national origin or ancestry [or] gives preferential treatment to some classes of persons in providing services or facilities in any public place of accommodation or amusement because of sex, race, color, creed, sexual orientation, national origin or ancestry.

Antigay Public Policy: Paragraph 175 and Colorado's Amendment 2

On June 28, 1935, the German government amended its constitution to prohibit homosexuality. Eventually, Paragraph 175 would be used to send gay men and lesbians to the concentration camps for execution. Even after the war, legal-minded Allied commanders returned homosexual prisoners back to prison to serve out their sentence.

175:

1. A male who indulges in criminally indecent activities with another male or who allows himself to participate in such activities will be punished with jail.

2. If one of the participants is under the age of twenty-one, and if the crime has not been grave, the court may dispense with the jail sentence.

(a): A jail sentence of up to ten years or, if mitigating circumstances can be established, a jail sentence of no less than three years will be imposed on.

1. any male who by force or by threat of violence and danger to life and limb compels another man to indulge in criminally indecent activities, or allows himself to participate in such activities;

2. any male who forces another male to indulge with him in criminally indecent activities by using the subordinate position of the other man, whether it be at work or elsewhere, or who allows himself to participate in such activities;

3. any male who indulges professionally and for profit in criminally indecent activities with other males, or allows himself to be used for such activities or who offers himself for same.

(b): Criminally indecent activities by males with animals are to be punished by jail; in addition, the court may deprive the subject of his civil rights.

In November 1992, the voters of Colorado passed Amendment 2 to the state constitution. It prohibited the state and municipalities from enacting antidiscrimination laws designed to protect lesbians and gay men. The amendment was challenged in court, and the U.S. Supreme Court in Romer v. Evans *declared it to be unconstitutional. Here is the Initiative.*

Amendment to the Constitution of the State of Colorado:

Be it Enacted by the People of the State of Colorado:

Article 2 of the Colorado Constitution is amended by the addition of Section 30, which shall state as follows:

No protected status based on homosexual, lesbian or bisexual Orientation.

Neither the State of Colorado, through any of its branches or departments, nor any of its agencies, political subdivisions, municipalities or school districts, shall enact, adopt or enforce any statute, regulation, ordinance or policy whereby homosexual, lesbian or bisexual orientation, conduct, practices or relationships shall constitute or otherwise be the basis of, or entitle any person or class of persons to have or claim any minority status, quota preferences, protected status or claim of discrimination. This Section of the Constitution shall be in all respects self-executing.

Natalie Meyer, Secretary of State

Co-parenting: The American Academy of Pediatrics

AAP is the largest professional organization in the United States devoted to the needs of health professionals working with children. It has issued many position papers.

Coparent or Second-Parent Adoption by Same-Sex Parents
Policy Statement, February 2002

ABSTRACT. Children who are born to or adopted by 1 member of a same-sex couple deserve the security of 2 legally recognized parents. Therefore, the American Academy of Pediatrics supports legislative and legal efforts to provide the possibility of adoption of the child by the second parent or coparent in these families. Children deserve to know that their relationships with both of their parents are stable and legally recognized. This applies to all children, whether their parents are of the same or opposite sex. The American Academy of Pediatrics recognizes that a considerable body of professional literature provides evidence that children with parents who are homosexual can have the same advantages and the same expectations for health, adjustment, and development as can children whose parents are heterosexual.

Reparative Therapy: The American Psychiatric Association, the Human Rights Campaign, and the National Association of Research and Therapy of Homosexuality

Psychiatric and psychological groups in the United States have come to the conclusion that it is impossible and unethical to attempt to change a person's sexual orientation. Religious-based reparative therapy groups disagree.

The APA declassified homosexuality as a mental illness in 1973. It is the largest and most powerful psychiatric association in the world and has worked toward normalizing homosexuality.

Fact Sheet: Gay, Lesbian, and Bisexual Issues

Is It Possible to Change One's Sexual Orientation? ("Reparative Therapy")

There is no published scientific evidence supporting the efficacy of "reparative therapy" as a treatment to change one's sexual orientation, nor is it included in the APA's Task Force Report, Treatments of Psychiatric Disorder. More importantly, altering sexual orientation is not an appropriate goal of psychiatric treatment. . . . Clinical experience indicates that those who have integrated their sexual orientation into a positive sense of self-function are at a healthier psychological level than those who have not.

The Human Rights Campaign (HRC) is one of the largest and most powerful lesbian and gay civil rights organizations in the United States. Here are its comments on reparative therapy.

Why Reparative Therapy and Ex-Gay Ministries Fail

By Kim I. Mills, Education Director, HRC, 1999.

The purveyors of "reparative therapy" are well outside mainstream research and thinking in the psychotherapeutic world. They rail constantly that their work is being subverted by the professional associations, which they claim were hijacked in the 1970s by activist gay members into removing homosexuality from the official lists of mental disorders.

We question how it could be that the American Psychiatric and American Psychological Associations—the pre-eminent professional associations in their fields—could have been held captive by these so-called gay activists for more than 20 years. Surely if there were clinical evidence that homosexuality *per se* were a mental illness, this information could not have been suppressed by so many bright minds for so long. In addition, the "reparative therapists" protest loudly and often that homosexuality was removed from the *Diagnostic and Statistical Manual* without empirical research. We submit that it was placed in the *DSM* originally without such evidence.

It is our studied belief that the purveyors of "reparative therapy" refuse to confront the underlying reasons for the apparent unhappiness of many of the gay people who seek their help. They presume that all gay people are mentally unwell, ignoring the hundreds of thousands of happy, well-adjusted, successful lesbians and gay men across this nation.

As for ex-gay ministries, our research found that many of them dangle impossible promises before troubled people in order to lure them into their programs. The clearest evidence that these programs are not effective are the "ex-ex gay" testimonials of people who once participated in them—and the fact that so many of the most prominent ex-gay leaders returned to their former gay lives, only to be replaced by people who were never gay themselves and therefore cannot create new public relations disasters. Like the so-called reparative therapists, these ministries play to guilt and unhappiness that have their roots in something other than people's intrinsic sexual natures.

The National Association for Research and Therapy of Homosexuality (NARTH) promotes psychological understanding of the cause, treatment, and behavior patterns associated with homosexuality and its cure.

NARTH's Purpose

During the last 25 years, powerful political pressures have done much to erode scientific study of homosexuality. As a result, there is now great misunderstanding surrounding this issue. Because of the angry tenor of the debate, many researchers have been intimidated, we believe, into trading the truth for silence.

As clinicians, we have witnessed the intense suffering caused by homosexuality, which many of our members see as a "failure to function according to design." Homosexuality distorts the natural bond of friendship that would naturally unite persons of the same sex. It threatens the continuity of traditional male-female marriage—a bond which is naturally anchored by the complementarily of the sexes, and long been considered essential for the protection of children.

In males, homosexuality is associated with poor relationship with father; difficulty individuating from mother; a sense of masculine deficit; and a persistent belief of having been different from, and misunderstood by, same-sex childhood peers. In adulthood we also see a persistent pattern of maladaptive behaviors and a documented higher level of psychiatric complaints.

Professionals who belong to NARTH comprise a wide variety of men and women who *defend the right to pursue change of sexual orientation.*

Most NARTH members consider homosexuality to represent a developmental disorder. Some of our clinician-members, however, do not consider the condition disordered, but simply defend the right to treatment for those who desire it.

It is NARTH's aim to provide a different perspective. Particularly, we want to clarify that homosexuality is not "inborn," and that gays are not "a people," in the same sense that an ethnic group is "a people"—but instead, they are (like all of us) simply individuals who exhibit particular patterns of feelings and behavior.

Statements for Gay Rights: Amnesty International, the American Psychiatric Association, the American Psychological Association, Dignity USA, the National Federation of Priests' Councils, and the Union of American Hebrew Congregations

Amnesty International conducts a worldwide campaign against torture. Lesbians, gay men, and bisexual and transgender people all over the world suffer persecution and violence simply for being who they are. They are tortured or intimidated by state officials to extract confessions of "deviance" and raped to "cure" them of it. They are attacked in their homes and communities because of their sexual orientation or gender identity. Amnesty International has issued this report, available on the web:

Crimes of hate, conspiracy of silence: Torture and ill-treatment based on sexual identity.

Section 8: Recommendations.

1. Repeal laws criminalizing homosexuality. Review all legislation which could result in the discrimination, prosecution and punishment of people solely for their sexual orientation or gender identity. This includes "sodomy" laws or similar provisions outlawing homosexual or transgender behavior; discriminatory age of consent legislation; public order legislation used to prosecute and punish people solely for their sexual identity; and laws banning the "promotion" of homosexuality which can be used to imprison LGBT rights advocates.

All such laws should be repealed or amended. Anyone imprisoned or detained solely for their real or perceived sexual orientation or gender identity should be released immediately and unconditionally. This includes those detained for same-sex sexual relations between consenting adults in private, those held for advocating LGBT rights, and those detained for their political beliefs or activities under the pretext of charges of homosexuality.

In 1973, the American Psychiatric Association's Board of Trustees removed homosexuality from its official diagnostic manual, the Diagnostic and Statistical Manual of Mental Disorders, Second Edition (DSM-II). *This action was taken following a review of the scientific literature and consultation with experts in the field. The experts found that homosexuality does not meet the criteria necessary to be considered a mental illness. The APA's prepared statement on homosexuality is available on the web.*

Fact Sheet: Gay, Lesbian, and Bisexual Issues

What Causes Homosexuality/Heterosexuality/Bisexuality?

No one knows what causes heterosexuality, homosexuality, or bisexuality. Homosexuality was once thought to be the result of troubled family dynamics or faulty psychological development. Those assumptions are now understood to have been based on misinformation and prejudice. . . . To date there are no replicated scientific studies supporting any specific biological etiology for homosexuality. Similarly, no specific psychosocial or family dynamic cause for homosexuality has been identified, including histories of childhood sexual abuse. Sexual abuse does not appear to be more prevalent in children who grow up to identify as gay, lesbian, or bisexual, than in children who identify as heterosexual.

What Position Has the American Psychiatric Association Taken Regarding This Stigma?

Whereas homosexuality per se implies no impairment in judgment, stability, reliability, or general social or vocational capabilities, the American Psychiatric Association calls on all international health organizations and individual psychiatrists in other countries, to urge the repeal in their own country of legislation that penalized homosexual acts by consenting adults in private. And further the APA calls on these organizations and individuals to do all that is possible to decrease the stigma related to homosexuality wherever and whenever it may occur.

How Do the Children of Gay/Lesbians Parents Fare?

Numerous studies have shown that the children of gay parents are as likely to be healthy and well adjusted as children raised in heterosexual households. Children raised in gay or lesbian households do not show any greater incidence of homosexuality or gender identity issues than other children.

In 1975, the APA followed its 1973 decision to resolve that "homosexuality per se implies no impairment in judgment, stability, reliability, or general social or vocation capabilities. . . .Over 25 years later the implications of this resolution have yet to be fully implemented in practice. There is a need for better education and training on mental health practitioner in this area." To that end, the APA issued guidelines (available on the web) to psychologists about the care of homosexual clients:

Guidelines for Psychotherapy with Lesbian, Gay, and Bisexual Clients

Attitudes toward Homosexuality and Bisexuality

Guideline 1. For over a century, homosexuality and bisexuality were assumed to be mental illnesses. Hooker's (1957) study was the first to question this assumption. She found no difference between nonclinical samples of heterosexual and homosexual men on projective test responses. Subsequent studies have shown no difference between heterosexual and homosexual groups on measures of cognitive abilities (Tuttle and Pillard 1991) and psychological well-being and self-esteem (Coyle 1993; Herek 1990; Savin-Williams 1990). Fox (1996) found no evidence of psychopathology in nonclinical studies of bisexual men and women. Further, an extensive body of literature has emerged that identifies few significant differences between heterosexual, homosexual, and bisexual people on a wide range of variables associated with overall psychological functioning (Pillard 1998; Rothblum 1994; Gonsiorek 1991). When studies have noted differences between homosexual and heterosexual subjects with regard to psychological functioning (DiPlacido 1998; Ross 1990; Rotheram-Borus, Hunter, and Rosario 1994; Savin-Williams 1994), these differences have been attributed to the effects of stress related to stigmatization based on sexual orientation. This stress may lead to increased risk for suicide attempts, substance abuse, and emotional distress.

The literature that classifies homosexuality and bisexuality as mental illness has been found to be methodologically unsound. Gonsiorek (1991) reviewed this literature and found serious methodological flaws including unclear definition of terms, inaccurate classification of subjects, inappropriate comparison of groups, discrepant sampling procedures, an ignorance of confounding social factors, and questionable outcome measures.

All major American mental health associations have affirmed that homosexuality is not a mental illness. In 1975, the American Psychological Association (APA) urged all psychologists to 'take the lead in removing the stigma long associated with homosexual orientations' (Conger 1975, p. 633). Subsequently, the APA and all other major mental health associations adopted a number of resolutions and policy statements founded on this basic principle, which has also been embodied in their ethical codes.

Dignity USA is a religious organization serving lesbian and gay Catholics. According to the Catholic Church, homosexuals must be chaste in order to be moral in the eyes of God. This was outlined in the church's document "Congregation for the Doctrine of the Faith—On the Pastoral Care of Homosexual Persons: Letter to the Bishops of the Catholic Church," October 1, 1986 (excerpted later in this chapter). Dignity USA responded to this letter on its website:

FAQs: Catholicism, Homosexuality, and Dignity

. . .

2. What is the official Catholic teaching about homosexuality?

The Catholic Church holds that, as a state beyond a person's choice, being homosexual is not wrong or sinful in itself. But just as it is objectively wrong for unmarried heterosexuals to engage in sex, so too are homosexual acts considered to be wrong. . . .

8. What options are open to a person who is homosexual and Catholic?

Official Catholic teaching requires that homosexual people abstain from sex. But the Catholic Church also teaches solemnly that people are obliged to form their conscience carefully and responsibly and to follow it as the bottom line in every moral decision. . . . Accordingly, and after much soul-searching, many gay and lesbian Catholics have formed consciences that differ from official Church teaching and have entered into homosexual relationships. In this respect they are exactly like the many married Catholic couples who cannot accept the official teaching on contraception. . . .

10. How could someone do what (the Church says) is wrong and not be living in sin?

As the Catholic Church understands it, wrong and sin are not the same thing. Wrong is harm, disorder, destruction; it is in the objective or external world. Sin is self-distancing from God; it is in the heart. . . . The Church teaches right and wrong but never says who is a sinner. Only God knows our hearts. Many homosexual people simply cannot believe that gay sex as such is wrong. So they do what for them is "the best they can do," though Church teaching says that homogenital acts are wrong. Still, according to the same Church's teaching on conscience, they do not sin in their hearts nor before God. Then they need not confess what is not sin, and they may participate in the Sacraments of the Church.

At a 1974 meeting, the National Federation of Priests' Councils (NFPC) adopted a progay resolution:
BE IT RESOLVED that the NFPC hereby declares its opposition to all civil laws which make consensual homosexual acts between adults a crime and thus urge their repeal: and BE IT FURTHER RESOLVED that the NFPC also express [*sic*] its opposition to homosexuality as such being the basis of discrimination against homosexuals in employment, governmental services, housing and child rearing involving natural or adoptive parents.

In 1977, the Union of American Hebrew Congregations passed a progay rights resolution.
Homosexual persons are entitled to equal protection under the law. We oppose discrimination against homosexuals in areas of opportunity, including employment and housing. . . . We affirm our belief that private sexual acts between consenting adults are not the proper province of government and law enforcement agencies.

Statements Opposing Gay Rights: The Boy Scouts of America, the Catholic Church, the Concerned Women for America, and God Hates Fags

On June 28, 2000, the U.S. Supreme Court in Boy Scouts of America v. Dale *(2000) held that requiring the Boy Scouts to include an open homosexual in its ranks would violate the organization's First Amendment right of "expressive association." The Court said: "We are not, as we must not be, guided by our views of whether the Boy Scouts' teachings with respect to homosexual conduct are right or wrong. Public or judicial disapproval of a tenet of an organization's expression does not justify the state's effort to compel the organization to accept members where such acceptance would derogate from the organization's expressive message."*

The Boy Scouts of America website lists two documents. The first statement gives its position on supporting diversity; the second is a resolution declaring that homosexuals cannot participate in the organization at any level.

On June 28, 2000, the United States Supreme Court reaffirmed the Boy Scouts of America's standing as a private organization with the right to set its own membership and leadership standards. The BSA respects the rights of people and groups who hold values that differ from those encompassed in the Scout Oath and Law, and the BSA makes no effort to deny the rights of those whose views differ to hold their attitudes or opinions. Scouts come from all walks of life and are exposed to diversity in Scouting that they may not otherwise experience. The Boy Scouts of America aims to allow youth to live and learn as children and enjoy Scouting without immersing them in the politics of the day.

Boy Scouts of America Resolution (February 6, 2002):

5. WHEREAS, the national officers agree with the report that "duty to God is not a mere ideal for those choosing to associate with the Boy Scouts of America; it is an obligation," which has defined good character for youth of Scouting age throughout Scouting's 92-year history and the Boy Scouts of America has made a commitment "to provide faith-based values to its constituency in a respectful manner"; and

6. WHEREAS, the national officers agree that "conduct of both Scouts and Scouters must be in compliance with the Scout Oath and Law" and that "membership is contingent upon one's willingness to accept the values and standards espoused by the Boy Scouts of America," and

7. WHEREAS the national officers further agree that homosexual conduct is inconsistent with the traditional values espoused in the Scout Oath and Law and that an avowed homosexual cannot serve as a role model for the values of the Oath and Law; and

8. WHEREAS, the national officers reaffirm that, as a national organization whose very reason for existence is to instill and reinforce values in youth, the BSA's values cannot be subject to local option choices, but must be the same in every unit; and

10. THEREFORE, the national officers recommend the National Executive Board affirm that the Boy Scouts of America shall continue to follow its traditional values and standards of leadership.

In 1986, the Catholic Church issued a letter to the bishops of the Catholic Church concerning the care of homosexuals. The church's position has not shifted since that time. This letter is available on the web and is excerpted here.

"Congregation for the Doctrine of the Faith—On the Pastoral Care of Homosexual Persons: Letter to the Bishops of the Catholic Church" (October 1, 1986)

5. . . .There is a clear consistency within the Scriptures themselves on the moral issue of homosexual behavior. The Church's doctrine regarding this issue is thus based, not on isolated phrases for official theological argument, but on the solid foundation of a constant Biblical testimony. . . . To be correct, the interpretation of Scripture must be in substantial accord with that Tradition.

6. . . .He fashions mankind, male and female, in his own image and likeness. Human beings, therefore, are nothing less than the work of God himself; and in the complementarily of the sexes, they are called to reflect the inner unity of the Creator. . . . The human body retains its "spousal significance" but this is now clouded by sin. Thus, in Genesis 19:1–11, the deterioration due to sin continues in the story of the men of Sodom. There can be no doubt of the moral judgement made there against homosexual relations. In Leviticus 18:22 and 20:13, in the course of describing the conditions necessary for belonging to the Chosen People, the author excludes from the People of God those who behave in a homosexual fashion.

7. . . .A person engaging in homosexual behavior therefore acts immorally. . . .

10. It is deplorable that homosexual persons have been and are the object of violent malice in speech or in action. Such treatment deserves condemnation from the Church's pastors wherever it occurs. . . .

12. What, then, are homosexual persons to do who seek to follow the Lord? . . . Christians who are homosexual are called, as all of us are, to a chaste life.

15. We encourage the Bishops, then, to provide pastoral care in full accord with the teachings of the Church for homosexual persons of their dioceses. No authentic pastoral program will include organizations in which homosexual persons associate with each other without clearly stating that homosexual activity is immoral. A truly pastoral approach will appreciate the need for homosexual persons to avoid the near occasions of sin.

Concerned Women for America (CWA) is one of the most powerful pro–traditional family organizations in the United States. Its members are outspokenly antihomosexual. Here is a statement by the organization's president.

Homosexuality

By Carmen Pate, President, June 26, 1998

"Extreme! Backward!" Those are the terms the White House chooses to describe millions of Christians across America who believe in the Biblical truth that homosexuality is a sin. As one of those Christians, I am outraged. White House Press Secretary Michael McCurry said that the subject is no longer a matter for conscience, but for science. How reputable is your scientific authority, Mr. McCurry, in comparison to Almighty God?

McCurry refers to the claims of the American Psychiatric Association who in 1973 declared homosexuality normal. . . . Dr. Charles Socarides reported the process by which the APA task force removed homosexuality from the category of abnormality. He says, "The APA rationale for removing homosexuality relied heavily on the work of Alfred Kinsey and his belief in the normality of homosexuality. . . ."

A closer look at the small hand-picked APA task force reveals that the declaration was strictly Kinseyan. . . . Members of the APA task force included Kinsey Institute Director (at the time) Paul Gebhard. . . . Also on the task force was Kinsey Institute advisor John Money . . . who in the 1991 *Journal of Pedophilia* called for legalizing all adult/child sex.

How dare Mr. McCurry call Christian values extreme and backward! Thousands of young men and women who want to leave the homosexual lifestyle, who desire to be free from the disease and death that awaits them, are being given a hateful message from the office of our nation's President. They are being told that they can't change, that they are doomed to live the rest of their lives without hope. Speaking the truth to homosexuals is the most compassionate thing one can do. . . . You can call it extreme—or even backward—Mr. McCurry, but they call it love.

Westboro Baptist Church maintains a webpage called God Hates Fags. Reverend Fred Phelps has staged hundreds, if not thousands, of protest demonstrations around the world, including one at the funeral of Matthew Shepard. The document here contains the WBC's stated purpose.

Purpose

Good afternoon gentle friend.

Welcome to the Westboro Baptist Church homepage. This page is dedicated to preaching the Gospel truth about the soul-damning, nation-destroying notion that "It is OK to be gay."

"God Hates Fags"—though elliptical—is a profound theological statement, which the world needs to hear more than it needs oxygen, water and bread. The three words, fully expounded, show:

1. the absolute sovereignty of "GOD" in all matters whatsoever (e.g., Jeremiah 32:17, Isaiah 45:7, Amos 3:6, Proverbs 16:4, Matthew 19:26, Romans 9:11–24, Romans 11:33–36, etc.),

2. the doctrine of reprobation or God's "HATE" involving eternal retribution or the everlasting punishment of most of mankind in Hell forever (e.g., Leviticus 20:13, 23, Psalm 5:5, Psalm 11:5, Malachi 1:1–3, Romans 9:11–13, Matthew 7:13, 23, John 12:39–40, 1 Peter 2:8, Jude 4, Revelation 13:8, 20:15, 21:27, etc.), and

3. the certainty that all impenitent sodomites (under the elegant metaphor of "FAGS" as the contraction of faggots, fueling the fires of God's wrath) will inevitably go to Hell (e.g., Romans 1:18–32, 1 Corinthians 6:9–11, 1 Timothy 1:8–11, Jude 7, etc.). (If you are concerned with our use of the word "fag," please click here to find out why we use this word.)

The only lawful sexual connection is the marriage bed. All other sex activity is whoremongery and adultery, which will damn the soul forever in Hell. Heb. 13:4. . . . Better to be a eunuch if the will of God be so, and make sure of Heaven. Mat. 19:12. Better to be blind or lame, than to be cast into Hell, into the fire that never shall be quenched. Mk. 9:43–48. Abstain, you fools.

Youth Suicide: The American Academy of Pediatrics

The American Academy of Pediatrics (AAP) is the largest professional organization in the United States devoted to the needs of health professionals working with children. It has issued many position papers. The one here focuses on youth suicide and is available from the web.

Suicide and Suicide Attempts in Adolescents (RE9928)

ABSTRACT. Suicide is the third leading cause of death for adolescents 15 to 19 years old.[1]

The number of adolescent deaths from suicide in the United States has increased dramatically during the past few decades. In

1997, there were 4,186 suicides among people 15 to 24 years old, 1,802 suicides among those 15 to 19 years old, and 2,384 among those 20 to 24 years old.[1] In 1997, 13 percent of all deaths in the 15- through 24-year-old age group were attributable to suicide.[1] The true number of deaths from suicide actually may be higher, because some of these deaths are recorded as "accidental."[2]

From 1950 to 1990, the suicide rate for adolescents in the 15- to 19-year-old group increased by 300 percent. [4] Adolescent males 15 to 19 years old had a rate 6 times greater than the rate for females.[1] Suicide affects young people from all races and socio-economic groups, although some groups seem to have higher rates than others. Native American males have the highest suicide rate, African American women the lowest. A statewide survey of students in grades 7 through 12 found that 28.1 percent of bisexual and homosexual males and 20.5 percent of bisexual and homosexual females had reported attempting suicide.[6]

Gay and bisexual adolescents have been reported to exhibit high rates of depression and have been reported to have rates of suicidal ideation and attempts 3 times higher than other adolescents.[20]

Notes

1. Centers for Disease Control and Prevention/National Center for Health Statistics. (1999). *Death Rates from 72 Selected Causes by 5-Year Age Groups, Race, and Sex: United States, 1979–1997.* Atlanta, GA: Centers for Disease Control and Prevention/National Center for Health Statistics; Table 291 A.

2. American Academy of Pediatrics, Committee on Adolescence. (1998). Suicide and suicide attempts in adolescents and young adults. *Pediatrics, 8*(1):322–324. . . .

4. Centers for Disease Control and Prevention. (1994). Programs for prevention of suicide among adolescents youth adults. *Morb Mortal Wkly Rep CDC Surveill Summ, 43*:1–7. No RR-6. . . .

6. Remafedi, G., French, S., Story, M., Resnick, M. D., and Blum, R. (1998). The relationship between suicide risk and sexual orientation: results of a population-based study. *Am J Public Health, 88*:57–60. . . .

20. Remafedi, G., Farrow, J. A., and Deisher, R. S. (1991). Risk factors for attempted suicide in gay and bisexual youth. *Pediatrics, 87*:869–875.

Case Summaries

Obscenity or Free Speech:
ONE, Inc. v. Olesen (1958)

Dorr Legg and his friends at the Mattachine Society decided to publish a national monthly newsletter under the new organization called the ONE, Incorporated. The newsletter began publication in January 1953 and served as the voice of the homophile movement during its early years. In 1954, the Los Angeles postmaster seized copies of ONE magazine and refused to mail them on the grounds that they were "obscene, lewd, lascivious and filthy." ONE editors challenged the seizure in court. Two lower courts upheld the actions of the postmaster but ultimately, the U.S. Supreme Court overturned the lower courts in 1958. This was a "legal and publishing landmark" (National Museum and Archive 1996, 13). Material containing homosexual themes and information was no longer automatically deemed obscene and could be distributed through the mail service. Without this favorable decision, the gay rights movement would have been significantly delayed.

Employment Rights: *Norton v. Macy* (1969)

The issue of homosexuality and federal employment came to court in 1969. Clifford Norton was employed by the National Aeronautics and Space Administration. He was arrested by officers of the District of Columbia Police Department's morals squad in Lafayette Square (directly across from the White House) for a traffic violation after they saw him attempt to make the acquaintance of another man. He was fired from his job. He sued and the Washington, D.C., circuit court agreed that the government had failed to show a specific connection between the employee's potentially embarrassing conduct and any reduction in the efficiency of the department for which he worked. On the basis of this and related decisions, the Civil Service Commission issued a directive to federal supervisors in December 1973 that stated that "you many not find a person unsuitable for Federal employment merely because the person is a homosexual or has engaged in homosexual acts" (*Civil Service Bulletin* 1973). Later this concept was expanded by the enactment of the Civil Service Reform Act of 1978. Supervisors were directed not to discriminate against employees on the basis of conduct that does not adversely affect the performance of others. Finally, in 1998 President Bill Clinton signed an executive order specifically banning discrimination based on sexual orientation in the federal civilian workforce.

Teachers' Rights: *Morrison v. State Board of Education* (1969)

Morrison engaged in noncriminal same-sex conduct. The school board deemed his behavior "immoral" and revoked his teaching credential. The California Supreme Court held that teaching credentials cannot be revoked because of homosexual conduct unless school authorities demonstrate an "unfitness to teach." Importantly, the court required factual evidence of fitness rather than mere speculation about immorality.

Gay Right to Organize: *Gay Students Org. v. Bonner* (1974)

Initially, when the Gay Activists Alliance sought to obtain corporation status in New York in 1972, its application was rejected because the secretary of state believed that the purpose of the organization was to promote activities that were illegal in the state. A New York court overruled the secretary of state, saying that it was not unlawful for individuals to peaceably agitate for repeal of any law.

Teachers' Rights: *Ancafora v. Board of Education* (1974)

When Ancafora applied to be a teacher, he did not include the lesbian and gay organizations to which he belonged for fear that doing so would disqualify him from the position. When he was discovered to be a homosexual, the board of education transferred him to an administrative position away from teaching. The school board reviewed his personnel file and discovered that he had left off membership in Homophiles of Penn State from his teaching application. The board fired him, claiming he had falsified his application. The Fourth District Court agreed that his intentional misrepresentation was sufficient grounds to qualify the board's decision for the transfer and dismissal.

Military Service: *Matlovich v. Secretary of the Air Force* (1976)

In this celebrated 1975 case, Leonard Matlovich sued the air force to be reinstated after being dismissed for homosexuality. His story made the cover of *Time* magazine and was later made into an NBC TV movie. His suit dragged on to 1980 when a federal judge ordered Matlovich reinstated. Instead of reentering the air force, he settled for financial restitution and became a gay rights activist.

Teachers' Rights: *Gaylord v. Tacoma School Dist. No. 10* (1977)

A Tacoma school district discovered that Mr. Gaylord was a homosexual. The officials believed that being known as a "gay teacher" would automatically impair his efficiency as the teacher. He sued when he was fired. During the trial, the U.S. Supreme Court resorted to encyclopedias, including the *New Catholic Encyclopedia*, to conclude that homosexuality was implicitly immoral. As such, the Court surmised that Gaylord could not be trusted to teach students about morality, and his presence was considered disruptive even though he had been a successful teacher for the previous twelve years. This Court's opinion about the immorality of homosexuality contradicted the conclusions reached by the state, which had repealed its antisodomy law by the time of the trial.

Coming Out as Free Speech: *Gay Law Students Ass'n v. Pacific Tele. and Tel. Co.* (1979)

Coming out, in some states, is considered a political act protected by the First Amendment and the Due Process Clause of the Fourteenth Amendment. The California Supreme Court ruled in this case that a person's affirmation of homosexuality was analogous to expressing a political view and as such was protected under the state labor code.

Gay Students' Rights: *Fricke v. Lynch* (1980)

In this celebrated case, Aaron Fricke wanted to bring his friend Paul Guilbert to the Cumberland High School senior prom. The principal denied the request, saying that there was a "real and present threat of physical harm" toward the two boys. Fricke sued. At the trial, the judge acknowledged that the principal's fears were real but said that the school should have looked into ways of increasing security and instituting other safety measures rather than denying the couple the right to attend. The court recognized that attendance at a prom is "symbolic speech," much like marching in a parade, and thus merits First Amendment protection.

Child Custody by Lesbian Parents: *In re Breisch* (1981)

The state of Pennsylvania took custody of a preschool boy who had a speech impediment. The mother had a masculine appearance and wore men's clothing. At the time of the hearing, she lived with another woman who had two children living with them. The mother took notes at meetings with the social workers and refused, as a condition of custody, not to live with her lover. Her actions were construed by the courts to be "uncooperative." The state took custody of her child. When the mother appealed, the Pennsylvania Supreme Court decided that restricting her from living with her lover was not an act of discrimination and interference with her lesbian relationship, but rather an attempt to establish order to the child's life and to bring the mother and son closer.

Teachers' Rights: *National Gay Task Force v. Board of Education of Oklahoma City* (1985)

Lesbian and gay teachers in the Oklahoma City school system brought suit against the state to rescind a state law permitting punishment of teachers for "public homosexual conduct." This conduct was defined as advocating, soliciting, imposing, encouraging, or promoting public or private homosexual activity in a manner that may bring it to the attention of schoolchildren or school employees. "Advocacy," the Court ruled, is squarely within the protection of the First Amendment. Thus, teachers have the right to take political action, including advocating for lesbian and gay rights.

Sodomy: *Bowers v. Hardwick* (1986)

Michael Hardwick was a twenty-eight-year-old white gay man who worked at one of the well-known gay bars in Atlanta, Georgia. After a long night at the bar, he left at 7:00 A.M. with a beer in hand. He decided he did not want the beer and disposed of it in a trash can outside the bar before getting in his car to drive home. Police officer Torrick pulled Hardwick over to the side of the highway. He asked Hardwick where he worked. Hardwick's answer indirectly indicated to the police officer that Hardwick was gay. Torrick suspected Hardwick of drinking and asked where he had disposed of his beer. Hardwick was placed in the rear of the police car while Torrick drove to where the beer was discarded. He did not find the trash receptacle, and Torrick issued a ticket to Hardwick for drinking in public.

The ticket Hardwick was given required him to appear in court. There was a discrepancy as to whether the court appearance was on a Tuesday or a Wednesday. Two hours after the Tuesday court date, a warrant for the arrest of Hardwick was issued. Officer Torrick came to Hardwick's home to arrest him, but he was not there. When Hardwick returned home later that day, his roommate informed him about the officer's visit. Hardwick went to the county clerk. The clerk said that was impossible that a warrant for his arrest could be issued so quickly because it usually took at least forty-eight hours to issue warrants. Later it was discovered that Torrick had personally processed the warrant, the first time this had been done in more than ten years. Hardwick paid the $50 fine and thought the case was closed.

About three weeks later, Officer Torrick returned to Hardwick's home at 3:00 A.M. with the arrest warrant. The door was open and Torrick was allowed to enter the home by a house-guest who was half asleep on the couch. He did not know that Hardwick and his companion were together in Hardwick's bedroom. Torrick walked into the bedroom and discovered Hardwick engaged in oral sex with another man. Torrick proceeded to arrest Hardwick and his companion for violating Georgia's sex statutes. Hardwick was entitled to bail within an hour after arriving at the jail, but instead he was held for twelve hours and was subjected to harassment by other prisoners because they had been informed of the charges against him.

Hardwick was charged. Gay activists saw this as a perfect test case, and Hardwick decided to challenge the Georgia statute in federal court. Because the Georgia sex statutes do not refer to the gender or marriage status of an offender, a married heterosexual couple attempted to join Hardwick's action, but the court dismissed the married couple's claim.

Hardwick lost his claim in federal court, but won on his appeal to the U.S. District Court for the Eleventh Circuit. The case was appealed to the U.S. Supreme Court by Attorney General Bowers for Georgia. In a 5–4 decision, the Court ruled against Hardwick, stating that claims for "homosexual sodomy" as a protected right to privacy are "facetious, at best." The Court therefore established that lesbians and gay men have no right to sexual expression under the U.S. Constitution.

Interestingly, Georgia's antisodomy law would later play a role in ending Bower's public career. In 1998, Bowers resigned as attorney general to seek the Republican nomination for governor. He presented himself as a moral crusader who had helped defend Georgia against homosexual sodomy. However, during the campaign, it came to light that Bowers was involved in a long-term extramarital affair—a violation of Georgia's archaic sex law against adultery. Bowers's hypocrisy put a nail in the coffin of his political career, and he lost the race.

Employment Rights: *Price Waterhouse v. Hopkins* (1989)

Ann Hopkins was a successful senior manager and a candidate for partnership at Price Waterhouse. When her nomination came up, many partners at Price Waterhouse reacted negatively and accused her of being "macho," of "overcompensat[ing] for being a woman" (233). They suggested she needed to take a "course in charm school" and that to improve her chances of becoming a partner, she should "walk more femininely, talk more femininely, dress more femininely, wear make-up, have her hair styled, and wear jewelry" (233). Hopkins sued and prevailed, with the court stating:

> An employer who objects to aggressiveness in women but whose positions require this trait places women in an intolerable and impermissible Catch 22: out of a job if they behave aggressively and out of a job if they do not. Title VII lifts women out of this bind. . . . She had proved discriminatory input into the decisional process, and had proved that

participants in the process considered her failure to conform to the stereotypes credited by a number of decisionmakers had been a substantial factor in the decision.

Family Issues: *Braschi v. Stahl Associates Co.* (1989)

A New York City gay man was faced with eviction from his apartment when his lover of eleven years died from AIDS. The survivor's name did not appear on the lease. Rent control provisions precluded landlords from evicting "either the surviving spouse of the deceased tenant or some other member of the deceased tenant's family who has been living with the tenant." The man argued that he was "family," and the New York Court of Appeals agreed with that position. The court's precedent-setting decision helped establish the idea that lesbians and gay men can form legitimate families.

Asylum from Torture: *Matter of Toboso-Alfonso* (1990)

In the first case of a gay male refugee to be considered for asylum, Judge Robert Brown of the Court of Immigration agreed in 1986 not to return Fidel Armando-Alfonso to Cuba because of the documented mistreatment of homosexuals by the communist government ("Gay Refugees Tell of Torture" 1980). The Board of Immigration Appeals upheld the decision in 1990, and Attorney General Janet Reno in 1994 designated this decision as precedent for all other requests for asylum by homosexual applicants. As such, lesbians and gay men who are persecuted by their governments may be eligible to remain in the United States. To date, only a few lesbians and gay men have secured asylum in the United States because meeting the criteria for asylum is extremely difficult.

Child Custody by De Facto Parents: *Alison D. v. Virginia M.* (1991)

The nonbiological mother, Alison D., sued to have visitation rights with the child carried by her lover, Virginia M. Although she was not the legal parent and had not adopted the child, she argued that she was a de facto parent. The New York Supreme Court said that she may, in fact, be a de facto parent, but that such a category had no legal claims, including visitation rights, to the child. Alison lost her right to visit the child.

Solicitation: *Commonwealth v. Wasson* (1992)

Jeffrey Wasson engaged in conversation with a man for twenty to twenty-five minutes during which he invited the other man to "come home" with him. The other man prodded Wasson to provide details about the sexual acts in which they would engage. What Wasson described violated Kentucky's sex statutes. Unknown to Wasson, the other man was an undercover police officer who was wired for sound and was taping the conversation. At the end of the conversation, the police officer arrested Wasson for "soliciting" to engage in unlawful sexual behavior.

Wasson moved to have the charges dropped against him on the grounds that the sex statutes violated the state constitution. The trial judge, appellate court, and, finally, the Kentucky Supreme Court all agreed with Wasson, stating that "the guarantees of individual liberty provided in our 1891 Kentucky Constitution offer greater protection of the right of privacy than provided by the Federal Constitution" (Robson 1997, 30). This was an important decision because the court rejected many of the points made by the majority in *Bowers v. Hardwick* and recognized that privacy extended to adult consensual sex regardless of whether it was homosexual.

Same-Sex Marriage: *Baehr v. Lewin* (1993)

In December 1990, the Hawaii Department of Health denied marriage licenses to three gay couples. The three gay couples sued the department. In September 1991, circuit court judge Robert Klein threw out the case, ruling that homosexual marriage was not a fundamental right. The ruling was appealed. In May 1993, the Hawaii Supreme Court reinstated the lawsuit and ruled that the state's denial of marriage licenses to the three couples violated their rights as a form of sex discrimination. Sex has suspect class status in the Hawaii constitution and thus requires the highest scrutiny in legal review. The state was required to show a compelling reason to justify the ban. Circuit court judge Kevin Chang ruled in 1996 that prohibiting same-sex couples from marrying violated the state constitution's equal protection clause. However, an amendment to the Hawaii Constitution was passed by the voters in November 1998 that restricted the definition of marriage to opposite-sex couples only. As a result, the state supreme court unanimously overturned Chang's 1996 decision.

Child Custody by Lesbian Parents:
Bottoms v. Bottoms (1995)

In 1993, a grandmother sought custody of Tyler, her two-year-old grandson. The mother, Sharon Bottoms, was a lesbian. The grandmother argued that Bottoms's lesbian relationship made her an unfit mother. Bottoms argued that she was a fit mother and did not want Tyler visiting the grandmother's home because the man who had sexually abused Bottoms while she was growing up lived there. The trial judge agreed with the grandmother, and Tyler was removed from Sharon Bottoms. This case caused tremendous outrage in the lesbian and gay community. Later, the Virginia appellate court reversed the lower court and gave custody of Tyler to the mother. The court said that Bottoms's sexual orientation as a lesbian did not make her unfit to have custody of her child.

Discrimination by Private Organizations:
Hurley v. Irish-American Gay, Lesbian and Bisexual Group of Boston (1995)

A gay marching contingent applied to participate in the Boston St. Patrick's Day parade and wanted to carry a banner indicating gay pride. The organizers refused the application and barred the group from the event because of its intent to express a message in the parade contrary to that of the parade organizers. The gay contingent sued. The U.S. Supreme Court upheld the First Amendment right of the organizers to exclude gays from their event, not because they were gay but because they intended to promote a political belief contrary to the beliefs of the private organizers of the event. The Court said that parades are a "form of expression" and private sponsors cannot be forced to include groups that "impart a message the organizers do not wish to convey."

Constitutionality of Antidiscrimination Statutes: *Romer v. Evans* (1996)

In 1987, Boulder citizens approved an antidiscrimination ordinance based on sexual orientation. In 1989, Colorado governor Roy Romer issued an executive order prohibiting discrimination against people with AIDS. In 1991, the Colorado Civil Rights Commission recommended that the state adopt antidiscrimination statues based on sexual orientation.

In response to these progay laws, three religious right activists—David Noebel, Tony Marco, and Kevin Tebedo—formed a new organization, Colorado for Family Values (CFV). Their goal was to repeal the governor's executive order and the antidiscrimination laws already on the books in Aspen, Boulder, and Denver, and to prevent any future efforts to pass antidiscrimination laws aimed at protecting lesbian and gay people elsewhere in the state. They drafted constitutional Amendment 2, which was passed by the voters in 1992 with 53 percent in favor. Nine days later, a group of activists filed a lawsuit in the Colorado District Court for Denver.

At the first hearing, a temporary injunction was granted to the plaintiffs barring the state from implementing Amendment 2. Six months later, the case was heard by the Colorado District Court for Denver, Judge Jeffrey Bayless presiding. The state gave six reasons that Amendment 2 was constitutional. Judge Bayless issued a sixteen-page ruling adhering closely to the six justifications and the evidence introduced at trial. He rejected all state claims, saying the state failed to demonstrate a compelling reason to abridge the fundamental rights of lesbian and gay citizens.

The state appealed Judge Bayless's decision to the Colorado Supreme Court, asking the court to reverse the fundamental rights analysis. By doing so, the state hoped to lower the burden of proof from a compelling one to a rational interest justification. The court rejected this approach and reiterated its view that Amendment 2's ultimate effect was to infringe on the fundamental rights of the plaintiffs by prohibiting the adoption of laws, regulations, ordinances, and policies against discrimination based on sexual orientation. The court provided a step-by-step analysis similar to that prepared by Judge Bayless.

In 1995, the U.S. Supreme Court agreed to review the Colorado Supreme Court's decision. Besides the two primary parties involved, the Court accepted more than two dozen friend-of-the-court briefs from almost 100 organizations, cities, and individuals. The Court debate was similar to the previous court arguments. The Court characterized Amendment 2 as "unprecedented in our jurisprudence" in that it identified "persons by a single trait and then denies them protection across the board. . . . A law declaring in general that it shall be more difficult for one group of citizens than for all others to seek aid from government is itself a denial of equal protection of the laws in the most literal sense" (637). Also, Amendment 2 "inflicts on [gay people] immediate, continuing, and real injuries that outrun and belie any legitimate justifications that may be claimed for it" (638). The Court ruled (6–1) that Amendment 2 appeared to violate the fundamental right of lesbians, gay men, and bisexuals to participate in the political process on a basis equal to other Coloradans. Justice Kennedy stated, "We conclude that Amendment 2 classifies homosexuals not to further a proper legislative end but to make them unequal to everyone else. This Colorado cannot do. A state cannot so deem a class of persons a stranger to its laws" (639).

Harassment of Gay Students: *Nabozny v. Podlesny* (1996)

Jamie Nabozny experienced terrible abuse from other students while attending an Ashland, Wisconsin, high school. He was wrestled to the classroom floor while his teacher was out of the room, and then two boys pretended to rape him while twenty other students watched and laughed. He was also urinated on in a bathroom and kicked so badly that he required surgery to stop the internal bleeding. His parents complained, but a school official told them that he "had to expect that kind of stuff" because he was a homosexual. Jamie eventually moved to Minneapolis, where he graduated with an equivalency degree, but he sued the Ashland School District in 1995. Initially, the case was dismissed, but the Seventh U.S. Circuit Court of Appeals could not find any rational reason for permitting one student to assault another based on the victim's sexual orientation and thus allowed the suit to continue. A jury found that school officials violated Jamie's rights under the Fourteenth Amendment's Equal Protection Clause, and the district was forced to pay $962,000 in damages.

AIDS and the Americans with Disabilities Act: *Bragdon v. Abbot* (1998)

Sidney Abbot went to the dental office of Randon Bragdon for an examination. She revealed that she was HIV-positive on the patient registration form. Dr. Bragdon performed a routine examination, determined that she had a cavity, and told her that he would not fill the tooth in his office because of his HIV policy. Rather, filling the tooth should be done in a hospital setting and at her expense. She declined his conditions and filed a complaint under Americans with Disabilities Act (ADA) and the Maine Human Rights Act (MHRA).

Both lower courts determined that Abbot's asymptomatic HIV was a physical impairment and that she was disabled as a matter of law under the ADA. The U.S. Supreme Court used the case-by-case method of analysis—first used in *Ennis v. National Ass'n of Business and Education Radio, Inc.* in 1995 where the court decided that the plain language of ADA required each case to be analyzed by itself.

The Court decided HIV infection is an "impairment from the moment of infection" (*Bragdon v. Abbot*, 2203–04). Second, the Court agreed that HIV infection "substantially limits . . . [a] major life activit[y]" [42 U.S.C. § 12102(2) (1997)]. The Court noted this position was further supported by the Equal Employment Opportunity Commission (EEOC) regulation for Title 1, which states that a physical or mental impairment is "[a]ny physiological disorder, or condition, . . . affecting any one or more of [a number of listed body systems]" [29 C.F.R. §1630.2 (h)(1) (1997)]. The Court upheld Abbot's claim of discrimination under ADA.

The *Bragdon* decision is exemplary for finding asymptomatic HIV a disability under ADA. However, the Court failed to explicitly state that HIV infection is a disability per se. Although a few lower courts have accepted the argument that HIV infection is a disability per se (*Hoepfl v. Barlow*), only the future will reveal if the U.S. Supreme Court agrees.

Same-Sex Sexual Harassment: *Oncale v. Sundowner Offshore Services, Inc.* (1998)

A male worker claimed sexual harassment by his male supervisor and two male coworkers on an offshore oil rig. All parties in the case presented themselves as heterosexual. The Court established that Title VII of the 1964 Civil Rights Act disallowing sexual harassment in the workplace applied to same-sex sexual harassment claims. However, the Court continued, "the conduct that is not severe or pervasive enough to create an objectively hostile or abusive work environment—an environment that a reasonable person would find hostile or abusive—is beyond Title VII's purview (Harris, 510 U.S., at 21, citing *Meritor*, 477 U.S., at 67). . . . In same-sex (as in all) harassment cases, that inquiry requires careful consideration of the social context in which particular behavior occurs and is experienced by its target" (79).

Transsexual Name Change: *In re McIntyre* (1998)

Until recently, only transsexuals who completed or nearly completed changing over, including surgery, could have their names changed. With the case of Robert Henry McIntyre, the Pennsylvania Supreme Court granted permission to Robert to change his name to Katherine Marie McIntyre even though he had not begun surgical reassignment. The court followed the reasoning in *Commonwealth v. Goodman* and *In re Grimes* that the main purpose of name change statutes is to prohibit fraud by those attempting to avoid financial obligations. Furthermore, in *In re Eck* the court determined that it is not a matter of governmental concern when someone wants to change a traditionally female or traditionally male name. Thus, in *In re McIntyre* the court found no public interest in denying McIntyre's request for a name change and determined that his transgender status had no bearing on the matter.

Civil Unions: *Baker v. State of Vermont* (1999)

In December 1999, the Vermont Supreme Court found that same-sex couples in Vermont are entitled to the same protections and benefits provided through law as are given opposite-sex married couples. The Vermont Constitution contains an equal protection clause that guarantees all citizens the same treatment under the law. These clauses are similar to the equal protection provision of the U.S. Constitution's Fourteenth Amendment, which was used to secure civil rights for racial minorities, women, and other groups.

The court did not decide that same-sex couples were entitled to civil marriage licenses. Instead, the court referred the matter back to the Vermont legislature to craft a solution for same-sex couples. The legislature decided against marriage and instead created a new category implemented under a "civil union" program. Immediately, the religious right and conservative representatives called for the impeachment of the judges making this decision and a reversal of the decision. However, many powerful Vermont politicians took great pride in the fact that Vermont was the first state to outlaw slavery in 1777 and believed that lesbians and gay men deserved to be treated fairly and equitably. Governor Howard Dean stated, "We will remain in the forefront of the struggle for equal justice under law" (Dean, 2000).

Diversity Training: *Altman v. Minnesota Department of Corrections* (1999)

Often, employees are required to attend diversity training courses. In Minnesota, three prison employees protested having to attend workplace training on sexual orientation. They believed that the mandatory program was "state-sponsored propaganda" promoting homosexuality. The three men said that homosexuality went against their religious beliefs and that same-sex intimacy was sinful. The men took their Bibles to the training program and read silently during class. Afterward, the employees received written reprimands for violating prison policies prohibiting improper conduct and prejudicial behavior. Supervisors further charged that the protest was an attempt to impede efforts to prevent sexual orientation harassment. The men sued. In August 1999, U.S. district judge Ann D. Montgomery of Minnesota ordered the state to withdraw the disciplinary notices. Judge Montgomery decided that the employees' First Amendment right to free expression of religion and the Minnesota Constitution's freedom of conscience clause had been violated by the prison's actions.

Safe Schools: *Godkin v. San Leandro School District* (1999) and *Berrill v. Houde* (1999)

These two cases illustrate a current trend in First Amendment arguments. In both situations, parents complained that teachers made comments in class that the parents believed violated their religious liberty. The California U.S. District Court dismissed a suit by parents who claimed their constitutional rights were violated when Godkin, their son's teacher, made progay remarks in class at a San Leandro public school. The court saw through the argument and said the teacher's discussion of homosexuality could not be legitimately characterized as the imposition of a theology. In Berrill's case, the teacher told her high school homeroom class that students were not allowed to use derogatory terms about gay people in her room. Parents of one of the girls in the class complained, writing the Brookfield Board of Education contending that her remarks constituted "homosexual recruiting" and a promotion of a "homosexual agenda." Berrill sued the parents for defamation and settled out of court.

Student Rights to Form Gay Clubs: East High Gay/Straight Alliance v. Board of Education (1999)

In 1995, a group of lesbian and gay students at East High in Salt Lake City, Utah, submitted an application to form a gay-straight alliance on campus. The school denied the application. The students sued, citing the Equal Access Act. This act requires federally funded public schools that provide access to noncurricular clubs to extend the opportunity to *all* clubs without discrimination. In April 1996, the board terminated forty-six school clubs not directly linked to the curriculum in an effort to block the alliance from meeting on school property. The clubs that were terminated included Students against Drunk Driving and the Young Republicans. Many in the community blamed the gay students and "gay agenda" for the cancellation of the extracurricular activities. The lesbian and gay students still met, but off campus.

However, when they learned that at least one noncurricular club was allowed to meet on school property in the 1997–1998 school year, they sued again. Federal district court judge Bruce S. Jenkins ruled that the school district had violated the federal Equal Access Act and the students' First Amendment rights ("Gay/Straight Alliance's Lawsuit to Proceed against Salt Lake School Board" 1999).

A few months later, a federal judge dismissed the student lawsuit against the Salt Lake City School Board because school officials produced definitive policy guarantees that allowed the right to express progay opinions. However, the lesbian and gay students still wanted to meet on campus. Thus, they reorganized their original club to link directly with the curriculum. In February 2000, the students petitioned the school to form the People Respecting Important Social Movements (PRISM) academic club. The goal of the club was to discuss history through gay and lesbian issues and expand and enhance the study and understanding of American history and government. The school denied the application. The students sued. U.S. judge Tena Campbell granted PRISM a preliminary injunction because school officials had violated their own policy and the Constitution.

Discrimination by Private Organizations: *Boy Scouts of America v. Dale* (2000)

James Dale was involved with the Boy Scouts for twelve years. He obtained the rank of Eagle Scout, was elected to the Order of the Arrow, and became assistant troop leader in 1990 at age twenty. He never made his homosexuality known to the Scouts, nor did he mention or discuss the topic of homosexuality. That same year, he was interviewed in a college newspaper and was identified as the copresident of a lesbian and gay student group at Rutgers University. The paper ran a photo of him marching in the local gay pride parade. When the Scouts Monmouth Council in New Jersey discovered this fact, it expelled him from the organization. The Scouts told Dale that it "does not admit avowed homosexuals to membership in the organization" (Asseo 2000). Dale was expelled not for acting inappropriately "on" or "off duty," but rather for simply being identified as a homosexual.

Dale sued the Monmouth Council and the national organization in 1992. He contended that their actions violated New Jersey's antidiscrimination law. The state court threw the case out, stating that the Boy Scouts was not a public accommodation and therefore was not bound by state antidiscrimination laws. The case was appealed, and the New Jersey Supreme Court ruled in Dale's favor. The court rejected the Scouts' position that allowing homosexuals to participate would violate the Scouts oath to remain "morally straight" and "clean." The court decided that Boy Scouts was a public accommodation and was subject to state regulation.

On June 28, 2000, the U.S. Supreme Court reversed the New Jersey Supreme Court decision. It held that requiring the Boy

Scouts to include Dale in its ranks would violate the organization's First Amendment right of "expressive association." The Court said: "We are not, as we must not be, guided by our views of whether the Boy Scouts' teachings with respect to homosexual conduct are right or wrong. Public or judicial disapproval of a tenet of an organization's expression does not justify the state's effort to compel the organization to accept members where such acceptance would derogate from the organization's expressive message" (722).

Student Rights to University Funding: *Board of Regents of the University of Wisconsin System v. Southworth* (2000)

Some students with antigay religious convictions have sued their universities to stop funding LGBT groups. They claimed their money was being used to fund organizations of which they morally disapproved and this violated their First Amendment right to free speech and association. In a unanimous decision by the U.S. Supreme Court, the Court upheld university-funding systems that use student fees for all student groups. Because students contribute to a neutral fund that supports all viewpoints rather than a particular ideology, the Court ruled that the university did not compel any speech or violate the First Amendment.

Transsexual Rights: *Schwenk v. Hartford* (2000)

Douglas Schwenk, a self-identified preoperative transsexual who went by the name Crystal and dressed as a woman, received repeated unwanted sexual overtures from prison guard Robert Mitchell. Mitchell attempted to rape Crystal anally in her prison cell. She filed a federal lawsuit claiming violation of her civil rights under the Eighth Amendment (cruel and unusual punishment) and the Gender-Motivated Violence Act (GMVA).

Judge Stephen Reinhardt of the Ninth Circuit Court of Appeals concluded that Schwenk was protected under the Eighth Amendment since precedent had been set in prior transsexual prisoner cases (*Farmer v. Brennan*). He rejected Mitchell's argument that GMVA did not apply to the case because it was part of the Violence Against Women Act (VAWA) and Schwenk was a man. Reinhardt noted that members of Congress made opinions that supported the terms of GMVA to protect all residents of the United States from gender-motivated violence. Reinhardt found that the Supreme Court had, in fact, collapsed the concept of sex and gender into one broad category—gender identity.

Laws, Statutes, and Executive Orders

Affirmative Action

The term *affirmative action* was first used by President John F. Kennedy when issuing Executive Order 10925, which created the Committee on Equal Employment Opportunity. Later, President Lyndon Johnson signed into law the Civil Rights Act of 1964, which included provisions for affirmative action programs that were enforced through Executive Order 11246 in 1965. The Civil Rights Act provided protections for a few categories of people based on race, color, religion, sex, and national origin. These are categorized as "suspect class" for the purpose of strict court scrutiny. Contrary to the claims of the religious right, no national gay and lesbian organization has campaigned to include sexual orientation in affirmative action plans.

Americans with Disabilities Act of 1990 (ADA) (Public Law 101–336)

In 1987, a Florida court decided that tuberculosis was a disability protected by law (*School Board of Nassau County v. Arline*). This was an important decision because AIDS, like tuberculosis, is an infectious disease that often causes people to lose their job and face other discriminations. This concept of protecting those with disabilities was further developed by Congress with the enactment of the Americans with Disabilities Act (ADA) of 1990. Although it was not enacted to cover only HIV-infected individuals, AIDS was clearly on the minds of congressional representatives during the debate over this measure. In enacting the ADA, Congress intended to "provide clear, strong, consistent, enforceable standards addressing discrimination against individuals with disabilities" [§12101(b)(2)]. However, court interpretation of HIV as being a disability has been anything but consistent.

Civil Service Reform Act of 1978, 5 U.S.C. §2302(b)(10)

On the basis of *Norton v. Macy* and related decisions, the Civil Service Commission issued a directive to federal supervisors in December 1973 that stated that "you many not find a person unsuitable for Federal employment merely because the person is a homosexual or has engaged in homosexual acts" (*Civil Service Bulletin* 1973). Later this concept was expanded by the enactment of the Civil Service Reform Act of 1978. Supervisors were directed not to discriminate against employees on the basis of conduct that does not adversely affect the performance of others.

Civil Unions (91 V.S.A. Chapt. 23, Eff. July 1, 2000)

Vermont became the first state to give full legal rights to same-sex couples similar to those enjoyed by opposite-sex married couples, called civil unions. For complete details, see www.sec.state.vt.us/pubs/civilunion.htm.

Communications Decency Amendment (CDA) and Child Online Protection Act (COPA)

Many parents, congressmembers, and conservatives wish to censor information from the Internet in the belief that some material is harmful to minors. To achieve this aim, Congress passed the Communications Decency Act in 1996, which was struck down in *ACLU v. Reno I* as being an unconstitutional restriction of the First Amendment. Congress tried again in 1998 and created the Child Online Protection Act (COPA). Even though it was more narrowly focused, U.S. district judge Lowell A. Reed, Jr. issued a preliminary injunction barring COPA from going into effect after he determined that the ACLU was likely to win the case against COPA (*ACLU v. Reno II*).

Court discussion showed that there were major questions about enforcing the act. For example, the act claimed to protect children from "harmful" materials, yet no one could give a clear definition of what constituted "harmful" or give evidence that such material actually harmed. Second, the act required adults to divulge personal information such as credit card numbers to gain access to adult sites. The judges recognized that this would produce a "chilling effect" and radically reduce usage of the sites since some people would be reluctant to give that information. Third, the act specified that "contemporary community standards" would be used to delineate "offensive" material. However, the government could not clearly indicate which community and which standards would be used, given that the Internet is worldwide. Judge Reed concluded that the government was relatively helpless in trying to solve the problem of children's access to material that might be harmful to them on the Internet. Any kind of censorship of the Internet has impact for the gay rights movement because historically LGBT materials and discussion were automatically deemed obscene and censored.

Defense of Marriage Act (DOMA) (5/96 H.R. 3396)

This act provides that no state will be required to honor a law of any other state with respect to same-sex "marriage." DOMA defines "marriage" and "spouse" as a legal union between one man and one woman as husband and wife. According to Section 1738C:

> No State, territory, or possession of the United States, or Indian tribe, shall be required to give effect to any public act, record, or judicial proceeding of any other State, territory, possession, or tribe respecting a relationship between persons of the same sex that is treated as a marriage under the laws of such other State, territory, possession, or tribe, or a right or claim arising from such relationship.

DOMA also amends Chapter 1, Title 1, of the U.S. Code as follows:

> In determining the meaning of any Act of Congress, or of any ruling, regulation, or interpretation of the various administrative bureaus and agencies of the United States, the word *marriage* means only a legal union between one man and one woman as husband and wife, and the word *spouse* refers only to a person of the opposite sex who is a husband or wife.

Many states have enacted their own version of DOMA. See the next section for a discussion of how DOMA may be found unconstitutional. Summary and analysis are available from the electric law library at www.lectlaw.com/files/leg23.htm.

Full Faith and Credit Clause

The U.S. Constitution, Article IV, Section 1, reads, "Full Faith and Credit shall be given in each State to the public Acts, Records, and judicial Proceedings of every other State." This has been interpreted to mean that each state must treat the judgments of other states as the judgment would be treated in the state in which it was made. The clause is a "nationally unifying force" (*Magnolia Petroleum Co. v. White*) that recognizes that states are required to "sacrifice particular local powers as the price of membership in a federal system" of government (*Sherrer v. Sherrer*, 356).

However, there are limits to the power that the federal government can exert over states to accept one another's laws. Judgments of other states do not need to be respected if they are (1) "obnoxious" to the public policy of the state or (2) if the state can show that there are important, rather than merely legitimate, state interests for rejecting the other state's claim. When courts are faced with competing state interests and laws, this becomes a choice of law.

Choice of law is a notoriously murky area. It is sometimes difficult to determine which state's laws apply to a particular situation. In general, the Hague court explained that "if a state has only an insignificant contact with the parties and the occurrence or transaction, application of its law is unconstitutional" (*Allstate Insurance Co. v. Hague*, at 310–311). Further, courts have recognized that frequently the laws of one state and the contrary laws of another state may apply equally. Unfortunately, the U.S. Supreme Court has not stepped in to help clear up the confusion over the Full Faith and Credit Clause. The Court believes such conflicts are "unavoidable" and has left it for other courts to "determine for [themselves] the extent to which the statute of one state may qualify or deny rights asserted under the statue of another" (*Allstate Insurance Co. v. Hague*, at 547). The Court has decided that the alternative to this confusion is worse.

The prospect of same-sex marriages set off a storm of controversy nationwide. Confusion over the Full Faith and Credit Clause led Congress to enact DOMA. It was clear, however, from the debate in Congress that there was no understanding of how the current system works. DOMA (as well as legislation enacted in many states) defined marriage as being between one man and one woman and allowed states to not recognize same-sex marriages of couples who move into their state. This was unnecessary since states already possessed this power. Legal theorists believe that when the federal DOMA is tested in court, it will be declared unconstitutional for a number of reasons.

Don't Ask, Don't Tell, Don't Pursue Policy, U.S.C. Chapter 37, Title 10, Sec. 546 (September 16, 1993)

On July 19, 1993, President Clinton issued military directives that stated the following:

> 1. "Servicemen and women will be judged based on their conduct, not their sexual orientation."
>
> 2. "The practice . . . of not asking about sexual orientation in the enlistment procedure will continue."
>
> 3. An "open statement by a service member that he or she is a homosexual will create a rebutable presumption that he or she intends to engage [in] prohibited conduct, but the service member will be given an opportunity to refute that presumption; in other words, to demonstrate that he or she intends to live by the rules of conduct that apply in the military service."

Behaviors that would no longer initiate an investigation, or serve as the basis for separation, included association with known homosexuals, presence at a gay bar, possession or reading of homosexual publications, participation in a gay rights rally, or the listing of someone of the same gender as the person to be contacted in case of emergency or as the beneficiary of an insurance policy.

Has the policy been effective in reducing lesbians and gay harassment? No! "Since the regulations took effect in early 1994, the number of gays dismissed from military service has climbed 42 percent" (Graham 1997). A Pentagon report released in February 2000 revealed that expulsion from the military in 1999 was 73 percent above the rate in 1993, the year preceding Don't Ask, Don't Tell ("New Gay Discharge Figures Up" 2000).

Quotations

AIDS

"AIDS is character-building. It's made me see all of the shallow things we cling to, like ego and vanity. Of course, I'd rather have a few more T-cells and a little less character."
—Randy Shilts, author of *And the Band Played On* (National Museum and Archive 1996, 74)

"AIDS is not the only issue in the nation tonight. Be concerned about AIDS, but also sickle-cell anemia. . . . Be concerned about the human rights of gays, but also Native Americans trapped on reservations and blacks in ghettos. I would urge you, as I urge black people, the bigger you get beyond yourselves, the more you protect yourselves."
—Jesse Jackson, influential African American leader, addressing a gay fund-raising dinner in New York City (National Museum and Archive 1996, 78)

"I've learned that God doesn't punish people. I've learned that God doesn't dislike homosexuals, like a lot of Christians think. AIDS isn't their fault, just like it isn't my fault."
—Ryan White, sixteen-year-old person with AIDS (National Museum and Archive 1996, 79)

Being Out

"Better than I've ever felt in my life."
—Representative Gerry Studds (D-MA) after being asked how he felt now that he'd come out (National Museum and Archive 1996, 75)

"Did you see those two fruits? They were holding hands! I wasn't going to wait on them even if the store manager saw me blow them off."
—Salesclerk in a study to determine the difference in treatment made by sales staff toward heterosexual or homosexual couples (Walters and Curran 1996, 138)

"Every gay person must come out. As difficult as it is, you must tell your immediate family, you must tell your relatives, you must tell your friends if indeed they are your friends, you must tell your neighbors, you must tell the people you work with, you must tell the people at the stores you shop in. And once they realize that we are indeed their children, that we are indeed everywhere—every myth, every lie, every innuendo will be destroyed once and for all. And once you do, you will feel so much better."

—Harvey Milk, openly gay supervisor of the City of San Francisco, who was assassinated in City Hall by Dan White in 1978, in a speech following the defeat of Proposition 6, which would have barred homosexuals from teaching in California public schools (National Museum and Archive 1996, 79)

"I get so tired of these stories about, 'Oh, the torture and torment of coming out.' There's no torment in coming out. The torment is in being in."

—Armistead Maupin, writer (National Museum and Archive 1996, 76)

"Would you ask me how I dare to compare the civil rights struggle with the struggle for lesbian and gay rights? I can compare them and I do compare them, because I know what it means to be called a nigger and I know what it means to be called a faggot, and I understand the difference in the marrow of my bone. And I can put that difference in one word: none."

—Mel Boozer, after being nominated for vice president of the United States at the Democratic National Convention in New York City in 1980 (National Museum and Archive 1996, 69)

"We believe an avowed homosexual is not a role model for the values espoused in the Scout Oath and Law."

—Letter signed by Irene Szinavel, Boy Scout Exective Director for the Des Plaines Valley Council, to the seven Scout groups in Oak Park, Illinois, informing them that they could not renew their charter agreement with the Boy Scouts because they agreed with the local school district to treat all people equally "without regard to race, color, creed, sexual orientation, age, national origin, gender or disabilities" (Brown 2001, A3)

Existence of Homosexuals

"All 34,000 homosexuals had been tested for the virus with negative results."

—Russian Counselor Office reporting in 1989 the first two cases of AIDS and saying that they "were both foreigners" (*Frontiers* 1989, 20)

"We don't have homosexuals in Uganda, so this is mainly heterosexual transmission."

—Ugandan president Yoweri Museveni at the Commonwealth Summit in Australia, where he accepted an award for his government's work in slashing the rate of HIV infection from 28 percent to less than 10 percent of the population (*Frontiers* 2002, 19)

Judicial Commentary

"Heterosexual activity [was] meant to sway [her] from her lesbianism."

—Judge explaining why he dismissed all charges of sexual battery, assault, and kidnapping of a nineteen-year-old Ohio lesbian (Comstock 1991, 201)

"Gays and lesbians should be put in some type of mental institution instead of having a law [marriage] like this passed for them."

—Mississippi Supreme Court justice Connie Wilkerson in a letter to the *George County Times*, which ran on March 28, 2002 ("Judge" 2002)

"[They were] just all-American boys."

—Judge explaining away the brutal beating of a gay man by teenage boys (Valente 1984, B1)

"No matter how much society appears to change, the law on this subject has remained steadfast from the earliest history of the law, and that law is and must be our law today. The common law designates homosexuality as an inherent evil, and if a person openly engages in such a practice, that fact alone would render him or her an unfit parent."

—Alabama chief justice Roy Moore in deciding to give custody of three teenagers to their father rather than to their lesbian mother ("Ala. Chief" 2002)

"We conclude that Amendment 2 classifies homosexuals not to further a proper legislative end but to make them unequal to everyone else. This Colorado cannot do. A state cannot so deem a class of persons a stranger to its laws."

—Supreme Court justice Anthony Kennedy, ruling in *Romer v. Evans* that Colorado's Amendment 2 violated the fundamental right of lesbians, gay men, and bisexuals to participate in the political process on a basis equal to other Coloradans (Stewart 2001, 236)

Love

"I am the love that dare not speak its name."

—Lord Alfred Douglas, 1894, describing his love for Oscar Wilde (National Museum and Archive 1996, 68)

"When he died, I went to pieces. I retreated into a shell. For nine months, I wouldn't speak to a living soul. I just clamed up. I wouldn't answer the telephone and I wouldn't leave the house."

—Tennessee Williams, playwright, on the death of his lover Frank Merlo, from lung cancer, in 1963 (National Museum and Archive 1996, 71)

Military

"After more than fifty years in the military and politics, I am still amazed to see how upset people can get over nothing. . . . Everyone knows that gays have served honorably in the military since at least the time of Julius Caesar. . . . There is no valid reason for keeping the ban on gays. . . . The conservative movement, to which I subscribe, has as one of its basic tenets the belief that government should stay out of people's private lives. . . . Legislating someone's version of morality is exactly what we do by perpetuating discrimination against gays. . . . Congress would best serve our national interest by finding the courage to rally the troops in support of ending this un-American discrimination."

—Former senator and one-time Republican presidential candidate Barry Goldwater (Goldwater 1993)

"Our biggest mistake was unconditionally believing in them, believing that they were really not lying to us, placing too much power and too much faith in them. We should never have put our fate in one individual's hands, especially in a non-gay individual's hands."

—David Mixner, campaign manager for President Clinton, on Clinton's reversal on lifting the military ban in 1994 (National Museum and Archive 1996, 77)

"When I was in the military, they gave me a medal for killing two men, and a discharge for loving one."

—Leonard Matlovich's headstone (Thompson 1994, 341)

"The one thing I hate is faggots and niggers."

—Private Clavin Glover explaining why he killed Private First Class Barry Winchell at Ft. Campbell, Kentucky ("Soldier Pleads Guilty" 1999)

Presidential Commentary

"I don't want to see this country go that way. You know what happened to the Greeks. Homosexuality destroyed them. Sure,

Aristotle was a homo, we all know that, so was Socrates. . . . You see, homosexuality, dope, uh, immorality in general: These are the enemies of strong societies."
—President Richard M. Nixon in recently released White House audiotapes from May 13, 1971 (Weingarten 2002, A4)

"I find it extremely outrageous and repugnant to my human conscience that such immoral and repulsive organizations, like those of homosexuals who offend both the laws of nature and the morals of religious beliefs espoused by our society, should have any advocates in our midst and even elsewhere in the world."
—Zimbabwe president Robert Mugabe (Predrag 2001, 56)

"The Republic of Namibia does not allow homosexuality [or] lesbianism here."
—President Sam Nujoma, speaking to students at the University of Namibia (Predrag 2001, 56)

"Police should eliminate gays and lesbians from the face of the Earth. . . . Police are ordered to arrest and deport [homosexuals] and imprison [them], too."
—Namibia minister Jerry Ekandjo (Predrag 2001, 56)

"Other Christians and the general public must not condone, even by silence, obnoxious attitudes, increasingly promoted among a few demagogic religious and political leaders. . . . We must make it clear that a platform of 'I hate gay men and women' is not a way to become president of the United States."
—Former U.S. president Jimmy Carter (Carter 1996)

The Religious Right

"Homosexuals and lesbians are not only a sickness, they are an abomination which should be removed from every city in the country, also from those districts where they feel protected like in Tel Aviv . . . [and] put to death."
—Rabbi David Batzri, religious leader in Jerusalem ("Rabbi Wants" 2002, 33)

"I agree with capital punishment and I believe that homosexuality . . . could be coupled with murder. . . . It would be the government that sits upon this land who will be executing the homosexuals."
—Dean Wycoff, director of the Moral Majority of Santa Clara County, California (Young 1982, 77)

"I know what you feel about these queers, these fairies. We wish we could get in our cars and run them down when they march. . . . We need an emotionally charged issue to stir up people. . . . I believe that the homosexual issue is the issue we should use."

—Robert Billings, the first executive director of the Moral Majority, recognizing the solicitation potential in using homosexuality (Young 1982, 78)

"The country was founded by Christians. It was founded as a Christian nation. They're trying to sell us this nonsense about separation of church and state. And that's what it is, it's a fanatical interpretation of the First Amendment. . . . We're going to win this battle but we've got to stand together, all the Christians in America need to join hands together and say we've had enough of this utter nonsense."

—Pat Robertson, founder and director of the Christian Coalition (White 1997)

"When the Christian majority takes control, pluralism will be seen as evil and the state will not allow anybody the right to practice evil."

—Gary Potter, Catholics for Christian Political Action (White 1997)

"You just wait until 1996, then you'll see a real right-wing tyrant."

—Patrick Buchanan describing a future for the presidency in 1996 (Corn 1995, 12)

For more pages of quotes from antigay sources, visit the organization HateCrime.org websites: www.wiredstrategies. com/narth. html,/ phelps.html, /aftah.html, /claremont.html, /sheldon.html, /laura.html, /robertson.thml, /frc.html, /exgayspeech.html, /cc. html, /cameron.html, /relycameron. html, and /afa.html.

References

ACLU v. Reno I, 117 S.Ct. 2329 (1997).

"Ala. Chief Justice Says Gays Evil, Unfit Parents." 2002. *Gay and Lesbian Times*, February 21, 27.

Alison D. v. Virginia M., 77 N.Y.2d 651, 572 N.E.2d 27, 569 N.Y.S.2d 586 (1991).

Allstate Insurance Co. v. Hague, 449 U.S. 302, 310–311 (1981).

Altman v. Minnesota Department of Corrections, No. 98-CV-1075 (D. Minn., Aug. 19, 1999).

American Academy of Pediatrics, Committee on Adolescence. 1998. "Suicide and Suicide Attempts in Adolescents and Young Adults." *Pediatrics 8,* no. 1: 322–324. Available at http://www.aap.org/policy/re9928.html.

American Academy of Pediatrics, E. C. Perrin, and the Committee on Psychosocial Aspects of Child and Family Health. 2002. "Coparent or Second-Parent Adoption by Same-Sex Parents." *Pediatrics* 109: 341–344.

American Psychiatric Association. 2000a. *Fact Sheet: Is It Possible To Change One's Sexual Orientation ("Reparative Therapy")?* Arlington, VA: APA. Available at www.psych.org/public_info/gaylesbianandbisexual-issues22701.pdf

———. 2000b. "What Causes Homosexuality /Heterosexuality /Bisexuality?" Available at: www.psych.org/public_info/gaylesbian andbisexualissues22701.pdf.

American Psychological Association. 1998. "Amicus Curiae Brief for *Janice Ann Delong v. Fredrick Joseph Delong III, Guardian ad Litem.*" Available at http://www.psyclaw.org/delongbrief.html.

———. Amicus Curiae Brief for *Kimberly Y. Boswell v. Robert G. Boswell.*

———. 2001. *Guidelines for Psychotherapy with Lesbian, Gay, & Bisexual Clients.* Washington, DC: American Psychological Association. Available at www.apa.org/pi/lgbc/guidelines.html.

Amnesty International. 2001. *Crimes of Hate, Conspiracy of Silence: Torture and Ill-Treatment Based on Sexual Identity.* New York: Amnesty International USA. Available at: www.amnesty.org/80256770002C7290/ 0E0160F89337B69 3E80256A7200554E56?OPEN.

Ancafora v. Board of Education, 491 F.2d 498 (4th Cir. 1974).

Asseo, L. 2000. "High Court Takes on Gays in Scouts." Associated Press, January 14.

Baehr v. Lewin, 852 P.2d 44 (Haw.), *reconsideration granted in part,* 875 P.2d 225 (Haw. 1993).

Baker v. State of Vermont, 1999 WL 1211709 (Vt. Sup. Ct., Dec. 20, 1999).

Benkov, L. 1994. *Reinventing the Family: The Emerging Story of Lesbian and Gay Parents.* New York: Crown.

Berrill v. Houde, Connecticut, 1997 Conn. Super. LEXIS 1272. Oct. 13, 1999. Unreported.

Board of Regents of the University of Wisconsin System v. Southworth, U.S. No. 98–1189 (March 22, 2000).

Boswell v. Boswell, 25 Family Law Reporter 1103 (Maryland Court of Appeals, 1998).

Bottoms v. Bottoms, 444 S.E.2d 276, 281–83 (Va. App. 1994), rev'd 457 S.E.2d 102 (Va. 1995).

Bowers v. Hardwick, 106 S. Ct. 2841, 2843 (1986).

Boy Scouts of America. 2000. *Position Statements: In Support of Diversity.* Irving, TX: Boy Scouts of America, National Council. Available at: www.scouting.org/excomm/positions/diversity. html.

Boy Scouts of America v. Dale, No. 99–699 U.S. (2000).

Bragdon v. Abbot, 118 S. Ct. 2196, 2201–02 (1998).

Braschi v. Stahl Associates Co., 74 N.Y.2d 201, 544 N.Y.S.2d 784, 543 N.E.2d 49 (1989).

Brown, M. 2001. "Scouts' Honor Is Undermined by Anti-gay Policy." *Chicago Sun-Times,* January 29, A3.

Buchanan, P. 1988. *Right from the Beginning.* Boston: Little, Brown.

Carter, J. 1996. "It's Fundamentally Christian to Reject Politics of Hate: No One Should Condone, Even by Silence, the Persecution of Homosexuals." *Los Angeles Times,* February 23, B9.

Catholic Church. October 1, 1986. *Congregation for the Doctrine of the Faith—On the Pastoral Care of Homosexual Persons: Letter to the Bishops of the Catholic Church.* Available at: www.newadvent.org/docs/df86ho.htm.

Centers for Disease Control and Prevention. 1994. "Programs for Prevention of Suicide among Adolescents and Young Adults." *Morbidity and Mortality Weekly Report CDC Surveillance Summary* 43: 1–7.

———. 1999. *Death Rates from 72 Selected Causes by 5-Year Age Groups, Race, and Sex: United States, 1979–1997.* Atlanta: Centers for Disease Control and Prevention/National Center for Health Statistics, Table 291A.

Civil Service Bulletin. December 21, 1973. Quoted in *Aston v. Civiletti,* 613 F.2d 923, 927 (D.C. Dir. 1979).

Colorado, State of. 1992. *Amends Article II, 30.b of the Colorado Constitution* (known as Amendment 2).

Commonwealth v. Goodman, 676 A.2d 234 (Pa. 1966).

Commonwealth v. Wasson, 842 S.W.2d 487 (Ky. 1992) (Wintersheimer, J., dissenting).

Comstock, G. D. 1991. *Violence against Lesbians and Gay Men.* New York: Columbia University Press.

Conger, J. 1975. "Proceedings of the American Psychological Association for the Year 1974: Minutes of the Annual Meeting of the Council of Representatives." *American Psychologist* 30: 620–651.

Coyle, A. 1993. "A Study of Psychological Well-being among Gay Men Using the GHQ-30." *British Journal of Clinical Psychology* 32, no. 2: 218–220.

Dean, H. January 5, 2000. "State of the State Address." Montpelier, Vermont.

Delong v. Delong, Case No. 80637 (Sup. Ct. Mo. 1998).

Dignity USA. 2002. *FAQs: Catholicism, Homosexuality, and Dignity.* Washington, DC: DIGNITY/USA. Available at: www.dignityusa.org/faq.html.

DiPlacido, J. 1998. "Minority Stress among Lesbians, Gay Men, and Bisexuals: A Consequence of Heterosexism, Homophobia, and Stigmatization." In G. Herek, ed., *Psychological Perspectives on Lesbian and Gay Issues: Vol. 4. Stigma and Sexual Orientation: Understanding Prejudice against Lesbians, Gay Men, and Bisexuals.* Thousand Oaks, CA: Sage, pp. 138–159.

East High Gay/Straight Alliance v. Board of Education, U.S. No. 2:98-CV-193J (November 30, 1999).

Ennis v. National Ass'n of Business & Education Radio, Inc., 53 F.3d 55 (4th Cir. 1995).

Farmer v. Brennan, 511 U.S. 825 (1994).

Fox, R. 1996. "Bisexuality in Perspective: A Review of Theory and Research." In B. Firestein, ed., *Bisexuality: The Psychology and Politics of an Invisible Minority.* Newbury Park, CA: Sage, pp. 3–50.

Fricke v. Lynch, 491 F.Supp 381 (R.R.I. 1980).

Frontiers. 1989. (September 25): 20.

———. 2002. (March 25): 19.

Gay Law Students Ass'n v. Pacific Tele. and Tel. Co., 24 Cal. 3d 458, 156 Cal. Rptr. 14, 595 P.2d 592 (1979).

"Gay Refugees Tell of Torture, Oppression in Cuba." 1980. *The Advocate,* November 27, 15.

Gay Students Org. v. Bonner, 367 F. Supp. 1088 (D.N.H.), *aff'd,* 509 F.2d 652 (1st Cir. 1974).

"Gay/Straight Alliance's Lawsuit to Proceed against Salt Lake School Board." 1999. Press release by the Lambda Legal Defense and Education Fund, October 8.

Gaylord v. Tacoma School Dist. No. 10, 559 P. 2d 1340 (WA. 1977), cert. denied 434 U.S. 879 (1977).

Godkin v. San Leandro School District, (U.S. Dist. Ct., Calif., Walker, J., Oct. 1999).

Gold, M. A., E. C. Perrin, D. Futterman, and S. B. Friedman. 1994. "Children of Gay or Lesbian Parents." *Pediatric Review* 15: 354–358.

Goldwater, B. (1993, June 10). "Ban on Gays Is Senseless Attempt to Stall the Inevitable." *Washington Post,* A2.

Gonsiorek, J. 1991. "The Empirical Basis for the Demise of the Illness Model of Homosexuality." In J. Gonsiorek and J. Weinrich, eds., *Homosexuality: Research Implications for Public Policy.* Newbury Park, CA: Sage, pp. 115–136.

Graham, B. 1997. "Military Reviews Allegations of Harassment against Gays." *Washington Post,* May 14, A1.

Herek, G. 1990. "Gay People and Government Security Clearance: A Social Perspective." *American Psychologist* 45: 1035–1042.

Hoepfl v. Barlow, 906 F.Supp. 317, 319 n.7 (E.D. Va. 1995).

Hooker, E. 1957. "The Adjustment of the Male Overt Homosexual." *Journal of Projective Techniques* 21: 18–31.

Hurley v. Irish-American Gay, Lesbian and Bisexual Group of Boston, No. 94–749, (1995, June 19).

In re Breisch, 434 A.2d 815 (Pa. Super. Ct. 1981).

In re Eck, 584 A.2d 859, 860–61 (N.J. Super. Ct. App. Div. 1991).

In re Grimes, 609 A.2d 158 (Pa. 1992).

In re McIntyre, 715 A.2d 400, 401 (Pa. 1998).

"Judge: Put Gays in Mental Institutions. Rights Groups File Ethics Complaint over Judge's Letter to Newspaper." 2002. ABC News, April 12, ABCNews.com.

Magnolia Petroleum Co. v. White, 320 U.S. 430, 439 (1943).

Matlovich v. Secretary of the Air Force, 414 F. Supp. 690 (D.D.C. 1976).

Matter of Toboso-Alfonso (A23 220 644) (March 12, 1990).

Mills, K. I. 1999. *Why Reparative Therapy and Ex-Gay Ministries Fail.* Washington, DC: HRC. www.hrc.org/publications/exgay_ministries/change.asp.

Mohr, R. D. 1988. *Gay/Justice—A Study of Ethics, Society, and Law.* New York: Columbia University Press.

Morrison v. State Board of Education, 82 Cal. Rptr. 175, 461 P. 2d 375 (Cal. 1969).

Nabozny v. Podlesny, 92 F.3d 446 (7th Cir. 1996).

National Association of Research and Therapy of Homosexuality (NARTH). 2002. *Purpose.* Encino, CA: NARTH. www.narth.com/menus/statement.html.

National Gay and Lesbian Task Force. 1990. *Who Supports the Gay and Lesbian Rights Movement?* Washington, DC: NGLTF.

National Gay Task Force v. Board of Education of City of Oklahoma City. 729 F.2d 1270 (10th Cir. 1984), aff'd by an equally divided court, 470 U.S. 903 (1985).

National Museum and Archive of Lesbian and Gay History, comp. 1996. *The Gay Almanac.* New York: Berkley Books.

"New Gay Discharge Figures Up 73% since 'Don't Ask, Don't Tell, Don't Pursue' First Implemented." 2000. Press release by the Servicemembers Legal Defense Network (SLDN), February 1. Available at sldn-list@digitopia.net.

Newton, D. E. 1994. *Gay and Lesbian Rights: A Reference Handbook.* Denver, CO: ABC-CLIO.

Norton v. Macy, 417 F.2d 1161 (D.C. Cir. 1969).

Oncale v. Sundowner Offshore Services, Inc, 523 U.S. 75 (1998).

One, Inc. v. Olesen, 355 U.S. 371 (1958).

Parks, C. A. 1998. "Lesbian Parenthood: A Review of the Literature." *American Journal of Orthopsychiatry* 68: 376–389.

Pate, C. June 26, 1998. *Homosexuality.* Washington, DC: Concerned Women for America. Available at: www.cwfa.org/library/family/1998–06–26_homo.shtml.

Patterson, C. J. 1997. "Children of Lesbian and Gay Parents." *Advanced Clinical Child Psychology* 19: 235–282.

Perrin, E. C. 1998. "Children Whose Parents Are Lesbian or Gay." *Contemporary Pediatrics* 15: 113–130.

Pillard, R. 1998. "Sexual Orientation and Mental Disorder." *Psychiatric Annals* 18, no. 1: 51–56.

Plant, R. 1986. *The Pink Triangle: The Nazi War against Homosexuals.* New York: Henry Holt.

Predrag, S. 2001. "Slow Progress Despite Changes in South Africa, Gays in Neighboring Countries Sorely Lack Rights." *Frontiers* (September 14): 56.

Price Waterhouse v. Hopkins, 490 US 228 (1989).

Purpose. 2002. Topeka, KS: Westboro Baptist Church (WBC). Available at: www.godhatesfags.com/main/purpose.html.

"Rabbi Wants to Execute Gays." 2002. *Gay and Lesbian Times,* January 31, 33.

Remafedi, G., J. A. Farrow, and R. S. Deisher. 1991. "Risk Factors for Attempted Suicide in Gay and Bisexual Youth." *Pediatrics* 87: 869–875.

Remafedi, G., S. French, M. Story, M. D. Resnick, and R. Blum. 1998. "The Relationship between Suicide Risk and Sexual Orientation: Results of a Population-Based Study." *American Journal of Public Health* 88: 57–60.

Robson, R. 1997. *Gay Men, Lesbians, and the Law.* New York: Chelsea House.

Romer v. Evans, 517 U.S. S. Ct. 620 (1996).

Ross, M. 1990. "The Relationship between Life Events and Mental Health in Homosexual Men." *Journal of Clinical Psychology* 46: 402–411.

Rothblum, E. 1994. "'I Only Read about Myself on Bathroom Walls': The Need for Research on the Mental Health of Lesbians and Gay Men." *Journal of Consulting and Clinical Psychology* 62, no. 2: 213–220.

Rotheram-Borus, M., J. Hunter, and M. Rosario. 1994. "Suicidal Behavior and Gay-Related Stress among Gay and Bisexual Male Adolescents." *Journal of Adolescent Research* 9: 498–508.

Savin-Williams, R. 1990. *Gay and Lesbian Youth: Expressions of Identity.* New York: Hemisphere.

———. 1994. "Verbal and Physical Abuse as Stressors in the Lives of Lesbian, Gay Male, and Bisexual Youths: Associations with School Problems, Running Away, Substance Abuse, Prostitution, and Suicide." *Journal of Consulting and Clinical Psychology* 62: 261–269.

School Board of Nassau County v. Arline, 480 U.S. 273 (1987).

Schwenk v. Hartford, 9735870, U.S. 9th Circuit Court of Appeals (March 11, 2000).

Sherrer v. Sherrer, 334 U.S. 343, 355 (1948).

"Soldier Pleads Guilty to Non-Premeditated Murder in Murder of Pfc. Barry Winchell." 1999. Press release by the Servicemembers Legal Defense Network (SLDN), December 7. Available at sldn-list@digitopia.net.

Stewart, C. 2001. *Homosexuality and the Law: A Dictionary.* Santa Barbara, CA: ABC-CLIO.

Tasker, F. 1999. "Children in Lesbian-Led Families: A Review." *Clinical Child Psychology and Psychiatry* 4: 153–166.

Thompson, M., ed. 1994. *Long Road to Freedom:* The Advocate *History of the Gay and Lesbian Movement.* New York: St. Martin's Press.

Tuttle, G., and R. Pillard. 1991. "Sexual Orientation and Cognitive Abilities." *Archives of Sexual Behavior* 20, no. 3: 307–318.

Valente, J. 1984. "Gay Community Seeks Judge Nunzio's Ouster." *Washington Post,* May 19, B1.

Walters, A. S., and M. Curran. 1996. "'Excuse Me, Sir? May I Help You and Your Boyfriend?': Salespersons' Differential Treatment of Homosexual and Straight Customers." *Journal of Homosexuality* 31, nos. 1–2: 135–152.

Weingarten, G. 2002. "Just What Was He Smoking?" *Washington Post,* March 25, A4.

White, M. 1997. "Selected Quotes from *The 700 Club.*" In *The Justice Report.* Special edition. Laguna Beach, CA: Soulforce.

Wisconsin, State of. 1981. *Chapter 12, Discrimination Appended.* Sexual Orientation Discrimination in Housing (Section 12), Employment (Section 17), or Business Preferential Treatment (Section 25).

Young, P. D. 1982. *God's Bullies: Native Reflections on Preachers and Politics.* New York: Holt, Rinehart & Winston.

6

Directory of National and International Organizations and Associations

This chapter provides contact information, historical descriptions, and statements of goals for major organizations focused on LGBT and HIV issues. Both progay and antigay organizations are included. In each case, the contact information has been verified to be accurate at the time of this printing. The organizations are listed by category—AIDS, Educational, Family, Legal Support, Libraries and Archives, Media, Military, Minority Focus, Political Action, Professional Organizations, Religious, Schools, and Transgender (Transsexual, Transgender, Intersex). The chapter concludes with a number of websites that contain links to other organizations.

AIDS

AIDS Treatment News
PO Box 411256
San Francisco, CA 94141
Phone: (800) TREAT-1-2
Voice-mail: (415) 255-0588
Fax: (415) 255-4659
E-mail: aidsnews@aidsnews.org
Website: http://www.aids.org/immunet/atn.nsf/page/o-about

Begun in 1986, *AIDS Treatment News* is published twice monthly by John S. James as a resource for physicians and people living with HIV/AIDS who are looking for current, authoritative information on new therapies. Community-based organizations, government agencies, social and clinical professionals, and national media have come to rely on *AIDS Treatment News* for its accurate and timely reporting.

Publications: *AIDS Treatment News* (twice monthly).

CDC National AIDS Hotline
PO Box 13827
RTP, NC 27709
Phone: (800) 342-AIDS (2437)
Spanish: (800) 344-7432
TTY: (800) 243-7889
Fax: (919) 361-4855

The CDC National AIDS Hotline is a toll-free, twenty-four hours a day, seven days a week telephone service that offers anonymous and confidential HIV/AIDS information. More than 3,000 phone calls a day are handled by trained specialists (speaking in English, Spanish, or TTY for the deaf). Besides answering questions about HIV infection, specialists make referrals to appropriate social, medical, educational, financial, and legal services in the United States. Since its inception in 1983, the hotline has handled more than 13 million phone calls.

Publications: The hotline offers many pamphlets, booklets, brochures, and posters originating from other offices of the CDC, American Social Health Association, and related governmental agencies.

NAMES Project Foundation
101 Krog Street
Atlanta, GA 30307
Phone: (404) 688-5500
Fax: (404) 522-1673
E-mail: info@aidsquilt.org
Website: http://www.aidsquilt.org/Newsite

During a 1985 annual candlelight march honoring those who had died from AIDS, Cleve Jones asked fellow marchers to write on placards the names of friends and loved ones who had died. At the end of the march, he and others stood on ladders taping these placards to the walls of the San Francisco Federal Building. This newly formed wall looked like a patchwork quilt. Thus, the Quilt was conceived. Jones teamed up with several similarly minded people to formally organize the NAMES Project Foundation in June 1987. Today about thirty-five NAMES Project chapters exist in the United States, and worldwide there are forty-six independent Quilt affiliates. Nominated for a Nobel Peace Prize in 1989, the Quilt is now the largest community art project in the world.

Publications: *The Aids Memorial Quilt* (quarterly) and brochures.

National Minority AIDS Council (NMAC)
1931 13th Street, NW
Washington, DC 20009
Phone: (202) 483-6622
Fax: (202) 483-1135
E-mail: info@nmac.org
Website: http://www.nmac.org

In response to the misconception that AIDS is an exclusively gay white male disease, NMAC formed in 1987 to help bring awareness of this spreading epidemic to the minority community. NMAC provides technical assistance to community-based AIDS organizations serving communities of color, focusing on management problems and corrective actions. Conferences are held several times a month to discuss the AIDS agenda and program management. NMAC offers services in the set up and maintenance of treatment-related programs at the community service level. Additionally, NMAC's prison initiative cultivates working partnerships for promoting a national standard of care in correctional settings.

Publications: *NMAC Lifeline* (quarterly), reference manuals, and brochures.

Educational

Campaign to End Homophobia
PO Box 382401
Cambridge, MA 02238-2401
E-mail: barbarazoloth@earthlink.net
Website: http://www.endhomophobia.org

The U.S. Supreme Court's decision in *Bowers v. Hardwick* motivated the members of the Gay Rights and Homophobia Task Group of the National Organization for Changing Men to launch the Campaign to End Homophobia in 1986. Since the beginning, they have held annual conferences drawing more and more participants from the United States, Canada, England, and Israel.

The campaign develops teaching materials, curricula, pamphlets, class activities, and other educational resources for anti-homophobia workshops. These materials are distributed by Creative Response in Nyack, New York. One- and two-day intensive seminars are provided by experienced trainers to people wishing to increase their skill at teaching about homophobia. The campaign has built a strong support network of people and organizations working together to end homophobia and heterosexism through education.

Publications: *Guide to Leading Introductory Workshops on Homophobia, Opening Doors to Understanding and Acceptance,* and various other books promoting reduction in homophobia and heterosexism.

Lesbian and Gay Law Association
of Greater New York (LeGaL)
799 Broadway, Suite 340
New York, NY 10003
Phone: (212) 353-9118
Fax: (212) 353-2970
E-mail: le-gal@interport.net
Website: http://www.le-gal.org

LeGaL is a nonprofit bar association of LGBT legal representatives in the New York metropolitan area committed to the advancement of LGBT legal professionals, public education on legal issues concerning LGBT people, the advancement of civil rights, and the elimination of homophobia in the justice system. As a nonprofit organization, it supports the publication of *Lesbian/Gay Law Notes,* the nation's most comprehensive monthly update of developments in LGBT civil rights law; a low-income law clinic; and the Dr. M. L. "Hank" Henry Judicial Internship Fund.

Publications: *Lesbian/Gay Law Notes* (eleven issues/year).

Matthew Shepard Foundation
191 University Boulevard, Suite 724
Denver, CO 80206-4613
Phone: (303) 368-9636
Fax: (303) 368-9614
E-mail: info@matthewshepard.org
Website: http://www.matthewshepard.org

The Matthew Shepard Foundation was created as a nonprofit organization in 1998 by Dennis and Judy Shepard to honor the memory of their son, who had been brutally murdered in a gay bashing. The goals of the foundation include supporting diversity programs in education and helping youth organizations establish environments in which young people can feel safe and be themselves. To these ends, the foundation sponsors Judy Shepard to share her thoughts and values of respect and dignity through a national speaking program. Also, an educational partnership with New Light Media has produced the award winning documentary *Journey to a Hate Free Millennium* and other multimedia programs for use in classrooms and elsewhere.

**National Association for Research
and Therapy of Homosexuality (NARTH)**
16633 Ventura Boulevard, Suite 1340
Encino, CA 91436-1801
Phone: (818) 789-4440
Fax: (818) 789-6452
Website: http://www.narth.com

Charles Socarides, Benjamin Kaufman, and Joseph Nicolosi founded NARTH in 1992. They believe they have been the targets of scientific censorship due to their work on homosexuality. NARTH provides the mechanism to continue their research. NARTH is dedicated to affirming the male-female model of gender and sexuality and considers homosexuality to represent a developmental disorder. NARTH helps homosexuals find the psychological therapy needed to change their sexual orientation and become heterosexual.

NARTH's ongoing projects include an international referral service in the United States, Canada, Europe, and Australia to licensed therapists offering sexual reorientation treatment; continued research into the psychological factors associated with the gay lifestyle and its deviance; a worldwide survey of homosexuals who have changed; lectures by respected mental health professionals; scholarly publications; distribution of educational materials to all levels of schooling; distribution of NARTH's own pamphlet, "All the Facts," to counter the progay propaganda given to 14,700 school superintendents in "Just the Facts"; information for students about the availability of ex-gay ministries and sexual reorientation therapy; and efforts to make the public aware that some homosexual people do seek and achieve change.

Publications: "All the Facts."

Family

Family Pride Coalition
PO Box 65327
Washington, DC 20035-5327
Phone: (202) 331-8015
Fax: (202) 331-0080
E-mail: pride@familypride.org
Website: http://www.familypride.org/index.html

At the first national March on Washington in 1979, a group of men formed the Gay Fathers Coalition. It received tax-exempt status in 1984 and soon after changed its name to the Gay and Lesbian Parents Coalition International (GLPCI), reflecting the changes in the organization through the inclusion of lesbian parents. By 1990, it had become apparent that children of lesbian or gay parents needed support, and Children of Lesbians and Gays Everywhere (COLAGE) was formed as a new program under GLPCI. The needs of straight spouses of gay or lesbian parents were accommodated through the addition of a board seat for the Straight Spouse Network in 1995.

But families include more than just heterosexuals or homosexuals; they also include bisexual, transsexual, intersex, and transgender parents. Thus, in 1998 GLPCI voted to change its name to Family Pride Coalition to reflect the inclusion of a wide diversity of family structures. The mission remains to support and advance the well-being of lesbian, gay, bisexual, and transgender parents and their families.

Publications: *The Family Tree* (quarterly).

Gay Parent Magazine and *Ripe Magazine*
PO Box 750852
Forest Hills, NY 11375-0852
Phone: (718) 997-0392
E-mail: info@gayparentmag.com
Website: http://www.gayparentmag.com
E-mail: info@ripemag.com
Website: www.ripemag.com

Gay Parent Magazine addresses the needs of lesbians, gay men, bisexuals, and transgender people who are parents. *GPM* provides articles and references about gay parents' legal status and struggles, child rearing, and the emotional and practical issues of being a gay parent in a culture that otherwise does not acknowledge his or her existence. *GPM* has applied for nonprofit status and will soon be a 501(c)3 corporation.

Ripe Magazine provides articles aimed at older lesbians and gay men, who are practically invisible in U.S. culture. *Ripe Magazine* includes practical articles on, for instance, how to talk with the Social Security Administration, Medicaid, or other organizations that do not have a history of understanding the needs of older lesbians and gay men and their partners.

Publications: *Gay Parent Magazine* (bimonthly) and *Ripe Magazine*.

Lesbian Mothers Support Society (LMSS)
PO Box 61 Station M
Calgary, Alberta T2P 2G9
Phone: (403) 265-6433
E-mail: lesbianmothers@home.com
Website: http://www.lesbian.org/lesbian-moms/index.html

LMSS is a Canadian nonprofit organization that assists lesbian families through peer sharing of experiences, potlucks, children's activities, and support in a positive environment. LMSS also provides legal, medical, and psychosocial referrals as needed. LMSS interests include rights of nonbiological parents, access to insemination for lesbians seeking to become parents, custody issues in lesbian family breakups, and equal treatment of lesbian families in society. The organization maintains a reference library of books, articles, and essays, and videos.

Parents, Friends, and Families of Lesbians and Gays (PFLAG)
1726 M Street, NW, Suite 400
Washington, DC 20036
Phone: (202) 467-8180
Fax: (202) 467-8194
E-mail: info@pflag.org
Website: http://www.pflag.org

While watching a local newscast, Jeanne Manford saw her son attacked during a gay rights protest and the failure of the police to intervene. Shortly after, she marched in the 1972 New York Gay Pride Day Parade alongside her son. It was an eye-opening experience. Many young gay men and lesbians ran up to Jeanne during the parade and begged her to talk to their parents. She responded by creating PFLAG, a support group for families with LGBT member(s). Now PFLAG is a national nonprofit organization with more than 80,000 members and supporters and is affiliated with more than 460 organizations throughout the United States. PFLAG is probably the most influential and respected LGBT organization addressing the needs of families and friends experiencing the coming-out process of a loved one.

PFLAG promotes the health and well-being of the LGBT community and its families and friends via support, education, and advocacy. PFLAG provides an opportunity for dialogue about sexual orientation and gender identity and acts to create a society that is healthy and respectful of human diversity.

Publications: *PFLAGpole* (quarterly) and many authoritative pamphlets, booklets, brochures, and posters.

Partners Task Force for Gay and Lesbian Couples
PO Box 9685
Seattle, WA 98109-0685
Phone: (206) 935-1206
E-mail: demian@buddybuddy.com
Website: http://www.buddybuddy.com

Partners was founded in 1986 to provide information, support, and advocacy for same-sex couples. Initially, Partners published the *Partners Newsletter for Gay and Lesbian Couples,* which evolved into the quarterly *Partners Magazine.* By the mid-1990s, the magazine was discontinued, and Partners focused on publishing special issues and videos. In 1995, Partners produced *The Right to Marry* video, which featured interviews with Reverend Mel

White, Evan Wolfson, authors Phyllis Burke and Richard Mohr, and other activists. Most of this material has been placed on the organization's website.

Publications: *Partners Newsletter, Partners Magazine,* and *The Right to Marry* (video).

OutProud, the National Coalition for Gay, Lesbian, Bisexual, and Transgender Youth
369 Third Street, Suite B-362
San Rafael, CA 94901-3581
E-mail: info@outproud.org.
Website: http://www.queer.com

Started in 1995, OutProud is a web-based organization providing advocacy, information, resources, and support for queer teens just coming to terms with their sexual orientation and for those contemplating coming out. OutProud "lets them [youths] know they're not alone by helping them find local sources of friendship and support." At the site are many links to local support groups, such as PFLAG, local lesbian and gay community centers, and school GLSEN organizations.

WeAreFamily Foundation (WAF)
PO Box 30734
Charleston, SC 29417
Phone: (843) 766-2123
E-mail: Ciri@waf.org
Website: http://www.waf.org

Established in August 1994, WeAreFamily works for acceptance of lesbians and gay men within the heterosexual world. WAF focuses on the plight of lesbian, gay, and questioning children, who most often feel completely alone in a hostile world. WAF provides advice and counsel through the use of direct mail to teachers, counselors, clergy, and parents to encourage them to accept these children. The WAF website contains important links to local services from which children may obtain educational information.

Legal Support

American Civil Liberties Union (ACLU)
125 Broad Street, 18th Floor

New York, NY 10004
Phone: (212) 549-2500
E-mail: @aclu.org
Website: http://www.aclu.org/issues/gay/hmgl.html

The ACLU was founded in 1920 by Crystal Eastman and Roger Baldwin. Civil liberties were not strongly enforced by courts at the time. Women had just gained the right to vote, activists were sent to prison for distributing antiwar literature, racial segregation was the law of the land, sex discrimination was firmly entrenched, and rights for lesbians and gay men were unthinkable. The ACLU has been at the forefront of many of the most historically significant legal battles in the United States—the 1925 *Scopes* case challenging the right to teach evolution, the 1954 *Brown v. Board of Education* case that outlawed racially segregated schools, and the 1973 *Roe v. Wade* case that affirmed women's right to reproductive choice, including abortion. The ACLU was again there in 1996 protecting the rights of lesbians and gay men to participate in the political process when it was successful at overturning Amendment 2 to the Colorado Constitution in *Romer v. Evans*.

The ACLU is one of the largest and most influential civil rights organizations in the United States and has many regional offices. It issues press releases, position papers, friend-of-the-court briefs, and more.

Publications: Many pamphlets and brochures.

Gay and Lesbian Advocates and Defenders (GLAD)
294 Washington Street, Suite 301
Boston, MA 02108
Phone: (617) 426-1305
E-mail: gladlaw@glad.org
Website: http://www.glad.org

GLAD is New England's only public interest legal organization that focuses on defending the rights of lesbians, gay men, bisexuals, transgender and intersex people, and people with HIV. Since its founding in 1978, GLAD has been involved in most of the significant court cases affirming gay rights. The AIDS Law Project began in 1984 and fights discrimination against people with HIV. The lawyers at GLAD choose cases they believe will set a good precedent and have broad implications for the gay community. Besides these impact cases, GLAD fields more than 3,000 requests for legal advice and assistance each year. GLAD operates mostly with a volunteer staff and cooperating attorneys in good standing with one of the New England state bar associations. Unpaid internships are available.

Some of the recent cases in which GLAD has been involved include *GLAD et al. v. Attorney General Thomas Reilly et al.* (challenging the constitutionality of antisodomy laws in Massachusetts), *Doe v. Kelley (State Police)* (presenting evidence of police harassment of gay men), *Ayer v. Sommi and Keller* (reviewing fairness of domestic violence as applied to same-sex couples), *In re John/Jane Doe* (affirming Connecticut's sex discrimination prohibitions apply to transgender people), *Crandall v. Boston Concession Group* (defending against employment discrimination), *Goodridge et al. v. Dept. Public Health* (defending the right of same-sex couples to marry), *Baker et al. v. State of Vermont* (establishing civil unions in Vermont), and *Rubano v. DiCenzo* (affirming co-parent rights).

Publications: English and Spanish materials regarding LGBT civil rights and how to access the legal system.

Lambda Legal Defense and Education Fund
120 Wall Street, Suite 1500
New York, NY 10005-3904
Phone: (212) 809-8585
Fax: (212) 809-0055
E-mail: legalhelpdesk@lambdalegal.org
Website: http://www.lambdalegal.org/cgi-bin/iowa/index.html

Lambda Legal Defense is the nation's oldest and largest legal organization dedicated to the civil rights of lesbians, gay men, and people with HIV/AIDS. From its beginnings in 1973 when it had to fight in court to overcome a New York court denial of Lambda's application to become a nonprofit legal organization (it won in the New York Supreme Court later that year), Lambda has used impact litigation, education, and public policy to make the nation a safer place for lesbians and gay men. Test cases are selected for their likelihood of success in establishing positive legal precedents. With offices in New York, Los Angeles, Chicago, and Atlanta, Lambda's attorneys work on an average of fifty cases at any given time.

Lambda has a long history with many successes in fighting discrimination in employment, housing, public accommodations, and the military as well as fighting for equal rights in laws that affect marriage, domestic partnership benefits, antisodomy laws, immigration issues, antigay initiatives, and free speech.

Publications: Monthly newsletter.

Marriage Project—Hawaii
PO Box 11690
Honolulu, HI 96828
Phone: (808) 944-4598
E-mail: MPH@hawaii.rr.com
Website: http://www.members.tripod.com/~MPHAWAII

In December 1990, two lesbian couples and one gay male couple applied for marriage licenses at the Hawaii State Department of Health. The applications were denied, and attorney Dan Foley filed suit (*Baehr v. Lewin*) in the Hawaii State First Circuit Court alleging that the couples' rights to privacy and equal protection under Hawaii's Constitution had been violated. The Marriage Project was formed as a nonprofit organization to help fund the ensuing ten-year court battle. Even thought the voters of Hawaii passed a constitutional amendment limiting marriage to heterosexual couples, the equal protection aspects of the earlier court decision have not been addressed. The project continues and predicts that lawsuits will chip away at the legal limitations and that eventually same-sex marriages will be allowed.

National Center for Lesbian Rights (NCLR)
870 Market Street, Suite 570
San Francisco, CA 94102
Phone: (415) 392-6257
Fax: (415) 392-8442
E-mail: info@nclrights.org
Website: http://www.nclrights.org

Since 1977, NCLR has fought for the rights of lesbians in child custody and same-sex adoption cases. As a progressive, feminist, multicultural legal center, it advances the rights of lesbians and their families. NCLR currently focuses on the areas of same-sex marriage, child custody and visitation, alternative insemination, immigration and asylum, domestic partnership, adoption, and youth.

Attorney Kate Kendell, executive director of NCLR, states: "The current climate facing lesbians is a dangerous one. Although we are greater in number than ever before, so too are those opposed to our equality. Each stride we make toward securing our civil rights spurs a hostile and, at times, dangerous response. The best defense against such well organized and particularly well funded actions is systematic legal challenges to change such discrimination."

Publications: Several LGBT civil rights leaflets.

Libraries and Archives

Canadian Lesbian and Gay Archives
PO Box 639, Station A
Toronto, Ontario M5W 1G2
Phone: (416) 777-2755
E-mail: queeries@clga.ca
Website: http://www.clga.ca

The Canadian Lesbian and Gay Archives was established in 1973 to aid in the recovery and preservation of Canadian LGBT histories. The archive's goal is to acquire, preserve, organize, and give public access to information and materials in any medium, by and about lesbians and gays, primarily produced in or concerning Canada. *The Body Politic*, published in 1971, forms the core of the archives, which has expanded to more than 7,200 titles. In 1980, the archives incorporated as an independent, nonprofit organization. As the archives grew, it moved to larger and larger facilities, finally settling in a 2,000-square-foot building in 1992. The archives also maintains major nonarchival collections, including a research library, international subject files, and an international collection of lesbian and gay periodicals.

Publications: *Lesbian and Gay Archivist* (monthly) and many books.

June L. Mazer Archives
626 N. Robertson Boulevard
West Hollywood, CA 90069
Phone: (310) 659-2478
E-mail: mazercoll@earthlink.net
Website: http://www.lesbian.org/mazer

The archives was founded in Oakland, California, in 1981 and was originally called the West Coast Lesbian Collections. Six years later, it moved to the Connexxus Women's Center/Centro de Mujeres in Los Angeles. When June Mazer died, the archives acquired her name to honor her work as a community activist and invaluable supporter of the archives.

The archives is the largest lesbian collection on the West Coast. It is a nonprofit organization staffed completely by volunteers. It is dedicated to preserving materials by and about lesbians of all classes, ethnicities, races, and experiences. It includes more than 2,300 books—some extremely rare, such as the 1895 *Norma Trist*, feminist novels of the 1970s and 1980s, and the immensely popular "pulps" of the 1950s and early 1960s. More than 250 periodicals and 200 feminist publications are available, in addition to audio- and videotapes and rare photographic collections. Possibly the most important holdings are the personal correspondence between lesbians. These give insight into the daily lives and loves of lesbians of different eras.

Publications: *In the Life* (monthly).

Kinsey Institute
Morrison 313
Bloomington, IN 47405
Phone: (812) 855-7686
E-mail: kinsey@indiana.edu
Website: http://www.kinseyinstitute.org

The Kinsey Institute for Research in Sex, Gender, and Reproduction was founded in 1947 and is a private, not-for-profit corporation affiliated with Indiana University. The institute's mission is to promote interdisciplinary research and scholarship in the fields of human sexuality, gender, and reproduction.

The institute began when Dr. Alfred C. Kinsey was asked to teach a course for students who were married or were contemplating marriage. He discovered that few scientific data existed on human sexual behavior. What did exist was either extremely value laden or based on very small samples. Kinsey decided to collect his own data. Eventually, he and his associates gathered more than 18,000 sexual histories based on in-depth, face-to-face interviews. The results of the data were presented in two ground-breaking books, *Sexual Behavior in the Human Male* (1948) and *Sexual Behavior in the Human Female* (1953). The institute became a nonprofit organization in 1947 to which Kinsey transferred all materials by deed for $1.00. The institute has since published other important books on the topic of human sexuality. It is currently located in Morrison Hall on the Bloomington campus of Indiana University.

Publications: *Sexual Behavior in the Human Male* and *Sexual Behavior in the Human Female,* as well as more recent publications and the monthly publication *Kinsey Today.*

Lesbian Herstory Education Foundation (LHEF)
PO Box 1258
New York, NY 10116
Phone: (718) 768-DYKE (3953)
Fax: (718) 768-4663
Website: http://www.datalounge.net/network/pages/lha//

The Lesbian Herstory Archives of New York City is the largest and oldest lesbian archives in the world. The founders believed that women, and particularly lesbian culture, were not fully appreciated by mainstream publishers, libraries, archives, and research institutions. Thus, the only way to preserve lesbian culture and history was to establish an independent archives governed by lesbians.

LHEF began in 1973 as an outgrowth of lesbian consciousness-raising with the Gay Academic Union. It moved to Joan Nestle and Deborah Edle's Upper West Side apartment in 1976. They created a traveling slide show and took it to homes, bars, churches, synagogues, and elsewhere. As word spread of its existence, the materials flowed in. Through years of effort, LHEF was able to buy a building and move the entire collection to larger quarters. LHEF is an all-volunteer organization that strives to make the archives accessible to all women. The collection is community based and collects materials from all lesbians, not just those who are famous or published. Funding comes from the community.

Publications: *Lesbian Herstory Education Foundation Newsletter* (biannual).

New York Public Library Gay and Lesbian Collection
Curator of Manuscripts
Manuscripts and Archives Division, Room 324
New York Public Library

5th Avenue and 42nd Street
New York, NY 10018-2788
Phone: (212) 930-0801
Fax: (212) 302-4815
E-mail: mssref@nypl.org
Website: http://www.nypl.org/research/chss/spe/
rbk/igic.html

Like most gay and lesbian archives, the New York Public Library
Gay and Lesbian Collection began through the efforts of private
individuals. The Gay Activist Alliance collected items for its History Committee that later incorporated in 1982 as the International
Gay Information Center (IGIC). It operated as a community-
based repository until 1988, when IGIC directors decided to give
the collection to the New York Public Library. The collection has
continued to grow and consists of 4,000 books, mostly published
after 1950; 2,000 separate periodical titles consisting of tens of
thousands of pieces; more than 300 audiotapes and 40 videotapes
of interviews, meetings, forums, lectures, radio broadcasts, and
public access cable channel programs; and hundreds of linear feet
of other materials consisting of flyers, posters, announcements,
and mailings. Many of the leaders of the gay rights movement
have donated their personal papers to the collection.

ONE Institute and Archives
909 W. Adams Boulevard
Los Angeles, CA 90007
Phone: (213) 741-0094
Fax: (213) 741-0220
E-mail: oneigla@usc.edu
Website: http://www.oneinstitute.org

ONE Institute and Archives (ONE) is the world's largest library
and collection of lesbian, gay, bisexual, and transgender books,
periodicals, and other memorabilia. With more than 19,700 books,
1,500 films, 3,000 videos, 1,000 audiotapes, and hundreds of linear feet of files totaling more than 1 million items, ONE has become a major research center on LGBT life and issues. Special collections include AIDS History Project Lesbian Legacy Collection;
Performing Arts Collection; Twice Blessed—Everything Gay/
Lesbian/Bisexual/Transgender and Jewish; and Art Collection
(including works of Don Bachard, Philip Core, Raymundo Meza,
and Tomata du Plenty). ONE holds more than 6,850 different pe-

riodical titles, including recent and rare issues such as the lesbian newsletter *Vice Versa* from the 1940s and complete runs of *ONE Magazine* and the *Mattachine Review* from the early 1950s. The collection includes more than 500 magazines in 25 different languages. ONE's collection includes some of the earliest gay European publications, such as *Arcadie* and *Der Kreis*, as well as significant runs of *Gai Pied, SEK, Homologie, Der Gay Krant, Revolt,* and *Vennen.*

ONE Institute and Archives had its genesis from two different sources. Jim Kepner began collecting LGBT items in the 1940s and founded the International Gay and Lesbian Archives (IGLA). In the 1950s, the Mattachine Society set up ONE, Inc. to publish a newsletter in January 1953. By the mid-1990s, ONE and IGLA merged and placed the combined collection in a 30,000-square-foot building provided by the University of Southern California.

Publications: *The One Institute Newsletter.*

Stonewall Library and Archives (SLA)
1717 North Andrews Avenue
Fort Lauderdale, FL 33311
Phone: (954) 763-8565
E-mail: info@stonewall-library.org
Website: http://www.stonewall-library.org

The Stonewall Library began in 1974 as a project of the Stonewall Committee under the direction of Mark Silber. A few years later, the committee disbanded and Silber took the library into his personal care. In 1984, Sunshine Cathedral Metropolitan Community Church in Fort Lauderdale provided the library with a space rent free. It merged with the Boca Raton-based Southern Gay Archives, changed its name to include archives, outgrew its space, and moved to a 1,000-square-foot suite adjoining the Gay and Lesbian Community Center (GLCC) of Greater Fort Lauderdale in 1997. Less than a year later, it was forced to move to a smaller temporary space, with much of the collection being spread to three remote locations. Finally, in 1999 GLCC provided 1,500 square feet with an additional 800 square feet of space adjoining the entrance of the center. For once, the entire collection is housed in one location.

SLA contains more than 8,000 books, thousands of newspapers, periodicals and journals, and many items that are unique to the southeastern United States. The collection is the largest south of Washington, D.C., and east of Houston, Texas. SLA assistance has been noted in scholarly works, including the 1998 book *Lonely Hunters: An Oral History of Lesbian and Gay Southern Life, 1948-1968* by James T. Sears.

Publications: *Archeion* (Monthly) and *The Legacy* (Monthly).

Media

American Family Association (AFA)
PO Box 2440
Tupelo, MS 38803
Phone: (662) 844-5036
Fax: (662) 842-7798
E-mail: afa@afa.net
Website: http://www.afa.net

Founded in 1977 by Don Wildmon, AFA focuses on the influence television and other media have had on society. AFA believes in traditional family values and opposes pornography and homosexuality. It believes there has been a decline in morals in the United States that can be directly attributed to the entertainment industry. For example, it believes the dramatic increase in teen pregnancies, sexually transmitted diseases such as AIDS, and abortion stems from twenty years of national entertainment "normalizing" and glorifying premarital sex and "normalizing" homosexuality. It holds accountable the sponsors of programs that attack traditional family values. AFA encourages its members to support companies that sponsor profamily programming by sending postcards or making phone calls.

Publications: *AFA Journal* (monthly) and *Life@Work* (bimonthly).

Gay and Lesbian Alliance against Defamation (GLAAD)
8455 Beverly Boulevard, Suite 305
Los Angeles, CA 90048
Phone: (323) 933-2240
Fax: (323) 933-2241
E-mail: glaad@glaad.org
Website: http://www.glaad.org

Before 1985, the mainstream media in the United States were blatantly antigay and sensationalized stories about AIDS. Most publications, television, and movies did not even use the word *gay* or *lesbian;* instead they used negative stereotypes when describing or portraying homosexuals. Against that backdrop, GLAAD was founded to overcome the negative language and stereotypes used against lesbians and gay men. Although GLAAD began in New York by protesting against the *New York Post,* chapters were soon formed in Los Angeles, Atlanta, Chicago, Dallas, Denver, Kansas City, San Diego, San Francisco, and the Washington, D.C., area. The early battles were tough. It was not until 1987 that the *New York Times,* after meetings with GLAAD, changed its editorial policy to use the word *gay.* Soon after, GLAAD was instrumental in getting the *Los Angeles Times* to modify its stylebook to eliminate derogatory terms for gays and lesbians. Television and movie studios finally met with GLAAD in 1990. In 1992, *Entertainment Weekly* named GLAAD one of Hollywood's most powerful entities, and the *Los Angeles Times* recognized GLAAD's success at lobbying the media for inclusion.

GLAAD has five main strategies: (1) respond to negative and positive media portrayals of LGBT through the Monitoring and Mobilization Program, (2) offer seminars as part of the Outreach to Media Professionals Program to improve understanding of the LGBT community, (3) work with other LGBT organizations to help them understand the media, (4) promote LGBT visibility with positive public education campaigns, and (5) study and articulate cultural and media-specific trends.

Publications: *IMAGES* (biannually), *GLAADAlert* (biweekly), and *Access Denied.*

Gay/Lesbian International News Network (GLINN)
1107 Key Plaza, Box 306
Key West, FL 33040
Phone: (305) 849-5020
Fax: (305) 296-2015
E-mail: mediamaster@gaydata.com
Website: http://www.glinn.com

Launched in 1989, GLINN attempted to provide news services to the lesbian and gay media. Associated Press (AP) and United Press International (UPI) also targeted these same markets. Because AP and UPI had larger staffs and the ability to be full-fledged news services, GLINN had no choice but to scale back to being a BBS service with news. Later, UPI virtually went bankrupt and all other attempts by smaller news services to target the gay media failed. But the Internet has changed all this. By the late 1990s, GLINN began providing direct contact between reporting professionals working on lesbian and gay news. GLINN could provide something AP could not—news reporting from a gay perspective. More and more lesbian and gay media outlets now get news reports from GLINN. Also, GLINN provides a central market where publications and freelance writers, photographers, and others come together to do business.

Outfest
3470 Wilshire Boulevard, Suite 1022
Los Angeles, CA 90010
Phone: (213) 480-7088
Fax: (213) 480-7099
E-mail: Outfest@outfest.org
Website: http://www.outfest.org

Many independent LGBT filmmakers explored the issues of coming out, sexual repression, hate crimes, and more, but had no commercial outlet for their work. They came together in 1982 to launch the first Gay and Lesbian Media Festival and Conference, held in conjunction with UCLA Film and Television Archives. Later, in 1994, the conference was renamed Outfest to better reflect the dynamics of the community. Outfest has grown to become the largest film festival in Southern California and now includes weekly gay-themed screenings.

Yankee Samizdat
PO Box 165
Austerlitz, NY 12017
E-mail: Staff@YankeeSamizdat.org
Website: http://www.yankeesamizdat.org

Samizdat is Russian for "self-publishing" and means an underground press used by dissidents to tell "truth" outside established media channels. The Yankee Samizdat confronts the American press by challenging its anti-intellectual propaganda regarding homosexuality, abortion, and other leftist issues. To that end, Yankee Samizdat points readers to sources of information to "protect your families and lead a life free from the seductive manipulation of the new materialists, the pragmatic atheists."

Publications: *Yankee Samizdat* periodical.

Military

Gay, Lesbian, and Bisexual Veterans of America (GLBVA)
PO Box 3755
Washington, DC 20007
Phone: (301) 438-3650
E-mail: hank_thomas@hotmail.com
Website: http://www.glbva.org

GLBVA is a nonprofit association of active, reserve, and veteran servicemembers dedicated to full and equal rights and equitable treatment for all present and former members of the U.S. armed forces. Lesbians, gay men, bisexuals, and transgender people have always participated in, and continue to participate in, the military to help defend the principles of the Declaration of Independence and the Constitution. GLBVA believes LGBT people should be allowed to join and serve in the military openly without discrimination. Since 1996, GLBVA has worked in conjunction with Servicemembers Legal Defense Network and the Military Law Task Force to lift the ban against gays and lesbians in the military.

Publications: *The Forward Observer* (quarterly).

Servicemembers Legal Defense Network (SLDN)
PO Box 65301
Washington, DC 20035-5301
Phone: (202) 328-3244
Fax: (202) 797-1635
E-mail: sldn@sldn.org
Website: http://www.sldn.org

SLDN is the primary organization dedicated to defending the rights of lesbian and gay men in the U.S. military. Since its beginnings in the early 1990s, SLDN has grown to a staff of fifteen full-time employees and an annual operating budget of $1.25 million, with more than 11,000 members making donations. As a nonprofit organization, SLDN has assisted more than 2,600 military members in all fifty states, at sixteen foreign bases, and in all branches of the military. It has intervened to stop dozens of witchhunts, was instrumental in obtaining fair investigations into the murder of PFC Barry Winchell and gay sailor Allen Schindler, has documented antigay harassment throughout the armed services, and has worked to secure a better environment for homosexual miltary personnel.

Publications: *Conduct Unbecoming Reports, Action Alert, Survival Guide,* and other booklets.

Minority Focus

**National Association of Black
and White Men Together (NABWMT)**
PO Box 73796, NW
Washington, DC 20056-3796
Phone: (202) 462-3599; (800) NA4-BWMT
Fax: (202) 462-3300
E-mail: nabwmt@mindspring.com
Website: http://www.nabwmt.com

NABWMT is committed to overcoming racial and cultural barriers in the gay community. Existing in more than thirty cities, NABWMT chapters identify themselves as Black and White Men Together, Men of All Colors Together, or People of All Colors Together. They engage in educational, political, cultural, and social activities as a means of addressing racism, sexism, homophobia, and HIV/AIDS discrimination.

Publications: *The Quarterly* (quarterly).

**National Latina/o Lesbian, Gay, Bisexual,
and Transgender Organization (LLEGÓ)**
1420 K Street, NW, Suite 200
Washington, DC 20006
Phone: (202) 408-5380
Fax: (202) 408-8478
E-mail: info@llego.org
Website: http://www.llego.org

A Latino caucus was formed at the 1986 International Lesbian and Gay People of Color Conference in Los Angeles, California. This led to the formation of the National Latino(a) Lesbian and Gay Activists, which incorporated as Latino(a) Lesbian and Gay Organization (LLEGÓ) at the 1988 Segundo Encuentro in Los Angeles. Ten years later, LLEGÓ officially changed its name to National Latina/o Lesbian, Gay, Bisexual, and Transgender Organization while still retaining the acronym LLEGÓ.

LLEGÓ is a nonprofit organization made up of approximately 172 Network of Allies (Afiliados and Aliados), LGBT Latina/o capacity-building organizations, and those who serve the Latina/o LGBT communities. LLEGÓ is one of the largest Latina/o providers of capacity-building assistance in the United States. It focuses on overcoming social, health, and political barriers due to sexual orientation, gender identity, and ethnic background. It works to empower LGBT Latinas/os to obtain access to culturally appropriate health and wellness services. It works with mainstream communities, including the non-LGBT Latino/Hispanic communities, in addressing homophobia and sexism. LLEGÓ is the first national Latina/o organization servicing the LGBT community to formally sign an agreement of cooperation with the Small Business Administration and is one of only twenty-two funded National Regional Minority Organizations to work in partnership with the Centers for Disease Control and Prevention (CDC) since 1994. Much of the organization's website is available in Spanish.

Political Action

ACT UP/ New York
332 Bleecker Street, Suite G5
New York, NY 10014
Phone: (212) 966-4873
E-mail: actupny@panix.com
Website: http://www.actupny.org

ACT UP was founded in March 1987 by a group of individuals united in anger and committed to ending the AIDS crisis through direct action. It brings AIDS issues to the attention of government and health officials, researches and distributes current medical information, and engages in protest demonstrations. Recent activities include zapping (disrupting a speech) of New York governor George Pataki over his cuts in New York State AIDS budgets (1999), a march and rally in New York City (2001) to encourage "Stop Global AIDS NOW," and a day-long protest by the Thai Network for People Living with HIV/AIDS demanding that the Thai government's AIDS program—"Thirty Baht Health Scheme"—include antiretroviral treatment for AIDS (2001). ACT UP and DIVA TV archives are available at the New York Public Library.

BiNet USA
4201 Wilson Boulevard, Suites 110-311
Arlington, VA 22203
Phone: (202) 986-7186
E-mail: BiNetUSA@aol.com
Website: http://www.binetusa.org

Seventy-five bisexuals marched in the 1987 March on Washington and later met to convene the first nationwide bisexual gathering. In 1990, a national organization was founded as the North American Bisexual Network, later becoming BiNet USA. Its mission is to end oppression based on sexuality and to create a sex-positive world that celebrates and supports all types of people, including bisexuals. Fund-raising is achieved through donations to Project 387.

BiNet USA was instrumental in convincing the 1992 March on Washington to include "Bi" in its name. *Newsweek* picked up on a BiNet USA media packet in 1995 and transformed it into a cover story. Soon after, in 1996, BiNet USA met with the White House liaison for gay and lesbian affairs. The Policy Institute of the National Gay and Lesbian Task Force has teamed up with Bi-Net USA to develop public policy on issues affecting bisexual people.

Christian Coalition
499 S. Capitol Street, SW, Suite 615
Washington, DC 20003
Phone: (202) 479-6900
Fax: (202) 479-4260
Website: http://www.cc.org

Pat Robertson founded the Christian Coalition in 1989 to give Christians a voice in government. It gives profamily perspectives to school districts, state legislatures, city and county councils, and Congress. In 1998, to resolve the issue of its tax-exempt status, the Christian Coalition split into two groups: the Christian Coalition International, which openly endorses candidates and makes campaign contributions, and the tax-exempt Christian Coalition of America (formerly the Christian Coalition of Texas).

Concerned Women for America (CWA)
1015 Fifteenth Street, NW, Suite 1100
Washington, DC 20005
Phone: (202) 488-7000
Fax: (202) 488-0806
E-mail: mail@cwfa.org
Website: www.cwfa.org

Beverly LaHaye was stirred to action while watching a television interview of Betty Friedan (founder of the National Organization for Women). LaHaye did not believe Friedan was speaking for the majority of women in America. LaHaye spoke later that year to 1,200 Christian women about defeating the Equal Rights Amendment. They were overwhelmingly supportive and came together to launch Concerned Women for America. Officially incorporated in 1979, CWA has been at the forefront in the battles over abortion, gay rights, sex education, pornography, and more. The mission of CWA is to promote and protect biblical values through prayer, education, and political means. As a protraditional Christian family organization, it is the leading organization fighting against gay rights. CWA was instrumental in funding the legal battles over same-sex marriage in Hawaii and Alaska, the federal passage of the Defense of Marriage Act (DOMA), the Boy Scouts case with the U.S. Supreme Court, and others. CWA has more than 500,000 members and 15,609 online subscribers.

Publications: *Family Voice* magazine (bimonthly).

Gay and Lesbian Victory Fund
1705 DeSales Street, NW, Suite 500
Washington, DC 20036
Phone: (202) 842-8679
Fax: (202) 289-3863
E-mail: jsiegel@victoryfund.org
Website: http://www.victoryfund.org

Founded in 1991, the Gay and Lesbian Victory Fund has become the leading national political organization that recruits, trains, and supports open lesbian, gay, bisexual, and transgender candidates and officials. The fund has supported qualified candidates in thirty-four states and the District of Columbia and has helped quadruple the number of openly gay officials. It has a membership of over 9,000 nationwide and is the largest nonconnected political action committee (PAC). Since its inception, the fund has raised more than $3 million to support the campaigns of qualified openly gay and lesbian candidates. Donors are able to target their donations to particular candidates, thus giving small donors a major impact that would otherwise be lost by donating to larger political parties.

Human Rights Campaign (HRC)
919 18th Street, NW, Suite 800
Washington, DC 20006
Phone: (202) 628-4160
TTY: (202) 216-1572
Fax: (202) 347-5323
E-mail: hrc@hrc.org
Website: http://www.hrc.org

Founded in 1980, HRC is the nation's largest gay and lesbian organization. HRC effectively lobbies Congress, mobilizes grassroots organizations in diverse communities, supports elections of fair-minded representatives, and increases public understanding of the issues through innovative educational programs. With more than 400,000 members, both gay and nongay, HRC is committed to equality based on sexual orientation and gender expression and identity. The organization works to make the United States safe for lesbians, gay men, bisexuals, and transgender people.

HRC has many programs aimed at (1) protecting gays from job discrimination, (2) protecting communities from hate violence, (3) advancing public policy on HIV/AIDS and lesbian health, (4) protecting families and advocating for fair treatment under federal law, and (5) ensuring a fair-minded judiciary. Members are kept updated through Action Networks from which tens of thousands of members receive regular *Action Alerts* on HRC's legislative and campaign efforts. HRC partners with statewide and national organizations to pass progay ballot measures and defeat antigay ones. HRC is also a major research institute conducting polls and other measures of the political landscape.

HRC Foundation, affiliated with HRC, provides educational programs for families and the workplace and was the original sponsor of National Coming-Out Day. The foundation is the publishing arm of HRC, with many books and pamphlets, including ones that review the failed effort by the religious right to obtain change in sexual orientation through reparative therapy.

Publications: *HRC Quarterly* (quarterly), many major pamphlets and brochures, and a Spanish-language booklet for coming out of the closet.

Log Cabin Republicans (LCR)
1633 Q Street, NW, Suite 210
Washington, DC 20009
Phone: (202) 347-5306
Fax: (202) 347-5224
E-mail: info@lcr.org
Website: http://www.lcr.org

Log Cabin Republicans was founded to fight the nation's first antigay ballot measure—Proposition 6 in California in 1978. LCR was able to enlist Republican Ronald Reagan to publicly oppose the measure—which was overwhelmingly defeated. Since then, LCR has become the nation's largest lesbian and gay Republican organization, with more than fifty chapters across the nation and a staffed office in Washington, D.C. LCR raises more than $100,000 per election for Republican candidates.

LCR believes in Republican values—limited government, individual liberty, individual responsibility, free markets, and a strong national defense. Its members also believe that these principles and the moral values that underlie them are consistent with the pursuit of equal treatment under the law for gay men and women. Further, LCR members believe that Republican core principles best serve the interests of the gay community.

Publications: *LCR Inclusion Wins* (weekly).

National Gay and Lesbian Task Force (NGLTF)
1700 Kalorama Road, NW
Washington, DC 20009-2624
Phone: (202) 332-6483
Fax: (202) 332-0207
TTY: (202) 332-6219
E-mail: ngltf@ngltf.org
Website: http://www.ngltf.org

NGLTF is one of the most influential LGBT organizations in the United States. It builds political strength through the use of proactive campaigns focusing on state-level legislative work and aligning with grassroots organizers to advocate for civil rights. NGLTF organizes activists, trains leaders, equips organizers, mobilizes voters, and builds coalitions. NGLTF is recognized as an expert in LGBT-related state and federal legislation and uses a comprehensive program to track, monitor, and report what is happening.

For example, in 1973 NGLTF worked to change the American Psychiatric Association's classification of homosexuality as a mental illness. In 1975 NGLTF worked on the introduction of the first gay rights bill in the U.S. Congress. In 2000, it helped coordinate Federal Partnerships Day, advocating federal funding of LGBT community centers.

Publications: *Discrimination Social y la Salud: El Caso de los Hombres Latinos Homosexuales y el Riesgo de Infección por HIV* (July 2001), *The 2000 National Election Study and Gay and Lesbian Rights: Support for Equality Grows* (June 2001), *Transgender Equality: A Handbook for Activists and Policymakers* (June 2000), *Legislating Equality: A Review of Laws Affecting Gay, Lesbian, Bisexual, and Transgendered People in the United States* (January 2000), and *Domestic Partnership Organizing Manual for Employee Benefits* (June 1999).

Oregon Citizens Alliance (OCA)
PO Box 9276
Brooks, OR 97305
Phone: (503) 463-0653
Fax: (503) 463-8745
E-mail: oca@oregoncitizensalliance.org
Website: http://www.oregoncitizensalliance.org

OCA grew out of the Joe Lutz for U.S. Senate campaign and was formed by Lon T. Mabon in February 1987. (Mabon is a Bible teacher and owns an adult retirement home in southern Oregon.) OCA launched the No Special Rights Committee the next year and was instrumental in passing Measure 8—revoking Governor Neil Goldschmidt's executive order giving equal legal protection based on sexual orientation. In 1990, OCA, in coalition with other organizations, sponsored an initiative that would have banned 95 percent of all abortions in Oregon. The initiative was defeated. In 1992, the No Special Rights Committee placed on the ballot a state initiative designed to prevent special rights for homosexuals. It, too, did not pass. The same initiative was reworded and placed on the 1994 ballot and again did not pass. As an alternative approach, OCA was successful in placing pro-OCA candidates into office in seven counties and nineteen cities. However, the state legislature passed a law that removed antidiscrimination ordinances from local authority, thus negating the local approach.

In November 2000, OCA placed on the ballot the Student Protection Act, which would have prohibited public schools from "promoting the homosexual lifestyle." The initiative lost by 3.5 percent. A second attempt was made in 2002 to place the Student Protection Act 2 on the ballot. It failed to get enough signatures.

Publications: *The Oregon Alliance.*

Stonewall Democrats
PO Box 9330
Washington, DC 20005
Phone: (202) 625-1382
Fax: (202) 625-1383
E-mail: info@stonewalldemocrats.org
Website: http://www.stonewalldemocrats.org

When the Stonewall Democrats began thirty years ago, neither the Republicans nor Democrats stood against the prejudice that blights the lives of LGBT people. Through years of campaigning, the Democratic Party has become a champion for gay rights. President Bill Clinton was very supportive and broke the barriers by appointing openly LGBT people to high federal office, issuing policies prohibiting discrimination in federal employment based on sexual orientation, and taking other actions. However, Clinton failed to support LGBT rights related to the military and marriage. The Republican Party has hardened its stance against LGBT rights and consistently blocks any attempts made by Democrats to gain equal rights for LGBT people.

The Stonewall Democrats is committed as Democrats to improving the rights and liberties of all persons. The organization works to help nominate Democratic candidates at every government level who are fully supportive of LGBT rights. Unlike other political organizations, it foresees a time when it will disband because all of its goals will have been met.

Publications: *The National Stonewall Democrats.*

Professional Organizations

Gay and Lesbian Medical Association (GLMA)
459 Fulton Street, Suite 107
San Francisco, CA 94102
Phone: (415) 255-4547
Fax: (415) 255-4784
E-mail: info@glma.org
Website: http://www.glma.org

GLMA is a nonprofit organization seeking to end homophobia in health care. Founded in 1981 as the American Association of Physicians for Human Rights (AAPHR), GLMA/AAPHR influenced public policy in developing equitable health care for lesbians and gays. GLMA created a successful campaign to ban discrimination based on sexual orientation within the American Medical Association. In 1998 GLMA set up GLMA*PAN, a physicians' advocacy network designed to influence public policy on issues crucial to LGBT health. GLMA has initiated diverse programs such as the Lesbian Health Fund (LHF), which focuses on education of primary care providers on lesbian health and conducts cultural sensitivity training. LHF has granted more than $335,000 to address the health concerns of lesbian patients.

Publications: *Journal of the Gay and Lesbian Medical Association* (quarterly) and *GLMA Report* (quarterly).

Golden State Peace Officers Association (GSPOA)
1125 McCadden Place
Los Angeles, CA 90038
Phone: (323) 962-5555
Fax: (323) 962-5500
E-mail: gspoa@gspoa.com
Website: http://www.gspoa.com

Beginning in 1979, a group of gay male San Francisco deputy sheriffs and police officers met for a yearly retreat at the Russian River, California. This party affectionately became known as "Pigs in Paradise." As it grew, a more structured organization evolved, and GSPOA incorporated in 1985. More than 400 men and women from both law enforcement and fire fighting have since joined. GSPOA holds monthly meetings, schedules social events, raises money through special events for distribution to other LGBT organizations, helps with recruitment with agency support, consults on academy diversity training, and sponsors a yearly educational conference. GSPOA maintains strict confidentiality of its membership and provides professional educational services to law enforcement and fire fighting agencies.

Publications: *Hogcaller* (newsletter).

International Association of Lesbian and Gay Judges (IALGJ)
Bronx Criminal Court
215 E. 161st Street
Bronx, NY 10451
Phone: (718) 590-2941
E-mail: mrsonberg@abanet.org
Website: http://home.att.net/~ialgj/

Twenty-five lesbian and gay judges and judicial officers met in April 1993 in suburban Washington, D.C., and formed IALGJ. They wanted to provide a forum in which judicial officers could meet and exchange views and promote education among members. They believed it was important to have openly LGBT judicial officers to serve as role models for other LGBT judicial officers and to bring their existences to general public attention. Most importantly, they want to ensure the equal treatment of all persons who appear in a courtroom as a litigant, juror, attorney, judge, or staff person. Within seven years, membership grew to sixty-one members from fourteen jurisdictions. Among its members are the Chief Justice of Guam's Supreme Court, two U.S. district court judges, a judge of the U.S. Tax Court, a chief tribal judge, a state's chief administrative law judge, and two judges from state intermediate appellate courts. Fifty-eight of its members are from nine states, the District of Columbia, and Guam. Two members are from Canada, and one is from the United Kingdom.

National Lesbian and Gay Law Association (NLGLA)
PO Box 180417
Boston, MA 02118
Phone/Fax: (508) 982-8290
E-mail: nlgla@aol.com
Website: http://www.nlgla.org

NLGLA, established in 1988, is a national association of legal professionals, law students, and LGBT legal organizations. NLGLA became an affiliate of the American Bar Association in 1992. NLGLA sponsors year-round regional and local events throughout the United States. It focuses on civil rights issues for the LGBT community at many levels of the legal profession. NLGLA has rapidly become a national voice for LGBT people in the legal profession.

Publications: *NLGLA Newsletter* (biannual).

National Organization of Gay and Lesbian Scientists and Technical Professionals (NOGLSTP)
PO Box 91803
Pasadena, CA 91109
Phone: (626) 791-7689
Website: http://www.noglstp.org

NOGLSTP, launched as a nonprofit educational organization in 1980, is dedicated to addressing stereotypes and discrimination based on sexual orientation in the scientific/technical professions. NOGLSTP was accepted into the American Association for the Advancement of Science (AAAS) in 1994 and is currently registered in the section Societal Impacts of Science and Engineering. NOGLSTP, acting as a cohort of the Los Angeles Lawyers for Human Rights, submitted an amicus brief asking for the rejection of the CIA's contention that sexual orientation is a security risk. Subsequently, it monitored security clearance suspensions and persuaded the AAAS to adopt a nondiscrimination policy. NOGLSTP shares in the dissemination of information with lesbian and gay support groups within corporations such as Aerospace Corp., Boeing, Caltech, DEC, Hewlett-Packard, the Jet Propulsion Laboratory, the National Academy of Science, the National Institutes of Health, the National Laboratories, RAND, TRW, and Xerox.

Publications: *NOGLSTP Newsletter* (quarterly), *Queer Scientists of Historical Note, Beyond Biased Samples: Challenging the Myths on the Economic Status of Lesbians and Gay Men,* and *Scientists and AIDS Research: A Gay Perspective.*

Religious

Affirmation: Gay and Lesbian Mormons
PO Box 46022
Los Angeles, CA 90046-0022
Phone: (323) 255-7251

E-mail: aff@sitedesignpros.com
Website: http://www.affirmation.org

Even before Stonewall, gay Mormons often formed small secret groups to meet others in a social setting away from the eyes of the Church of Latter-Day Saints. However, these organizations were short-lived. In 1978, Matthew Price formed a group in Salt Lake City and named it "Affirmation—Gay Mormons United." This got press coverage in *The Advocate* and encouraged others to join and form chapters in other cities. Ultimately, the chapter in Los Angeles headed by Paul Mortensen became the primary spokesperson for Affirmation. Representatives marched in the Los Angeles Gay Pride Parade in 1979, which brought national attention to their efforts, and representatives from other chapters of Affirmation met in Los Angeles later that year and changed the organization's name to Affirmation: Gay and Lesbian Mormons. Since then, it has grown, with affiliations in major cities and other countries. Matthew Price states, "We firmly believe that Affirmation has a place in the plan of our Father in Heaven and His Kingdom, and that the Holy Spirit is still with us." Affirmation sponsors annual conferences and retreats to build local chapters, conducts local and worldwide chapter meetings, supports a group dedicated to gay Mormon fathers (Gamofites), and conducts an active electronic mailing of gay Mormon issues.

Publications: *Affinity* (monthly magazine).

Affirmation United Methodist
PO Box 1021
Evanston, IL 60204
Phone: (847) 733-9590
E-mail: umaffirmation@yahoo.com
Website: http://www.umaffirm.org

In 1972, a delegation of openly gay men attended the United Methodist Church General Conference. They engaged in conversations concerning the acceptance of homosexuality within the church but were not well received. By the end of the conference, a new statement of social principles by the church held, "We do not condone the practice of homosexuality and consider this practice to be incompatible with Christian teaching."

Out of frustration with the church, Gay United Methodists formed in 1975 to insist that homosexuality is a gift from God and not rebellion against His will. Later, in 1976, the name was changed to Affirmation, in preparation for what members believed to be a decades-long struggle for inclusion in the church.

In 1984, the church adopted a specific provision against the ordination or appointment of "self-avowed practicing homosexuals." Affirmation responded by creating the Reconciling Congregation Program (RCP). RCP has become the second-largest LGBT Christian organization, with hundreds of congregations and thousands of individuals reconciling United Methodists. Affirmation continues to promote the inclusion of homosexuals in the United Methodist Church.

Affirmation is an independent, nonprofit organization; it has no official ties to the United Methodist Church and does not receive support from the church.

Publications: *General Conference* newsletters.

American Family Association
c/o Abiding Truth Ministries
6060 Sunrise Vista Drive, Suite 3050
Citrus Heights, CA 95610
Phone: (916) 676-1057
E-mail: info@abidingtruth.com
Website: http://www.abidingtruth.com

The American Family Association of California has as its mission to glorify God through the promotion of Christian views regarding human sexuality and the family and to fight evil with good as revealed in the Bible. To these ends, a number of support organizations have been formed. The Pro-family Law Center provides the profamily movement with legal advice and assistance on public policy and matters of law. It is the nation's only law-oriented organization devoted exclusively to promoting strategies opposing homosexuality. The Pro-family Resource Center works in concert with the law center by directing profamily activists to resources that oppose homosexuality. These include a resource guide with links to other websites and archives. To fund these activities, The Pro-family Charitable Trust was established and is managed by Abiding Truth Ministries and gives grants for pro-family projects deemed to have promise at increasing grassroots activism or other goals that oppose homosexuality.

Publications: *The Poisoned Stream, The 7 Steps to Recruit-Proof Your*

Child, The Pink Swastika, Why and How to Defeat the Gay Movement, and other related books.

Association of Welcoming and Affirming Baptists (AWAB)
PO Box 2596
Attleboro Falls, MA 02763-0894
Phone: (508) 226-1945
Fax: (508) 226-1991
E-mail: Mail@WABaptists.org
Website: http://www.wabaptists.org

The Association of Welcoming and Affirming Baptists (AWAB) comprises churches, organizations, and individuals who are willing to go on record as welcoming and affirming all people without regard to sexual orientation and who have joined together to advocate for the full inclusion of lesbian, gay, bisexual, and transgender people within Baptist communities of faith. Begun at a gathering of pastors at the 1991 American Baptist Biennial in Charleston, West Virginia, AWAB has grown to more than forty-five churches and organizations throughout the United States.

Publications: *The InSpiriter* (quarterly).

Cathedral of Hope
5910 Cedar Springs
Dallas, TX 75235
Phone: (214) 351-1901
E-mail: hope@cathedralofhope.com
Website: http://www.cathedralofhope.com

Cathedral of Hope is dedicated to removing exclusive language from Christian worship. It believes exclusive language is sinful and just as unacceptable as sexism, bigotry, classism, or ageism. It does not view God as a "man" or a "woman" but rather an embodiment of both. Similarly, the Cathedral of Hope does not view God as either homosexual or heterosexual, but rather embracing of both. Furthermore, the Cathedral of Hope asks why issues such as judgment, pride, and hypocrisy (on which the scriptures say a great deal) are not vehemently condemned, whereas homosexuality (a topic on which the Bible has little to say) is vigorously attacked by Christian fundamentalists. The Cathedral of Hope is a gay-affirming congregation and hosts a nationally syndicated television program.

Publications: *National Newsletter.*

Dignity USA
1500 Massachusetts Avenue, NW, Suite 11
Washington, DC 20005
Phone: (800) 877-8797
Fax: (202) 429-9808
E-mail: dignity@aol.com
Website: http://www.dignityusa.org

Dignity USA is the largest and most progressive gay, lesbian, bisexual, and transgender Catholic organization in the United States. It serves as a proactive voice for reform in the Catholic Church and is supportive of same-sex marriages, women's ministry, AIDS ministry, and the elimination of hate crimes. Contrary to official Catholic teaching, which requires people to abstain from homosexual behaviors, Dignity believes these teachings to be incorrect and a misinterpretation of history and scripture. Dignity does not consider homosexual behaviors or relationships to be sinful.

Father Patrick Nidorf, OSA, founded Dignity USA in 1969 as a counseling group in Los Angeles. By 1973, it had become an independent nonprofit organization with a national office located in Washington, D.C., and local chapters throughout the United States. After the Vatican issued its 1986 document "Congregation for the Doctrine of the Faith—On the Pastoral Care of Homosexual Persons," many chapters of Dignity were evicted from Catholic churches and had to find accommodations elsewhere. In response, Dignity became a founding member of Catholic Organizations for Renewal (COR), which hosts a biennial national convention that attracts thousands of members. Dignity believes that "God created us, Christ died for us, and the Holy Spirit sanctified us in Baptism."

Publications: *Dignity USA News* (monthly).

Exodus International North America
PO Box 77652
Seattle, WA 98177
Phone: (206) 784-7799
Fax: (206) 784-7872
E-mail: info@exodusnorthamerica.org
Website: http://www.exodusintl.org

Exodus International was founded in 1976 on the belief that freedom from homosexuality is possible through the power of Jesus

Christ. As an interdenominational Christian organization, it has grown to include over 100 local ministries in the United States and Canada, with links to an additional 135 ministries in 17 countries. Exodus is the largest Christian organization dealing with homosexual issues. It challenges those who claim homosexuality as a valid sexual orientation. It believes that homosexuals who accept Jesus Christ into their lives can change their sexual orientation and find peace as heterosexuals.

Exodus provides referrals and information on homosexuality. Most members are "lay" (nonprofessional) ministries. These ministries engage in "spiritual counseling" to lead homosexuals out of the "darkness of their depravity." Each year, more than 1,000 ex-gays, therapists, spouses, parents, friends, and pastors attend an annual conference. Many workshops are presented to help guide homosexuals and their families through difficult times of change.

Publications: *Update* (monthly).

Gay and Lesbian Atheists and Humanists (GALAH)
PO Box 34635
Washington, DC 20043
E-mail: writegalah@bellatlantic.net
Website: http://www.galah.org

GALAH is the only national lesbian, gay, bisexual, and transgender organization devoted to atheism and humanism. GALAH strongly supports separation of church and state and believes "religion promotes fear, limits freedom, oppresses the poor, and suppresses knowledge. Religion is authoritarian, sexist, and homophobic." As such, GALAH opposes political support of religious "morality," particularly that espoused by the religious right and others who advocate the eradication of homosexuals. GALAH keeps its members updated on the activities of the religious right by e-mail and a monthly newsletter. It holds meetings in many major cities in the United States.

Publications: *The GALAH Newsletter* (monthly).

God Hates Fags
Westboro Baptist Church (WBC)
3701 W. 12th Street
Topeka, KS 66604-1730

Phone/Fax: (954) 337-0400
E-mail: ghf-info@godhatesfags.com
Website: http://www.godhatesfags.com

Founded in 1955 as an Old School (or Primitive) Baptist Church by Reverend Fred Phelps, WBC preaches against all forms of sin, such as fornication, adultery, and sodomy. Members believe that Christians have been lied to when they are told that "God loves everyone" and "Jesus died for everyone." Instead, WBC believes that God is vengeful and that the "homosexual lifestyle" is soul-damning and nation-destroying filth. WBC engages in daily sidewalk demonstrations at homosexual parades, funerals ("of impenitent sodomites like Matthew Shepard"), and other public places. WBC claims to have conducted more than 20,000 such demonstrations since 1993 throughout the United States, Canada, and Iraq. The unique picketing ministry of WBC has received much media attention. WBC believes its gospel message to be the world's last hope.

Publications: Many books and pamphlets.

Homosexuals Anonymous (H.A.)
PO Box 7881
Reading, PA 19603
Phone: (610) 921-0345
E-mail: ha_devotions@yahoo.com
Website: http://members.aol.com/hawebpage

H.A. is a Christian fellowship of men and women who help each other to live free of homosexuality. H.A. believes that homosexual activity is not in harmony with the will of God and the universal creation norm of heterosexuality. Through weekly meetings and a fourteen-step program, members attempt to heal their spiritual and intrapsychic relationship with Christ, thereby attaining freedom and recovery from homosexuality. H.A. does not believe that a change in homosexual inclination is required for the acceptance of God or the church. However, the degree to which a person accepts Christ will be the degree to which that person is healed of homosexuality.

Publications: Many books and pamphlets.

Lutherans Concerned/North America (LC/NA)
PO Box 10197

Chicago, IL 60610
E-mail: ric@lcna.org
Website: http://www.lcna.org

LC/NA is an independent membership organization founded in 1974 and supported entirely by donations. It accepts all Lutheran affiliations as well as other Christian denominations. LC/NA believes in employing the Gospel's principles of inclusiveness and justice while celebrating God's gift of sexuality and diversity. LC/NA maintains that homosexuality, heterosexuality, and all other sexual orientations are part of the spectrum of God's human creation and that sexuality is not a consciously made choice. Rather, the choice is in how it is expressed. LC/NA helps people reconcile their spiritual and sexual conflicts in uplifting ways and calls on its members to be visible advocates for gay, lesbian, bisexual, and transgender people.

Publications: Various brochures and a handbook.

New Ways Ministry
4012 29th Street
Mt. Rainier, MD 20712
Phone: (301) 277-5674
Fax: (301) 864-6948
E-mail: newwaysm@aol.com
Website: http://members.aol.com/newwaysm

New Ways Ministry provides a gay-positive ministry of advocacy and justice for LGBT Catholics and reconciliation within the larger Christian and civil communities. Founded in 1977 by Sister Jeannine Gramick, SSND, and Father Robert Nugent, SDS, New Ways was incorporated as a nonprofit organization seeking to promote the full and equal acceptance of lesbians and gay men into the Catholic Church. Because of the founders' actions, the Vatican decided to silence them in May 23, 2000. Gramick and Nugent were ordered to no longer speak or write about homosexuality or about their eleven-year harassment by the Vatican.

Publications: *Bondings* (quarterly).

Presbyterian Parents of Gays and Lesbians, Inc. (PPGL)
PO Box 600882
Dallas, TX 75360-0882
Phone: (214) 750-7186

E-mail: ppglinfo@presbyterianparents.org
Website: http://www.presbyterianparents.org

Jane Loflin, the mother of a gay son, saw the need for a ministry for mothers and fathers within the Presbyterian Church to come together to share their experiences in an environment of concern, compassion, and spiritual nurturance when coping with having homosexual children. In 1993, the clergy and lay leaders at Grace Presbytery assisted her in creating PPGL. Soon, other groups formed in Dallas, Texas; La Cañada/Glendale, California; Raleigh, North Carolina; Seattle, Washington; Albany/Watervliet, New York; and Norwalk, Connecticut. The group welcomes parents of all faiths, beliefs, and backgrounds. The goal of PPGL is to provide a support network of pastoral care and information about homosexuality to parents of gay and lesbian children in an environment of faith that is safe, nurturing, and confidential. It guides parents toward understanding, acceptance, and affirmation of themselves and their sons and daughters.

Rainbow Baptists
American Baptists Concerned for Sexual Minorities (ABC)
PO Box 3183
Walnut Creek, CA 94598
Phone: (925) 439-4672
E-mail: abc-sfba@rainbowbaptists.org
Website: http://www.rainbowbaptists.org

Honesty
c/o Jeff Street Baptist Community at Liberty
800 East Liberty Street
Louisville, KY 40205
Phone: (502) 635-1905
E-mail: ambaptists@aol.com
Website: http://www.rainbowbaptists.org

Rainbow Baptists is a website cooperative for American Baptists Concerned for Sexual Minorities and Honesty. Both organizations provide support, education, and advocacy for gay, lesbian, bisexual, and transgender Baptists with a Southern Baptist background. They believe that LGBT people are wholly loved and accepted as they are by the Creator. Both organizations bring a voice of enlightenment, hope, and encouragement to all Baptists. ABC has assembled two booklets, one focusing on coming-out issues and experiences of LGBT youths and the other telling the stories of parents and families of LGBT people.

Publications: *Voice of the Turtle* (quarterly).

Scriptures for America
PO Box 766
LaPorte, CO 80535
Phone: (307) 745-5913
Fax: (307) 745-5914
E-mail: preacher@fiberpipe.net
Website: http://www.scripturesforamerica.org

Scriptures for America is an international outreach ministry of the LaPorte Church of Christ. Pastor Peter J. Peters believes his church is engaged in a struggle between good and evil, Christ and anti-Christ, as exemplified by the struggle between hetero-sexuals and homosexuals. Peters believes homosexuals are to be judged and killed. For details, see *Death Penalty for Homosexuals Is Prescribed in the Bible* by Peter J. Peters (www.voy.com/28938/5.htm). Scriptures for America broadcasts on short-wave, main-tains a website, and publishes a newsletter.

Soulforce
PO Box 4467
Laguna Beach, CA 92652
Phone: (877) 705-6393
Fax: (949) 455-0959
E-mail: garynixon@soulforce.org
Website: http://www.soulforce.org

Soulforce is named for Mohandas Gandhi's teaching of *satya-graha*, "truth force" or "soul force," a plan of action that develops inner lives while working to transform society. Founded by Rev-erend Mel White and his partner, Gay Nixon, in 1998, Soulforce aims to help end the suffering of lesbian, gay, bisexual, and trans-gender people; change the minds and hearts of religious leaders whose antihomosexual campaigns lead to suffering; and help heal society from homophobia and heterosexism.

Soulforce engages in direct action by meeting with religious leaders and, when need be, by nonviolent picketing. Its first stage was a campaign to stop spiritual violence. It trained 1,000 volun-teers on site at the national conventions of the United Methodist,

Southern Baptist, and Presbyterian Churches, and the National Conference of Catholic Bishops. After silent, candlelight vigils, more than 500 Soulforce members were arrested in carefully planned acts of nonviolent dissent. The second stage is a noncooperation campaign; that is, to encourage people not to cooperate with evil religions by cutting off donations.

Soulforce produces films and other educational materials. Also, White and Nixon have been tracking for more than a decade antigay rhetoric in television and radio programs, using letter writing campaigns to respond to the negative misinformation.

Publications: *Stranger at the Gate* (book), *Soulforce* (video), *How Can I Be Sure That God Loves Me, Too?* (video), and other videos.

Universal Fellowship of Metropolitan Community Churches (UFMCC)

8704 Santa Monica Boulevard, 2nd Floor
West Hollywood, CA 90069
Phone: (310) 360-8640
Fax: (310) 360-8680
E-mail: info@MCCchurch.org
Website: http://www.ufmcc.com

Reverend Troy Perry founded the Universal Fellowship of Metropolitan Community Churches (commonly known as MCC) of Los Angeles in 1968 to serve the spiritual needs of gay and lesbian people. This was before the Stonewall Riots and the national pride festivals and parades. His Pentecostal church had defrocked him for his homosexuality and for a suicide attemp. His first worship service was attended by eleven men and one woman—encompassing people with Protestant, Catholic, and Jewish backgrounds, including one Latino and one heterosexual couple. This foreshadowed the diversity that would characterize MCC in the coming years.

MCC has grown to include more than 300 churches around the world, with a membership exceeding 40,000 in 18 countries. In many small communities, MCC is the only local lesbian- and gay-oriented organization. Because of it longevity and central support, MCC has been the birthplace of dozens of different gay and lesbian organizations and social justice projects across the world.

Publications: Many pamphlets.

Schools

American Federation of Teachers (AFT)
555 New Jersey Avenue, NW
Washington, DC 20001
Phone: (202) 879-4400
E-mail: online@aft.org
Website: http://www.aft.org

Beginning in the basement of a teacher's home in Winnetka, Illinois, in 1916, AFT has grown to more than 1 million current members. It holds strong democratic ideals and has long been known for taking risks and taking a stand on controversial issues. As early as 1918, AFT called for equal pay and representation for African American teachers. In 1954, it filed an amicus brief in *Brown v. Board of Education* supporting the end of segregated schools. In 1957, AFT required all affiliated local unions to fully integrate or be expelled from the organization. Nearly 7,000 members left the small fledgling union at that time, but the AFT board believed it was "worth it."

AFT has a gay and lesbian caucus. It has issued a position paper denouncing discrimination against homosexuals and includes sexual orientation antidiscrimination language in its constitution.

Publications: *Inside AFT* (monthly).

Gay, Lesbian, and Straight Education Network (GLSEN)
PO Box 5392
Albany, New York 12205
Phone: (518) 228-3251
E-mail: glsencr@nycap.rr.com
Website: http://www.glsen.org

GLSEN is the leading national organization focused on ending antigay bias in K–12 schools. It strives to ensure that every student, teacher, administrator, and staff member in every school community is respected regardless of his or her sexual orientation or gender identity/expression. GLSEN believes that heterosexism and homophobia undermine a healthy school climate and negatively impact educational achievement.

GLSEN members also believe that education is the key to ending antigay prejudice and hate-motivated violence. It advocates educating not only gay and lesbian students but also their families, friends, teachers, and others on issues of sexual orientation and gender identity so that they can work together to reform America's educational system. Thousands of volunteers working through a national network of local chapters have made a significant impact. The public policy program works with elected officials and educational policy leaders to ensure basic protections for LGBT students, teachers, and families. GLSEN has successfully mounted a number of nationally significant court battles. GLSEN helps students organize their own gay-straight alliances at their schools in an effort to help change the environment from the inside out. GLSEN has also created teacher training materials and inclusive curricular resources.

Publications: *Respect* (quarterly).

**National Consortium of Directors of
LGBT Resources in Higher Education**
Website: www.lgbtcampus.org

This consortium aims to support colleagues and develop curriculum to enhance professional standing, to improve campus climate by reducing homophobia and heterosexism, and to advocate for policy change. The consortium communicates with members through its listserv. Members meet twice a year—once at the NGLTF Creating Change conference and once at another location. Overall, the consortium hopes to achieve environments in higher education in which LGBT students, faculty, staff, administrators, and alumni have equality with all other people in every respect.

**National Education Association Gay
and Lesbian Caucus (NEA)**
1201 16th Street, NW
Washington, DC 90036
Phone: (202) 833-4000
E-mail: webmaster@nea-glc.org
Website: http://www.nea-glc.org

The National Education Association is the oldest and largest organization in the United States devoted to the cause of public education. Founded in 1857, it has more than 2.5 million members working at every level of education, from preschool to university graduate programs. The Gay and Lesbian Caucus was established in 1987 and represents public education employees who are concerned about sexual orientation issues and their impact on students and the school employees who work with them. The caucus helps educate state education associations on issues of sexual orientation and promotes nondiscriminatory policies and actions that support LGBT persons. Also, the caucus is involved in developing legal response protocols, domestic partnership benefit programs, training, curriculum, and family life education.

Publications: *Caucus Connection* (quarterly), *Strengthening the Learning Environment,* and *A School Employee's Guide to Gay and Lesbian Issues.*

Stonewall Center
256 Sunset Avenue
Crampton House, SW
Amherst, MA 01003
Phone: (413) 545-4824
Fax: (413) 545-6667
E-mail: stonewall@stuaf.umass.edu
Website: http://www.umass.edu/stonewall/resources/campus

A series of homophobic incidents on the Amherst campus of the University of Massachusetts in 1984 led to disturbing protest demonstrations. The college conducted systematic research about heterosexism and homophobia on campus and issued the report "The Consequences of Being Gay: A Report on the Quality of Life for Gay, Lesbian, and Bisexual Students at the University of Massachusetts at Amherst." One of the key recommendations was the creation of the Program for Gay, Lesbian, and Bisexual Concerns. When established in 1985, this was only one of three such college centers across the United States.

Since then, the Stonewall Center has grown in size and scope. Besides students, faculty, and staff, the center now serves the surrounding community by providing cultural and educational programming; video, audio, and text library holdings; educational resources; referral services; responses to harassment and discrimination; training; advocacy; newsletters; and web service.

Publications: *In Newsweekly* (weekly), *Bay Windows* (biweekly), *Voice Male* (quarterly), and other such LGBT periodicals.

Transgender (Transgender, Transsexual, Intersex)

Female-to-Male International (FTM)
1360 Mission Street, Suite 200
San Francisco, CA 94103
Phone: (415) 553-5987
E-mail: info@ftm-intl.org
Website: http://www.ftm-intl.org

FTM provides support for women who desire to act on their feelings and beliefs that they are men. The support includes a monthly newsletter and other publications, a hotline, mailing lists, links, monthly meetings, and special events. FTM operates with volunteers who are at different stages of transitioning and encourages each person to take the path with which he is most comfortable. FTM does not push any member to take the expensive and potentially dangerous medical approach. The members of FTM range in age from teens to seventies and include people who are just beginning to examine gender issues and those who are experts on the topic.

Publications: *Trans Forming Families: Real Stories about Transgendered Loved Ones, The Transsexual Phenomenon*, and other books and articles on transgender.

Intersex Society of North America (ISNA)
PO Box 301
Petaluma, CA 94953
Phone: (707) 283-0420
Fax: (707) 283-0419
E-mail: info@isna.org
Website: http://www.isna.org

ISNA is aimed at ending the shame, secrecy, and unwanted genital surgeries for people born with atypical reproductive anatomies. Until recently, the medical establishment believed it was necessary to "correct" reproductive anomalies in children within the first few months and years of life. In the United States alone, five children are subjected to harmful, medically unnecessary sexual surgeries every day. ISNA challenges the medical status quo by citing research to show that early genital surgery has a high failure rate and often results in sexual dysfunction. ISNA urges physicians to adopt patient-centered, rather than concealment-centered, practices. Because of the efforts of ISNA and other intersex organizations, the basic philosophy of medical management of sexual ambiguity is being reevaluated toward leaving the child unaltered.

Publications: *ISNA News* (monthly), *Hermaphrodites with Attitude* (quarterly), and many pamphlets and brochures in English and in Spanish regarding intersex people.

Transgender Fund
PO Box 2313
Vineyard Haven, MA 02568
Phone/Fax: (508) 696-6767
E-mail: tgfund@tgforum.com
Website: http://www.tgfund.org

The Transgender Fund is a nonprofit organization devoted to financially supporting initiatives advancing the interests of the transgender community. It supports collaborative education, research, and public awareness programs. One of its major efforts is the creation and maintenance of the Transgender Forum, which allows other transgender organizations to link into one large resource (called a webring, at www.trangender.org).

Web Resources

Most of the foregoing organization websites contain links to other organizations. However, there are a number of websites that provide links to hundreds and sometimes thousands of other websites or have unique links. These "master" directory websites are very helpful in locating local, national, and international organizations. The reader is cautioned that web addresses change often, and no guarantee is made that these addresses are still valid.

Blackstripe
Website: blackstripe.com/index.html

This is the Internet's leading resource for news, information, and culture affecting LGBT people of African descent.

GayLawNet
Website: www.gaylawnet.com/main.html

This site is dedicated to providing general information and resources concerning the law as it affects the global LGBT community and the simplest access to LGBT or LGBT-friendly lawyers.

Gay/Lesbian International News Network (GLINN)
Weblink: www.glinn.com/books/lar1.htm

This site has a list of LGBT archives and libraries across the United States.

Gay/Lesbian Politics and Law: WWW and Internet Resources
Website: www.indiana.edu/~glbtpol/

This site contains a selected, annotated guide designed by students at Indiana University, to the best and most authoritative resources on politics, law, and policy.

Gayscape
Website: www.jwpublishing.com/gayscape

This site lists more than 68,000 mostly commercial indexed sites by topics.

International Gay and Lesbian Human Rights Commission (IGLHRC)
Weblink: www.iglhrc.org/world/resources/index.html

This site contains a list of international LGBT organizations.

Lesbian.org
Website: www.lesbian.org

This site promotes lesbian visibility on the Internet.

Queer Resources Directory
Website: www.qrd.org

This is one of the oldest and largest websites devoted to linking to everyone possible. It contains more than 26,000 files. However, this directory is often not current.

Transgender Forum's Community Center
Website: www.transgender.org

This website has links to transgender organizations in the United States.

UC Davis—Sexual Orientation: Science, Education, and Policy
Website: psychology.ucdavis.edu/rainbow/

This site lists major books on the topic.

University of Washington Libraries
Website: faculty.washington.edu/alvin/gayorg.htm#ARCHIV

Here is a listing of national and international LGBT organizations and publications.

7

Selected Print and Nonprint Resources

Books

Academic Research

Altman, D. 1982. *The Homosexualization of America, the Americanization of the Homosexual.* New York: St. Martin's Press.

This work examines the progress made in the gay movement by individual gay men and lesbians in the United States of the late 1970s and early 1980s. The gay movement is analyzed through a cultural focus and not solely in terms of politics.

Badgett, M. V. L. 1998. *Income Inflation: The Myth of Affluence among Gay, Lesbian, and Bisexual Americans.* Washington, DC: National Gay and Lesbian Task Force. Available free at www.ngltf.org.

The stereotype is that lesbians and, even more, gay men have higher than average incomes in the United States. This stereotype is often used to claim that antidiscrimination policies are not needed. Lee Badgett, professor of economics at the University of Massachusetts at Amherst, conducted research using the national census and other publicly funded economic studies to show that LGBT people actually earn decidedly less than heterosexual Americans.

Blumenfeld, W. J., and D. Raymond. 1993. *Looking at Gay and Lesbian Life.* Rev. ed. Boston: Beacon Press.

When this book came out, it was the first comprehensive overview of lesbian and gay research, history, law, health, and culture. This book could be used as the core text for introductory courses on homosexuality. It reads easily and is well documented.

Cahill, S., and K. T. Jones. 2001. *Leaving Our Children Behind: Welfare Reform and the Gay, Lesbian, Bisexual, and Transgender Community.* Washington, DC: National Gay and Lesbian Task Force. Available free at www.ngltf.org.

This is the first comprehensive report to critically analyze welfare's impact on poor gay, lesbian, bisexual, and transgender people. The report shows parallels to the attacks made by right-wing conservatives on the gay community.

Cory, D. 1951. *The Homosexual in America.* New York: Greenburg.

This is one of the most important early books to be written on homosexuality. Unlike the sentiments at the time that condemned homosexuality as an illness and criminal activity, Cory presented gay culture as a positive force in the United States of the 1940s. He demonstrated a sociological and psychological understanding of the times. Also as a complement to his thesis, the appendix lists federal and state laws regulating homosexual behavior.

Cruikshank, M. 1992. *The Gay and Lesbian Liberation Movement.* New York: Routledge, Chapman, and Hall.

Using feminist analysis, Cruikshank discusses existing conflicts between lesbians and gay men within the gay and lesbian liberation movement. She proclaims a radical new departure from antiquated ideas in politics regarding sexual freedoms. The book is one of the series Revolutionary Thought/Radical Movements.

Dawson, J. 2000. *Gay and Lesbian Online.* 4th ed. Los Angeles: Alyson Publications.

Encyclopedic in nature, this book provides a useful guide to sites of interest to lesbians and gay men on the Internet. The author has written for *Macworld, The Net,* and *MacHome Journal* and brings his expertise to the ever-changing world of the Internet.

D'Emilio, J. 1983. *Sexual Politics, Sexual Communities: The Making of a Homosexual Minority in the United States.* Chicago: University of Chicago Press.

Although many lesbians and gay men believe the modern gay liberation movement began with the Stonewall Riots, a handful of men and women laid the groundwork more than two decades earlier. D'Emilio traces the beginnings of the Mattachine Society, the Daughters of Bilitis, and other early gay organizations.

Dynes, W. R. 1990. *Encyclopedia of Homosexuality.* New York: Garland.

The encyclopedia deals with topics as diverse as economics, anthropology, art, gender, relationships, and several others all related to homosexuality. The book's format lends itself to a quick reference or leisure reading.

Garnets, L. D., and D. C. Kimmel, eds. 1993. *Psychological Perspectives on Lesbian and Gay Male Experiences.* New York: Columbia University Press.

This was one of the major textbooks written in the 1990s. It is a comprehensive review of what was known about the psychology of homosexuality. It is still worth reading since there has not been a similar volume published by anyone else.

Gonsiorek, J. C., and J. D. Weinrich, eds. 1991. *Homosexuality: Research Implications for Public Policy.* Newbury Park, CA: Sage.

Although other books have reviewed the research into homosexuality, the selected articles in this book look at the impact such research has on government and organizational policies. Topics include the origins of human sexuality, the medicalization and "deviancy" of homosexuality, cross-cultural analysis, a review of law, reparative therapy, lesbian and gay relationships, and families. The book is well written and aimed for college-level readers.

Greenberg, D. 1988. *The Construction of Homosexuality.* Chicago: University of Chicago Press.

David Greenberg is a physicist who turned his attention to the development of homosexuality. He believes same-sex sexual and personal relationships have always existed and gives many cultural examples to prove the point. But it has been politics that has given special emphasis to the supposed "difference" in homosexuals, and that difference has been constructed through language, customs, and law. This important work is quite long and written at a high academic level.

Heger, H. 1994. *The Men with the Pink Triangles: The True, Life-and-Death Story of Homosexuals in the Nazi Death Camps.* Rev. ed. Trans. David Fernbach. Los Angeles: Alyson Publications.

This important work first appeared in Germany in 1972 and should be considered a primary source for studying the persecution and execution of homosexuals under Adolf Hitler. The writer recounts the concentration camp experiences of an Austrian man who remains anonymous because of continued persecution. Unlike other subsequent books detailing the Nazi holocaust against homosexuals, this book contains greater personal details of what happened.

Herek, G. M., ed. 1997. *Stigma and Sexual Orientation: Understanding Prejudice against Lesbians, Gay Men, and Bisexuals.* Newbury Park, CA: Sage.

Herek discuses the nature of antigay prejudice, stereotypes, and behaviors; the consequences of homophobia; and the critical need for science and psychology to examine homophobia and related issues.

International Gay Association. 1985. *IGA Pink Book, 1985.* Amsterdam: COC-Magazine.

This is a directory of various worldwide organizations whose focus is on gay civil rights.

Katz, J. N. 1996. *The Construction of Heterosexuality.* New York: Penguin.

Katz's review of historical documents demonstrates that modern heterosexuality is a new social arrangement. This is an important finding because it blasts the heterosexual presumption of normalcy and an ahistorical status. Since social forces have created heterosexuality, it can be refashioned into one that is less exclusive and more embracing of human sexual diversity.

Marcus, E. 1999. *Is It a Choice? Answers to 300 of the Most Frequently Asked Questions about Gay and Lesbian People*. San Francisco: Harper.

This popular book is easy to read and gives concise answers to frequently asked questions about homosexuality.

Marotta, T. 1981. *The Politics of Homosexuality*. Boston: Houghton Mifflin.

This thorough academic overview of the first decade of gay civil rights and liberation is based on the author's dissertation and research, but has been revised to make it easier to read. Excellent endnotes and index make the book useful to academic researchers.

Mills, K. I. 1999. *Mission Impossible: Why Reparative Therapy and Ex-Gay Ministries Fail*. Washington, DC: Human Rights Campaign. Available at www.hrc.org/publications/exgay_ministries/change.asp.

Although the religious right has adopted reparative therapy as a significant program in its intention to eliminate homosexuality, it continues to fail at this goal. Those engaging in reparative therapy claim to be successful, but they do not publish their results or have their work corroborated by others. This paper explores these failures and demonstrates the real political purpose of reparative therapy—to disenfranchise LGBT people and to raise money.

National Museum and Archive of Lesbian and Gay History, comp. 1996. *The Gay Almanac*. New York: Berkley Books.

This is a wonderful resource on the gay community, its history, famous people, quotes, glossary, statistics, and other topics. It contains a comprehensive list of lesbian and gay community centers and a national directory of lesbian and gay organizations.

Pharr, S. 1988. *Homophobia: A Weapon of Sexism*. Little Rock, AR: Chardon Press.

This small book powerfully demonstrates that homophobia is a major tool for maintaining sexism in U.S. culture. Told from her experience of conducting group counseling, Pharr shares her deep insight into how the fear of being labeled a dyke keeps women in their place.

Remafedi, G. 1994. *Death by Denial: Studies of Suicide in Gay and Lesbian Teenagers.* Los Angeles: Alyson Publications.

A federal study in 1989 found that lesbian and gay teenagers are three times more likely to attempt suicide than their peers. The report was squelched by the Bush administration. Here it is printed in its entirety, along with other studies documenting the difficulties teenagers face when coming out.

Rothblum, E. D., ed. 1996. *Preventing Heterosexism and Homophobia.* Newbury Park, CA: Sage.

The contributors to this volume propose methods for eliminating heterosexual bias in many settings—health care, therapy, communities, corporate America, and education. They explore the risks and joys of being gay, lesbian, or bisexual and how heterosexism affects the lives of all people.

Sandfort, T., J. W. Schuyf, J. Duyvendak, and J. Weeks, eds. 2000. *Lesbian and Gay Studies: An Introductory, Interdisciplinary Approach.* Newbury Park, CA: Sage.

This timely book introduces readers to the interdisciplinary approaches to the field while asking, What is lesbian and gay studies? When did it emerge? What are the goals and achievements of the research agenda?

Tierney, W. G. 1997. *Academic Outlaw: Queer Theory and Cultural Studies in the Academy.* Thousand Oaks, CA: Sage.

Until recently, even considering a lesbian or gay topic for research was fatal to an academic career. Tierney reviews the cultural changes that have allowed academic institutions to incorporate queer studies into their curriculum. However, Tierney warns readers that doctoral research and publishing on LGBT topics are considered of lesser value than mainstream topics and that selecting such topics will negatively affect professional progress. Much of the book is difficult to read due to the heavy use of feminist terminology.

Woog, D. 2001. *Gay Men, Straight Jobs.* Los Angeles: Alyson Publications.

Journalist Woog, who has written on the intersection of sexual orientation and class (*Jocks* and *School's Out*), brings his observational skills to the issue of gay men working and coping in jobs that traditionally have attracted straight men. Some of the stories are liberating, whereas others are frightening and sometimes tragic.

Zuckerman, A. J., and G. F. Simons. 1995. *Sexual Orientation in the Workplace: Gay Men, Lesbians, Bisexuals, and Heterosexuals Working Together*. Newbury Park, CA: Sage.

This excellent book demonstrates how individuals' sexual orientation may affect both how well they are accepted by coworkers and how they react to coworkers. Included are a variety of simple tools and exercises to help readers develop the skills to work effectively and realistically with a diverse workforce.

AIDS

Herek, G. M., and B. Green, eds. 1995. *AIDS, Identity, and Community: The HIV Epidemic and Lesbians and Gay Men*. Newbury Park, CA: Sage.

Most of the chapters of this volume reflect study findings from AIDS-related research, including discussions of AIDS in large urban centers and in less populated settings. The specific topics explore the relationship between AIDS and gay and bisexual men of color, lesbian women, gay and lesbian youths, public policy, volunteerism, and long-term survival as it relates to AIDS awareness and education.

Shilts, R. 1987. *And the Band Played On: Politics, People, and the AIDS Epidemic*. New York: St. Martin's Press.

Shilts traces the efforts to identify the cause of AIDS in this compelling story of intrigue, professional rivalry, sorrow, and hope. Written in journalistic style, this award-winning book was later made into a popular movie of the same title.

Antigay Sources

American Family Association. n.d. *The Pink Swastika*. Citrus Heights, CA: Abiding Truth Ministries. Available at http://www.abidingtruth.com.

In response to *The Pink Triangle* (1987), by Richard Plant, which documents the arrests and death of homosexuals in Nazi concentration camps, *The Pink Swastika* attempts to show how the upper echelon of the Nazi Party and German military were homosexuals. Full of inaccuracies and assumptions, the book is rejected by respected academics. In response to this document, the Citizens Allied for Civic Action commissioned a professional annotation of *The Pink Swastika* (*The Annotated Pink Swastika* is available at www.glinn.com/pink). *The Pink Swastika* belongs to the crypto-history genre, which uses out-of-context selective quoting from respectable authors and extensive quoting from disreputable ones although claiming that one's position has been purposefully suppressed by evil powers. This book is interesting reading for those aware of its inaccuracies and reveals a deeper understanding of those who hate lesbians and gay men.

————. n.d. *The Poisoned Stream.* Citrus Heights, CA: Abiding Truth Ministries. Available at http://www.abidingtruth.com.

This large document traces select elements of world history in an attempt to show a correlation between the practice of homosexuality and the downfall of society. It is extremely inaccurate and makes unsupportable claims with which no respected academic would agree, such as homosexuality was the cause of the fall of the Roman Empire. Nevertheless, this book has had a major influence on the religious right. Its lack of acceptance by respected academics is considered by members of the religious right as proof that this document is true but is being suppressed by a conspiracy of silence.

————. n.d. *The 7 Steps to Recruit-Proof Your Child.* Citrus Heights, CA: Abiding Truth Ministries. Available at http://www.abidingtruth.com.

Fears of religious right members concerning the "recruitment" of children by gay militants has resulted in this pamphlet being printed. It relies on false stereotypes to model behaviors that supposedly will protect children. For example, boys are encouraged to play sports to build their masculine characters (the pamphlet denies, of course, that gay men play sports), whereas girls are to be on the alert for lesbian coaches coercing them into homosexuality. The book easily could have been the blueprint for the movie farce *But I'm a Cheerleader.* Unfortunately, this book is taken seriously and surely discourages children from accepting diversity in gender and sex roles.

————. n.d. *Why and How to Defeat the Gay Movement.* Citrus Heights, CA: Abiding Truth Ministries. Available at http://www.abidingtruth.com.

This small pamphlet begins with the basic religious right belief that homosexuality is deviant and that homosexuals should not be entitled to basic political rights. The text then develops a number of strategies designed to hinder or stop the gay rights movement. Much of the strategies discussed involve simple political steps, including electing conservative members to school boards and local offices, distributing educational materials, organizing antigay religious groups, and more.

Bryant, A. 1977. *The Anita Bryant Story: The Survival of Our Nation's Families and the Threat of Militant Homosexuality.* Old Tappan, NJ: Revell.

Bryant provides an outline of her fear of "the militant homosexual agenda." In doing so, she reviews the battle she undertook in 1977 to override gay rights legislation in Dade County, Florida. This important book sheds light on the psychology of religious right leaders.

Falwell, J. 1980. *Listen, America!* Garden City, NY: Doubleday.

Falwell presents his views on "traditional morality" and the antigay beliefs promulgated by the Moral Majority. He warns of the destruction of America by evil forces, including homosexuality.

Gramick, J., and P. Furey. 1988. *The Vatican and Homosexuality.* New York: Crossroad.

In 1986, the Catholic Church issued its "Congregation for the Doctrine of the Faith—On the Pastoral Care of Homosexual Persons." This book contains this letter, along with twenty-five articles analyzing and responding to it. The authors of the book agree with the sentiments of the letter. They explain that lesbians and gay men should not try to claim civil rights and that violent hate crimes directed at them are "understandable" given their "promotion of immoral causes."

Magnuson, R. J. 1990. *Are Gay Rights Right? Making Sense of the Controversy.* Portland, OR: Multnomah Press.

Magnuson presents arguments as to why the gay rights movement has no legal legitimacy.

Peters, P. J. 1992. *Intolerance of, Discrimination against, and the Death Penalty for Homosexuals Is Prescribed in the Bible.* La Porte, CO: Scriptures for America. Posted on the web 5/7/01 at www.voy.com/28938/6.html by D. R. W. Wadsworth.

This article is cited by extreme Christian right groups and purports to give biblical evidence as to why homosexuals should be put to death. Peters further argues that the 1982 joint resolution of both houses of the U.S. Congress declaring that the "Bible is the Word of God" authorizes it to carry out the execution of homosexuals.

Rodgers, W. D. 1977. *The Gay Invasion: A Christian Looks at the Spreading Homosexual Myth.* Denver: Accent Book.

Rodgers outlines the spread of homosexuality and analyzes the threat to society posed by "militant homosexuals." Rodgers makes specific suggestions as to what steps Christians can take to stop this threat.

Bisexuality

Firestein, B. A., ed. 1996. *Bisexuality: The Psychology and Politics of an Invisible Minority.* Newbury Park, CA: Sage.

Written for academics, *Bisexuality* discusses many of the political issues that arise from stereotypes and myths concerning bisexuality.

Hutchins, L., and L. Kaahumanu, eds. 1991. *Bi Any Other Name: Bisexual People Speak Out.* Los Angeles: Alyson Publications.

Bisexuals have had difficulty in being accepted in the gay rights movement. Slowly, bisexuals have gained limited acceptance and have launched their own campaign for civil rights. This book details their struggle and discusses many of their issues.

Coming Out

Barber, K., and S. Holmes, eds. 1994. *Testimonies: A Collection of Lesbian Coming Out Stories.* Los Angeles: Alyson Publications.

Lesbians speak with their own voices about their experiences coming out to family and friends. This nontechnical book is aimed at the average reader.

Bono, C., with B. Fitzpatrick. 1999. *Family Outing.* Boston: Little, Brown.

Bono is the lesbian daughter of Sonny Bono and the famous entertainer Cher. Although Cher has spent a lifetime working with lesbians and gay men and is an icon of gay male culture, having a lesbian daughter challenged her concept of family. In this book, Bono gives insight into the process of coming out when one's every action is recorded by the tabloids. Cher proved to be supportive of her daughter and her lesbianism.

Borhek, M. 1993. *Coming Out to Parents.* New York: Pilgrim Press.

Probably the most frightening thing any lesbian or gay young adult faces is coming out to her or his parents. This little book provides encouragement for this important step and gives effective suggestions for doing so.

Groff, D., ed. 1997. *Out Facts: Just about Everything You Need to Know about Gay and Lesbian Life from* Out *Magazine.* New York: Universe Publishing.

Written like a travel guide, this book provides the basics about what it is like to be openly gay. Sometimes witty, sometimes serious, the topics include clothing styles, what to look for to avoid discrimination at work and elsewhere, health and AIDS, safer sex, gay culture, lesbian culture, and coming out.

Holmes, S., and J. Tust, eds. 2002. *Testimonies: Lesbian Coming-Out Stories.* Los Angeles: Alyson Publications.

Nearly two dozen women recount their coming-out experiences. The women represent different ethnic, social, racial, and economic classes. This is better written than most coming-out stories.

Saks, A., and W. Curtis, eds. 1994. *Revelations: A Collection of Gay Male Coming Out Stories.* Los Angeles: Alyson Publications.

Coming out is a frightening process. This collection of coming-out stories provides insight into the emotional turmoil many men go through when deciding to share their sexual orientation with others. Fear, self-hate, understanding, tears, anger, and hope distinguish coming out. Ultimately, each writer shows great strength of character by being true to himself.

Signorile, M. 1995. *Outing Yourself: How to Come Out as Lesbian or Gay to Your Family, Friends, and Coworkers.* New York: Random House.

Although similar in content to other books on the process of coming out, *Outing Yourself* addresses the additional issue of coming out at work and personal public safety. Each topic is well written and nonacademic.

Counseling

DeCrescenzo, T. 1997. *Gay and Lesbian Professionals in the Closet: Who's in, Who's Out, and Why.* Binghamton, NY: Harrington Park Press.

Although one would think that professional counselors, psychologists, and psychiatrists would be honest about their sexual orientation, that is often not the case. This book explores why many in the helping professions are not open about their sexual orientation.

Kominars, S. B., and K. D. Kominars. 1996. *Accepting Ourselves and Others: A Journey into Recovery from Addiction and Compulsive Behavior for Gays, Lesbians, and Bisexuals.* Center City, MN: Hazelden.

Internalized homophobia leads many lesbians and gay men into chemical addiction and compulsive behavior. It is important for professional counselors to recognize internalized homophobia and how it manifests itself instead of wrongly trying to treat homosexuality. This book is quite academic and is aimed at the working professional counselor.

Ryan, C., and D. Futterman. 1998. *Lesbian and Gay Youth, Care and Counseling.* New York: Columbia University Press.

Counselors, unfortunately, are often unaware that their clients are lesbian or gay. This book brings awareness to this topic and gives specific guidelines for appropriate services.

Cultural Diversity

Battle, J., C. J. Cohen, D. Warren, G. Fergenson, and S. Audam. 2002. *Say It Loud: I'm Black and I'm Proud.* Washington, DC: National Gay and Lesbian Task Force. Available free at www. ngltf.org.

This study examines the family structure, political behavior, experiences of racism and homophobic bias, sexual identity, and the policy priorities of more than 2,500 black LGBT people who participated in black gay pride celebrations.

Constantine-Simms, D., ed. 2000. *The Greatest Taboo: Homosexuality in Black Communities.* Los Angeles: Alyson Publications.

Constantine-Simms has compiled twenty-eight essays by academics and writers of different ethnic heritages, genders, and sexualities to discuss the often-volatile relationship between black gay men and lesbians and others of their race. Histories from nineteenth-century slave quarters to postapartheid South Africa, from RuPaul to Wu Tan Clan, from 1920s Harlem to the Million Man March on Washington in 1995 provide settings to discuss the transformation and continued repression of black gay men and lesbians.

Greene, B., ed. 1997. *Ethnic and Cultural Diversity among Lesbians and Gay Men.* Thousand Oaks, CA: Sage.

A diverse group of authors provide empirical, clinical, and theoretical discussions concerning diversity within the lesbian and gay community. The volume includes a number of personal narratives that offer poignant insight into the complexities, pressures, and losses experienced by lesbians and gay men as a result of the closed fist of bigotry.

Hinsch, B. 1990. *Passions of the Cut Sleeve: The Male Homosexual Tradition in China.* Berkeley: University of California Press.

Legend tells of Han Emperor Ai cutting the sleeve of his shirt to keep from waking his lover Dong Xia, who was sleeping soundly in his arms. As a result of this legend, homosexuals in China have long been called "those of the cut sleeve." In this book Hinsch explores homosexual norms in China. For those who have never thought about homosexuality in terms other than those of Western culture, this book is an eye-opening experience.

Williams, W. 1992. *The Spirit and the Flesh: Sexual Diversity in American Indian Culture.* Boston: Beacon Press.

Although numerous books have examined other cultures with respect to homosexuality, *The Spirit and the Flesh* is probably the best. Written for the high school or college-level reader, the book reads easily, yet is authoritative. For people studying homosexuality, a book such as this provides a better understanding of the diversity in human sexuality, which is greater than the simple binary heterosexual-homosexual paradigm. It may surprise readers to learn that in some cultures everyone engages in homosexual relationships for the majority of life. This demonstrates the flexibility of human sexuality.

History and Biographies

Cowan, T. 1992. *Gay Men and Women Who Enriched the World.* Rev. ed. Los Angeles: Alyson Publications.

This fascinating collection of biographies has been recently updated to include more biographies and address some of the controversies caused by the earlier editions. Biographies include Plato, Colette, Bessie Smith, Andy Warhol, Laurence Olivier, and Barbara Jordan.

Duberman, M. 1991. *About Time: Exploring the Gay Past.* Rev. ed. New York: Meridian.

Duberman presents a collection of gay commentaries dating from 1826 to his own personal essays. This is enlightened reading from the past.

Duberman, M., M. Vicinus, and G. Chauncey, Jr., eds. 1990. *Hidden from History: Reclaiming the Gay and Lesbian Past.* New York: Meridian.

This is one of the major books written in the 1990s. It discusses the history of many different cultures and their acceptance of homosexuality. Designed for the college classroom, it is fully cited and won many literary awards.

Faderman, L. 1981. *Odd Girls and Twilight Lovers: A History of Lesbian Life in Twentieth-Century America*. New York: Penguin.

Faderman wrote one of the first books to look at lesbian life in the United States. *Odd Girls* is widely cited for its content and research and is recommended for use in college classrooms.

Harris, D. 1997. *Rise and Fall of Gay Culture*. New York: Hyperion.

The reception of this book was mixed when released. The author argues that as lesbians and gay men are accepted into society, much of the uniqueness of the gay community has been lost. The book looks primarily at the gay male experience, and many book reviewers complained that it lacked a global view. It is interesting to read when these caveats are taken into consideration.

Katz, J. 1976. *Gay American History: Lesbians and Gay Men in the U.S.A.* New York: Thomas Y. Crowell.

This authoritative book includes more than 200 source documents related to homosexuality in America dating back to 1566. Many pivotal documents of the gay rights movement are included, such as the founding in 1924 of the Chicago Society for Human Rights in Illinois—the first gay rights group to obtain nonprofit corporation status.

———. 1983. *Gay/Lesbian Almanac: A New Documentary*. New York: Harper and Row.

Katz accumulated more information on American history than he could include in his book *Gay American History*. These documents are included in this book and are a must for any student of gay history studying the period between 1607 and 1950.

Liebman, M. 1992. *Coming Out Conservative*. San Francisco: Chronicle Books.

What would it be like to hold conservative values your entire life and then, at age sixty-seven, to have the public become aware of your same-sex attraction? Liebman led such a double life, having had close ties to right-wing conservatives such as William F. Buckley, Jr. and Ronald Reagan. He shares inside views about antigay politics from in and out of the closet.

Perry, T. D., and T. L. P. Swicegood. 1991. *Profiles in Gay and Lesbian Courage.* New York: St. Martin's Press.

Perry and Swicegood have written biographies of eight gay men and lesbians who have "achieved recognition" in various fields. These are Ivy Bottini, Barbara Gittings, Harry Hay, Gilberto Gerald, Harvey Milk, Jean O'Leary, Elaine Noble, and Leonard Matlovich.

Plant, R. 1987. *The Pink Triangle: The Nazi War against Homosexuals.* New York: New Republic Books/Henry Holt.

Plant writes about the personal experiences of those who suffered in Nazi concentration camps. Included in the appendixes is Paragraph 175, which outlawed homosexuality, and a chronology of the German gay civil rights movement concluding with the German Nuremberg trials.

Rector, F. 1981. *The Nazi Extermination of Homosexuals.* New York: Stein and Day.

Rector chronicles the changes in gay German society from the heyday of the 1920s to the brutality of the concentration camps two decades later. Rector shows what life was like under these circumstances and includes testimonials from gay men who survived the camps. This stirring book is emotionally difficult to read.

Rutledge, L. W. 1992. *The Gay Decades.* New York: Plume.

Rutledge tells hundreds of narratives to weave a tapestry of the U.S. gay social movement from 1969 to the present. It is a delight to read and contains social, legal, historical, political, and psychological data not available in any other source.

Shilts, R. 1982. *The Mayor of Castro Street: The Life and Times of Harvey Milk.* New York: St. Martin's Press.

This was Shilts's first major work and received wide accolades. The book tells the personal story of Harvey Milk, his political career in San Francisco, and his subsequent murder by Dan White. Shilts is able to write in a way that keeps the reader's interest.

Simpson, R. 1976. *From the Closet to the Courts: The Lesbian Transition.* New York: Richard Seaver/Viking Press.

Simpson presents a personal view of the early gay rights movement from the position of a lesbian who was directly involved in it beginning in 1969.

Timmons, S. 1990. *The Trouble with Harry Hay: Founder of the Modern Gay Movement.* Los Angeles: Alyson Publications.

This is a well-written biography of one of the central figures in the development of the modern gay movement. Hay was responsible for the founding of the Mattachine Society; ONE, Inc.; and the Radical Fairies.

Tobin, K., and R. Wicker. 1972. *The Gay Crusaders.* New York: Paperback Library.

Biographical sketches are presented of fifteen men and women who were politically active during the early stages of the modern gay rights movement. These include Jim Baker, Del Martin, Jim Owles, Michael McConnell, Franklin Kameny, Troy Perry, Barbara Gittings, and Phyllis Lyon.

Weeks, J. 1977. *Coming Out: Homosexual Politics in Britain, from the Nineteenth Century to the Present.* London: Quartet Books.

This is the best-written chronology of the gay rights movement in Britain. Weeks provides historical listings and analyzes the changes occurring in British culture.

Weiss, A., and G. Schiller. 1988. *Before Stonewall: The Making of a Gay and Lesbian Community.* Tallahassee, FL: Naiad Press.

This is a reprint of the script used to make the award-winning documentary film of the same name. Stills from the film highlight the book.

Humor

Cohn, M. 1995. *"Do What I Say": Ms. Behavior's Guide to Gay and Lesbian Etiquette.* Boston: Houghton Mifflin.

This is a marginally funny book that pokes fun at lesbian and gay stereotypes.

Eisenback, H. 1996. *Lesbianism Made Easy.* New York: Crown.

This book has nonstop laughs as it guides readers into becoming full-blown lesbians.

Hanes, K. 1994. *The Gay Guy's Guide to Life: 463 Maxims, Manners, and Mottoes for the Gay Nineties.*

This book is witty and funny, with many quotes and mottoes to choose from. Unfortunately for the academic, the sources are not clearly identified.

Instructional Guides and Curricula

Besner, H. F., and C. I. Spungin. 1995. *Gay and Lesbian Students: Understanding Their Needs.* Washington, DC: Taylor and Francis.

This is a small book that talks about the difficulties of being a lesbian or gay male student in public schools. It includes a detailed outline for a six-hour faculty workshop on homophobia, but fails to provide the content of the workshop.

Blumenfeld, W. 1992. *Homophobia: How We All Pay the Price.* Boston: Beacon Press.

Blumenfeld first discusses the impact of homophobia on our society and the individual. The final chapters present his teaching program for reducing homophobia. It is considered one of the best short courses available.

Gallos, J., V. J. Ramsey, and Associates. 1997. *Teaching Diversity: Listening to the Soul, Speaking from the Heart.* San Francisco: Jossey-Bass.

Here, teachers who have faced the challenges of teaching diversity tell their experiences. Most are candid, telling us what worked and what bombed. A few of the stories are funny and ultimately encouraging. Each writer provides gems of ideas for educators faced with the daunting task of developing their own diversity training programs.

Gay, Lesbian, Straight Education Network (GLSEN). n.d. *Advanced Anti-Homophobia Training.* Watertown, CT: GLSEN. Available at http://www.glsen.org.

GLSEN is the largest organization devoted to the needs of lesbian and gay students and their allies in K–12 education. This training manual is designed to help teachers and others conduct antihomophobia training. Much of this material has been repackaged by GLSEN in its Lunchbox Series—literally, a yellow lunchbox with all materials and activities placed on cards for ease of use.

Jennings, K. 1994. *Becoming Visible: A Reader in Gay and Lesbian History for High School and College Students.* Los Angeles: Alyson Publications.

Jennings is the major force behind GLSEN and has put together a reader applicable for high school and college students on LGBT issues.

Lipkin, A. n.d. *A Staff Development Manual for Anti-Homophobia Education in the Secondary Schools.* Cambridge, MA: Harvard Graduate School of Education.

Massachusetts mandated statewide antihomophobia training in all secondary schools. This book is the result of that mandate. It speaks about the need and rationale for antihomophobia training and presents a workshop model appropriate for secondary school personnel. Unfortunately, the book does not contain the content required for the course and expects teachers to be familiar with the facts and data.

McNaught, B. 1993. *Gay Issues in the Workplace.* New York: St. Martin's Press.

McNaught is a leading authority on LGBT issues in the workplace. Based on almost twenty years of practical experience, this book is an invaluable resource for human relations departments. It discusses the needs of lesbian, gay, and bisexual workers. In the final chapters of the book, McNaught presents a teaching model he has found to be effective in meeting the goals of the corporation and the personal needs of workers.

Mitchell, L., ed. 1998. *Tackling Gay Issues in School.* Watertown, CT: Gay, Lesbian, Straight Education Network (GLSEN). Available at http://www.glsen.org.

This book discusses many of the controversies concerning lesbian and gay issues in K–12 schools. Although not a training manual, it contains insights helpful to those contemplating an antibias program that includes LGBT issues.

National Education Association (NEA), Human and Civil Rights Division. n.d. *Affording Equal Opportunity to Gay and Lesbian Students through Teaching and Counseling: A Training Handbook for Educators.* Washington, DC: NEA.

The National Education Association is the largest educational organization in the United States. This handbook was a collaborative effort by many educators who have experience in developing antibias educational programs. This book is invaluable to educators faced with the challenges of providing safe environments for all students—including lesbian and gay students.

Riddle, D. 1994. *Alone No More: Developing a School Support System for Gay, Lesbian and Bisexual Youth.* Appendix A. St. Paul: Minnesota Department of Education.

This program was funded by the Minnesota Department of Education and gives a broad discussion of the issues of lesbian, gay, and bisexual youths in school. This is not a curriculum but rather gives suggestions to school administrators and staff on developing support systems to meet the needs of LGBT students.

Stewart, C. 1995a. *The Efficacy of Sexual Orientation Training in Law Enforcement Agencies.* UMI: 9614075. Los Angeles: University of Southern California.

This is the only research to review educational programs and their efficacy at reducing bias. Although based on law enforcement environments, the findings are applicable to other areas. Stewart pulls no punches about what does not work and, more importantly, what does. Academic and sometimes difficult to read, the book contains important messages for educators faced with developing and delivering antibias programs.

———. 1995b. *Training for Law Enforcement: Gay and Lesbian Cultural Awareness.* Rev. ed. Los Angeles: L.A. Gay and Lesbian Police Advisory Task Force.

This is the only training manual on lesbian and gay issues in law enforcement that has been sold nationwide. Each topic focuses on the unique needs of law enforcement, including points of contact and the law.

———. 1999. *Sexually Stigmatized Communities—Reducing Het-*

erosexism and Homophobia: An Awareness Training Manual. Thousand Oaks, CA: Sage.

This is the most comprehensive and thorough training manual for developing and delivering educational programs to reduce heterosexism and homophobia. It provides everything an educator would need for an antibias training program. Chapters 1 and 2 present educational theory, research findings, and a step-by-step model. Chapter 3 contains over 100 topic papers concisely presenting what is known about homosexuality. Chapter 4 contains 23 overhead transparencies, and Chapter 5 contains 47 classroom activities—many with worksheets. The materials are designed for high school or college-level students.

Legal Resources

Cain, P. A. 2000. *Rainbow Rights.* Boulder, CO: Westview Press.

Cain has written a readable book about the history and development of LGBT civil rights. Instead of simply listing what laws and rights exist in specific jurisdictions, she expands on the politics that created legal situations and influenced court decisions. The book is written for all those interested in the law and its development.

Editors of the Harvard Law Review. 1990. *Sexual Orientation and the Law.* Cambridge, MA: Harvard University Press.

Written as a guide for legal professionals, this book presents topics on criminal justice, employment, education, same-sex couples, family, immigration, and others with a concise explanation of the law and some of the controversy. It does not contain academic research on homosexuality. Although outdated, the book is still useful.

Eskridge, W. N., Jr. 1999. *Gaylaw: Challenging the Apartheid of the Closet.* Cambridge, MA: Harvard University Press.

This is an impressive historical review of the politics and changes in U.S. law that constructed the modern gay closet. It is written for law and college students. At the end of the book, Eskridge discusses many of the paradoxes surrounding sex, consent, and the law and their future implications. The unique appendix traces the changes in sex statutes from the 1600s to the present. The appendix alone is worth the price of the book. In many ways, this is an update of the well-written book *Intimate Matters: A History of Sexuality in America* (1988).

Hunter, N. D., S. E. Michaelson, and T. B. Stoddard. 1992. *The Rights of Lesbians and Gay Men: The Basic ACLU Guide to a Gay Person's Rights.* 3rd ed. Carbondale and Edwardsville: Southern Illinois University Press.

This small handbook is a concise summary of the laws and court cases relating to lesbians and gay men in the United States. It desperately needs to be updated, yet it is still usable to guide researchers in their own work. It is written for both the lay reader and the legal professional.

Keen, L., and S. B. Goldberg. 1999. *Strangers to the Law: Gay People on Trial.* Ann Arbor: University of Michigan Press.

This book traces the development of Colorado's Amendment 2 and its ultimate defeat by the U.S. Supreme Court in 1996 in *Romer v. Evans.* Written by Goldberg, lawyer for the Lambda Legal Defense and Education Fund, and Keen, editor for the *Washington Blade*, the book is a captivating glimpse of the struggles Colorado experienced with the attempt to block antidiscrimination laws for lesbians and gay men. It is well written and appropriate for high school and college students. It contains much of the Supreme Court dialogue and the complete written decision.

Marotta, T. 1981. *The Politics of Homosexuality.* Boston: Houghton Mifflin.

Although this is an old book, it has one of the best historical accounts of the founding of the modern gay civil rights movement. It reviews the founding of the Mattachine Society and subsequent activists groups such as the Gay Liberation Front, the Gay Activists Alliance, Radicalesbians, and the Daughters of Bilitis. More than anything, this book shows how a handful of activists was able to make significant strides toward gaining equal rights. These achievements were not made through intimidation, but rather through educating the heterosexual establishment about gay and lesbian issues and concerns. This is a "must-have" book for any student of gay history.

Mohr, R. D. 1988. *Gay/Justice—a Study of Ethics, Society, and Law.* New York: Columbia University Press.

Written for the legal professional, this book engages in deep legal analysis of a number of issues, including discrimination, sodomy, privacy, gay rights, and AIDS. It is perfect for class debates about legal gay issues. Although the laws regarding homosexuality have changed considerably since the publication of this book, it contains many of the classic arguments on freedom and social responsibility.

Richards, D. A. J. 1998. *Women, Gays, and the Constitution: The Grounds for Feminism and Gay Rights in Culture and Law.* Chicago: University of Chicago Press.

Written for the legal analyst and college student, this book makes the argument that sex statutes are examples of "moral slavery." Richards develops his thesis by tracing the writings of early first-wave feminists and their analysis of slavery. Ultimately, Richards provides arguments as to why sexual orientation should be made a suspect class, gay marriages should be made legal, and other topics. This book is perfect for a college law class.

Robson, R. 1997. *Gay Men, Lesbians, and the Law.* New York: Chelsea House.

This thin book is probably the best-written book for the lay reader or high school student. It reviews in nontechnical terms sex statutes, discrimination, education, families, criminal justice, health concerns, and the legal profession. It was written mainly to present the current legal status of gay men, lesbians, and the law. However, its brevity limits the depth of the topics discussed.

Stewart, C. 2001. *Homosexuality and the Law: A Dictionary.* Santa Barbara, CA: ABC-CLIO.

This is the most recent and comprehensive book covering the legal status of gay and lesbian people in the United States. The volume blends sociological, psychological, and medical research on human sexuality and discusses historical and political forces that affect the legal status of homosexuality. It is the first book to examine transsexual, transgender, and intersex legal issues in detail. It is written in language understandable by the layperson.

Strasser, M. 1997. *Legallywed: Same-Sex Marriage and the Constitution.* Ithaca, NY: Cornell University Press.

This book focuses on the controversy of same-sex marriage. Written for the college-level reader, the book contains a detailed discussion of the legal aspects of marriage, full faith and credit, the Defense of Marriage Act, and the impact same-sex marriage would have on child custody and adoptions. It is easy to read and not overburdened with references.

Students of the Tulane University School of Law, eds. n.d. *Law and Sexuality: A Review of Lesbian, Gay, Bisexual, and Transgender Legal Issues.* New Orleans, LA: Tulane University School of Law. Available at http: www.law.tulane.edu/journals.htm.

This excellent law journal is written for law students and practicing judges and lawyers. Each volume is reasonably priced. Volume 8 contains a comprehensive state-by-state summary of statutes dealing with HIV and AIDS as well as other topics.

Van der Meide, W. 2000. *Legislating Equality: A Review of Laws Affecting Gay, Lesbian, Bisexual, and Transgendered People in the United States.* Washington, DC: National Gay and Lesbian Task Force. Available at http://www.ngltf.org.

The Policy Institute Research of NGLTF has written a comprehensive report on the extent to which laws and regulations throughout the United States have been enacted to provide protection and equality for the LGBT community.

LGBT Parenting

Arnup, K. 1995. *Lesbian Parenting: Living with Pride and Prejudice.* Charlottetown, PEI: Gynergy.

Lesbian mothers face discrimination because they are lesbian, and have lower incomes because they are women. These issues affect parenting choices. This book concisely addresses these issues while at the same time giving support to lesbian mothers in their struggles.

Barret, R., and B. Robinson. 1990. *Gay Fathers.* Lexington, MA: Lexington Books.

Groundbreaking when it was released, *Gay Fathers* gives voice to gay men who are fathers through marriage or adoption. Questions such as, When do I tell my children I am gay? and Do I tell the school administration? are addressed through example.

Drucker, J. 1998. *Families of Value: Gay and Lesbian Parents and Their Children Speak Out.* New York: Plenum.

Drucker surveyed lesbian and gay parents and their children about their family experiences. Each story is presented to show the wide range in responses to the issue of homosexuality and family. No other book on gay families gives as much first-person reporting.

Johnson, S. M., and E. O'Connor. 2001. *For Lesbian Parents.* New York: Guilford Press.

This highly regarded book provides guidance on the numerous special questions lesbian parents face, such as when and how to come out to their child, interfacing with school officials, teasing at school, and more. Written with clarity and wit, Johnson and O'Connor bring to the book their knowledge as Ph.D.s in psychology as well as their personal experience as lesbian mothers.

LGBT Seniors

Adelman, J., ed. 1993. *Lambda Gray: A Practical, Emotional, and Spiritual Guide for Gays and Lesbians Who Are Growing Older.* North Hollywood, CA: Newcastle.

Lesbian, gay, bisexual, and transgender older people are often ignored by the dominant culture. *Lambda Gray* discusses some of the dynamics associated with growing older, along with practical ideas for dealing with these issues.

LGBT Youths

Bass, E., and K. Kaufman. 1996. *Free Your Mind: The Book for Gay, Lesbian, and Bisexual Youth and Their Allies.* New York: HarperPerennial.

Because of the controversy concerning homosexuality and youths, few books address the needs of young gays and lesbians and their allies. This book contains many first-person accounts that envision a world without homophobia.

Day, F. A. 2000. *Lesbian and Gay Voices: An Annotated Bibliography and Guide to Literature for Children and Young Adults.* Westport, CT: Greenwood Press.

The world of literature for children and young adults that addresses the issue of homosexuality has exploded. This bibliography provides annotations to help readers select materials suitable for young readers.

Heron, A., ed. 2001. *Two Teenagers in Twenty: Writings by Gay and Lesbian Youth.* Los Angeles: Alyson Publications.

More than a decade ago, Heron published the writings of lesbian and gay youths in *One Teenager in Ten*—the first time LGBT youths had written about their lives in their own words. Now she asks another group of youths to tell their stories and finds that the fears and feelings of isolation have not abated with the new generation.

Pollack, R., and C. Schwartz. 1995. *The Journey Out: A Book for and about Gay, Lesbian, and Bisexual Teens.* New York: Puffin Books.

Although there are a number of excellent books on the topic of gay, lesbian, and bisexual youths, this one is structured more to assist youths in coming to terms with their sexuality and growing into happy, adjusted adults whose sexual orientation is an integral part of their lives.

Rench, J. 1990. *Understanding Sexual Identity: A Book for Gay and Lesbian Teens.* Minneapolis: Lerner Publications.

Much of the literature on sexual identity is written for adults and academics. This accessible book brings this important topic to the reading level and understanding of teenagers. Important information on coming out, sexual development, masculinity and femininity, and more is covered.

Sonnie, A., ed. 2000. *Revolutionary Voices: A Multicultural Queer Youth Anthology.* Los Angeles: Alyson Publications.

This collection of queer youths' experiences, ideas, and dreams expressed through poetry, letters, prose, diaries, and artwork gives an indication of the diversity of future queer society.

Marriage

Cabaj, R. P., and D. W. Purcell, eds. 1998. *On the Road to Same-Sex Marriage: A Supportive Guide to Psychological, Political, and Legal Issues.* San Francisco: Jossey-Bass.

This collection of articles is one of the most comprehensive reviews of the topic of same-sex marriage. In addition to the legal implications of same-sex marriage, the psychological and political impacts are discussed. Even when same-sex marriage is finally approved, it will take time for members of the lesbian and gay community to come to view this as a desirable arrangement for their relationships, not simply a replication of heterosexual coupling.

Eskeridge, W. N., Jr. 1996. *The Case for Same-Sex Marriage: From Sexual Liberty to Civilized Commitment.* New York: The Free Press.

Eskeridge presents solid arguments as to why legalizing same-sex marriage is important for maintaining civil liberties within a democracy. Denying lesbians and gay men the right to marriage has serious implications for other freedoms and for the maintenance of equality between citizens. Written for academics, the book is well cited.

Graff, E. J. 1999. *What Is Marriage For? The Strange Social History of Our Most Intimate Institution.* Boston: Beacon Press.

Our current concept of marriage in the United States is but one of many forms that marriage has taken over human history. This book reviews many different cultures from many different regions and with many different religions and shows that marriage is a social construction used to solidify power. This is important to remember when the discussion of same-sex marriage is debated in our modern media.

Kohn, S. 1999. *The Domestic Partnership Organizing Manual for Employee Benefits.* Washington, DC: National Gay and Lesbian Task Force. Available at http://www.ngltf.org.

This report provides comprehensive information on what domestic partnerships benefits are, why employers should adopt them, and how employees and citizens can organize effectively for policy change.

Men and Gay Men Issues

Fanning, P., and M. McKay. 1993. *Being a Man: A Guide to the New Masculinity.* Oakland, CA: New Harbinger.

The men's movement has brought forth a flood of writings. This book looks at contemporary America and discusses what it means to be a man. The authors address the issue of sexual orientation, which, to the surprise of many men, is not related to masculinity.

Hemphill, E., ed. 1991. *Brother to Brother: New Writings by Black Gay Men.* Los Angeles: Alyson Publications.

Black activist Hemphill follows in the footsteps of Joseph Beam with this powerful anthology of essays, poetry, and fiction. Contributors include Marlon Riggs, Assoto Saint, Melvin Dixon, and Craig G. Harris.

Lowenthal, M., ed. 1997. *Gay Men at the Millennium: Sex, Spirit, and Community.* New York: Tarcher/Putnam.

Many gay men struggle with their masculinity in an environment in which major religions tell them that they are not legitimate men or that they do not have an enlightened spirit. This book explores more diverse understandings of masculinity and seeks to encourage a spiritual revolution toward greater acceptance of sexual and gender diversity.

Nardi, P. M., ed. 1999. *Gay Masculinities.* Newbury Park, CA: Sage.

The articles in this collection attempt to explain how contemporary gay men in the United States engage in, contest, and modify notions of masculinity. The writers explore how gay men form masculine identities in business, church, home, the community, and interpersonal relationships. This is a fascinating and thought-provoking book.

Outland, O. 2000. *Coming Out: A Handbook for Men.* Los Angeles: Alyson Publications.

Outland is the author of *The Principles: The Gay Man's Guide to Getting (and Keeping) Mr. Right, Death Wore a Smart Little Outfit,* and

Death Wore a Fabulous New Fragrance. He brings his wit and insight to the topic of coming out.

Penn, R. 1997. *Gay Men's Wellness Guide: The Natural Lesbian and Gay Health Association's Complete Book of Physical, Emotional, and Mental Health and Well-Being for Every Gay Male.* New York: Henry Holt.

Similar to other wellness guides, this one focuses on the needs of gay men. It is very helpful, with many resources.

The Military

Benecke, M. M., C. D. Osburn, and K. Gilberd. 1997. *Survival Guide.* Washington, DC: Servicemembers Legal Defense Network (SLDN). Available at http://www.sldn.org.

This guide was developed by SLDN to help military personnel who have been accused of being lesbian or gay, or of being supportive of gay rights to protect themselves from harassment and persecution. This is an excellent and comprehensive resource.

Bérubé, A. 1990. *Coming Out Under Fire: The History of Gay Men and Women in World War Two.* New York: The Free Press.

Bérubé provides a retrospective outlook on military attitudes regarding homosexuality and studies the roles that lesbians and homosexual men played in World War II.

Dyer, K. 1990. *Gays in Uniform: The Pentagon's Secret Reports.* Los Angeles: Alyson Publications.

Dyer makes comments and reprints two different studies carried out by the Pentagon regarding gays and lesbians in the military. The reports were squelched by the military because they both proved that the antigay policies of the military are unjustified.

Hippler, M. 1989. *Matlovich: The Good Soldier.* Los Angeles: Alyson Publications.

This is an autobiography about the trials and tribulations of Matlovich, the first soldier to come out while still in the military.

Shilts, R. 1993. *Conduct Unbecoming: Lesbians and Gays in the U.S. Military.* New York: St. Martin's Press.

Shilts, one of America's finest gay journalists, writes a popular history of U.S. policies concerning gays and lesbians in the military. Shilts reveals the hypocrisy demonstrated by the military on this topic. Many of the leading spokespersons during the 1993 congressional battles over gays in the military are documented as giving different positions when speaking on or off the record. Further, Shilts reviews the military's own findings that lesbians and gay men make excellent military personnel.

Political Activism

Currah, P., S. Minter, and J. Green. 2000. *Transgender Equality: A Handbook for Activists and Policymakers.* Washington, DC: National Gay and Lesbian Task Force. Available at http://www.ngltf.org.

This handbook provides the tools for activists and policymakers to pass transgender-inclusive nondiscrimination and antiviolence legislation.

Yang, A. S. 2001. *The 2000 National Election Study and Gay and Lesbian Rights: Support for Equality Grows.* Washington, DC: National Gay and Lesbian Task Force. Available at http://www.ngltf.org.

Using data from the 2000 National Election Study, researcher Yang shows that support for LGBT rights has substantially increased among all people of all political ideologies.

Religion and Homosexuality

Balka, C., and A. Rose, eds. 1989. *Twice Blessed: On Being Gay and Jewish.* Boston: Beacon Press.

Written with a sense of humor, this book gives historical, sociological, and psychological research on homosexuality and Jewish culture.

Boswell, J. 1980. *Christianity, Social Tolerance, and Homosexuality: Gay People in Western Europe from the Beginning of the Christian Era to the Fourteenth Century.* Chicago: University of Chicago Press.

Boswell's groundbreaking research looks at various opinions regarding homosexuality in the first twelve centuries of the Christian church. He shocked the world with the discovery that same-sex marriages were not only sanctioned by the early Christian church but were also celebrated in marriages between same-sex clergy.

Denman, R. M. 1990. *Let My People In.* New York: Morrow.

Denman recounts her personal trials and tribulations in being a lesbian minister in a United Methodist Church. In 1987 she was dismissed from the church due to her sexuality. Shortly after her removal from the church, she was ordained in the Unitarian Universalist Association, a church that does not disenfranchise members and clergy based on sexual orientation.

Glaser, C. R. 1988. *Coming Out as Sacrament.* 1991. *Coming Out to God.* Louisville, KY: Westminster/John Knox Press.

These two books are connected through the meditations of Chris Glaser. He explores what it means to be gay and religious. They clearly show that lesbians and gay men do not have to give up their spirituality to live an openly gay life.

Hasbany, R., ed. 1990. *Homosexuality and Religion.* New York: Haworth Press.

This was one of the first books to review many different world religions and their positions on homosexuality. It is well written and easy to read.

Helminiak, D. 2000. Rev. ed. *What the Bible Really Says about Homosexuality.* San Francisco: Alamo Square Press.

Helminiak discusses many of the arguments and counterarguments concerning the Bible and its supposed condemnation of homosexuality. He reviews the successive translations of the Bible from Hebrew to Greek, to Old English, to Modern English and how these have impacted our understanding of homosexuality. He concludes that the Bible does not condemn homosexual sex as we understand it today. This is an extremely important contribution to gay and biblical studies.

Johnson, T. 2000. *Gay Spirituality: The Role of Gay Identity in the Transformation of Human Consciousness.* Los Angeles: Alyson Publications.

Once many lesbians and gay men discover that the social conventions concerning sexuality and sex roles are wrong, they are inclined to question other social norms—such as religion. Johnson contends that this experience provides a kind of enlightenment that is unique to being gay and can help lead the way to religious transformation.

Kolodny, D. R., ed. 2000. *Blessed Bi Spirit: Bisexual People of Faith.* New York: Continuum.

A bisexual person involved in an opposite-sex relationship is welcomed with open arms by major religious organizations. However, when the same person is involved in a same-sex relationships, these doors are often closed. The author explores the emotional and spiritual impact that religious hypocrisy has on bisexual people.

National Gay and Lesbian Task Force, Political Research Associations, and Equal Partners in Faith. 1998. *Calculated Compassion.* Washington, DC: NGLTF. Available at http://www.ngltf.org.

The ex-gay movement presents itself as being a caring haven for "healing the homosexual." Actually, the ex-gay movement serves to camouflage and retool the religious right assault on legal protections against discimination for LGBT persons. *Calculated Compassion* traces the roots of this political change and reveals that the goal of the religious right is to create a theocratic government in the United States.

Perry, T. D. 1997. *The Lord Is My Shepherd and He Knows I'm Gay.* Los Angeles: Universal Fellowship Press.

Perry's long history with the Metropolitan Community Church (MCC), which he founded, gives him a unique perspective on religion and homosexuality. Here, he shares his understanding and supports the full acceptance of lesbians and gay men by major religious institutions.

Perry, T. D., and T. L. P. Swicegood. 1990. *Don't Be Afraid Anymore.* New York: St. Martin's Press.

The book retells Perry's life and the founding of MCC, the first gay church.

White, M. 1994. *Stranger at the Gate: To Be Gay and Christian in America.* New York: Simon and Schuster.

White worked for many years as a writer for members of the religious right, such as Pat Robertson. As a spiritual man coming to terms with his homosexuality, White eventually left that work to become a pastor for the Metropolitan Community Church. He toured America with his message of hope for lesbians and gay men. He was shocked by the blatant hatred espoused by many Christians toward him and other homosexuals. This book shares his experiences of this tour and contains quotes from religious leaders explicitly stating that homosexuals should be put to death. This book is excellently written and easy to read.

Young, P. D. 1982. *God's Bullies: Native Reflections on Preachers and Politics.* New York: Holt, Rinehart, and Winston.

Young was a reporter assigned to cover the Evangelical movement in the United States during the development of the Moral Majority and other fundamentalist religious groups. He was there for many of the founding meetings and includes many interviews and quotes from these leaders. As such, he observed the hatred many of these leaders expressed concerning homosexuality and gay rights. The book is excellently written and documents personal beliefs of these leaders that their followers rarely hear.

School Issues

Fricke, A. 1981. *Reflections of a Rock Lobster: A Story About Growing Up Gay.* Los Angeles: Alyson Publications.

Fricke's autobiography details his court battles over his desire to attend a high school prom with a male date.

Harbeck, K. M., ed. 1992. *Coming Out of the Classroom Closet: Gay and Lesbian Students, Teachers, and Curricula.* Binghamton, NY: Harrington Park Press.

This was the first book aimed at educational issues. It contains research articles on the attitudes and beliefs of educational professionals, a legal review of cases and statutes as they apply to students and staff, suggestions on curriculum development, and a number of personal experiences. Everyone interested in the school setting should read this book.

Howard, K., and A. Stevens, eds. 2002. *Out and About Campus: Personal Accounts by Lesbian, Gay, Bisexual, and Transgendered College Students.* Los Angeles: Alyson Publications.

This collection—the first of its kind—allowed twenty-eight lesbian, gay, bisexual, and transgender college students to describe how they survived college and, more importantly, how they fought, endured, and *changed* it.

Jennings, K. 1994a. *Becoming Visible.* Los Angeles: Alyson Publications.

Jennings, executive director of GLSEN, has written a 2,000-year history of lesbians and gay men. It is a welcomed general reader and is appropriate for high school students.

———. Jennings, K., ed. 1994b. *One Teacher in 10.* Los Angeles: Alyson Publications.

Jennings, executive director of GLSEN, has compiled stories written by gay and lesbian teachers about their professional experiences. The book chronicles both the struggles and victories these educators experienced in their fight for visibility.

———. 1998. *Telling Tales Out of School: Gays, Lesbians, and Bisexuals Revisit Their School Days.* Los Angeles: Alyson Publications.

More than thirty men and women share their experiences—some written with wry humor, others with acknowledged pain. Most discovered they are still trying to overcome the self-hate they learned in school. The stories are varied, detailing valiant struggles in pre-Stonewall days, the isolation experienced by tomboys and sissies, and the constant threat of violence.

National Gay and Lesbian Task Force (NGLTF). 1996. *LGBT Campus Organizing: A Comprehensive Manual.* Washington, DC: NGLTF. Available at http://www.ngltf.org.

This is an invaluable how-to manual to help with the creation of student, faculty, staff, or alumni LGBT groups on college campus.

Windmeyer, S. L., and P. W. Freeman, eds. 2001a. *Out on Fraternity Row: Personal Accounts of Being Gay in a College Fraternity.* Los Angeles: Alyson Publications.

Thirty gay men share their stories of coming out or staying silent while belonging to a fraternity. Many of the stories are emotionally charged, detailing the struggles of trying to belong while at the same time being true to themselves.

————. 2001b. *Secret Sisters: Stories of Being Lesbian and Bisexual in a College Sorority.* Los Angeles: Alyson Publications.

Thirty-two women share their personal accounts of pain and isolation resulting from being lesbian or bisexual while belonging to a college sorority. The book also provides a resource guide on organizations designed to promote greater tolerance of sexual diversity within the college Greek system.

Sports

Kopay, D., and P. D. Young. 1977. *The David Kopay Story.* New York: Arbor House.

A closeted professional football player of the 1960s and 1970s, Kopay tells his experiences and his views on antigay discrimination in professional sports.

Louganis, G., with E. Marcus. 1995. *Breaking the Surface.* New York: Random House.

Louganis became the most celebrated Olympic diver of all time. This biography details his dyslexia and discrimination, battles with low self-esteem, bouts of depression, and conflicts over his sexuality. It is also the story of a man who learns to live with HIV and the media intrusion into his life.

Pallone, D., with A. Steinberg. 1990. *Behind the Mask: My Double Life in Baseball.* New York: Viking Press.

Pallone began his career in major league baseball as a closeted umpire in the National League. After many faltering attempts to conceal his sexuality, he finally announced that he was gay. He was fired and wrote this book to explore his feelings and expose the antigay culture that pervades professional baseball.

Sanford, W. R., and C. R. Green. 1993. *Billie Jean King.* New York: Crestwood House.

This biography pulls no punches about tennis immortal King and her lesbianism.

Woog, D. 2001. *Jocks: True Stories of America's Gay Male Athletes.* Los Angeles: Alyson Publications.

Is there life for gay athletes after they come out to their team? Is there life before coming out? This collection of stories by journalist Woog explores what it means to be a gay male athlete in American sports.

Young, P. D., and M. Duberman. 1995. *Lesbians and Gays and Sports.* New York: Chelsea House.

This book gives biographical information about many sports personalities who are lesbian or gay. This is a nice overview, with discussion about homophobia within sports.

Zwerman, G. 1995. *Martina Navratilova.* New York: Chelsea House.

Unlike other biographies of tennis star Martina Navratilova, this one shows a caring and touching side of her struggle regarding her sport, love, and media intrusion.

Straight Parents, Family, and Friends

Aarons, L. 1995. *Prayers for Bobby: A Mother's Coming to Terms with the Suicide of Her Gay Son.* San Francisco: Harper.

Bobby Griffith committed suicide by jumping off a bridge over a freeway. He came from a religious family that was concerned that its religion had let it down. This book tells how his mother came to terms with his suicide, and identifies the hate spread by religious leaders as the source of his pain.

Cohen, S., and D. Cohen. 1989. *When Someone You Know Is Gay.* New York: M. Evans and Company.

This classic self-help book provides basic information on homosexuality in terms of how to be helpful to the person coming out. It is easy to read and is supportive of the coming-out process.

DeGeneres, B. 2000. *Just a Mom.* Los Angeles: Alyson Publications.

Written by the mother of television and motion picture star Ellen DeGeneres, this book tells of her trials and tribulations watching many in the media alternately slam and then support her daughter in her decision to come out as a lesbian on national television.

Herdt, G., and B. Koff. 2000. *Something to Tell You—the Road That Families Travel When a Child Is Gay.* New York: Columbia University Press.

When a child comes out gay or lesbian, the family also comes out. It has to face possible ridicule and discrimination from religious leaders, employers, and friends. This book details many of the common problems families with gay children experience.

Miller, D. A. 1993. *Coping When a Parent Is Gay.* New York: Rosen Publishing.

Often not discussed are families in which one or more of the parents are homosexual. This book is designed for children of homosexual parents. It answers many questions about homosexuality and assures children that they are not the cause of their parent's sexual orientation. Although somewhat dated and limited because of a focus on middle-class family structure, the book is still relevant today.

Woog, D. 1999. *Friends and Family: True Stories of Gay America's Straight Allies.* Los Angeles: Alyson Publications.

Friends of people who come out lesbian or gay face a coming out of their own. This book tells the stories of straight people who learned to cope with and admire the strength of their loved ones who came out.

Straight Spouses

Buxton, A. P. 1994. *The Other Side of the Closet: The Coming-Out Crisis for Straight Spouses and Families.* New York: John Wiley and Sons.

Spouses who discover or are told that their partner is lesbian or gay may be overcome with feelings of guilt, hatred, sadness, and more. This book gives some basic information on homosexuality and hopes to guide the couple into a deeper dialogue to address this important junction in the relationship.

Corley, R. 1990. *The Final Closet: The Gay Parent's Guide for Coming Out to Their Children*. Miami: Editech Press.

Gay or lesbian parents often lead hidden lives. Coming out, and coming out to their own children, may seem to be an insurmountable hurdle. This book gives support and advice to parents wanting to tell their children of their sexual orientation.

Transgender and Intersex People and Their Families

Boenke, M., ed. 1999. *Trans Forming Families: Real Stories about Transgendered Loved Ones*. Imperial Beach, CA: Walter Trook.

First-person accounts are used to describe the challenges faced by families in which one or more members are transgender. In some cases, the stories are tragic, whereas others show the indomitable strength of family love. Each story helps shed light on this otherwise hidden phenomenon.

Brown, J., and C. A. Rounsley. 1996. *True Selves: Understanding Transsexualism for Family, Friends, Coworkers, and Helping Professionals*. San Francisco: Jossey-Bass.

This book takes a middle ground between academic research and general public knowledge of transsexualism to provide information to those who want to gain a basic understanding.

Bullough, V., and B. Bullough. 1993. *Crossdressing, Sex, and Gender*. Philadelphia: University of Philadelphia Press.

The Bulloughs are one of the preeminent academic research teams on human sexuality, with many books to their credit. Here, they give a good academic review of gender and how it is expressed through sex and culture.

Burke, P. 1996. *Gender Shock: Exploding the Myths of Male and Female*. New York: Doubleday.

Male and female are considered by most to be self-evident and fixed. They are not. Human sexuality spreads across a wide spectrum of expression. This book reviews some of the sociological, anthropological, and psychological research on gender.

Dreger, A. D., ed. 2000. *Intersex in the Age of Ethics.* Hagerstown, MD: University Publishing Group.

Intersex activists are challenging the status quo concerning sexual assignment, particularly the surgery performed on infants to make them conform to the binary male-female paradigm. Intersexuality brings to the forefront ethical questions concerning gender, sexual orientation, and violence. This book gives an excellent overview of these dynamics.

Greenberg, J. A. 1999. **"Defining Male and Female: Intersexuality and the Collision Between Law and Biology."** *Arizona Law Review* 41 (Summer): 265.

This is what is termed the "mother" of all articles—that is, it reviews all previous articles and research on the subject of intersexuality. It contains medical definitions and examines the impact intersexuality has on sex statutes, legal identity, and documents. It is important for its legal analysis and the impact of the law in defining gender, sex, and sexual orientation.

Mallon, G. P. 1999. *Social Services with Transgendered Youth.* Binghamton, NY: Harrington Park Press.

Too often transgendered youths have been viewed as simply being confused about their gender because of inexperience. This view is changing with the recognition that anyone with a will and personality strong enough to go against cultural norms of gender is probably sincere in his or her belief. This book addresses many of the issues related to transgendered youths, promotes acceptance, and does not advocate attempting to change deep-seated gender identity.

Paisely, C., and S. Minter. n.d. *Transgender Equality: A Handbook for Activists and Policymakers.* San Francisco: National Center for Lesbian Rights. Available at http://www.nclrights.org.

The National Center for Lesbian Rights has produced this booklet to guide activists and policymakers who seek to gain equality for transgender people. Many practical applications are discussed, and resources that could be used in this effort are listed.

Walworth, J. 1998. *Transsexual Works: An Employer's Guide.* Westchester, CA: Center for Gender Sanity.

This is an excellent resource on the issue of transsexual workers. It gives many practical suggestions and some review of the law. Every business should have a copy of this book.

Violence

Bowker, L. H., ed. 1997. *Masculinities and Violence.* Thousand Oaks, CA: Sage.

This collection of essays explores the connection between the cultural norms of masculinity and violence. Men are trained to use violence to ensure conformity to gender norms. Because lesbians and gay men do not conform to these norms, they experience a greater level of bias-motivated violence. Written for the academic, the essays are well documented.

Comstock, G. D. 1991. *Violence against Lesbians and Gay Men.* New York: Columbia University Press.

This is an excellent book reviewing the research on antigay violence. It provides a historical overview, empirical data on victims and perpetrators, and an understanding of the patriarchal underpinnings of antigay violence, and it analyzes the connection between conservative religious beliefs and antigay violence. This book is well written and documented for college readers. For complementary materials, see the works of Gregory Herek.

Herek, G. J., and K. T. Berrill, eds. 1992. *Hate Crimes: Confronting Violence against Lesbians and Gay Men.* Newbury Park, CA: Sage.

This is a collection of essays on the psychological and sociological dimensions of antigay hate crimes. Suggestions for overcoming the problems are included.

Women and Lesbian Issues

Boston Women's Health Book Collective. *Our Bodies, Ourselves for the New Century: A Book by and for Women.* 1998. New York: Simon and Schuster.

Our Bodies is one of the better health books written for women. With many updated references, it should be in the library of all women and those interested in providing quality health care to women.

Brill, S., and K. Toevs. 2002. *The Essential Guide to Lesbian Conception, Pregnancy, and Birth*. Los Angeles: Alyson Publications.

This book, the first of its kind, provides a step-by-step guide to the physical and emotional aspects of conception as these are related to the unique needs of lesbians. Resources in the appendix include lists of fertility centers, legal and medical guidance, legal forms and contracts, and fertility charts.

Gruskin, E. P. 1998. *The Care and Treatment of Lesbian and Bisexual Women: A Guide for Health Professionals*. Thousand Oaks, CA: Sage.

Lesbian and bisexual women have unique health needs that are often ignored by health professionals. This book addresses many of these issues and provides appropriate guidance for their care.

Landrine, H., and E. A. Klonoff. 1997. *Discrimination against Women: Prevalence, Consequences, Remedies*. Thousand Oaks, CA: Sage.

Women experience a high level of discrimination based upon their gender. Lesbians are subjected not only to sexism but also to homophobia. This academic book documents the level of sexism in the United States and proposes many remedies. It is written for policymakers and academics.

Strock, C. 2000. *Married Women Who Love Women: The Secret Life of Married Women and the Power of Female Attraction*. Los Angeles: Alyson Publications.

Strock interviewed more than 100 women and their husbands and children to explore the emotional consequences of married women who suddenly discover they are attracted to other women. How do they cope? How is making love with another woman different from making love with men? The topic remains largely taboo but is explored here with discreet concern and understanding.

White, J., and C. Martinez, eds. 1997. *The Lesbian Health Book: Caring for Ourselves*. Seattle: Seal Press.

Women's health issues are overlooked by our culture, and lesbian health is virtually ignored. This book provides an excellent

overview of the health needs of lesbians. It argues that neglect by
the medical establishment makes it even more important that lesbians take care of themselves and their lesbian community. This
is an excellent resource.

Bookstores

Most major bookstore chains and college bookstores have lesbian
and gay sections. There are a handful of bookstores that are exclusively gay. These include:

A Different Light Bookstores (www.adlbooks.com):
151 West 19th Street
New York, NY 10011
Phone: (212) 989-4850; (800) 343-4002
489 Castro Street
San Francisco, CA 94114
Phone: (415) 431-0891
8853 Santa Monica Boulevard
West Hollywood, CA 90069
Phone: (310) 854-6601

Lambda Rising Bookstore
1625 Connecticut Avenue, NW
Washington, DC 20009-1013
Phone: (202) 462-6969; (800) 621-6969

Periodicals

If you search the web for LGBT periodicals, you will find thousands. Many no longer exist or have merged with others, and it is
difficult to verify who or what they are. Some are so specialized
that they really are newsletters of small groups. The better place
to search is Gay/Lesbian International News Network (GLINN).
It keeps lists of periodicals from around the world that are substantial enough to attract contributing writers. Still, there are
more than 500 periodicals meeting that criterion.

Following is a selection of approximately 150 periodicals that
are either large, old, uniquely serve a particular geographic location, or serve a subpopulation of the LGBT community.

Most periodicals are broad in scope. They report on political progress, current events, entertainment news, and medical advances, and they provide self-help articles. Regional periodicals focus on local events, whereas national publications take a broader view. Journals, as opposed to periodicals, are typically more academically oriented. The international periodicals listed are ones for which English is the primary language. Thus, many of the major international periodicals are not listed because they are not in English.

The periodicals listed are mostly commercial. Publications of nonprofit organizations are often the only print media available in restricted countries or area of limited populations.
Note: Biweekly refers to every other week; bimonthly refers to every other month.

Journals

AIDS Clinical Care
Massachusetts Medical Society
1440 Main Street
Waltham, MA 02154-1600
Mail to: PO Box 9085
Waltham, MA 02254-9081

Ambitious Amazons, Lesbian Connection
PO Box 811
East Lansing, MI 48826-0811
Phone: (517) 371-5257 #09244
E-mail: elsiepub@aol.com

BiFocus
4213 Baltimore Avenue
Philadelphia, PA 9104-4411

Campaign
PO Box A228
Sydney South
NSW 2000
Australia
Phone: 61 2 332-3620
Fax: 61 2 361-5962

Common Lives—Lesbian Lives
1802 7th Avenue Court
Iowa City, IA 52240-6436
Phone: (319) 335-1486

Cross Dresser's Information Guide
PO Box 566065
Atlanta, GA 30356
Phone: (404) 333-6455

De Gay Krant
Postbus 161
NL-5680 AD Best
The Netherlands

Defiance
c/o Women's Resources
PO Box 645
Delaware Water Gap, PA 18327-9999

Disability Rag
PO Box 145
Louisville, KY 40201-0145

Diversity
PO Box 323
Boise, ID 83701-0323
Phone: (208) 323-0805; (208) 386-3870

Empathy
PO Box 5085
Columbia, SC 29250-5085
Phone: (803) 791-1607

The Evergreen Chronicles
PO Box 8939
Minneapolis, MN 55408-0939

Feminist Bookstore News
PO Box 882554
San Francisco, CA 94188-2554
Phone: (415) 626-1556
Fax: (415) 626-8970

The Feminist Press
City University of New York
311 E. 94th Street
New York, NY 10128-5603
Phone: (212) 360-5790

Feminist Studies Program
University of Maryland
College Park, MD 20742-0001
Phone: (301) 405-7413

Fireweed: A Feminist Quarterly
PO Box 279, Station B
Toronto, ON M5T 2W2
Canada
Phone: (416) 504-1339; (416) 323-9512

Gay Community News
Hirschfeld Centre
10 Fownes Street
Dublin 2, Ireland
Phone: 353 1 671-9076
Fax: 353 1 671-3549

Gay Community News
PO Box 37083
Honolulu, HI 96837-0083
Phone: (808) 526-3000

Homo-en lesbiennejongerenkrant
Lange Leemstraat 337
B-2018 Antwerpen
Belgium-Belgique
Phone: 03 230 37 64

Journal of Gay and Lesbian Psychotherapy
Haworth Press
10 Alice Street
Binghamton, NY 13904-1580
Phone: (607) 722-5857
Fax: (800) 895-0582; (607) 722-6362
E-mail: getinfo@haworth.com
Website: http://www.haworth.com

Journal of Gay and Lesbian Social Services
Haworth Press
10 Alice Street
Binghamton, NY 13904-1580
Phone: (607) 722-5857
Fax: (800) 895-0582; (607) 722-6362
E-mail: getinfo@haworth.com
Website: http://www.haworth.com

Journal of Homosexuality
The Haworth Press, Inc.
10 Alice Street
Binghamton, NY 13904
Phone: (800) 429-6784
Fax: (607) 771-0012
E-mail: getinfo@haworth.com
Website: http://www.haworthpressinc.com

Journal of Lesbian Studies
4202 E. Fowler Avenue, CPR 107
Tampa, FL 33620-9900
Phone: (813) 974-2550

Lambda Book Report
PO Box 73910
Washington, DC 20056-3910
Phone: (202) 462-7924
Fax: (202) 462-7257
E-mail: lambdabookreport@his.com

Lesbian Ethics
PO Box 4723
Albuquerque, NM 87196-4723

Lesbians in Colorado
PO Box 533
Denver, CO 80201-0533
Phone: (303) 399-3544

New Voice of Nebraska
PO Box 3512
Omaha, NE 68103-0512

Northeast Directory
PO Box 2357
Princeton, NJ 08543-2357

Northwest Gay and Lesbian Reader
1501 Belmont Avenue
Seattle, WA 98122-3711
Phone: (206) 322-4609

Out and About
PO Box 5691
Portsmouth, NH 03802-5691

Ozark Feminist Review
PO Box 1662
Fayetteville, AR 72702-1662
Phone: (501) 846-3740

Resources for Feminist Research, OISE
252 Bloor Street W.
Toronto, ON M5S 1V6
Canada

Rocky Mountain Oyster
PO Box 27467
Denver, CO 80227-0467
Phone: (303) 985-3034

SAGE: A Scholarly Journal on Black Women
PO Box 42741
Atlanta, GA 30311
Phone: (404) 223-7528

Sojourner
42 Seaverns Avenue
Boston, MA 02130-2865
Phone: (617) 524-0415

Woman of Power Magazine
PO Box 2785
Orleans, MA 02653
Phone: (508) 240-7877

Women's Review of Books
Wellesley College Center for Research on Women
Wellesley, MA 02481
Phone: (617) 283-2555

WomenSource
PO Box 8230
Pittsburgh, PA 15217-0030

Womyn's Community Newsletter
PO Box 75025
Charleston, WV 25375-0025

Womyn's Community Newsletter
852 River Trail Terrace, Apt. 717
Salt Lake City, UT 84123-7787
Phone: (801) 484-6325

Legal Journals

Georgetown Journal of Gender and the Law
600 New Jersey Avenue, NW
Washington, DC 20001
Phone: (202) 662-9460
E-mail: gigl@law.georgetown.edu

*Law and Sexuality: A Review of Lesbian,
Gay, Bisexual, and Transgender Legal Issues*
Tulane Law School
6329 Freret Street
New Orleans, LA 70118
Phone: (504) 865-5835
Fax: (504) 862-6748
Website: www.law.tulane.edu/journals/l&s/contact.htm

National Journal of Sexual Orientation Law (on-line journal)
E-mail: gaylaw@e-mail.unc.edu
Website: sunsite.unc.edu/gaylaw

Queer Law (on-line listserv)
E-mail: queerlaw@abacus.oxy.edu

Popular Magazines

The Advocate
PO Box 4371
Los Angeles, CA 90078
Phone: (323) 871-1225
Fax: (323) 467-0173
E-mail: letters@advocate.com
Website: http://www.advocate.com
Monthly

Alternative Family Magazine
PO Box 5650
River Forest, IL 60305-5650
Phone: (708) 386-4770
Fax: (708) 386-5662
E-mail: info@altfammag.com
Website: http://www.altfammag.com
Bimonthly

Art and Understanding Magazine
25 Monroe Street, Suite 205
Albany, NY 12210
Phone: (800) 841-8707; (518) 426-9010
Fax: (518) 436-5354
E-mail: editor@aumag.org
Website: http://www.aumag.org
Monthly

Cybersocket Web Magazine
7510 Sunset Boulevard, Suite 1203
Los Angeles, CA 90046
Phone: (323) 650-9906
Fax: (323) 650-9926
E-mail: editor@cybersocket.com
Website: http://www.cybersocket.com
Bimonthly

Gay and Lesbian Review Worldwide
PO Box 180300
Boston, MA 2118
Phone: (617) 421-0082

E-mail: editor@glreview.com
Website: http://www.glreview.com
Bimonthly

Gay Parent Magazine
PO Box 750852
Forest Hills, NY 11375-0852
Phone: (718) 997-0392
E-mail: info@gayparentmag.com
Website: http://www.gayparentmag.com
Bimonthly

Genre
145 West 28th Street, 8th Floor
New York, NY 10001
Phone: (212) 594-8181
Fax: (212) 594-8263
E-mail: benreadv@aol.com
Website: www.genremagazine.com
Monthly

Girlfriends
3415 Cesar Chavez, Suite 101
San Francisco, CA 94110
Phone: (415) 648-9464
Fax: (415) 648-4705
E-mail: editorial@girlfriendsmag.com
Website: http://www.gfriends.com
Monthly

Identity's Rainbow Borealis
PO Box 200070
Anchorage, AK 99520-0070
Phone: (907) 258-4777
E-mail: northvue@pobox.alaska.net
Website: http://www.alaska-net/~identity/northvue.htm

OUT
110 Green Street, Suite 600
New York, NY 10012
Phone: (212) 334-9119
Fax: (212) 334-9227

E-mail: outm@kable.com
Website: http://www.out.com
Monthly

Out World Magazine
1104 North Nova Road, Suite 251
Daytona Beach, FL 32117
Phone: (904) 441-5367
Fax: (904) 441-5604
E-mail: senioreditormatt@aol.com
Website: http://www.ourworldmag.com
Monthly

POZ
PO Box 1965
Danbury, CT 06813-1965
Website: http://www.posmag@aol.com

QV Magazine
PO Box 9700
Long Beach, CA 90910
Phone: (818) 766-0023
Fax: (818) 985-5106
E-mail: qv@qvmagazine.com
Website: http://www.qvmagazine.com
Bimonthly

XY Magazine
4104 24th Street, Suite 900
San Francisco, CA 94114
Phone: (877) 996-0930
Fax: (415) 552-6664
E-mail: wazup@xy.com
Website: http://www.xy.com
Bimonthly

Publications by State

Alabama
Alabama Forum
205 32nd Street S, Suite 216

Birmingham, AL 35233
Phone: (205) 328-9228
E-mail: alforum@aol.com

Arizona
Heatstroke Gay and Lesbian News
PO Box 33430
Phoenix, AZ 85067
Phone: (602) 264-3646
Fax: (602) 294-9695
E-mail: alkalphx@aol.com
Biweekly. Free.

The Source
2750 W. McDowell Road
Phoenix, AZ 85009
Phone: (602) 278-5600
Fax: (602) 278-6600
E-mail: info@gaysource.com
Website: http://www.gaysource.com

California
Bay Area Reporter
395 Ninth Street
San Francisco, CA 94103-3831
Phone: (415) 861-5019
Fax: (415) 861-6534
E-mail: barpaper@aol.com
Website: http://www.ebar.com

Community Yellow Pages
2305 Canyon Drive
Los Angeles, CA 90068-2411
Phone: (213) 469-4454
Website: http://www.gaycommunitydirectory.com

fab!
6363 Wilshire Boulevard, Suite 350
Los Angeles, CA 90048
Phone: (323) 655-5716
Fax: (323) 655-1408
E-mail: editor@gayfab.com

Website: http://www.gayfab.com
Biweekly

Frontiers News Magazine
7985 Santa Monica Boulevard, Suite 109
West Hollywood, CA 90046
Phone: (323) 848-2222
Fax: (323) 656-8784
E-mail: gaynewsla@aol.com
Website: http://www.frontiersweb.com

Gay and Lesbian Times/Uptown
3911 Normal Street
San Diego, CA 92103
Phone: (619) 299-6397
Fax: (619) 299-3430
E-mail: editor@uptownpub.com
Website: http://www.gaylesbiantimes.com

Lavender Reader
PO Box 7293
Santa Cruz, CA 95061
Phone: (408) 423-8044
E-mail: scotty@cruzio.com

Lesbian News
PO Box 55
Torrance, CA 90507
Phone: (562) 438-4444
Fax: (310) 787-1965
E-mail: theln@earthlink.net
Website: http://www.lesbiannews.com
Monthly

Mom, Guess What Newspaper
1725 L. Street
Sacramento, CA 95814
Phone: (916) 441-6397
Fax: (916) 441-6422
E-mail: info@mgwnews.com
Website: http://www.mgwnews.com
Biweekly

Orange County and Long Beach Blade
PO Box 1538
20754 Los Zorillas Canyon Road
Laguna Beach, CA 92652
Phone: (949) 376-9880
Fax: (949) 494-6945
E-mail: bladeedtr@aol.com
Website: http://www.metrog.com

Florida
Lavender Community Pages
2031 Wilton Drive, Suite C
Ft. Lauderdale, FL 33305
Phone: (954) 567-1616
Fax: (954) 567-1611
E-mail: kprigal@aol.com
Website: http://www.lavender.com

Georgia
David Atlanta Magazine
575 Juniper Street
Atlanta, GA 30308
Website: http://www.davidatlanta.com
Weekly

Eclipse Magazine
1095 Zonolite Road, Suite 100
Atlanta, GA 30306
Phone: (404) 876-0789
Fax: (404) 876-2709
E-mail: editor@eclipsemag.net
Website: http://www.eclipsemag.net
Weekly

Hawaii
Out in Maui
PO Box 5042
Kahului, HI 96733-5042
Phone: (808) 248-4022
Fax: (808) 248-7501
E-mail: gaymaui@maui.net
Website: http://www.maui-tech.com/glom
Monthly

Illinois
Gay Chicago Magazine
3121 North Broadway
Chicago, IL 60657
Phone: (773) 327-7271
Fax: (773) 327-0112
E-mail: gaychimag@aol.com

Indiana
The Word
225 E. North Street, Tower 1, Suite 2800
Indianapolis, IN 46204-1349
Phone: (317) 579-3075
Fax: (317) 687-8840
Website: www.the-word-online.com
Monthly

Iowa
Gay and Lesbian Resource Center Newsletter
PO Box 7008
Des Moines, IA 50309
Phone: (515) 277-7884
E-mail: outword414@aol.com
Website: http://www.glrc-dsm.org

Kansas
Liberty Press, Wichita, KS
PO Box 16315
Wichita, KS 67216
Phone: (316) 652-7737
Fax: (316) 685-1999
E-mail: editor@libertypress.net
Website: http://www.libertypress.net
Monthly

Kentucky
The Letter
PO Box 3882
Louisville, KY 40201
Phone: (502) 636-0935
Fax: (502) 635-6469
E-mail: willNich@aol.com

Maryland
Baltimore Gay Paper
PO Box 2575
Baltimore, MD 21203
Phone: (410) 837-7748
Fax: (410) 837-8512
E-mail: editor@bgp.org
Website: http://www.bgp.org
Biweekly

Massachusetts
The Amazonian
PMB 118, 351 Pleasant Street
Northhampton, MA 01060
Phone: (413) 529-0083
Fax: (877) 510-2363
E-mail: editors@amazonian.net
Website: http://www.amazonian.net

Bi Women
PO Box 400639
Cambridge, MA 02140
Phone: (617) 424-9595
E-mail: nellythrustmon@aol.com
Website: http://www.biresource.com/bbwn

Gay Community News
29 Stanhope Street
Boston, MA 02116
Phone: (617) 262-6969

Michigan
Between the Lines
20793 Farmington Road, Suite 25
Farmington, MI 48336
Phone: (248) 615-7003
Fax: (248) 615-7018
E-mail: pridepblis@aol.com
Website: http://www.betweenthelinesnews.com
Weekly

Minnesota
focusPOINT
3105 Bloomington Avenue S.
Minneapolis, MN 55407
Phone: (612) 722-8800
Fax: (612) 722-1192
E-mail: focuspointe-mail@aol.com
Website: http://www.gaydata.com/db/focus.htm
Weekly

Mississippi
Mississippi Voice
PO Box 7737
Jackson, MS 39284
Phone: (601) 873-8610

Missouri
Current News
809 W. 39th Street, Suite 1
Kansas City, MO 64111
Phone: (816) 753-4300
Fax: (816) 753-2700
E-mail: current@currentnews.com
Website: http://www.currentnews.com
Weekly

Liberty Press, Kansas City
1509 Westport Road, Suite 203B
Kansas City, MO 64111
Phone: (816) 931-3060
Fax: (816) 931-1420
E-mail: kc@libertypress.net
Website: www.libertypress.net
Monthly

Nevada
Las Vegas Bugle
714 E. Sahara Avenue, Suite 220
Las Vegas, NV 89104
Phone: (702) 369-6260
Fax: (702) 369-9325
E-mail: bugle@lvbugle.com

Website: http://www.lvbugle.com
Biweekly

Lesbian VOICE
714 E. Sahara Avenue, Suite 210
Las Vegas, NV 89104
Phone: (702) 650-0636
Fax: (702) 650-0641
E-mail: lesbianvoice@hotmail.com
Website: http://www.lesbianvoice.com
Monthly

New York
New York Blade
242 West 30th Street, 4th Floor
New York, NY 10001
Phone: (212) 268-2711
Fax: (212) 268-2069
E-mail: editor@nyblade.com
Website: http://www.nyblade.com
Weekly

Outcome
266 Elmwood Avenue, PMB 226
Buffalo, NY 14222
Phone: (716) 441-7476
Fax: (716) 883-2756
E-mail: outcomewny@aol.com
Monthly

North Carolina
Carolina Lesbian News
PO Box 11776
Charlotte, NC 28220
Phone: (704) 559-5991
Fax: (704) 333-9316
E-mail: clesbiann@aol.com
Website: http://www.sarahsplace.com/cln

Ohio
Gay People's Chronicle
PO Box 5426

Cleveland, OH 44101
Phone: (216) 631-8646
Fax: (216) 631-1052
E-mail: chronicle@chronohio.com
Website: http://www.cleveland.com/community/gay
Weekly

Outlook News
700 Ackerman Road, Suite 600
Columbus, OH 43202
Phone: (614) 265-8525
Fax: (614) 261-8200
E-mail: editor@outlooknews.com
Website: http://www.outlooknews.com
Biweekly

Oklahoma
Gayly Oklahoman
PO Box 60930
Oklahoma City, OK 73146
Phone: (405) 528-0800
Fax: (405) 528-0796
E-mail: gaylyok@aol.com
Website: http://www.gayly.com

Oregon
Just Out
PO Box 14400
Portland, OR 97293-0400
Phone: (503) 236-1252
Fax: (503) 236-1257
E-mail: marty@justout.com

Pennsylvania
Access Philadelphia
2 Penn Center Plaza, Suite 200
Philadelphia, PA 19102
Phone: (215) 854-6447
Fax: (509) 694-1533
E-mail: editor@accessphilly.net
Website: http://www.accessphilly.net
Weekly

Lavender Letters (Womyn Events)
PO Box 266
Mechanicsburg, PA 17055
Phone: (717) 975-0464
E-mail: lavlet4wym@aol.com
Website: http://www.lavenderletter.com

Out Magazine, Philadelphia, PA
1000 Ross Avenue
Pittsburgh, PA 15221
Phone: (412) 243-3350
Fax: (412) 243-7987
E-mail: out@outpub.com
Website: http://www.outpub.com
Monthly

South Carolina
In Unison
PO Box 8024
Columbia, SC 29202
Phone: (803) 771-0804
Fax: (803) 799-6504
E-mail: nunison@aol.com

Tennessee
Family and Friends
PO Box 771948
Memphis, TN 38177-1948
Phone: (901) 682-2669
Fax: (901) 685-2234
E-mail: familymag@aol.com
Website: http://members.aol.com/familymag/homepage.html
Monthly

Texas
Dallas Voice
3000 Carlisle Street, Suite 200
Dallas, TX 75204
Phone: (214) 754-8710
Fax: (214) 969-7271
E-mail: editor@dallasvoice.com
Website: http://www.dallasvoice.com

Houston Voice
500 Lovett, Suite 200
Houston, TX 77006
Phone: (713) 529-8490
Fax: (713) 529-9531
E-mail: editor@houstonvoice.com
Website: http://www.houstonvoice.com
Weekly

Outsmart Magazine
3404 Audubon Place
Houston, TX 77006
Phone: (713) 520-7237
Fax: (713) 522-3275
E-mail: dennise@outsmartmagazine.com
Website: http://www.outsmartmagazine.com
Monthly

Vermont
Out in the Mountains
PO Box 1978
Richmond, VT 5477
Phone: (802) 434-6486
Fax: (802) 434-7046
E-mail: editor@mountainpridemedia.org
Website: http://www.mountainpridemedia.org
Monthly

Virginia
Blue Ridge Lambda Press
PO Box 237
Roanoke, VA 24022
Phone: (540) 989-8016

Eros Magazine
PO Box 321
Alexandria, VA 22313-0321
Phone: (301) 717-3313
Fax: (703) 549-3879
E-mail: info@eroswebmag.com
Website: http://www.eroswebmag.com
Weekly

West Virginia
Out and About
152 6th Avenue
Huntington, WV 25701
Phone: (304) 522-9089

Wisconsin
In Step Magazine
1661 N. Water Street, Suite 411
Milwaukee, WI 53202
Phone: (414) 278-7840
Fax: (414) 278-5868
E-mail: instepnews@aol.com
Website: http://www.instepnews.com
Biweekly

Publishers

Although most of the larger publishers print books on lesbian and gay subjects, there are a handful that make a major effort to target the LGBT reader.

Alyson Publications
PO Box 4371
Los Angeles, CA 90078
Phone: (213) 860-6065
Fax: (213) 467-0173
E-mail: mail@alyson.com
Website: http://www.alyson.com.

Chelsea House Publishers
1974 Sproul Road, Suite 400
Broomall, PA 19008
Phone: (800) 848-BOOK
E-mail: info@chelseahouse.com
Website: http://www.chelseahouse.com

Gay Sunshine Press/Leyland Publications
PO Box 410690
San Francisco, CA 94141
Phone: (415) 626-1935
Fax: (415) 626-1802

Haworth Press, Inc.
10 Alice Street
Binghamton, NY 13904
Phone: (800) 429-6784; (607) 722-5857
Fax: (800) 895-0582; (607) 771-0012
E-mail: getinfo@haworthpress.com
Website: http://www.haworthpressinc.com

Sage Publications
2455 Teller Road
Newbury Park, CA 91320
Phone: (805) 499-0721
Website: http://www.sagepub.com

Radio and Television

Many public and college radio stations have broadcast LGBT programs since the beginnings of the modern gay civil rights movement. Today, there are a few stations that devote significant time to LGBT news, interviews, and entertainment. There are even plans to launch an all-gay cable channel. Here is a list of a few of the radio programs that have heavy LGBT content.

Radio

Colorado OUT Spoken
PO Box 9901
Denver, CO 80209
Phone: (303) 861-0829
Fax: (303) 861-0829
E-mail: lambdacom@tde.com
Website: http://www.coloradoOUTspoken.org

Q'zine Radio Program
3905 Spruce Street
Philadelphia, PA 19104-6005
Phone: (215) 898-6677
Fax: (215) 573-6094
E-mail: qzine@xpn.org
Website: http://www.xpn.org

This Way Out Radio Program
PO Box 38327
Los Angeles, CA 90038-0327
Phone: (818) 986-4106
Fax: (818) 763-7526 at TWO
E-mail: TWOradio@aol.com
Website: http://www.qrd.org/grd/www/media/radio/thiswayo

Television Shows

Queer as Folk (British version). 1999. Original British TV show that spawned the U.S. version. Source: Wolfe Video; tlavideo.

Queer as Folk (U.S.) 2001-2002. Smash hit TV show on Showtime. Source: general; Wolfe Video.

Queer as Folk Two—Same Men. New Tricks (British version). 2001. Original British TV show that spawned the U.S. version. Source: Wolfe Video; tlavideo.

Video and DVD Resources

The number of movies, video, and DVD titles with gay and lesbian themes has exploded. Prior to the Stonewall Riots of 1969, homosexuals depicted in movies were always self-loathing, were criminals, and were either murdered or committed suicide by the end of the story. *The Children's Hour* is a classic early 1960s movie in which two teachers, played by Audrey Hepburn and Shirley MacLane, were accused of being lesbians. The character played by MacLane, who at the end of the movie revealed her lesbian inclinations, hung herself because of the shame. Likewise, the central figure under investigation by the U.S. Senate in *Advise and Consent* (1962) committed suicide.

In the 1970s and early 1980s, movies began to portray homosexuals as human beings, although ultimately as lost souls doomed to a hidden underground. Martin Sheen played the handsome boyfriend of the older, married, coming-out Hal Holbrook in the made-for-TV movie *That Certain Summer.* They were never allowed to show affection, and the story implied that Hal Holbrook was giving up everything good to live a gay life. *Desert*

Hearts (1986) explored the subject of a married woman (Helen Shaver) coming to terms with her lesbianism, but she was presented as a pathetic figure. Similarly, in *Making Love* (1982), a young married physician (Michael Ontkean) discovered his homosexual feelings, became involved with a care-free but somewhat closeted writer (Harry Hamlin), told his wife (Kate Jackson), divorced, and moved to New York. Audiences were made to feel that both the wife and husband were tragic victims. Also, seeing two men, with their shirts off, embrace and kiss in a scene that faded to black sent audiences squirming.

Even with this shift toward normalizing lesbians and gay men through the telling of coming-out stories, an occasional movie punctuated this trend. Gays went from being victims to being portrayed as both victims and victimizers. Homosexuality was seen as a strange evil power that people could not resist. The 1980 film *Cruising* reinforced these points. In it gay men were shown to be pathetic creatures obsessed with sadomasochistic sex and sadistic murders. Al Pacino played a cop investigating a series of brutal murders committed by a deranged man. The power of gay sadomasochism influenced Pacino's character to explore his own sadomasochistic leanings. Many gay organizations called for a general boycott of *Cruising*.

Another shift occurred in sentiments toward lesbians and gays in movies of the late 1970s and 1980s. Gay or transgender people became a source of comedy. Although gay people were the source of comedy in the movies of the 1930s through the 1950s, they were not out or easily identified. Beginning with *La Cage aux Folles* (French 1978) and three films in 1982 (*Partners, Tootsie, Victor/Victoria*) audiences laughed as long as gay people or crossdressers conformed to bitchy stereotypes using witty repartee. An exceptional film was Mel Brooks's 1983 comedy *To Be or Not To Be*, which was the first time the persecution and extermination of gay people by Nazis during World War II were mentioned in mainstream media. This pattern continued with the release of more mainstream comedies such as *Torch Song Trilogy* (1988); *The Adventures of Priscilla, Queen of the Desert* (1994); *Jeffrey* (1995); *Birdcage* (1995, an American remake of *La Cage aux Folles*); *In and Out* (1997); and *But I'm a Cheerleader* (1999).

Most mainstream gay films focused on white male experiences and portrayed mostly effeminate men. Independent filmmakers began to explore the issues of coming out, sexual repression, hate crimes, racism, violence, and more serious issues as related to the gay community. Filmmakers came together in 1982 to launch the first Gay and Lesbian Media Festival and Conference, held in conjunction with UCLA Film and Television Archives. The festival was renamed Outfest in 1994 to better reflect the dynamics of the community. Outfest has grown to become the largest film festival in Southern California, and it now includes screenings of movies with gay themes.

Likewise, Sundance and other international film festivals included more and more entries that focused on gay and lesbian themes. Many films that once would have been shown only at art houses have made their way to television via cable TV. Now, anyone with access to HBO, Showtime, Sundance, Starz, and other cable channels can see a wide range of gay-themed films, from mainstream comedies such as *Trick*, to Spanish-language films *Nico and Dani* and *Before Night Falls*, to lesbian experimental filmmaking in *Go Fish*, to an exploration of the intersection of race and sexual orientation in *The Wedding Banquet*, or to dramatizations of hate crimes such as the murder of transgender Teena Brandon in *Boy's Don't Cry* (1999), which garnered the Academy Award for best actress for Hilary Swank, or the murder of Matthew Shepard in *The Laramie Project* (2001).

AIDS became a popular topic for filmmakers in the 1990s. Although the made-for-television film *An Early Frost* (1985) addressed the anguish that a closed-minded family experienced on discovering their son was gay and dying of AIDS, it was not until 1993 that Randy Shilts's book on the history of AIDS, *And the Band Played On*, was made into a movie. The discrimination experienced by AIDS sufferers was personalized in *Philadelphia* (for which Tom Hanks won the Academy Award for best actor in 1993), the story of an attorney who was fired because he had AIDS. *In the Gloaming* (1997), Christopher Reeve's (*Superman*) directorial debut, brought the horrors of AIDS to an intimate family level by telling the story of a young man who returned home to die and how his parents and siblings responded.

TV has made great strides in the inclusion of lesbians and gay men, although mostly in comedies. The first show with a main character who was gay was *Soap* (1970s). Billy Crystal played an over-the-top parody of a gay man who eventually married a woman. The 1980s cable TV show *Brothers* focused on the interactions of Cliff, the gay brother, with his two other brothers and their outrageously flamboyant gay friend, Donald. This was truly the first gay-focused TV show. By the 1990s, *Ellen* became the first prime-time network show to have the main character come out on television. There was much controversy when Ellen came out and the show was cancelled within a year. In none of these shows could lesbian or gay characters show physical affection toward someone of the same gender.

Immediately after the cancellation of *Ellen*, NBC launched *Will & Grace* to much success. As a comedy, it teamed an openly gay man with a straight woman. It played along with gay stereotypes, with gay men acting like straight women or swishy queens. Again, none of the gay characters displayed physical affection or kissed on screen. In 2001, Showtime broke new ground with *Queer as Folk*, an hour-long program that contained explicit full-body nudity, explicit sex, and explicit language among a cast composed mostly of gay and lesbian characters. Critics of the show claim that it focused on gay white male fantasies and reinforced stereotypes that all gay men are promiscuous.

The prevalence of gay male roles makes it seem that many male actors in Hollywood want to claim on their resume that they have played a gay role—even John Goodman from *Roseanne* fame played the gay male lead in the failed television show *Normal, Ohio*. Unfortunately, many female actors and directors, whether gay or straight, are still treated as second-class citizens, with fewer opportunities. In the 2000s, many television shows have openly gay characters in secondary roles that do not reinforce antigay stereotypes.

Given how mainstream gay and lesbian films have become, the list here does not begin to describe the thousands of films available. Instead, the list focuses on three categories of films: (1) recent or classic films of general interest that could be obtained from a local video store and are shown often on cable TV; (2) biographic, and historic films, and international/foreign-language films obtainable from select video distributors who target gay audiences; and (3) educational films/videos that can often be obtained only from the producing organization. Pornography has not been included in this list, although some of the titles contain adult material. Here are some video distribution companies that target gay audiences:

Flying Focus Video Collective
3439 N.E. Sandy Boulevard, PMB 248
Portland, OR 97232
Phone: (503) 321-5051

Fax: (503) 239-7456
E-mail: ffvc@agora.rdrop.com
Website: http://www.rdrop.com/~ffvc

Intermedia
1700 Westlake Avenue N., Suite 724
Seattle, WA 98109
Phone: (800) 553-8336
Website: http://www.intermedia-inc.com

Strand Releasing
1460 Fourth Street, Suite 302
Santa Monica, CA 90401
Phone: (310) 395-5002
Fax: (310) 395-2502
E-mail: strand@strandreleasing.com
Website: http://www.strandreleasing.com

Telling Pictures
121 Ninth Street
San Francisco, CA 94103
Phone: (415) 864-6714
Website: http://www.tellingpix.com

TLA Entertainment Group, Inc.
234 Market Street, 4th Floor
Philadelphia, PA 19106
Phone: (800) 333-8521, ext. 1
Fax: (215) 733-0668
E-mail: customer.service@tlavideo.com
Website: http://www.tlavideo.com

TRB Production
PO Box 2014
Provincetown, MA 02657
Phone: (508) 487-3700
Website: http://www.brian-mcnaught.com

Wolfe Video
PO Box 64
New Almaden, CA 95042
Phone: (408) 268-6782

Fax: (408) 268-9449
E-mail: info@wolfevideo.com
Website: http://www.wolfevideo.com

Women Vision Library
22-D Hollywood Avenue
Hohokus, NJ 07423
Phone: (800) 343-5540

Women's Educational Media
2180 Bryant Street, Suite 203
San Francisco, CA 94110
Phone: (415) 641-4616

Each of the following video listings indicates a possible source as
general (video store) and/or as the name of the *distributor* or *producer*.

AIDS

And the Band Played On (140 min.) 1993. Randy Shilts's best-
seller on the history of HIV was made into this film. Matthew
Modine plays Dr. Don Francis, a researcher at the Centers for Disease Control, who uncovers the source of a number of mysterious
deaths. The film chronicles the political and scientific background
of the developing AIDS epidemic. It is an unforgettable tale of
scientific struggle, corruption, media manipulation, deceit, and
tragedy. *Source:* general; Wolfe Video.

Common Threads: Stories from the Quilt (73 min.) 1992. This
Academy Award-winning film uses powerful stories from the
NAMES Project AIDS Quilt to recount the tumultuous history of
the first decade of the AIDS epidemic in America. *Source:* Telling
Pictures.

An Early Frost (97 min.) 1985. This is the first film, whether for
TV or movie theater, to explore one family's struggle with the
news that their son (Aidan Quinn) is gay and has AIDS. Although
almost twenty years old, the film is still relevant today. *Source:*
Wolfe Video.

In the Gloaming (62 min.) 1997. Christopher Reeve made his directorial debut with this heart-warming family drama about a

young man coming home to die from complications of AIDS. Taut acting and picturesque country scenes make this an updated version of *An Early Frost*. *Source:* general; Wolfe Video.

It's My Party (120 min.) 1995. Nick, played by Eric Roberts, discovers that he has untreatable brain lesions due to AIDS that will leave him unable to care for himself in a short few weeks. He decides to throw one last party before committing suicide by taking a drug overdose. Family and friends come to the party, and, unexpectedly, his former live-in who could not handle Nick's HIV-positive diagnosis but who desires a last rapprochement. Based on a true story, this is a finely acted but weepie film. *Source:* general; Wolfe Video.

Longtime Companion (100 min.) 1990. This film was hailed as the first mainstream film to put a human face on the AIDS epidemic. The film traces a group of friends in New York as they experience, over the course of the early 1980s, the onslaught of friends becoming ill and dying from a mysterious "gay cancer." Those who survived are redefined by unconditional displays of love, courage, and hope. *Source:* general; Wolfe Video; tlavideo.

My Own Country (106 min.) 1998. This unique story follows the experiences of a medical doctor from India who moves his family to Johnson City, Tennessee, to set up practice. At the same time, the first documented case of AIDS rocks the city. The doctor makes AIDS his personal crusade and is overwhelmed with patients from surrounding states. This places a strain on his marriage. He struggles with making the adjustment to a new country and having compassion for a class of patients no one else will treat. *Source:* Wolfe Video.

Philadelphia (119 min.) 1993. Tom Hanks leads in this Academy Award-winning film (best actor for Hanks). Hanks's character contracts AIDS and is fired from his prestigious law firm. Hanks joins forces with another lawyer played by Denzel Washington and successfully sues Hanks's former employer for AIDS discrimination. In addition to excellent acting, the film contains a fine score. *Source:* general; Wolfe Video.

Rock the Boat (84 min.) 1998. This documentary chronicles a crew of HIV-positive men who participate in the Get Challenged

Team of the 1997 TransPacific Yacht Race. The mostly amateur sailors experience numerous squalls, mishaps, and clashes of egos. A mixture of black comedy, adventure, and intimate human drama, this film is an unforgettable portrait of ordinary guys and their will to live. The film was an Academy Award nominee for best documentary. *Source:* Wolfe Video.

Silverlake Life (99 min.) 1994. This is a video diary of the last days of two men, one dying from AIDS. This film is gritty, touching, and difficult to watch. *Source:* Wolfe Video.

Coming Out

And Then Came Summer (115 min.) 1999. A couple of teenage boys discover their homosexual feelings for each other, only to have their families find out. Once exposed, one of the boys reveals that he was previously institutionalized for his homosexuality. *Source:* Wolfe Video.

Beautiful Thing (89 min.) 1995. In this sweet British film of two teenage boys falling in love, Jamie, the more outgoing lad, helps protect his next-door neighbor, Steve, from being physically abused by his father and brother. It is refreshing to see a film about love between average guys without the element of class struggle. *Source:* general; Wolfe Video; tlavideo.

But I'm a Cheerleader (90 min.) 2001. This is a hysterical comedy about a high school cheerleader who is accused by her friends and parents of being a lesbian. They ship her off to an isolated ranch, where she is forced to participate in a behavioral modification program to make her straight. Of course, it all fails in a series of funny mishaps, and the local gay group helps organize a rescue mission. *Source:* general; Wolfe Video.

Change of Heart (96 min.) 1998. This made-for-television movie tackles the problem of a woman discovering that her husband is having an affair with another man. The woman is stunned, and the children are unable to deal with their father's homosexuality. This better-than-average film delves into how each member of the family must deal with the unexpected changes in his or her life. Especially noteworthy is the change the "Stepford wife" must address when given a dose of reality. *Source:* Wolfe Video.

The Delta (85 min.) 1997. A white teenager, Lincoln Bloom, leads a double life in Memphis, partying with his friends and girlfriend and then going off to the city's gay pick-up spots. Lincoln meets John, an older Asian immigrant from Vietnam whose father is an unknown black American GI. The two have a brief romantic encounter, but the impossibility of their situation leads to tragic consequences. *Source:* Wolfe Video; tlavideo.

Desert Hearts (91 min.) 1986. One of the first positive lesbian films, *Desert Hearts* tells the story of a repressed English professor who goes to Reno for a quick divorce in 1959. While waiting for the papers to be processed, she meets and falls in love with Cay, a beautiful young casino worker. The movie has a fabulous 1950s soundtrack featuring Elvis Presley, Patsy Cline, and Patti Page. *Source:* general; Wolfe Video; tlavideo.

Edge of Seventeen (100 min.) 1999. Eric, a teenager in Sandusky, Ohio, goes through the many levels of coming out—thinking he is bisexual; having a girlfriend; hiding the attraction he has for men; meeting and falling in love with Rod, who tosses him aside after a short time; and coming out to his parents. This is one of the better coming-out films because it does not sanitize the experience. *Source:* general; Wolfe Video; tlavideo.

Get Real (108 min.) 1999. This British film explores the coming out of sixteen-year-old Steven. He knows that he is gay and goes to the local park to meet men in the bathroom. There, he meets John, the school's handsome superjock. The two get involved, but Steven's desire to be open about his relationship with John threatens John's carefully constructed closet. It all comes to a head when Steven wins a writing contest and comes out to the school during his acceptance speech. *Source:* general; Wolfe Video; tlavideo.

In and Out (92 min.) 1997. This is a big-budget movie with mainstream actors in a Hollywood fantasy of one man coming out in middle America. Actor Kevin Kline plays Howard Brackett, a local teacher who is engaged to be married in three days, when, on a national broadcast of the Oscars, the acceptance speech given by the best actor "outs" Brackett. Everyone in town is devastated, including Howard, and the media turn the situation into a circus. Howard eventually comes to realize that he really is gay and tells his fiancée during the marriage ceremony. *Source:* general; Wolfe Video.

The Incredibly True Adventure of Two Girls in Love (94 min.) 1995. This is a touching and comic story of the first love between two girls in high school. Randy Dean, the rebellious tomboy, falls in love with Evie Roy, a beautiful and smart African American. The romance leads them to decide to run away together. A series of comic misadventures culminates with family and friends converging on a motel to keep the lovers from leaving. *Source:* general; Wolfe Video.

Journey of Jared Price (90 min.) 2000. Nineteen-year-old Jared Price leaves home in Georgia for Southern California on a journey of self-realization and sexual discovery. He stumbles through a Hollywood youth hostel and discovers that his prostitute roommate wants more than a platonic friendship. Jared gains employment with a wealthy, older, blind woman and falls into a deceptive relationship with her affluent older son, Matthew. The two men's relationship becomes personally destructive, and Jared faces the difficult decision of abandoning the relationship. *Source:* Wolfe Video.

Lost Language of Cranes (90 min.) 1992. This BBC adaptation of David Leavitt's literary masterpiece shows a family in crisis as Philip, their college son, tells the family of his homosexuality. Doing so brings up long-hidden secrets concerning homosexuality and infidelity of the parents. The rigid, angular movement of construction cranes becomes a metaphor for the emotional remoteness within this dysfunctional family. *Source:* general; Wolfe Video.

Maurice (139 min.) 1987. Adapted from E. M. Forster's novel of the same name, *Maurice* tells the story of the love that develops between two upper-class Cambridge College students. Their love exceeds the bounds of "decent society" in sexually repressed pre-World War I Britain, yet they never cross the line into physical intimacy. Eventually, Clive is unable to overcome his privileged upbringing and marries, ending the relationship with Maurice who then moves to America. The film was produced by the Academy Award-nominated creators of *Remains of the Day* and *Howard's End*. *Source:* general; Wolfe Video.

Trevor (18 min.) 1995. This Academy Award–winning short film tells the story of a thirteen-year-old boy, his emerging sexuality, and his realization that he is gay. *Source:* Intermedia.

Culture and Education

Always My Kid: A Family Guide to Understanding Homosexuality (74 min.) 1994. Parents and children of PFLAG recount their experiences. *Source:* Triangle Video Productions, 550 Westcott, Suite 400, Houston, TX 77007, (713) 869-4477.

Both of My Moms' Names Are Judy (10 min.) 1994. This film is composed of a powerful and moving series of interviews with children (aged six to eleven) who have gay or lesbian parents. Training materials for overcoming homophobia in the elementary classroom are also available. *Source:* Lesbian and Gay Parents Association, 260 Tingley Street, San Francisco, CA 94112, (415) 522-8773, lgpasf@aol.com

Combating Homophobia (30 min.) 1991. This is a video of a homophobia workshop in which fourteen gay couples talk about their desire to be married. *Source:* Flying Focus Video Collective.

Disarming the OCA (30 min.) 1992. A panel discusses attempts by the Oregon Citizens Alliance to curb gay rights. Donna RedWing and Suzanne Pharr are on the panel. *Source:* Flying Focus Video Collective.

The Gay Agenda (19 min.) 1990. This is one of the most famous antigay videos ever made. It weaves together clips from gay pride parades showing simulated sex and sadomasochistic behaviors with testimony from "expert" witnesses on the deviancy of homosexuality. Currently, *The Gay Agenda* seems impossible to locate, but it is available for viewing at some libraries. *Source:* Stonewall Center, 256 Sunset Avenue, Crampton House SW, Amherst, MA 01003-9324, (413) 545-4824, (413) 545-6667 (fax), e-mail: stonewall@stuaf.umass.edu, website: http://www.umass.edu/stonewall/library/videos/tvcoverage.html. Also at the ONE Institute and Archives, 909 W. Adams Boulevard, Los Angeles, CA 90007, (213) 741-0094, (213) 741-0220 (fax), e-mail: oneigla@usc.edu, website: http://www.oneinstitute.org.

Gay Issues in the Workplace (25 min.) 1993. A cross-section of gay, lesbian, and bisexual workers speak for themselves in this engaging and enlightening discussion. Hosted by Brian Mc-Naught. *Source:* TRB Production.

Gay Lives and Culture Wars (27 min.) 1994. Gay youths tell their stories against the backdrop of antigay propaganda used in Oregon's Ballot Measure 9. *Source:* Democracy Media, PO Box 82777, Portland, OR 97282, (503) 235-5036.

Homophobia in the Workplace (57 min.) 1993. Brian McNaught explains why companies need to address issues of concern to gay, lesbian, and bisexual employees. *Source:* TRB Production.

It's Not Gay (30 min.) 2002. This video produced by the religious right provides an uncompromising, yet "compassionate" look at the "tragic consequences of homosexual life." Ex-gays share their experiences and the emotional pain and brokenness that led to their empty lives and to AIDS. *Source:* American Family Association, PO Box 2440, Tupelo, MS 38803, (626) 844-5036, (662) 842-7798 (fax), e-mail: webmaster@afa.net.

A Little Respect (30 min.) 1991. This video is intended to help college students combat homophobia. *Source:* Rutgers University, Department of Health Education, University Heights, 249 University Avenue, Newark, NJ 07102, (973) 353-1236.

On Being Gay (57 min.) 1994. In this highly praised two-part presentation, Brian McNaught explains the unique aspects of growing up gay. He addresses often cited but erroneously interpreted biblical quotes. This can be used in twenty-minute segments. *Source:* TRB Production.

Out at Work (60 min.) 1998. This is the best documentary detailing people who experienced job discrimination for being lesbian or gay. Also included is the Cracker Barrel case. *Source:* HBO Consumer Affairs, 1100 Avenue of the Americas, New York, NY 10036, (212) 512-1000, (212) 512-5451.

Out for a Change: Addressing Homophobia in Women's Sports (27 min.) 1996. Open lesbian sports figures describe their experiences and discuss what needs to change in sports. *Source:* Women Vision Library.

The Right to Marry (72 min.) 1996. Here are interviews with Mel White, Phyllis Burke, Richard Mohr, and Kevin Cathcart discussing the issues around lesbian and gay men's right to marry. *Source:* Partners Task Force for Gay and Lesbian Couples, PO Box 9685, Seattle, WA 98109-0685, (206) 935-1206, e-mail: demian@ buddybuddy.com.

Straight from the Heart (24 min.) 1995. This work contains moving accounts of parents' struggles with homophobia on learning that their child is lesbian or gay. It uses simple stories told by real people: a police chief who talks about his pride in his lesbian daughter, a Mormon family whose son is believed to be the first person to die from AIDS in Idaho, a mother who talks about her two lesbian daughters and how she has been told that they are "that way" because they caught the "predilections from white people." Academy Award nominee. *Source:* Wolfe Video; Women Vision Library.

Teaching Respect for All (52 min.) 1996. A project of the Gay, Lesbian, and Straight Education Network, this is a "Homophobia 101" workshop. *Source:* GLSEN, 122 W. 26th Street, Suite 1100, New York, NY 10001, (212) 727-0135, www.glsen.org.

TransFamily. 2001. Having a transgender member of the family is explored. *Source:* PFLAG Transgender Network, c/o Mary Boenke, 180 Baily Boulevard, Hardy, VA 24101.

What Lesbians Have Done for America (60 min.) 1999. Historian Lillian Faderman examines lesbians' contributions to the positive history of the United States since the 1800s. *Source:* Flying Focus Video Collective.

Who's Afraid of Project 10? (23 min.) 1989. This video contains interviews with Virginia Uribe, founder of Project 10; gay and lesbian students; political and religious opponents of the program; and the mother of a teen who committed suicide over being gay. *Source:* Friends of Project 10, 115 W. California Boulevard, Suite 116, Pasadena, CA 91105, (626) 577-4553.

Why and How to Defeat the "Gay" Movement. Based on the book of the same name by Scott Lively, this video provides a "straightforward, nonsectarian plan for rolling back the gay agenda and restoring the natural family to primacy in America." *Source:* Abiding Truth Ministries, 6060 Sunrise Vista Drive, Suite 3050, Citrus Heights, CA 95610, (916) 676-1057, website: http://www.abidingtruth.com.

Gay Male Comedy

The Adventures of Priscilla, Queen of the Desert (102 min.) 1994. *Priscilla* is the simple story of two drag queens and one female transsexual taking a trip across the great expanse of the Australian outback. Taking their drag show to a gig in rural Alice Springs, they find that their camp show, outrageous costumes, disco music, and dancing get interesting responses from the locals at every stop they make. This was one of the big hits of 1994. *Source:* general; Wolfe Video; tlavideo.

Billy's Hollywood Screen Kiss (89 min.) 1998. Sean Hayes, of TV's *Will & Grace* fame, plays Billy, who dreams of meeting Mr. Right through the viewfinder of his instamatic camera. He meets and falls for handsome coffeehouse waiter Gabriel, who is unsure of his sexuality. Billy asks Gabriel to pose for a series of photos re-creating Hollywood's great screen kisses. It is then that Billy discovers the truth about Gabriel. This is one of the better-written and acted gay male comedies. *Source:* general; Wolfe Video; tlavideo.

Broadway Damage (108 min.) 1998. Three friends are determined to take New York City by storm. Marc dreams of his Broadway break, Cynthia dreams of landing her fantasy job at the top, and Robert dreams of Marc. Reality intervenes and the fun begins in this tale of unrequited love and relentless optimism. *Source:* general; Wolfe Video.

I Think I Do (90 min.) 1997. Two college roommates meet five years later at a straight mutual friend's wedding. The roommate who was openly gay in college brings his boyfriend, whereas the other roommate has recently come out, unbeknownst to the others. Romantic entanglements ensue. This is a screwball comedy in the 1930s style. *Source:* Strand Releasing; tlavideo.

Jeffrey (92 min.) 1995. With a big budget and a star-studded cast (including Patrick Stewart and Sigourney Weaver in the supporting cast), *Jeffrey* comes from the acclaimed writer Paul Rudnick

(*In and Out, The Addams Family*). It is a hilarious boy-meets-boy romantic comedy adapted from the stage play of the same name. Because of AIDS, Jeffrey (Steven Weber of television show *Wings* fame) swears off sex—until he meets sweet, hunky, sensitive Steve. However, once passions ignite, Steve reveals that he is HIV-positive, leaving Jeffrey to choose between what may be true love or solitude. *Source:* general; Wolfe Video.

Kiss Me, Guido (86 min.) 1997. Franki Zito, a straight as an arrow pizza maker from the Bronx, decides to leave home and hunt for an apartment. He sees an ad that says GWM and figures it means "guy with money," not knowing that it means "gay white male." This is the setup for a movie with plenty of laughs and good-hearted intentions. *Source:* general; Wolfe Video.

Love! Valor! Compassion! (115 min.) 1996. Based on Terrance McNally's Tony Award-winning play, this film tells the story of eight gay friends who leave the city to spend three weekends out at a country home. It becomes a mix of strong personalities, outrageous camp, and poignant reflections. Jason Alexander (from television show *Seinfeld*) is in a leading role. *Source:* general; Wolfe Video.

Psycho Beach Party (95 min.) 2000. Based on Charles Busch's long-running stage play, *Psycho Beach Party* is a wickedly funny satire of Hollywood movie genres. Characters include a burnt-out surf guru, dreamy surfboys, a stylish homicide detective, drag queens, good-bad split personalities, and more. *Source:* general; Strand Releasing.

Relax . . . It's Just Sex (110 min.) 1998. This Hollywood-studded cast dramatizes tangled relationships among a group of close-knit friends. Tara is a sexy straight woman whose biological clock is ticking and who wants a child from her boyfriend, who is not ready. Vincey, Tara's best friend, is looking for Mr. Right and has a violent clash with street thugs. Longtime couple Megan and Sarina break up over Megan's affair with a man. Add a couple of hopeless crushes and you have a hilarious romantic comedy with a twist ending. *Source:* general; Wolfe Video.

The Sum of Us (95 min.) 1994. In this humorous and touching Australian film, Russell Crowe (*Gladiator*) plays a gay son whose father tries to help him find "Mr. Right." *Source:* general; tlavideo.

Torch Song Trilogy (126 min.) 1988. Tony Award-winning actor and playwright Harvey Fierstein (*Bullets over Broadway*) re-creats his role as Arnold Beckoff in this film adaptation of the smash Broadway play of the same name. Arnold is a drag queen looking for love who gets involved first with a closeted man who wants to be heterosexually married and then with a young fashion model (Matthew Broderick). Arnold has a complicated relationship with his mother (Anne Bancroft). Arnold also has a keenly developed sense of humor and piercing wit. *Source:* general; Wolfe Video.

Trick (90 min.) 1999. The simple premise of two men meeting and trying to arrange a quickie becomes, instead, a chance for them to get to know each other and develop something deeper. Each time they try to find a place for sex, they are thwarted in some humorous situation. Tori Spelling has a memorable part as the bulldozing best friend. *Source:* general; Wolfe Video; tlavideo.

Gay Male Experience

Advise and Consent (139 min.) 1962. This is one of the classic black-and-white movies in which the gay character must commit suicide. The president's choice of a candidate for secretary of state divides the Senate. When the candidate is threatened with the revelation that he is gay, he commits suicide. The film is based on Allen Drury's novel and was controversial for its time. *Source:* general.

Big Eden (107 min.) 2001. A New York artist returns to his hometown of Big Eden, Montana. He confronts his unrequited love for his high school best friend and his feelings about being gay in a small town. He is surprised to find the town residents quietly conspiring to help him with his romance. Big Eden's residents defy the stereotype of "small town, small minds." The movie explores the universal longing and hope of finding a place where we are unconditionally loved. *Source:* general; Wolfe Video.

Boys Life (90 min.) 1994. This is actually three short films on coming out and growing up: *Pool Days, Friend of Dorothy,* and *The Disco Years.* The series includes *Boys Life 2* and *Boys Life 3. Source:* general; Strand Releasing.

Common Ground (105 min.) 2000. This film tells the stories of three generations of gays living in the tiny town of Hormer, Connecticut. The all-star cast includes Donna Deitch, Beau Bridges, Ed Asner, Helen Shaver, Margot Kidder, and Jonathan Taylor Thomas. *Source:* Wolfe Video.

Finding North (95 min.) 1997. Rhonda, a love-starved girl, spots her ideal man, Travis. Unfortunately, Travis is a naked gay man in the process of jumping off a bridge to commit suicide. In a quirky chain of events, they end up on the road driving to Texas in a tale of misconceptions and mistaken identities. The journey becomes an exploration of self-worth and life. *Source:* general; Wolfe Video.

Green Plaid Shirt (87 min.) 1996. Back in 1978, Phillip and Guy were experiencing the exhilaration of first love, sharing life experiences with their friends Devon, Jerry, and Todd. Ten years later, all have died except Phillip, who tries to make sense of the joys and sorrows of life, while looking hopefully to a new future. *Source:* Wolfe Video.

The Hanging Garden (91 min.) 1997. William, a once inept young man, returns home confident in his gay life. Yet he must address old demons and family dynamics. This film is a lyrical and humorous approach to the topic of gay men attending family reunions. *Source:* Wolfe Video.

Hollow Reeds (106 min.) 1995. A gay man attempts to save his son from abuse. However, the father is then subjected to the harsh scrutiny of the court. This film is a heart-stirring dramatic thriller. *Source:* Wolfe Video.

Lilies (95 min.) 1996. *Lilies* won four Canadian Genie Awards (equivalent to the Oscar) in 1996, including best picture, and is found on many ten best movies lists. In 1952, a Catholic bishop visits a prison to hear a dying prisoner's last confession. There, he is confronted by Simon, a childhood friend, who, along with other prisoners, takes the bishop hostage. Simon and his cohorts reenact Simon's version of events that took place in 1912 in the rural village in which the bishop and Simon grew up. The action moves back and forth between the crude prison enactment and the actual events of 1912, culminating in the tragic night when both men's fates were sealed. *Source:* general; Wolfe Video.

My Beautiful Laundrette (93 min.) 1985. This British film explores the relationship between a Pakistani and his white working-class childhood friend. They are lovers, and neither family nor friends approve. (Daniel Day Lewis gives an excellent performance as the white Brit.) *Source:* general.

My Own Private Idaho (105 min.) 1991. Mike (River Phoenix) is a narcoleptic street hustler searching for his mother and possessed by his idyllic memories of his childhood. He meets Scott (Keanu Reeves), who is a runaway rich kid on a personal quest to find the meaning of life while waiting to inherit his father's estate. Together, Mike and Scott travel through a bizarre world of wealthy strangers, male prostitutes, and more. *Source:* general; Wolfe Video.

The Opposite of Sex (100 min.) 1998. Dedee is a sixteen-year-old runaway who goes to live with her gay half-brother, Bill. He is a caring teacher in a small town. She turns his quiet existence upside-down and interferes with his attempt to date a new boyfriend. *Source:* Wolfe Video.

Parallel Sons (93 min.) 1995. A white teenager who identifies completely with blacks (he wears his blond hair in dreadlocks, likes hip-hop, and treats *The Autobiography of Malcolm X* as his bible) falls in love with a young black man who has been wounded escaping from prison. This film received the Grand Jury Award at Outfest. *Source:* Strand Releasing.

Querelle (106 min.) 1983. Set in a surreal *Barbarella*-style seaport, Brad Davis plays a sailor who discovers and explores homosexual sadism. This is a surprising early gay film. *Source:* general; Wolfe Video.

Rites of Passage (95 min.) 1999. The Farraday family men unexpectedly end up at the family's mountain cabin. Conflict arises among them, and the father (Dean Stockwell) comes to realize that his homophobia is pushing his youngest son (Jason Behr of *Roswell*) into the arms of a much deadlier father. From writer/director Victor Salva (*Powder*). *Source:* general; Wolfe Video.

Under Heat (90 min.) 1994. A family reunion between an eccentric mother (played by Lee Grant) and her two sons (one straight and one gay) becomes an explosive mix. The compelling musical score is by Obie Award-winner Elizabeth Swados. *Source:* Wolfe Video.

World and Time Enough (92 min.) 1995. Winner of the 1994 audience award at the San Francisco International Lesbian and Gay Film Festival, this clever and bittersweet comedy offers a glimpse into gay coupledom rarely seen—young, midwestern, and not chic. Mark is a radical artist-activist, and Joey is a garbage collector. They encounter many issues—family obligations, HIV status, temporary jobs, and more. In spite of everything, they are, inexplicably, a happy couple. *Source:* Strand Releasing.

Foreign

Aimee and Jaguar (126 min.) 1997. Lilly Wust leads a comfortable life as a married woman in her late twenties with four children and a Nazi husband. It is 1943 and Berlin is under constant bombing. At a concert she meets Felice. Eventually, the two women fall in love. They write to each other using the pseudonyms Aimee (Lilly) and Jaguar (Felice). Unknown to Lilly, Felice is Jewish and works for the underground resistance. Lilly divorces her husband, and the two women move in together. On a hot August day in 1944, the Gestapo waits in the apartment for the women to return from swimming and playing along the banks of the Havel. This film was nominated for a Golden Globe award. German with English subtitles. *Source:* Wolfe Video; tlavideo.

Beloved Friend (90 min.) 2001. Official selection of the Berlin International Film Festival, *Beloved Friend* tells the story of an accomplished professor of medieval literature who is fixated on one of his students, David. He is surprised when, in response to a call for an anonymous callboy, David arrives at his door. A dysfunctional relationship begins between the two men. The professor risks his career and faces the possibility of cruelty and violence at the hands of heartless David. Spanish with English subtitles. *Source:* Strand Releasing.

Coming Out (108 min.) 1989. *Coming Out* is the only film to show gay life in communist East Germany. Phillip has strong feelings for his best male friend, but puts that behind him to live with a girl in a "normal" relationship. Yet Phillip finds he cannot deny his passionate desires for men. German with English subtitles. *Source:* Wolfe Video.

Don't Tell Anyone (111 min.) 1998. A young man searches for honesty and sexual identity against the backdrop of modern Catholic Peru. Spanish. *Source:* Wolfe Video.

East Palace, West Palace (90 min.) 1996. This is one of the first Chinese-language films to address the issue of homosexuality. A police officer arrests a young man found cruising on the grounds of the Forbidden Palace in Beijing. At the police station, the young man tells a tale of sexual oppression and sexual torture. The police officer seems intrigued, if not actually interested in pursuing the young man. There is tension between the officer and young man as they jockey for sexual dominance, a metaphor for the authoritarian regime and its helpless citizens. Mandarin Chinese with English subtitles. *Source:* general; Strand Releasing; Wolfe Video.

Entre Nous (112 min.) 1983. Academy Award for best foreign-language film, *Entre Nous* tells the story of two married women who challenge the social rules of their time to develop a rare, loving friendship. French with English subtitles. *Source:* general; Wolfe Video.

Fire (108 min.) 1996. Banned in India for its lesbian content, *Fire* tells the story of two sisters-in-law who abandon their loveless marriages to be with each other. Hindi with English subtitles. *Source:* Wolfe Video.

Full Speed (82 min.) 1996. Rick and Samir had a friendship they thought would last forever. One rowdy night, Rick is killed and Samir is left to overcome the guilt associated with being the one who survived. French with English subtitles. *Source:* Strand Releasing; Wolfe Video.

Happy Together (97 min.) 1996. Director Wong Kar-Wai chronicles the stormy affair of a gay Chinese couple living as expatriates in Buenos Aires. Chinese with English subtitles. *Source:* Wolfe Video.

Le Jupon Rouge (90 min.) 1987. Shifting attractions among three women of different ages are played out in this lesbian drama.

Jealousy and intrigue place this film alongside other European lesbian favorites such as *November Moon* and *Another Way*. French with English subtitles. *Source:* Strand Releasing.

Nico and Dani (105 min.) 2001. Nico visits his best friend, Dani, in Barcelona during summer vacation. They engage in homosexual play. Dani comes to realize that he is sexually attracted to Nico, but for Nico, it is just play. Dani begins to associate with other homosexuals, which places Nico in the awkward position of seeing his friend head on a different life path. The film is well done and told without condemnation. Spanish with English subtitles. *Source:* general; Wolfe Video; tlavideo.

Salut Victor (83 min.) 1989. *Salut Victor* breaks ground with its portrait of romance between two older gay men. Phillipe, a straight-laced loner, checks into a stately nursing home to die. There he meets Victor, the resident rebel who is openly gay. Phillipe is inspired to share his secrets and falls in love with Victor. French with English subtitles. *Source:* Strand Releasing.

Show Me Love (89 min.) 1999. Sweden's 1999 entry for the Academy Award for best foreign-language film, *Show Me Love* is a sensitive and funny coming-of-age drama about two teenage girls living in a small town called Amal. Elin is the school debutante, popular and cool. Agnes is an outcast. She accidentally goes to the wrong party, where she is challenged to kiss Elin. The kiss transforms them both, and they fall in love. Swedish with English subtitles. *Source:* Strand Releasing; Wolfe Video.

Steam (96 min.) 2000. Francesco arrives in Turkey to oversee the disposition of an estate left to him by his recently deceased aunt. The property is a *hamam*, a traditional Turkish steam bath. Letters and friends' accounts help Francesco learn how remarkable and passionate his aunt was. The beautiful son of the hamam's custodian, Mehmet, introduces Francesco to the sultry world of the Turkish baths and men's erotic love for each other. Francesco decides to stay in Istanbul and restore the hamam. Turkish with English subtitles. *Source:* general; Strand Releasing; tlavideo.

Via Appia (90 min.) 1992. Frank, a former Lufthansa steward, goes to Rio to look for Mario, a young man with whom he had a one-night stand. Before he left, Mario scrawled on the bathroom mirror, "Welcome to the AIDS club." It seems that whenever Frank arrives at a location, he is told that Mario has just left. Via Appia is the nickname given to the district in Rio where male prostitutes hang out. German, Portuguese, and English with English subtitles. *Source:* Strand Releasing; Wolfe Video.

Wedding Banquet (111 min.) 1993. A gay Taiwanese yuppie living in New York with his American lover tries to end his parents' endless matchmaking by announcing he is engaged to a woman—actually, a tenant in one of his buildings who is an illegal Chinese alien in need of a green card. Within days the parents fly to meet the bride and arrange a traditional wedding. The gay couple strips the apartment of all things gay and tries to pull off the charade. Hilarious with many twists and turns. *Wedding Banquet* is an interesting examination of Chinese and American cultures and their views on homosexuality. English and Chinese. *Source:* general; Wolfe Video.

Westler: East of the Wall (94 min.) 1986. Felix is a West Berliner who falls in love with Thomas, an East Berliner. As Felix journeys back and forth to East Berlin, he comes under increasing suspicion. Their love grows stronger despite the distance between them, and they plan for Thomas's escape to West Berlin. This film was awarded best feature film at the San Francisco International Lesbian and Gay Film Festival. German with English subtitles. *Source:* Strand Releasing.

Wild Reeds (110 min.) 1994. This is a poignant coming-of-age story of four young teenagers in a nation torn apart by war. Franscois finds himself attracted more to his male classmate Serge than to his platonic girlfriend Maite. Henri, an older boy, is drawn into the circle of friends, complicating the relationships. There are sexual and political conflicts that mark their passage into adulthood. French with English subtitles. *Source:* Wolfe Video.

History and Biography

Before Night Falls (133 min.) 2000. The late Cuban poet Reinaldo Arenas fought for personal expression by defying censorship and persecution. A largely international cast, including Johnny Depp, Sean Penn, Cunningham O'Keefe, Javier Bardem, and Olivier Martinez tells his story. This was considered one of the best foreign films of the year. *Source:* general; Wolfe Video.

Bent (104 min.) 1997. Based on Martin Sherman's play, the film reenacts the forgotten persecution of homosexuals during the Nazi reign of terror. The arrest and incarceration of a gay male couple bring the audience face-to-face with the atrocities of the concentration camps. *Source:* general; Wolfe Video.

Brandon Teena Story (85 min.) 1998. This documentary uses interviews and still shots to recreate the story of Brandon Teena, a fresh-scrubbed young man who was biologically a woman. Only twenty years old, Brandon dated woman and dressed and acted as a man. When uncovered as a woman by former friends, he was beaten, raped, and later killed. Much of the material in this film was the basis for the fictional film *Boys Don't Cry. Source:* Wolfe Video.

Breaking the Surface (95 min.) 1996. This documentary profiling the life of Greg Louganis, Olympic gold medalist in diving, chronicles his overbearing father; his achievements in diving; his abusive relationship with his lover Tom Barrett, who later dies from AIDS; and Louganis's own HIV status. This is a heroic story of a man overcoming personal demons and personal turmoil while being a public figure. *Source:* general; Wolfe Video.

Celluloid Closet (102 min.) 1995. This documentary, narrated by Lily Tomlin, presents a dazzling 100-year history of lesbians and gay men in the movies. *Source:* general; Wolfe Video.

Coming Out under Fire (71 min.) 1994. This documentary profiling the experiences of nine gay and lesbian veterans combines declassified documents and rare archival footage with interviews and photographs. It is moving to hear first-person accounts of men and women who fought for their country, only to later be persecuted and expelled from the military for being homosexual. *Source:* Wolfe Video.

Dear Jesse (82 min.) 1997. Filmmaker Tim Kirkman returns home to North Carolina to rediscover his roots. He turns his camera on the pervasive homophobia personified in Jesse Helms. Kirkman interviews openly gay elected officials, a civil rights leader, writers, and others on their opinions about Helms. Kirkman explores how he and Helms had similar upbringings, yet hold such different views concerning gay men. *Source:* general; Wolfe Video.

Execution of Justice (103 min.) 1999. Based on Emily Mann's play, *Execution of Justice* dramatizes the people and events leading to the assassinations of San Francisco mayor George Moscone and City Supervisor Harvey Milk. Tim Daly plays killer Dan White. The light sentence received by White triggered the worst riots in San Francisco's history. *Source:* Wolfe Video.

Extramuros (120 min.) 1985. During the Spanish Inquisition Sister Angela, along with her lover, Sister Ana, decides to fake stigmata to help save her convent from ruin. The scam brings unexpected notoriety as well as enemies who want to destroy the women's relationship. The film is strange, beautiful, and serious. The struggle for political power is contrasted with the smoldering passion between the sisters. Spanish with English subtitles. *Source:* Wolfe Video.

Gods and Monsters (105 min.) 1998. This is a fictional account of the last few weeks in the life of Hollywood's only openly gay director in the 1930s—James Whale (*Frankenstein, Bride of Frankenstein, Showboat*). Openly gay British actor Sir Ian McKellen portrays the confusion experienced by Whale, who had a brain illness. A gardener (Brendan Fraser) is a character used to dramatize Whale's life and his conflicts over being openly gay. This excellently written and acted film was nominated for numerous Oscars. *Source:* general; Wolfe Video.

The Life and Times of Harvey Milk (50 min.) 1984. Produced and written by Robert Epstein and Richard Schmiechen, the film uses gay politics in San Francisco during the 1970s and 1980s as a backdrop to recount the events surrounding the assassination of City Supervisor Harvey Milk. *Source:* Telling Pictures.

Living with Pride: Ruth Ellis at 100 (60 min.) 1999. Ruth Ellis, at 100 years old, is the oldest "out" African American lesbian. This documentary includes rare film footage and interviews of this inspiring woman. *Source:* Wolfe Video.

The Man Who Drove with Mandela (98 min.) 1998. Cecil Williams was a white gay man who fought against South Africa's apartheid and homophobia from the 1940s to the 1960s. The film documents the economic disparity created by racism and the development of apartheid after World War II. The most dramatic moment in the film is when Williams helps Nelson Mandela sneak back into South Africa by having Mandela pose as his chauffeur. It is through Williams's work and that of many others that South Africa became the first country in the world to give constitutional equality to gay men and lesbians. *Source:* Wolfe Video.

Out of the Past (70 min.) 1998. This powerful and instructional film tells the history-making story of a high school student in Salt Lake City who formed a gay-straight alliance in her public school. *Source:* Wolfe Video.

Paragraph 175 (81 min.) 2001. A mix of interview, rare film footage, and still photographs, *Paragraph 175* tells the story of the Nazi persecution of homosexuals. The survivors relate bitter stories infused with a powerful will to endure. The film won the audience award for best documentary at the San Francisco Lesbian and Gay Film Festival. In English, German, and French with English subtitles. *Source:* Wolfe Video.

Paris Was a Woman (75 min.) 1995. This film re-creates the exciting and magical time when women writers, artists, and photographers flocked to the Left Bank of Paris in the early decades of the twentieth century. *Source:* Wolfe Video.

The Real Ellen Story (52 min.) 2002. The inner workings of the sitcom industry are revealed as we watch the development and subsequent controversy over Ellen coming out on national TV in the "Puppy Episode." Footage of Ellen, Oprah, Anne Heche, Bill Clinton, and others provides a fascinating picture of what it meant to be out in the 1990s. *Source:* Wolfe Video.

Serving in Silence: The Margarethe Cammermeyer Story (91 min.) 1995. Glenn Close stars as Margarethe Cammermeyer, a decorated army colonel who challenged the U.S. military's antigay policy (Judy Davis stars as her lover). Based on a true story, the film won Emmy Awards for best actress, best supporting actress, and best screenplay. *Source:* general; Wolfe Video.

Silent Pioneers (30 min.) 1984. Produced by Patricia Ginger Snyder, this work shows elderly gays and lesbians talking about their struggles. *Source:* Filmsmaker Library, 133 East 58th Street, New York, NY 10022, (212) 355-6545.

Stolen Moments (92 min.) 1998. Lesbian history from Sappho's poems in ancient Greece, to Gertrude Stein's Parisian salon, to Stonewall and beyond, is brought to life in this acclaimed film. *Source:* Wolfe Video.

Stonewall (99 min.) 1995. This is a fictional retelling of the events leading up to the 1969 Stonewall Riots, often marked as the event launching the modern gay liberation movement. The story follows Matty Dean, a self-made hustler who becomes involved with gay activists in New York. *Source:* general; Wolfe Video.

Tongues Untied (64 min.) 1991. Through the use of poetry, personal testimony, rap, and performance, *Tongues Untied* describes the homophobia and racism that confront black gay men. Many of the stories are difficult to watch, such as black men being refused entry into gay white bars or a gay black man being left on the street after a gay bashing. The film explores the rich diversity of the gay black male experience—from smoky bars, to protest marches, to the language of the "snap diva" and Vogue dancer. The film became a source of controversy when many public television stations refused to air it during their POV programs and it was excerpted by Republican presidential candidate Patrick Buchanan as part of his muckraking campaign. *Source:* Strand Releasing; Wolfe Video.

Twilight of the Golds (92 min.) 1997. An all-star cast appears in this riveting science fiction story of how a family deals with a husband who wants to abort a fetus that genetics has determined will be gay. Brendan Fraser plays the gay brother-in-law who fights for the life of the unborn child and who must confront the long simmering antigay feelings of his own parents. *Source:* general; Wolfe Video.

Wilde (116 min.) 1997. Stephen Fry plays Oscar Wilde from his days as a celebrated London socialite to his banishment to prison for being openly gay. This is one of the better Oscar Wilde biographies and film treatments. *Source:* general; Wolfe Video; tlavideo.

Lesbian Experience

Better Than Chocolate (101 min.) 1999. Maggie, played by Karyn Dwyer, is a college dropout who is living with her lover. Maggie has not told her flighty mother that she is a lesbian. Her mother, Lila, who is recently divorced, comes along with her son to live with Maggie. Maggie tries to pass off her girlfriend as a roommate. At the same time, Lila comes to discover sex toys. Very funny, but also educational. *Source:* general.

Bound (107 min.) 1996. This romantic thriller of two girls in love who attempt to foil the Mob was hailed as one of the best films of the year by Roger Ebert. *Source:* Wolfe Video.

Boys on the Side (117 min.) 1994. Whoppie Goldberg plays Jane, an unemployed lesbian singer who befriends Robin (Mary-Louise Parker) for a road trip to California. They pick up addle-brained Holly (Drew Barrymore), who just accidentally killed her drug-crazed abusive beau with a baseball bat to the head. The threesome are on the run from the cops and emotionally bond as a family. They also face two huge secrets—one is pregnant and another of the women has AIDS. Strong performances and cool soundtrack make up for a rather trite movie premise. *Source:* general; Wolfe Video.

Chutney Popcorn (92 min.) 2000. Reena and Lisa are two young women in love. But when Reena agrees to be a surrogate mother for her childless sister, a rift develops between Reena's Indian family and her lesbian life. *Chutney Popcorn* is a delightful and heartfelt comedy illustrating the struggles between immigrant parents and their Americanized children. *Source:* general; Wolfe Video.

Claire of the Moon (102 min.) 1992. Claire, a famous satirist, attends a writer's conference in the Pacific Northwest. She is heterosexual and extremely promiscuous. There, she shares a cabin with Dr. Noel Benedict, a solemn sex therapist. They engage in extended philosophical discussions that slow the pace of the movie. Claire finds the discussions challenging and is disturbed to find that she is falling for Noel. An intricate courting "dance" takes place between the women as they address their fears of same-sex intimacy. *Source:* general, Wolfe Video.

Dyke Drama (89 min.) 1993. Four lesbian short stories investigate couples, exploration, and cruising. *IFE, MAYA, Things We Said To-day*, and *A Certain Grace* originated from the esteemed San Francisco Lesbian and Gay Film Festival. *Source:* Wolfe Video.

Family of Women (36 min.) 1995. This work explores, through interview and video footage, three women-only communities. The women are asked why they have chosen to separate from mainstream society to live in an exclusively female society. *Source:* Wolfe Video.

Framing Lesbian Fashion (90 min.) 1992. Changes in lesbian identity are reflected in dress codes—butch/femme, corporate drag, leather, androgyny, lipstick, flannel, queer fluorescence, and more. This documentary uses archival photographs, interviews, and contemporary "shocking" footage of lesbian sex clubs. The film shows a butch/femme contest before 400 dykes, poet Kitty Tsui getting a military flat top, ACT UP Crystal Mason having her tongue pierced, and stand-up comic Mimi Freed modeling clothing required at lesbian sex clubs. *Source:* Wolfe Video.

Fresh Kill (80 min.) 1987. Two young lesbian parents get caught up in a global crisis of nuclear refuse, household pets glowing ominously, the sky snowing soap flakes, and people speaking in tongues. A multinational corporation is implicated, and the couple's infant daughter mysteriously vanishes. After uncovering censored information, our lesbian parents team up with a group of young New Yorkers to strike back. *Source:* Strand Releasing.

Go Fish (83 min.) 1994. Filmed in black and white, this lesbian experimental film traces the changes in an older lesbian who "punks" out for her new younger girlfriend. The film is a classic lesbian movie, with love, comedy, gossip, dating, and matchmaking. *Source:* Wolfe Video.

If These Walls Could Talk 2 (90 min.) 1996. Presented as a HBO drama, this film contains three short films about and for lesbians. *Source:* general; Wolfe Video; tlavideo.

It's in the Water (100 min.) 1996. In the small southern town of Azalea Springs, a tipsy comment starts the rumor that the local drinking water turns anyone who drinks it gay. An outrageous comedy with a queer twist ensues. *Source:* Wolfe Video; tlavideo.

Johnny Greyeyes (76 min.) 2001. This is a powerful story of a Native American woman struggling to maintain strength, love, and spirit while confined to prison for the shooting death of her father. She falls in love with her cellmate and struggles with maintaining that relationship in light of her impending release. The film was nominated for best picture at the 2000 American Indian Motion Picture Awards. *Source:* Wolfe Video; tlavideo.

Lavender Limelight (60 min.) 1997. America's most successful lesbian movie directors discuss their sexual identities, working in Hollywood, and more. The conversations are intimate, with clips of their work. *Source:* Wolfe Video.

Monkey's Mask (93 min.) 2000. A bisexual married woman is pulled into a torrid love affair with a women private investigator searching for the murderer of a young woman. Staring Kelly McGillis (*The Accused, Witness*), *Monkey's Mask* is a smoldering story of two lovers whose lives are irrevocably changed. This film contains frequent, steamy sexual situations. *Source:* Strand Releasing.

My Femme Divine (54 min.) 1999. From the creator of *Framing Lesbian Fashion*, director Karen Everett explores contemporary butch/femme lesbians, contrasted with her own explosive love affairs. *Source:* Wolfe Video.

Out in Suburbia (28 min.) 1989. Eleven lesbians aged twenty-three to sixty-seven tell about their families, friends, and loves. *Source:* Wolfe Video.

Personal Best (128 min.) 1982. Mariel Hemingway stars as a promising hurdler who falls in love with her female mentor. As passions increase, the potential for conflict rises as both vie for a spot on the U.S. Olympic team. This film is considered a classic lesbian movie. *Source:* general; Wolfe Video.

Salmonberries (94 min.) 1990. Beautifully shot in Alaska and Germany, *Salmonberries* tells the story of two women who form an unusual and unexpected relationship. Kotz, an androgynous young Eskimo (k. d. lang) is attracted to Roswitha, a German expatriate and town librarian. Roswitha initially rebuffs the younger woman, but persistence gradually wins her over. *Source:* Wolfe Video.

Short Shorts (135 min.) 1999. This is a collection of short stories for lesbians. *Source:* Wolfe Video.

The Sticky Fingers of Time (82 min.) 1997. A very 1990s nod to lesbian chic, *The Sticky Fingers of Time* is an elaborate tale of passion between two women as they travel through the hazards of nonlinear time. Tucker is a modishly sexy, 1950s pulp fiction novelist who time-travels. She collides with present-day Drew, a writer who has attempted suicide and is confused about what she wants. The film constantly shifts in style from science fiction to film noir. *Source:* Strand Releasing.

The Truth about Jane (91 min.) 2001. In this Lifetime movie with the highest ratings in five years, Jane meets Taylor and falls in love. She realizes that she is lesbian. Her classmates and family have trouble adjusting to her "experiment." Jane faces her mother (played by Stockard Channing) who cannot or will not accept her daughter's lesbianism. That could end their relationship. *Source:* Wolfe Video.

Two in Twenty (330 min.) 1996. This film is a five-part episodic soap opera following the complex lives of two lesbian households. With suspense and humor, the film tackles topics such as child custody, AIDS, lesbian parenting, racism, monogamy, substance abuse, crushes, bisexuality, lust, coming out, sex, and therapy. The film contains fictional commercials rooted in feminist and lesbian humor. *Source:* Wolfe Video.

Walk on the Wild Side (114 min.) 1962. In this drama (which won an Academy Award for best song), a man searches for his long-lost love in 1930s New Orleans, only to find her working as a prostitute. He fights to free her from the wicked lesbian madame (played by Barbara Stanwyck). *Source:* general.

West Coast Crones (28 min.) 1990. Nine older lesbians (over sixty) tell their stories. The film includes footage from the Gay Games and gay and lesbian pride marches in which senior lesbians participate. *Source:* Wolfe Video.

Religion

All God's Children (25 min.) 1986. This film is a celebration of black churches as they embrace and acknowledge the spiritual value of their gay and lesbian members. *Source:* Women Vision Library.

Eve's Daughters (27 min.) 1996. Documentary look at the lives of five lesbians who create a supportive religious community in the face of antigay Christian leaders condemnations. *Source:* Leonardo's Children, Inc., 26 Newport Bridge Road, Warwick, NY 10990, (914) 986-6888.

License to Kill (80 min.) 1997. This disturbing documentary profiles religious gay hatred. Director Arthur Dong interviews men who have killed gay men. *Source:* Deep Focus Production, 4506 Palmero Drive, Los Angeles, CA 90065-4237, (213) 254-7072, (213) 254-7112 (fax), e-mail: adongla@aol.com, website: http://film-mag.com/community/adong.

Maybe We're Talking About a Different God (28 min.) 1996. A woman pastor is barred from serving her Presbyterian church when she is discovered to be lesbian. The film interviews congregation members who were overwhelmingly in support of her work and records the Rochester religious court hearings. The documentary is skillfully crafted and shows that homophobia in the church may be overcome through the experiences of human love. *Source:* Leonardo's Children, Inc., 26 Newport Bridge Road, Warwick, NY 10990, (914) 986-6888.

One Nation under God (50 min.) 1994. This funny video looks at the religious-sponsored reparative therapy movement. *Source:* Video Finder (for Public Television), 425 E. Colorado Street, Suite B-10, Glendale, CA 91205, (800) 328-7271.

Portrait of Courage (60 min.) 2000. Produced by Courage, an apostolate of the Roman Catholic Church, the video teaches homosexuals how to develop an interior life of chastity so that they can move beyond the confines of their homosexual identity to a more complete one in Christ. *Source:* Courage, c/o Church of St. John the Baptist, 210 West 31st Street, New York, NY 10001, (212) 268-1010, e-mail: webmaster@courageRC.net, website: CourageRC.net.

The Rhetoric of Intolerance (30 min.) 1996. Dr. Mel White was once a ghostwriter for leaders of the religious right. He later acknowledged that he was gay. In this video, he addresses intolerance spread by the religious right. *Source:* The Justice Report, 1280 Bison, Suite B9-431, Newport Beach, CA 92660, (714) 224-9392.

Your Mom's a Lesbian: Here's Your Lunch, Have a Good Day (27 min.) 1980. This is a beautiful and moving portrait of a woman coming to embrace her lesbianism and her family's journey of acceptance and love. A true documentary that is highly recommended for children and families. *Source:* Leonardo's Children, Inc., 26 Newport Bridge Road, Warwick, NY 10990, (914) 986-6888.

Safe Sex

She's Safe (55 min.) 1994. This compilation of woman-to-woman safer-sex videos from around the world is sexually explicit and contains *Girls Will Be Boys* and *Cunt Dykula*. *Source:* Wolfe Video.

Well Sexy Women (50 min.) 1993. This frank presentation of the practices and sensuality of safer sex for lesbians was made by and for lesbians. Six women demonstrate safer-sex techniques and present the facts without sermonizing. *Source:* Wolfe Video.

Transgender

Boys Don't Cry (114 min.) 1999. Hilary Swank won an Oscar for best actress for her portrayal of Teena Brandon, a female-to-male transgender youth who was brutally murdered for passing as a male. Based on the documentary *Brandon Teena Story, Boys Don't Cry* is excellent and disturbing. *Source:* general; Wolfe Video.

Crying Game (112 min.) 1992. *Crying Game* is a complex blend of violence, love, betrayal, guilt, and redemption. It tells the story of an IRA terrorist who befriends the girlfriend of a soldier he held hostage. A surprising twist made this little film into one of the highest-grossing films of the year. *Source:* general.

Different for Girls (97 min.) 1996. In this funny and poignant film, Paul, a loser deliveryman in his early thirties, bumps into Kim and takes an interest in her. He is unaware that Kim is a postoperative transsexual who was a schoolmate of his fifteen years earlier. They form a stormy relationship that results in Kim being outed at work. *Source:* general; Wolfe Video.

Flawless (110 min.) 1999. Director Joel Schumacher took a real situation and turned it into a second-rate melodrama, complete with ridiculous subplots and stereotypes. Walt (Robert De Niro) is a retired cop living in the same building as Rusty, a flamboyant drag queen. Walt is injured and requires speech therapy. He does not like "sissy" men, but turns to Rusty to give him singing lessons. Slowly, Walt overcomes his homophobia and befriends Rusty and his fellow drag queens. *Source:* general; Wolfe Video.

A Gaudi Afternoon (88 min.) 2000. An American woman, Casandra (Judy Davis), working in Barcelona is approached by a glamorous American woman, Frankie (Marcia Harden), and offered a large sum of money to help locate Frankie's husband. Soon, Cassandra finds herself ensnarled in a web of mistaken identities and double-crossing families besides discovering that Frankie's husband is really a woman. *Source:* general, Wolfe Video.

Hedwig and the Angry Inch (95 min.) 2001. Based on the long-running New York smash hit play, *Hedwig and the Angry Inch* is a wickedly funny high-powered rock musical that tells that story of how a German glam-rock diva traveled to the United States to find love and stardom only to find himself abandoned in a trailer park. *Source:* Wolfe Video; tlavideo.

Wigstock (82 min.) 1995. This film documents the tenth anniversary of New York's most notorious underground event. *Wigstock* is a spoof of Woodstock. *Source:* general; Wolfe Video.

Youth

Gay Youth (40 min.) 1993. Here are poignant stories of two adolescents: one who committed suicide, the other who is openly gay in high school. The video (with a classroom guide) shows that information, acceptance, and support can make a significant difference in the lives of young people. *Source:* Wolfe Video.

Growing Up Gay and Lesbian (57 min.) 1993. This is a wonderful presentation by Brian McNaught about what it is like to grow up gay in a heterosexist society. *Source:* TRB Production.

Hate, Homophobia, and Schools (60 min.) 1995. **Sexual Orientation: Reading between the Labels** (30 min.) 1993. These films contain discussions between gay and antihomosexual youths and adults about what it is like to grow up gay in this society. Unfortunately, both films are slow paced and uninvolving. *Source:* NEWIST/CESA 7, IS 1040, University of Wisconsin at Green Bay, Green Bay, WI 54311, (920) 465-2599, (800) 633-7445, e-mail: newist@uwgb.edu, website: http://www.uwgb.edu/~newist.

It's Elementary: Talking about Gay Issues in School (78 min. or shorter 37 min. version) 1997. This feature-length documentary film shot in schools across the United States makes a compelling case for including gay issues in multicultural education. *Source:* Women's Educational Media; Women Vision Library.

Live to Tell (30 min.) 1995. This video documents the first lesbian and gay prom in America. *Source:* Wolfe Video.

Planet Out Shorts (92 min.) 2001. This collection of award-winning short films sponsored by Planet Out contains *Girls Shorts* and *Boys Shorts. Source:* Wolfe Video.

Speaking for Ourselves: Portraits of Gay and Lesbian Youth (27 min.) 1994. The lives of five lesbian and gay youths are explored. *Source:* Intermedia.

What If I'm Gay? (55 min.) 1987. This CBS Schoolbreak Special dramatizes the problems faced by youths who come out as gay. *Source:* Coronet/Phoenix Film and Video, 2349 Chaffee Drive, St. Louis, MO 63146, (800) 777-8100.

Glossary

gay Gay, rather than homosexual, is the preferred term for reference to a same-gender sexual orientation and is comparable to the distinction between black or African American and Negro. Gay is preferred to homosexual because homosexual implicitly emphasizes the sexual and diminishes the other aspects of gender orientation. Stylistically, gay is often paired with straight, meaning "heterosexual." Similarly, homosexual is paired with heterosexual. The history of the word gay is confused. It is thought that gay was used in eighteenth-century England to connote the conduct of a playboy. Later, in the nineteenth century, gay, when applied to women, came to mean "of loose morals; a prostitute." By the early twentieth century in the United States, the use of gay to refer to male homosexuals was becoming more prevalent, and this definition was first printed in 1933 in Noel Ersines's *Dictionary of Underground Slang* as "geycat" (Dynes 1985, 58).

gay agenda Antigay people often claim that lesbians and gays are seeking special rights. But lesbians and gays are seeking protections for themselves as workers, homeowners, and citizens—rights that other Americans have. These are not special rights but rather equal rights. Unfortunately, the term "gay agenda" has been used to mislead the public into believing that lesbians and gays are seeking legal rights greater than those possessed by heterosexuals, greater than those available through affirmative action, or both. None of the national gay rights organizations, community services centers, college resource centers, or academic writers has ever made claims for special rights.

heterosexism and homophobia Heterosexism is the assumption, both explicit and implicit, that everyone is heterosexual. It is "the continual promotion by major social institutions of heterosexuality and the simultaneous subordination" of lesbians, gay men, and bisexuals (Neisen 1990, 36). It is also the conscious or unconscious bias that heterosexuals are

375

more important than gay people, or that gay people do not exist, or both. For example, offering medical and other benefits to the spouses of married employees denies the fact that gay employees have partners. Homophobia is a strong negative emotional attitude toward gay people. It manifests itself in four ways: overt homophobia, institutional homophobia, societal homophobia, and internalized homophobia.

homosexual panic defense The homosexual panic defense is a legal strategy used by perpetrators of violence against gays in which they claim to have panicked and reacted with violence toward a gay person who "came onto them" (also known as a "gay advance"). Homosexual panic was considered a psychological disorder by the APA in versions of the *Diagnostic and Statistical Manual* before the fourth revised edition based on the Freudian theory that persons with latent homosexual tendencies would react with extreme and uncontrollable violence when propositioned by a homosexual (Chuang and Addington 1988). No court has ever acquitted a defendant based solely on the homosexual panic defense. However, the defense has been instrumental in obtaining reduced sentences in murder cases involving gay victims. Recently, judges have denied defendants the use of the homosexual panic defense, as demonstrated in the Matthew Shepard murder.

homosexuality Homosexuality is a primary sexual attraction to members of the same gender. For men, the preferred terms are gay man and gay male. For women, the preferred terms are gay woman, gay female, and lesbian. It is acceptable to use gay to mean both men and women in the context of the gay community, but the term should not be overused. Instead, when referring to women as well as men, writers should use both lesbian and gay and the gay community. Also, it is important not to overlook bisexual, transgender, transsexual, or intersex people. Using the all-encompassing term gay community does not provide recognition of their important issues.

intersexed Intersex people have partially or fully developed genitalia, gonads, or chromosomes that are not distinctly male or female but are some combination of both. The archaic term hermaphrodite is inaccurate because it implies that an intersexed person has genitalia that is equally male and female. Intersex people are born between (inter) the sexes. There are roughly eight classifications and forty subclassifications of intersexuality. It is estimated that from 1 to 4 percent of the population have a hermaphroditic condition, which means there are approximately 2.8–12 million intersex people in the United States alone (Fausto-Sterling 1993).

lesbian Lesbian is the term for a female with a same-gender orientation. The regular and conscious use of lesbian, as in "lesbians and gay
men," affirms the equality and independence of women within the gay
community. Reference to gay people and the gay community as inclusive
of lesbians and gay men is acceptable if not used exclusively. Many lesbians prefer the term gay woman or dyke. When in doubt, it is best to ask
the woman directly what label, if any, she wants to be called.

National Coming-Out Day October 11 was designated by the Human
Rights Campaign as National Coming-Out Day. Begun in 1988, this day
has grown into thousands of events held nationally to encourage people
to come out to family, friends, neighbors, and coworkers about being lesbian, gay male, bisexual, transgender, transsexual, or intersex. It has been
found that visibility, that is, being seen and known to be homosexual, is
the most effective way to change societal attitudes toward and increase
the acceptance of homosexuality.

outing Outing is when public disclosure is made to reveal the sexual orientation of a closeted gay person. Outing is very controversial both in and
out of the lesbian and gay community. Many lesbians and gay men believe
that outing is never acceptable. Others believe that outing public figures is
OK and, in fact, necessary to break the wall of silence that surrounds homosexuals and their relationships. By doing so, the world becomes aware of
how many lesbians, gays, and bisexuals there are. Some believe that outing
should only be used against public figures who are closeted homosexuals
whose job is to persecute gays and lesbians (such as in the military). Others
believe that everyone who is homosexual needs to be outed so as to destroy
the last vestiges of secrets that lead to discrimination.

public accommodations Public accommodations, which involve services, items, or benefits offered to the public, commonly include hotels
and motels, restaurants, stores, and other businesses or organizations
catering to the public. Local, state, and federal laws regulate public businesses under public accommodation statutes. However, the legal definition of public accommodation varies from jurisdiction to jurisdiction. A
business subject to ordinances against discrimination in one jurisdiction
may be exempt in other jurisdictions.

What constitutes a "private" club is an area of continuing litigation
in our society. For example, the Boy Scouts has been sued for excluding
lesbian and gay members. Some courts have ruled that the Boy Scouts
has the right to discriminate, whereas other courts have ruled that the
organization is a public entity and must accommodate lesbian and gay
members. Ultimately, the Supreme Court decided that the Boy Scouts'

right to determine policy overruled the applicability of government rules concerning antidiscrimination.

queer   Queer was probably the most common mid-twentieth-century U.S. abusive slang term for homosexual. The word is most likely rooted in the use of the word for counterfeit money and coins, as in "queer as a three-dollar bill." Queer implied not being authentic. When applied to male homosexuals, queer meant that the man was not an authentic male and not normal. Queer was rarely applied to women.

In the early 1990s, the word began to be appropriated by the lesbian and gay community. Queer Nation was an activist anarchist group that staged in-your-face confrontations with political, business, and educational leaders. Similar to ACT UP, which brought media attention to the problem of AIDS, Queer Nation brought attention to the problems of homophobia and heterosexism.

Queer became mainstreamed into academic parlance. Instead of writing the phrase lesbian, gay, bisexual, transgender, transsexual, and intersex people, *queer* became a shorthand way of referring to all people who are not heterosexual. Many college and academic conferences on lesbian and gay issues became queer conferences. However, the lesbian and gay community has not wholeheartedly embraced the term. For many, the term is still negative in much the same way the word faggot is.

The process of appropriating epithets by stigmatized groups is well documented. For example, the word black was an epithet that Negroes and colored people once detested. The Black Panthers appropriated the term in the 1960s. Now, black no longer has the sting it once had and can be used neutrally to refer to African Americans. This same process may happen with queer, but at this time it is not universally accepted by the lesbian and gay community and should not be used by heterosexuals in reference to homosexuals.

safe sex   Safe sex involves specific sexual practices that reduce the transmission of sexually transmitted diseases (STD). With the advent of AIDS, health professionals developed safe-sex guidelines to reduce the risk of people contracting HIV. Safe-sex campaigns have proven effective. The rate of infection for gay men has dropped significantly. "Gay males have changed their behavior on an unprecedented scale" (Gonsiorek and Shernoff 1991, 237).

sexual preference   Sexual preference should not be used as a synonym for sexual orientation. Sexual preference suggests that sexual orientation is a choice. No person would choose to become a stigmatized outcast of society. A better term is sexual orientation.

transgender   A transgender person is one whose outward gender presentation (being feminine or masculine) does not conform to his or her biological sex (being female or male). Transgender people may self-identify as butch, femme, drag king, drag queen, intersex person, transvestite, transgenderist, androgyne, or transsexual.

transvestite   A transvestite is a person who chooses to wear clothing that society deems appropriate for the opposite gender. German sexologist Magnus Hirschfeld introduced the term in 1910. Transvestitism is prevalent among both heterosexuals and homosexuals. When transvestites dress in the clothing of the opposite sex, they are attempting to "pass" as the opposite sex. Homosexual transvestites are popularly known as drag queens or drag kings. Mixing clothing and hairstyles of both genders at one time is known as camp.

References

Chuang, H. T., and D. Addington. 1988. "Homosexual Panic: A Review of Its Concept." *Canadian Journal of Psychiatry* 33(7) (October): 613–617.

Dynes, W. 1985. "Homolexis: A Historical and Cultural Lexicon of Homosexuality." *Gai Saber Monographs 4*. New York: Scholarship Committee of the Gay Academic Union.

Fausto-Sterling, A. 1993. "How Many Sexes Are There? Intersexuality Is a Biological Condition, Not a Disease, and Medical Policy toward It Should Be Reevaluated." *New York Times*, March 12, A15(N), A29(L).

Gonsiorek, J. C., and M. Shernoff. 1991. "AIDS Prevention and Public Policy: The Experience of Gay Males." In J. C. Gonsiorek and J. D. Weinrich, eds., *Homosexuality: Research Implications for Public Policy*. Newbury Park, CA: Sage, pp. 230–243.

Neisen, J. 1990. "Heterosexism or Homophobia?" *Out/Look* 3(2) (Fall): 36.

Index

Proms
and same-sex couples,
60
Proposition 6 (California), 17
Pseudonyms, 8
Psychology
and homosexuality, theories of,
2, 10, 11–12
Public attitude, 54–55
and culture war, 26
Public employment
discrimination, 14, 46, 47
and gay demonstrations, 9
and police officers,
employment as, 18
See also Employment;
Employment discrimination
Public Morals Section of NYPD
and Stonewall riots, 12–13
Publishers Weekly, 150

Quaker Academy (New York),
129
Queensberry, Marquis of, 172
Queer in America: Sex, the Media,
and the Closets of Power
(Signorile), 164
Queer Resources Directory, 129,
135, 274
Queer World, 162

Radcliffe College, 159
Radical Faeries, 144
Rainbow Baptists, 266
Raleigh North Carolina Times,
145
Reagan, Ronald, 17
and AIDS, 19–20
Redwood Records, 157
Reed College, 168
Religious conservatives, 18
and APA, and homosexuality,
as mental illness, 16
and domestic partnership
programs, 45
and emotional hysteria, 17

and free speech and
association, right to, 64
See also Christian conservatives;
Christian fundamentalists;
Religious right
Religious freedom
and free speech and
association, right to, 64
Religious groups, 18
in schools, 59
Religious right
and AIDS, 19
and AIDS prevention
programs, 37
and antidiscrimination statutes,
38–39, 47
and APA, and homosexuality,
as mental illness, 16
and Bryant, Anita, 134
and Cameron, Paul
Drummond, 41, 137
and culture war, 26–27
and domestic partnership
programs, 52
and ex-gay movement, 26–27
formation of, 18
and homosexuality, causes of,
34
and public attitude, about gays
and lesbians, 55
and same-sex marriage, 22,
51–52
and special rights, 23. See also
Special rights
See also Christian conservatives;
Christian fundamentalists;
Religious conservatives
Rensselaer Polytechnic Institute,
135
Rent control statutes, 48
Rent stabilization statutes,
48
Reparative therapy, 55–58
APA position on, 178
(document)
See also Ex-gay movement

About the Author

C huck Stewart received his Ph.D. from the University of Southern California School of Education, along with a certificate in women's studies. He specialized in intercultural education and was funded by the California Commission on Peace Officers Standards and Training (POST) to conduct research into effective means to reduce heterosexism and homophobia through the design and implementation of educational programs. His master's thesis, "Homosexuality and Public Education Law," led to the Police Advisory Task Force hiring him to write the curriculum and teaching materials for use on sexual orientation training within the Los Angeles Police Department. He wrote the award-winning book *Sexually Stigmatized Communities—Reducing Heterosexism and Homophobia: An Awareness Training Manual* for Sage (1999). For ABC-CLIO, he wrote *Homosexuality and the Law,* which was released in 2001 to rave reviews. He is a twenty-year member and cochair of the Los Angeles Gay and Lesbian Scientist, administrative assistant to the Lesbian and Gay Psychotherapy Association and Southern California Lambda Medical Association, member of the America Civil Liberties Union Gay and Lesbian Caucus, and research fellow for the ONE Institute and Archives. He was the newsletter editor for both the Los Angeles Unified School District Gay and Lesbian Education Commission and University of Southern California Lambda Alumni. He teaches ballroom and western dancing and founded Out Dancing Ballroom, a performing group that brings the delights of ballroom dancing to the gay community.

In his previous life (the 1970s and 1980s), he worked as a research physicist, built cars for the custom car circuit, and worked as a professional classical ballet dancer (at the same time—yes, he was a dancing physicist—how eclectic). Visit his website for articles, reviews, and pictures at http://members.aol.com/ckstewar/CStewart.html.